Red, cream and a touch of Gray

The <u>WESTERN WELSH</u> story

By Colin Scott

BRYNGOLD

BOOKS

www.bryngoldbooks.com

First published in Great Britain in 2012
by Bryngold Books Ltd.,
100 Brynau Wood, Cimla,
Neath, South Wales SA11 3YQ.

www.bryngoldbooks.com

Typesetting, layout,
editing and design
by Bryngold Books

ISBN 978-1-905900-26-8

Printed and bound
in Wales by
Gomer Press,
Llandysul, Ceredigion.

Reliability, Efficiency, Comfort and Courtesy

— the company motto

Dedication

This book is for my wife Sue, without whose support and encouragement it would not have been possible. It is also a tribute to the men and women whose efforts made Western Welsh such a legend.

About the author

Colin Scott grew up in the bustling town of Bridgend, at the very heart of Western Welsh territory and from an early age became aware that the company's buses provided the first important link with almost every journey he would make from his home.

What developed from this was an enthusiasm with buses in general and a lifelong passion for

his beloved Western Welsh, one of the largest passenger road transport companies in Wales. His memories range from those fuelled by days spent watching the comings and goings at his home depot of Bridgend, to the hours when he sneaked into Ely Works and feasted his eyes on so many Western Welsh wonders from all corners of its territory. Colin's quest to complete this book has been a long and sometimes arduous one, but the information, facts, figures and photographs it contains combine to document the rise and fall of an iconic and legendary leader in the transport world. Alongside this are the down-to-earth tales of life on the buses which offer a clue to why pride was the watchword of Western Welsh. Since his days of chasing buses, Colin enjoyed a long career in local government as a draughtsman, graphic designer, and surveyor.

Early retirement brought with it the opportunity to bring to fruition the long term project that has resulted in publication of a book that most will agree is as close as it gets to being a definitive history.

Colin maintains an interest in most forms of transport, not least railways, which led to the publication of his first book — Diesels, Dragons & Daffs — but his love affair with Western Welsh, the company with which he began travelling almost before he could walk, endures to this day.

Contents

Nostalgia is a different country, they say, 'it's alright to visit, as long as you don't live there'. Well, having read Colin Scott's book about Western Welsh, it's not at all a bad place to visit, especially, as in my case, the journey there would be in a Leyland Tiger in the Glory Days.

I'm put in my place in Colin's work, for, compared to his passion, courtship and love affair with buses, in this case Western Welsh, my interest is, clearly, just a flirtation. It's an extraordinary piece of historical archive tempered with a lovely human touch. Not only is this a scholarly record of a bus company, but it is an insight on society itself and the integral, vital place of public transport on people's everyday lives across South Wales.

Thinking back to my younger days, Gwaun Cae Gurwen was my 'Check Point Charlie'. Although I lived in Brynaman, G.C.G. was the gateway to the rest of the world. From there you could get a bus, with connections to all points of the compass. South

Foreword by Roy Noble

Wales Transport, James & Sons, United Welsh and, of course, Western Welsh, all travelled through G.C.G. My father worked, for some 12 years, for James & Sons. The South Wales Transport was the regular bus ride to

Swansea if a big item was required, like a suit for a funeral or school uniform. The United Welsh was not used as much by our family, because it went to Swansea via Ystalyfera, a longish, roundabout route, but Western Welsh was the bus to take you to an exciting far away land. Western Welsh seemed to go further, they stretched your limited horizons. They went to Cardiff, Lampeter and Carmarthen and their buses had fabric seats, so they were regarded as 'posh', a cut above the rest. Before the days of pit-head baths, miners returned from work in dirty clothes and, generally, Western Welsh did not pick them up, because of the problem of coal dust getting into those seats. The slatted wooden seats of the utility Guy Arabs of James & Sons were far better suited for miners' transport. Western Welsh took over the responsibility for James & Sons in 1950 and the Leylands in their fleet fitted in well.

My holiday every year was a week's stay, with my parents, at my grandparents' house in Tenby, so the exciting prospect always started with a bus to G.C.G. and then the Western Welsh to Carmarthen for the Ebsworths' connection to Tenby. Buses were full in those days and the one consistency of the trip to Carmarthen was that my father always had to stand up en-route, no seats being available.

On the Lampeter run, it was a Western Welsh bus that put us off just east of the Dolau Cothi Roman gold mines, at the road junction to the village of Caio, where my great aunts Marged and Hannah lived, both married to men named Dafydd. I recall those days with pleasure, the bus ride, crossing the river seven times on the road just beyond Llanwrda, and the final long walk into the village, and back again in the evening to catch the bus back to Ammanford.

The interior of Western Welsh buses were 'a cut above the rest' for Roy Noble — and many others, of course — and the company rarely ran work buses for miners because the coal dust soiled the 'posh' seats. This peep inside Weymann saloon 404 (FUH 404) will revive the memory for many. *George Wedlake*

roaring tigers!

The squat, flat roofed all-Leyland saloon wasn't chosen by Western Welsh, but two vehicles, new in 1952/3, were absorbed from Ebsworth of Laugharne in 1954. Here, 470 (GTH 956) is seen at Carmarthen soon after the takeover. As a child, Roy Noble travelled to Tenby on one of these vehicles. Both buses survived until 1965. *Geoff Morant*

During college days in Cardiff, the Western Welsh again became part of my life and movements. I caught the bus at 'Check Point Charlie' and then off to the Capital City, via Victoria Gardens, Neath, sometimes breaking the routine by getting off there and jumping on the N. & C. Coaches for a bit of luxury for the long final leg.

So, the Western Welsh with their golden interwoven double 'W' badge was part of my travelling scene, part of my life's fabric. Colin, in this book, has warmly reminded me of those halcyon formative years. He has done so much more than that, of course, because his tome has covered the entire Western Welsh world, from the Valleys to the Vale, to the towns and to the large rural stretches of Carmarthenshire, Pembrokeshire and Cardiganshire.

The detail is incredible, from the start as Albert Gray's South Wales Commercial Motors in 1919, with the new sliding roofs of 1922, to the acquisition of so many other smaller companies, to the wartime years and on to the 1948-68 Glory days... my days actually. The work is a masterly record of a large public transport company, but I especially loved the human touches within the vast framework. Every combine is really about its people, and this is certainly so. The staff are the lifeblood. The tales of drivers being fined for haring along at 14 mph in Cardiff and 16 mph in Neath, one of them being crossed in love, so he was clearly tense and over-wrought, or a conductor being caught overloading a 32 seater with over 50 people, all paint cold facts of fares and schedules with a colourful hue. There was also the difficulty of collecting fares in the blackout years of the war, using a torch light, and the meths drinkers of Penarth Road, based in a former Vincent's Daimler. Then the gentle tale of developing love for a sick driver who just happened to sit next to a young lady on a trip and the bus driver helping to ease love's uncertain shy way towards marriage. The famed Singing Busmen, Barber Shop style, of the Bridgend depot — the human tales unfold to glitter the main tale and Colin regales us with many other stories of characters, in many depots, who played their part in the ever-developing saga that is the history of the Western Welsh, milestones and millstones all.

When I first came to live in Aberdare, following a woman, as men do, the Western Welsh depot was on the Gadlys. The building has been knocked down and a Lidl store now fills the site. I can never pass the shop without thinking of the buses once based there. Colin Scott's book has rekindled the memory in all the warming parts of the recalling mind. It is a definitive work, academic in its research, information and detail. It is, also, so much more, in that it gives clues as to the company's place in the South Wales of the 1920s to the late 1960s. For most people, bus companies played a vital part in their work and play; without them, communities would have been insular and confined; with them, the world could come to their door and they could go beyond the far horizon. The buses were liberating and the Western Welsh was a cog in that turning wheel. Colin is to be congratulated on this fine book. Bus enthusiasts, social commentators and those who just visit nostalgia now and again will be enthralled with the tale.

Roy Noble

OBE, DL, O.St.J.
Aberdare

Ticket for a special tour

Welcome aboard — enjoy the trip!

ONE of the best things about nostalgia is sharing it with others who remember, or are interested in the past. It can be attached to a whole variety of aspects of our daily lives; for many it will focus on the much missed Western Welsh bus company.

Those yet to reach the age of 50 may not remember the arrival of their family's first TV. It has always been there, and a colour one at that. Before that, entertainment meant visiting a cinema or dance hall. Few would have had a car at their disposal, and if they did it would have been used exclusively by dad except, perhaps, for Sundays — when everything was closed! Taxis were unheard of for days out which just left the bus. You went to school by bus, to work, to town, and to the cinema or theatre. You relied on buses and will probably remember their sights, sounds and smells with considerable affection — and what sights, sounds and smells they were!

Passengers had an allegiance to their bus company, as long as their vehicles were smart, comfortable and reliable, and their crews friendly. Many may even have holidayed by coach — quite often provided by the same operator. The larger companies such as Western Welsh had the resources and experience to organise interesting itineraries as well as buying power with the best hotels.

To its management, staff and passengers alike, Western Welsh was an institution. It was a way of life that every day affected thousands of people across south and west Wales for almost half a century. Few bus undertakings covered an operating area as widespread and varied as that served by the company. Its territory ranged from the bustling coastal towns that stretched between Newport and Neath, through the heavily industrialised valleys of Monmouthshire and Glamorgan, to the sparsely populated rural shires of Brecon, Carmarthen, Cardigan and Pembroke. Western Welsh was a big company by anyone's standards, but from its earliest days it retained a family feel which could be attributed to the efforts of Albert Gray, its first general manager. Gray was the founder of the company's predecessor, South Wales Commercial Motors (SWCM). As with the Great Western Railway (GWR) who launched it, there was an immense feeling of pride and commitment by its staff at all levels. While not unique, it was a quality that others envied. It flourished as the company expanded and acquired new businesses, often enhancing services to an extent that could never have been dreamed of. In rural west Wales particularly, where early railway closures had unsettled communities, there also developed a sense of security that 'The Western' would always be there when needed, both as a public service and employer. Good management from both near and far meant long-term stability, vulnerable routes often receiving funds from the many lucrative ones, even if they were 100 miles further east.

Western Welsh was a major player at a time when buses ruled the road. It operated a variety of types of traditionally constructed chassis, engines and bodies, invariably of British manufacture. In its heyday the company owned more than 700 vehicles which were housed in 18 area depots. It had a head office and large central workshops in Cardiff along with dozens of booking offices and outstations dotted around its empire. The company's land holdings were considerable and included many prime, town centre sites that would realise valuable income once the glory days were over.

There weren't many people in south and west Wales, especially in rural areas, whose lives didn't depend on some form of contact with Western Welsh. In the mid-1930s one technical writer described the company's operating area as: "A virtual monopoly of some 4,000 square miles, embracing most of South Wales and as far north as Aberystwyth, Builth Wells and Hay-on-Wye." This was not exactly correct, as the company's share of passengers within this vast territory probably amounted to around only one fifth of the total. The services inherited from the GWR had been intended to fill gaps in its rail network and were based at its stations. While commercially minded, they were never intended to penetrate areas in the way that other bus operators had done, and for the most part Western Welsh services were thinly spread out. In truth, they shared nearly all of their busiest routes with other companies. Some were small and soon absorbed, but others such as James of Ammanford, Red & White (R&W), White's, and Cardiff

The head office of Western Welsh, at 253 Cowbridge Road West, Cardiff, was built in 1931 on an island formed by the approach drives to Ely Works. It was a striking double fronted building featuring a balustrade with three flagstaffs and hipped roof. Its frontage was flanked by decorative wrought iron railings. This early 1950s view shows the original building with the works behind.
Stewart Williams

Typical of the quality of British vehicle manufacturing in the 1930s was this Brush - bodied Leyland TS7. Bus 129 (KG 5623) is factory fresh and awaiting delivery in July 1935. *Stewart Williams*

Corporation Transport (CCT), were large and powerful. The latter had the city sewn up, though Western Welsh had some picking-up rights established long before these areas became part of the City of Cardiff. Because the company's buses were seen everywhere, to the casual onlooker this may have appeared as though it had a monopoly.

The first decade, up until 1939, saw almost continuous expansion as a variety of businesses were absorbed. The result of this was that the company gained new routes, often obtaining a monopoly on former joint operations. Even at its formation, Western Welsh buses appeared almost everywhere, although a notable void in the centre of its operating area was filled by Rhondda Transport while further west, British Electric Traction (BET) group associate, South Wales Transport (SWT) was firmly ensconced in Swansea and Llanelli. However, there were encroachments. Acquisition of White's took the company into the heart of Rhondda territory, while at Neath and Port Talbot,

A gathering of Crosskeys drivers and conductors at Newport in 1953. *Stewart Williams*

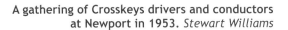

11

Western Welsh management quickly realised the benefit of advertising and capitalised on this method of increasing business. Its campaigns were sensible and conservative, never brash. They were straight and to the point. New developments were covered by newspapers and often linked with promotion by local agents and a demonstration ride for the press. Considerable effort was also made to publicise express services and tours.

Vehicle advertising on behalf of other companies, a valuable source of revenue, was also tackled in a conservative manner that never allowed buses to be plastered with posters as they often were elsewhere.

Western Welsh was never one to actively promote its suppliers. For example the Leyland badges on the radiators of its buses were more often than not replaced by cast badges on which appeared the company name. Later, economies dictated that the bus livery was simplified with the use of cream relief and black lining-out eliminated. Nevertheless the vehicles were still overhauled and repainted every two years and so it was rare to see a shabby bus in service.

It was paramount to the company's directors and managers that staff at all levels should take pride in their jobs, and through the pages of a monthly Staff Bulletin were kept informed of developments, whether at head office or in a far-flung corner of the Western Welsh empire. They were also reminded of the importance that management attached to public relations. The stream of appreciative letters that was received almost daily at head office reflected, with great credit, the happy state of affairs that existed. Over the years a succession of

SWT was left behind by its expanding neighbour. Here the tentacles inherited from the GWR brought the company close to Swansea on three sides. On the fourth of course, was the sea!

In 1950s Britain, public transport was the only means of getting around for the majority of people. By 1952 buses and coaches accounted for around 75 per cent of the total mileage driven on Britain's roads. This was a figure that had increased dramatically since the end of the Second World War. By 1955 trains, trams, buses and trolleybuses thrived as the demand for travel increased, even though the number of cars had risen to nearly four million. Gradually the motor bus took the place of trams and trolleybuses. For many years it was perceived to be in competition with the railways rather than the private car. The statistics may be dull, but there is a fascinating story behind them. The bus was — and still is — versatile and didn't need the specialist infrastructure that the other systems demanded. As wartime restrictions eased and new buses became available once again, enthusiastic Western Welsh area managers seized every opportunity to expand into new housing estates, shopping centres and recreational areas. Above all, at a time when cars were largely for officialdom and the well-off, the company's buses were classless. In keeping with the spirit of the times, they were practical, friendly and unstuffy. There was a grand feel to it all — and Western Welsh vehicles looked the best! Attention to detail and even their chosen shade of red made the competition look second rate by comparison.

Fitters at Neath check over a PS1 in 1949. A lump hammer would solve most bodywork problems in the good old days! *Stewart Williams*

Western Welsh's 'Andy Cappers' in party mood as they set off on their annual outing to Symonds Yat in 1962.
Graham Bravey

general managers were genuinely pleased to commit an individual reply to every letter received.

Management also encouraged social activity among the company's staff by supporting hobbies and sports. This led to the formation of an educational club with which Leslie Gray was particularly associated. Its main aim was to increase the knowledge and appreciation of just about everything Welsh. It attracted employees of all levels. Outings — by coach naturally — were regular and most club visits included a pub stop at some point. There were many reports of sing-a-longs on the journey home! A cricket club was also formed, partly as a result of the enthusiasm for the sport of RT Ebury during his time as general manager.

The Staff Bulletin, as the popular monthly newsletter was titled, was instrumental in alerting the employees at all depots to a variety of activities. As the sports and social side flourished, with inter-depot tournaments ranging from draughts to soccer, the bulletins always covered events with reports and photographs. Senior management was always on hand to meet the staff to present trophies. There was also an annual field day, held alongside dismantled body shells and redundant chassis on the spare ground behind Ely Works. The fancy dress, helter-skelter, egg 'n' spoon race, Punch and Judy, as well as the ice-cream, were not to be missed! On the road, the competitive spirit extended to the presentation of the buses themselves. Perhaps this explains the area-based system of coloured diamonds applied to buses from around the company's many, widespread depots.

Of the staff clubs that were formed, none was more significant than the Andy Capp Club which had no rules and held no meetings, but behind the humourous front 'The Cappers' did a great deal of good work protecting the income of members who had lost wages through illness. They paid out £5 for every four weeks' absence from duty, and ran an annual outing to the Symonds Yat Hotel. Even the hotel proprietors became members. At the same time, the company's educational club, in the course of many trips around Britain, formed a strong bond with the Sporvejenes Engelsk Klub of the Copenhagen Transport Company. Exchange visits began in 1949, and when it was the turn of Western Welsh to entertain the Danes, the company rolled out the latest additions to the fleet, bedecked with flags, for a tour around a variety of attractions in the area, ranging from Llandarcy oil refinery to Cardiff Arms Park.

Good housekeeping was often a topic aired in the Staff Bulletins. This was tackled in typically competitive style. Monthly fuel and oil consumption figures were given, and to encourage thriftiness, each depot's position was published in a league table. This was something that many never really understood. The terrain and range of vehicles operated didn't seem to be taken into account, and perhaps it isn't surprising that Brecon would top the charts and Bridgend prop up the bottom, when their monthly mileages differed by 300,000. To those at

 Western Welsh had developed a proud and successful corporate identity long before the days of graphic designers and media relations agencies. It devised a brilliant logo — although the term probably didn't exist then — that filled an otherwise empty space on the rear domes and fronts of its buses, appeared on its depots and offices and of course featured on its publicity and stationery. This was almost heraldic, a regal crest consisting of an interwoven 'WW' monogram crowned with orbs and coronets set above a proud banner motto.

Running in from Penarth Road depot on its first day of service, July 6, 1954, Leyland Tiger Cub 1070 (JBO 70) in Wood Street, on the way to work the Lower Penarth route from St Mary Street. The route was a joint enterprise with Cardiff Corporation.

Bridgend, the league table was a real niggle. Staff there knew their efforts would never win them top spot.

In most bulletins there would usually be a serious message to get across. For example, in 1953 general manager TG Davies flew the flag for road safety. He suggested that there should be no let up in the intensive campaign to make the roads of Britain safe. Happily, Western Welsh had an outstanding record of safe driving, something of which it could be understandably proud.

Conversely, in 1964 the company wasn't afraid to admit that its vehicles were involved in 1,567 accidents of all kinds, major and minor, in which four people were killed and 291 injured. There were 1,238 incidents of damage and the cost of repairs amounted to around £10,000 with vehicles out of action for around 3,100 days. The cost of third party claims amounted to £17,706. 'Resolve here and now to exercise that extra degree of caution when you are driving,' was the manager's advice.

In some ways Western Welsh was different to other British bus companies. The high proportion of rural operation, together with the multitude of low railway bridges in the valleys, meant it had a smaller double-deck fleet than was the norm elsewhere. Although double-deckers were never plentiful a sizable number of Leyland Atlanteans was in operation by the end of 1962. The company operated the largest fleet of Leyland Tiger Cub saloons in the world. Excluding those absorbed with

Publicity for early Western Welsh coaches boasted 'pneumatic tyres, spring seats, heavy foot mats and travelling rugs', although surprisingly little attention was given to ventilation or heating. As time passed increased engine power and improved braking, suspension and steering gave a much better ride for passengers and drivers alike and coach tours grew in popularity.

the Rhondda company in 1970, an impressive 349 were delivered new over the years. The predecessor ranks of Leyland TS7s and TS8s surely broke some records too. For most people, mention of the company conjures up an image of one or other of these vehicle types. Even allowing for this standardisation, Western Welsh had an interesting mix of vehicles, usually grouped in big batches. As well as the single deck Leylands that ruled the roost, the AEC marque was commonplace and the preferred option for double-deckers and coaches. No doubt there were debates as to the allocation of particular vehicle types to particular depots, but in reality there seemed to be a few of everything at each depot.

Rural services were relied upon in a totally different way to that of the urban and inter-urban routes. Many people will have their own fond memories. For me, recollections are clear of a childhood ride through the Vale of Glamorgan to Llantwit Major when the informal 'hail and ride' approach saw the bus stopping at farm gates and the odd oak tree. The Tiger Cub on this trip — 1070 — had an early form of one-man operation where a 'Pay Here' sign was slotted onto the cab door. The bus wound its way through the narrow lanes of Marcross and Monknash without meeting a single car, and upon arrival at Llantwit, passengers for Penarth strolled across the road for a cuppa in the Yacht Café. A conveniently timed crossing service allowed westbound passengers to do the same. Then, suitably refreshed, the journey continued with the

drivers having swapped vehicles so as not to stray too far from home.

The company's tours department was considered of special importance even in the early years, with the drivers chosen for their inter-personal skills as well as seniority. Only top-class hotels and restaurants were selected, and itineraries were carefully planned to strike a balance between travel and sightseeing time.

Attractive leaflets, posters and window displays were produced in-house and distributed around booking offices and agencies. They were given generous counter space in an era before the travel market became saturated by cheap continental package holidays.

In the 1930s, coaches became more identifiable. The bodywork began to appear in a style far different to the run of the mill buses. Fashion and flare began to play their part. The new coaches featured curtains, enclosed luggage accommodation and roll-open roofs. Better still was the luxurious, armchair-style seating and extra spaciousness.

They were very interesting times because there was a wide variety of chassis available, of both heavyweight and lightweight construction. Coachbuilders vied with each other to provide the most distinctive and eye-catching styles with streamlined effects.

Colourful artwork was a valuable selling point of the 1954 extended tours brochure.

Viv Corbin

Two set off on a

Author's boyhood trip

We were just lads, like any others at the time, but in our case we were united by a brother-like bond. We shared a love of buses — Western Welsh buses in particular and we had hatched a plan for an exciting adventure.

It was early in 1966 and the school holidays were beginning to drag. So we decided to embark on a mission to that place where, at one time or another in their lives, all Western Welsh buses would have to visit. We decided that we would make a pilgrimage to Ely Works.

It was a trip that was planned with military-like precision. We had decided to take flight from Bridgend bus station aboard an N&C Express coach, our next favourite mode of passenger transport. Timetables were checked, money for fares pocketed, along with a few bob for refreshments along the way, and watches were synchronised.

At first all went well. We boarded the N&C and soon after, it eased its way out of its bay and into the afternoon traffic and we handed a grateful conductor the exact fare.

Other passengers were chatting about the coming World Cup football tournament. For us the topic was what might lay behind the doors of our transport target. So much so that the first leg of our journey seemed to be over in no time at all. From here we quickly transferred to a No 14 Cardiff Corporation trolleybus to accomplish the U-turn that took us back on to Cowbridge Road West and our destination. This doubling up was necessary because the Brown Bombers weren't allowed to set down on their run into the city.

As the trolleybus pulled away we nervously turned around on the pavement to be confronted with our temple of transport — Western Welsh head office and central works. There was no shortage of vehicles on which to feast our eyes as we confidently

Inside Ely Works during the 1940s. There is a general feel of light and airiness about the place. Most of the machining was carried out in the shops situated around the building's perimeter. This left an uncluttered shop floor for the vehicles themselves. *Christine Davies*

strode down the concrete driveway clutching the latest South Wales edition of British Bus Fleets. My pal gave a cry of exclamation as he spotted an elusive vehicle, but before I could add to this there was another shout. Our progress down the driveway hadn't gone un-noticed and the realisation that our seemingly well-founded plans were about to fail soured our excitement, replacing it instead with bitter disappointment.

Leslie Gray himself — although we didn't realise at the time — had seen us walk down the drive, and despite our polite pleas and protestations we were unable to look around and given our marching orders. All was not lost,

however, as we returned home armed with the latest comprehensive fleet list. Priced at 2/6d, it swallowed what remained of the week's pocket money in one fell swoop. Our appetite for the wonders of Ely Works had been whetted and with nothing better than disappointment to fire fresh determination we decided a visit was more than worthy of a second attempt. So the following Sunday, back we trekked. This time aboard a smart new Tiger Cub on service 301, which, unlike the N&C, stopped outside the works. There was a definite feel good factor about these vehicles. The rich blue and ivory livery, blue and red tartan moquette seats, and dark blue trim all played their part

secret mission

to bus heaven

Telegraphic Address:
"CARDIFF 71327"

WESTERN WELSH
OMNIBUS COMPANY LIMITED
LAG/RD.

Telephone:
71327

ENGINEERING DEPARTMENT,
253 COWBRIDGE ROAD WEST,
CARDIFF.

16th January 1967.

C. Scott Esq.,
32 Jubilee Road,
Bridgend,
Glam.

Dear Sir,

    Your enquiry of the 11th inst., will have consideration
if you give the reason for your request to come to these Works.

    It is not usual to allow visitors here for a few days
monthly, but we could give permission for two of you to see the Works
on a Friday afternoon, subject to the usual conditions concerning
accidents etc.

    Yours faithfully,

L.A.Gray
Asst. Chief Engineer.

Following his Ely adventure the author wrote to head office asking for permission to visit 'legally'. This is the reply he received.

in that. This time our intrusion avoided detection. Our first taste of what lay within was parked in the yard — considerably fuller than in mid-week. There were buses in varying condition from the care-worn to those that were sparkling fresh out of the paint shop following overhaul. Peering through the doors of the first building, all we could see was plastic sheeting cocooning dozens of coaches. We walked among the mothballed ranks of Harringtons and Weymanns, all spotless in blue and ivory, ready for unveiling with the arrival of the tour season. Passing through another door, we entered the main workshops in the vicinity of the paint shop. It was a thrill to find buses in all states of repair, some of which could only be identified by the number plates, resting nearby. We saw several green-diamond vehicles from West Wales which were

Atlantean 329 (VKG 329) at Ely in 1966 after an argument with a low bridge.

much-needed 'cops' — there would be much underlining to do in our fleet books when we returned home! There were buses in every corner of the works. Eventually we left through a sliding door into the adjacent garage where there were several more coaches — the licensed ones, mainly Plaxtons — and a few more buses including a decapitated Atlantean. We gingerly climbed its staircase, our shoes crunching on the splinters of broken glass, to view the wreckage on the top deck. Our detective skills identified blood

splashes on some of the seats, a sobering sight. Many dreams were born of that day and the excitement it brought. It was a thrill I, nor probably, my mate have never forgotten. Little did I realise that the fleet list bought on our first visit to Ely Works and which wiped out a week's pocket money would, nearly 50 years later, form part of a book I would write on our favourite company!

Western Welsh management participated in the company's tours. Albert Gray's eldest son, Leslie, captured the proceedings in colour on cine film, so that in the winter months a series of talks over coffee and biscuits promoted the tours to many would-be customers who gathered in selected hotels for the event. A sort-of timeshare holiday campaign, but without the spivs! Remember, there was no commercial TV or radio reaching out to potential customers in their living rooms.

Western Welsh tours remained firmly on home soil — leaving the rest of Europe to an adventurous South Wales Transport — and so avoided the indignity of hoisting the coach by crane aboard a cross-channel ferry as the passengers scrambled up an open gangway from the quayside. In those days you needed an overnight stop before reaching Cornwall, and the Scottish tours often ran up the east side of England, or spent a night or two in the Lake District before they reached the border. In 1960 a grand tour to Loch Maree and John O'Groats started. For the princely sum of £50 you had 14 uninterrupted days of travel — think of the poor driver whose day continued beyond the driving to include unloading the cases, sweeping out and washing the coach! The tour left on a Sunday for Buxton, and by Monday had reached Whitby. Two nights at Dunbar followed, then a night each at Dalwhinnie and Helmsdale, followed by two nights at Dingwall. Returning down the west coast, single nights at Tyndrum and Oban preceded two at Prestwick, then came

The Tondu Road forecourt of Bridgend RFC became a useful overflow parking area, firstly after flooding in December 1960, then in the following year during bus station redevelopment when 425 (FUH 425) is pictured 'on the bench' awaiting selection. *Paul Redmond*

the final night at Windermere, by which time there would have been some tearful goodbyes, but happy memories of the Falls of Measach, Inverewe Gardens, Staffa, Iona and the Isle of Arran. What a shame that today, major bus operators have no time for coaching pursuits.

There was also a flourishing summer business in day trips, and in its heyday the fleet included around 50 coaches for use on tours and private hire work. Many people came back year after year, drawn by the company's colourful publicity, comprehensive route planning and steady

Many a happy hour was spent by the author as a teenager, observing scenes such as this at Bridgend bus station, perched on the railings at stand 18, between the frequent visits of the N&C coaches. Leyland PD2A, fleet No. 917 (917 DBO) is fuelled and washed, having returned from a works duty in March 1968. Hopefully the conductor remembered to shut the windows! *Mike Street*

Tiger Cub 1149 (MUH 149) at the depot yard in Fishguard on July 25, 1961. The green diamond, which would have identified the depot, is absent. *Paul Redmond*

growth in available destinations. Then there were the newcomers influenced by recommendations from satisfied friends and neighbours – or perhaps the promotional film shows.

During the winter months, considerably fewer coaches were required and the majority were delicensed and kept under wraps. Later they were stored within Ely works. Many coaches spent six months of the year mothballed in this way. In the summer Ely became an operational depot and on Monday mornings the elite touring driver/couriers reported there to collect their coaches before proceeding in convoy to Cardiff's central bus station to await feeder services from the west. Most of them then headed east, radiating away to Abergavenny, Usk, Chepstow or, with the coming of the Severn Bridge, Alveston. The Emerald Isle and Welsh Wonderland tours headed in the opposite direction.

On one occasion, a coach leaving Bridgend bus station by the entrance instead of the exit, turned right against the one-way traffic. The poor Pontypool-based driver/courier had never negotiated the town's traffic system before!

It is easy to forget just how much fun a bus journey could be in the days when services were planned for passenger needs as well as those of the operators. Days when local management decisions and common-

sense operation meant it was possible to enjoy a spirit of adventure in a simple bus journey. For example, where today would you find yourself jumping down from the bus inside the garage, or remaining aboard with smoking passengers as the bus refuelled, or hurriedly closing the windows before passing through the bus wash? Some will recall the excitement, in the heart of Bridgend bus station, where it seemed every other journey on the 240 or 302 went via the garage and did all of those things! While today's car-wash can evoke much, the trail of water from the average car will never match that of a

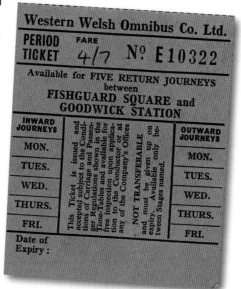

Leyland PD2 as it sped away from the washers and leaned into the corner of Market Street! Simple pleasures, maybe, but a world apart from open-air compounds in business parks, Hi-Vis safety wear and the dozens of 'Passengers Must Not' signs in the fully enclosed, super-sanitised bus stations of today.

Considering both the extent of operations and popularity of Western Welsh, regrettably there is very little today to serve as a lasting reminder of its existence. Many depots have long-since been redeveloped as high-density residential or light industrial parks,

The official opening of a new building always resulted in a souvenir brochure. This one was produced when Milford Haven's new garage and bus station opened in 1962.

and any sign of their former splendour has been obliterated. However, the occasional gem remains. Cwmbran depot still fulfills the function it was designed for while the garages at Barry, Brecon, Carmarthen, Neath, Newcastle Emlyn and Fishguard also survive, albeit in a variety of uses. Barry depot has become a working bus museum. This is remarkable when you consider the predecessor of the current town council bore such animosity towards Western Welsh!

The fleet at its formation consisted almost entirely of Commer cars, chain-driven and with gate gear changes. As the company began to absorb smaller, sometimes one-man businesses a variety of little-known and largely forgotten vehicle types were acquired. These vehicles were basic and all petrol driven returning miles per gallon that rarely exceeded single figures. Despite this the manufacturers had given them colourful names such as Star Flyers, AJS Pilots, Gilford Swifts, Thornycroft Darings, Vulcan Blackpools, Maudslay Marathons, Commer Corinthians, Guy Vixens and Arabs. Alongside them were Conquests, Wallaces, Beans, Dodges, and Tilling-Stevens.

As time went on AEC and Leyland became the dominant names in the fleet. With the growth in the popularity of public transport vehicle design changed significantly.

It would be great to see some of these early vehicles today to show just how different things were in those distant days. What a pity then, that only a few of the company's vehicles survive in preservation — or in store as long-term restoration projects — a mere fraction of

Carmarthen's town service between Blue Street and Bryn Meurig took all of five minutes end-to-end and in this quiet scene, the driver of 1233 (LKG 233) even had time to photograph his bus. There were 10 return trips each weekday in 1964. *Arnold Richardson/Photobus*

With Leyland's Tiger Cub production at an end, the 1971 intake of dual-purpose saloons consisted of 10 Leopards. The last of the batch, 1510 (TKG 510J) was the final vehicle to receive the splendid peacock blue and royal ivory colours. Unlike the earlier designs, lack of room at the front of the Willowbrook body prevented use of the WW crown and only the coach-style script could be fitted in. However, accident repairs to 1510 resulted in the 'V' beading being cut off, which allowed use of the lozenge-style fleet name. This was rapidly replacing the crown, proudly worn by the fleet since day one, as seen on 1315 (ABO 315B) alongside at Penarth Road in November, 1972. *Andrew Mann*

those of London Transport, Devon General, Southdown and Western National, to name a few, that are frequently seen at bus rallies. Nevertheless we should be thankful to those groups and individuals whose commitment and dedication to bus preservation allows us to view a real Western Welsh bus at events up and down the country. In particular John Wiltshire (WKG 284), Keith Severn (ABO 145B) Brian Catchpole (ABO 147B) Paul Burgess (FUH 370D) and Tony & Viv Jenkins (BKG 713B) have painstakingly achieved their ambitions to restore their vehicles at no small cost to themselves, and continue to work, often single-handedly, to keep them pristine and roadworthy for us all to enjoy. On the horizon, and funds permitting, CUH 856, LKG 678, OUH 107, TUH 13, KKG 215F and OUH 177G will one day join in the fun.

Another feature of the rally scene is the memorabilia that can sometimes be found among the enthusiast stalls. Old timetables and excursion pamphlets can and do command a hefty sum. But what has happened to all the company records? The efficiency of the fleet depended on them. The history of every vehicle was kept on its own particular card at head office. In the days when vehicles were licensed and delicensed continually throughout the year, such records, along with certificates of fitness, and drivers' public service vehicle (PSV) licences, were meticulously recorded. Full information on any vehicle or member of staff was available. Tragically much of this

information along with so much more of the company's heritage has disappeared in the years that have elapsed since Western Welsh finally died.

Like all successful public service businesses, people mattered most in the Western Welsh story. Many of the events and topics featured in the Staff Bulletins, of which management was so justifiably proud, are now recounted once again and hopefully will enable as complete a picture as possible to be painted. The nuts and bolts, people and personalities all earned their mention. They all played a part in the company that was Western Welsh.

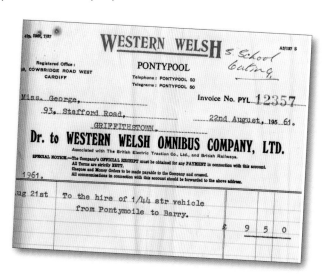

A bus route to success

Pioneering spirit of inventor Albert

If there is one name that is synonymous with the story of Western Welsh it is that of Albert Gray. He was there at the very start and it was his combination of determination, intuition and business acumen that, more than anything else, led to the creation of what became one of the country's biggest bus companies.

There had been few motor buses in Wales before the First World War and they were regarded as nothing more than a novelty. When hostilities ceased however, there was a flood of Army surplus vehicles. Two things occurred to the entrepreneurial Gray at this time. He realised that this would be an easy way of acquiring vehicles and at the same time spotted the potential for transforming them into passenger carriers. He persuaded his employers to buy a number of vehicles and never looked back. Gray was not one for standing still, but little could he have realised when he set out on an engineering career with

the Bellis & Moorcom company the route that this would take. In 1900 he joined the Star Engineering company at Wolverhampton and became involved in production of the 3½hp Star-Benz Dog Cart. Four years later he joined the Ariel Motor company, Birmingham and then in 1906 became transport manager and engineer with Cardiff brewers William Hancock. There, his role was the maintenance of their fleet of Milnes-Daimler and Dennis lorries. With the advent of the First World War he was appointed transport engineer to the South Wales and Monmouthshire Coal Owners' Association and oversaw the movement of pit props in Wales and the south west of England. Under his control was a fleet of petrol lorries, steam wagons and steam tractors.

Gray's inventive skills appear to have known no bounds. In 1912 he patented the Notax paraffin carburettor and two years later he designed the United induction pipe for vaporising heavy oils.

Albert Gray, first general manager of Western Welsh and the genius behind it all. *Christine Davies*

The war had been an ideal proving ground for motorised road transport. The practicality and reliability of many makes of vehicle were established this way and led to the production of many successful chassis types.

But it wasn't this that interested Gray when he returned to Hancock's in 1919. Instead he spotted the opportunity presented by the surplus wartime vehicles. He felt that not only was it a useful way of boosting the brewery's transport fleet, but by turning them into buses it was a way of generating more income for his employers.

1920

Early in the year, Gray persuaded the Hancock company to finance the creation of South Wales Commercial Motors as a vehicle sales and repair facility. The enterprise was eventually launched in May with Gray as general manager. Before long he was joined by Ernest S Mountain as works manager. The business operated from leased premises in Penarth Road and Crawshay Street, Cardiff. It began with a franchise for the sales

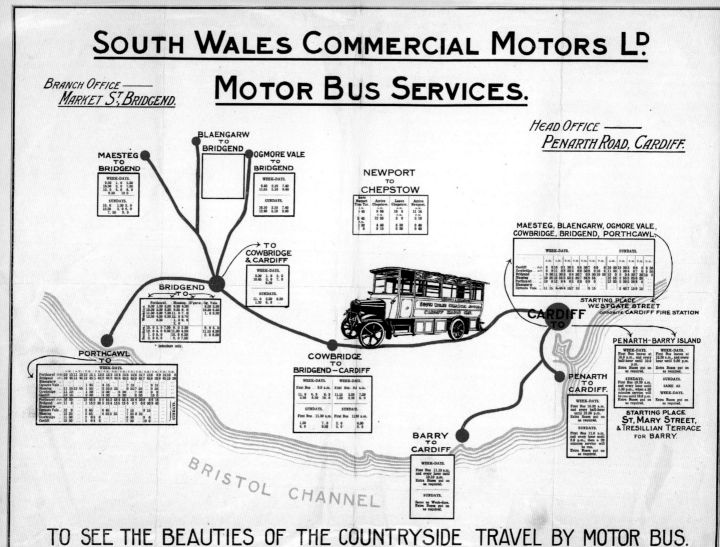

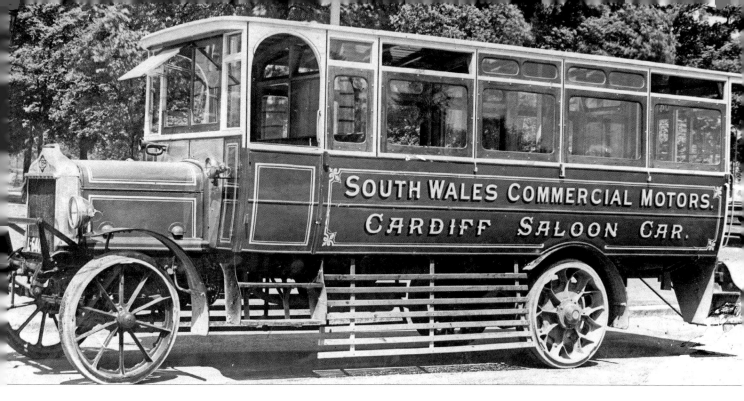

and service of Commer vehicles, the Hancock company's preferred manufacturer, and with it came the opportunity to start a bus operation.

On Good Friday, April 1, the inaugural service began between Cardiff and Penarth. It was of an hourly frequency and used two vehicles. Driver Tom Willis left the Terminus Hotel in St Mary Street at 10am behind the wheel of a chain-driven Commer bus. This was to be the ticket to Gray's future.

These pioneering Commers were basic vehicles, and the completion of a day's work — or even a return journey — without breakdown was by no means assured. Rudimentary spares were carried on the vehicles, and conductors sometimes had to lie along the mudguard to flood the carburettor in order to get back! Nevertheless, the drivers and conductors took great pride in their vehicles. On arrival at terminal points, they would often spend the layover time polishing radiators and lamps, cleaning the paintwork and generally tinkering with their vehicles. Every conductor counted a tin of Brasso and dusters as part of his equipment, often buying them out of his own pocket.

With solid tyres, oil lamps and slatted seats, these red and white saloons carried their intrepid passengers at a steady 12mph for three-and-a-half miles along Penarth Road, a privilege for which the return fare was 1/6d.

This first regular service marked the modest beginning of a business which seized each and every opportunity that presented itself throughout the 1920s, a decade which saw tremendous growth in the provision of bus services. There were many operational shortcomings, but people

This beautifully presented AEC YC was the pride of the SWCM fleet when new in 1920. No. 32 (L6404) was the oldest vehicle to pass to Western Welsh at its formation in 1929. *Viv Corbin*

weren't bothered by this and gave the new company their full support. Business thrived as the Penarth service increased to half-hourly frequency and a second route, from Cardiff to Cowbridge, began in December. This success was to grow steadily for the remainder of the decade to a point where the company began to attract outside attention.

In those early days, duty scheduling was comparatively simple and allowed buses to be allocated regularly to the same crews, who came to regard their vehicles with

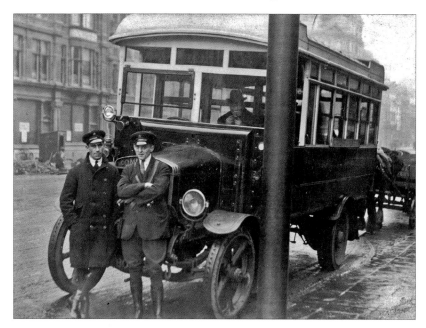

The proud crew of South Wales Commercial Motors' Commer bus No. 1 (BO 2935) about to set off on another pioneering journey in the early 1920s. The post looks as though it could cause some serious damage if those tiny tyres lost their grip on the road. *Viv Corbin*

affection. Realising that this engendered loyalty, pride and a happy workforce, it was fully encouraged. There can be no doubt that SWCM was a happy organisation.

In a hand-written ledger dated June 18, SWCM's wage bills for the week in the body shop amounted to £48 19s 9d; fitters received a total of £55 9s 9d; office staff £9 10s; haulage cost £4 4s 8d; welding £8 17s 4d; National Insurance payments were 10s 10d and the charwoman received the sum of 17 shillings.

South Wales Commercial Motors was formally registered in November with capital of £20,000 in £1 shares. It had four directors, each of whom received 5,000 shares and an annual salary of £250.

Driver Charles Perrin of Penarth Road depot was fined for speeding, having been accused of tearing along at the breakneck speed of 14 mph. He was described as 'a bachelor by chance, having been crossed in love by a girl who could not be happy with love in a cottage'. Now that's creative journalism, and there was absolutely no phone-hacking! 'Nowadays he can discipline his roving eye and he prefers his glass of beer.' You couldn't invent it!

1921

A two-hourly service, between Cardiff's Tresillian Hotel and Dinas Powis via Cogan began in February and was soon extended to Barry. Despite fierce competition from White's and Thomas Motor Services, the frequency had become hourly by April.

A route between Rodney Road, Newport and Chepstow began operation in April, for which a garage was rented at Caerwent. Newport Corporation's refusal to allow SWCM's service to start from the town centre resulted in an appeal to the Ministry of Transport. Eventually, the

corporation reluctantly agreed, but continued to make life difficult for the company by imposing many operational restraints.

A parcel service began in August, co-ordinated by Inspector AE Smith. He had started his career producing timetables which, with canvassed sponsorship from local businesses, were printed and widely distributed for the princely sum of one penny.

With the company facing increased competition from a number of other enthusiastic operators, Gray took the decision to abandon the route from Cardiff to Barry and informed Barry Urban District Council (UDC) that they no longer required the licences. Attention then focussed on the Bridgend area, with the town becoming the hub of a service from Porthcawl to Pontypridd. The Cardiff to Cowbridge route was also extended to Bridgend to connect with this. An office was leased in the town centre, and garages for seven vehicles rented at Free School Lane. Gray later regretted his decision to withdraw from Barry, as within a few years the town had become a popular seaside resort.

1922

The ever-inventive Albert Gray designed a sliding roof for saloon vehicles, for which he obtained patents in Britain, America and Canada. The prototype 'sunshine roof' was eventually fitted to a Commer 3P saloon the following year. Northern Counties took the design up and within two years the all-weather roof was an option on all their coach bodies. Within a decade this type of roof, whether consisting of sliding metal or canvas material, would become the norm for touring coaches.

Conveying parcels on buses was a profitable sideline which recorded a profit of £253 for SWCM in its first year. Agencies were established in every town and village served. Parcels could also be handed to conductors. It soon became necessary to levy an extra charge on large and bulky items, and to carry them only on the proviso that there was room on the bus.

Operations at Bridgend grew rapidly to such extent that a larger garage for 12 buses was quickly brought into use at Brackla Street. Services to Caerau, Blaengarw and Ogmore Vale were introduced. In the Llynfi valley, SWCM paid Maesteg UDC a fee for running buses through their area. They were not obliged to do this under the 1920 Roads Act, and it was later revealed that the council should not have accepted payment. Meanwhile, Newport Corporation agreed, subject to certain conditions, that the company could start its Chepstow service from the

This is how they were on the inside. Commer BO 5194 with SWCM bodywork shows off Albert Gray's patented roll-top sunshine roof. It was the first PSV in the country to have such a feature. *Viv Corbin*

One of the three SWCM Commer 3P charabancs with home-made bodies which found its way to Western Welsh in 1929 was No.16 (BO 3944). *Viv Corbin*

junction of Alfred Street and Church Street instead of the tramway terminus, but this was later withdrawn and, following public meetings, a terminus at Skinner Street was mutually agreed early in 1923.

1923

From March of this year, SWCM became the regional agent for Lancia vehicles. Within a month and possibly by coincidence, Commercial Cars Ltd (Commer) went into receivership. At the time, SWCM held 1,000 10 per cent debentures in the latter company and it continued to trade under the Receiver until eventually it was bought by Humber in 1926. Most of the fleet still consisted of Commers. There were 20 at this time.

South Wales Commercial Motors can also lay claim to opening the first bus station in Wales on leased ground in Market Street, Bridgend. A summer service from there to Ogmore-by-Sea and Southerndown began along with an advertising campaign for private hire. The vehicles used for parties were charabancs, and these often doubled up on local stage carriage services when not engaged on private hire work. When working on charabancs, conductors would have to climb along the running board

to move from one compartment to another while the vehicles travelled at anything up to 20mph!

A new service was started by SWCM, from Porthcawl to Port Talbot, although it was short lived and abandoned in December. In November an application to operate from Bridgend to Kenfig Hill via Laleston was refused. The Cridlands company was already operating this route and continued to hold sway in the Port Talbot area until 1929 when their services were acquired by Western Welsh, the company born out of SWCM. In December a Saturday service started from the Old Post at Bonvilston to Llancarfan, while freehold land was bought for a new garage at 'Green Talbot'.

Captain GT Wilcox was succeeded as Bridgend area manager by E Rees who continued the loyal and enthusiastic fight to establish services in the area. These were competitive times on nearly every route that was opened up. The company fought hard to maintain the gains that were made, and in doing so laid the firm foundation of what would eventually become the Western Welsh company's largest centre of operation.

In May, the location of the Newport terminus had been moved again. In future the routes that it handled would operate from Rodney Street.

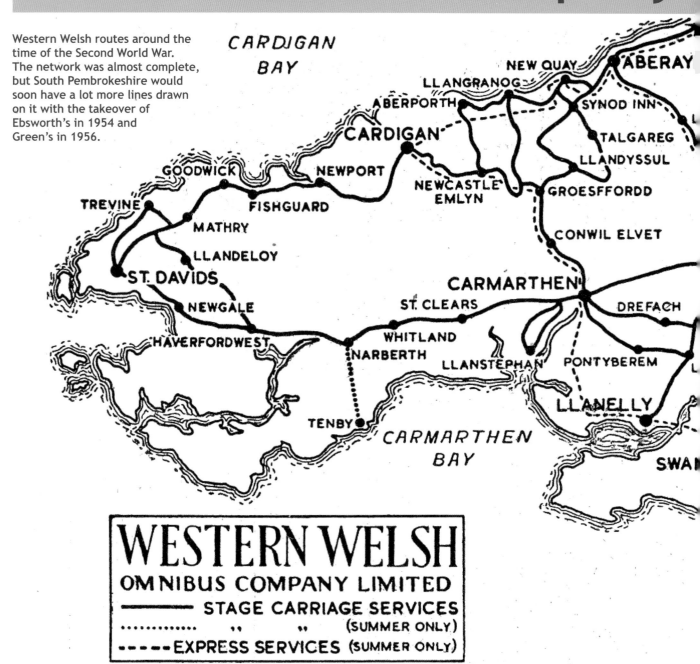

Western Welsh routes around the time of the Second World War. The network was almost complete, but South Pembrokeshire would soon have a lot more lines drawn on it with the takeover of Ebsworth's in 1954 and Green's in 1956.

EXPRESS SERVICE

(Summer Season Only)
From all parts of South Wales to ABERYSTWYTH with connections for North Wales

DAY & HALF-DAY

EXCURSIONS

From numerous centres in the Company's operating area

served its people

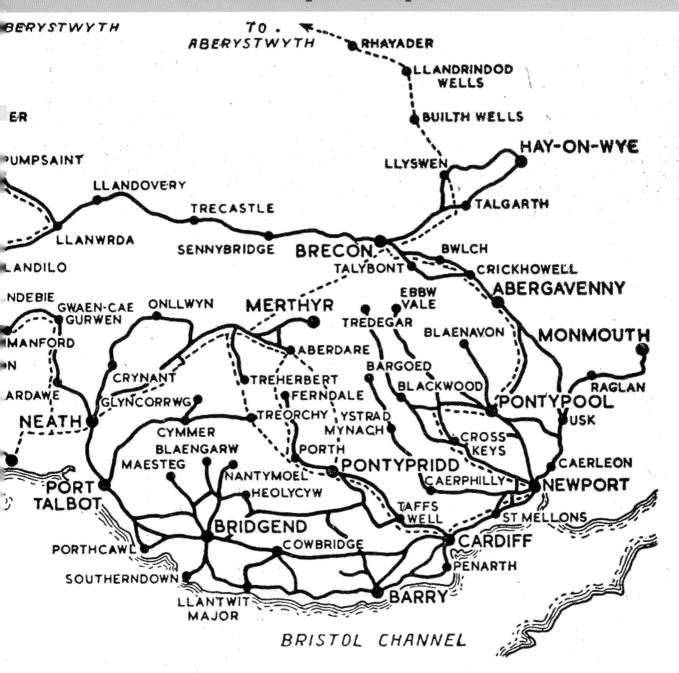

EXTENDED TOURS

(Summer Season Only)
Inclusive of FIRST CLASS
HOTEL ACCOMMODATION
operated to ALL PARTS OF
BRITAIN

PRIVATE HIRE

We shall be pleased

to quote for your

party

1924

Pneumatic tyres were now becoming available for commercial vehicles and buses, and a Lancia saloon became the first vehicle in the fleet to be equipped with them. From here on they began to replace solid-tyred front wheels much to the delight of drivers who welcomed the improved ride and steering. Front wheel brakes followed during the year, further improving control of vehicles.

The mid-1920s saw a period of consolidation, but the company could not afford to rest on its laurels as many one-man businesses were being set up in direct competition. These would undercut fares and poach customers. However, a persistent and genuine desire to provide a good public service shone through and the company stood out among its competitors.

In April, services started between Bridgend and Sarn, and from Bridgend to Kenfig Hill via Aberkenfig. There was strong competition from Cridlands over the latter section and it was this that resulted in the withdrawal of the Western Welsh Porthcawl to Port Talbot service. In the same month a 21-year lease was agreed on the Armoury Garage, Cowbridge, and in October the Talbot Green depot was completed. Meanwhile, consolidation in the Monmouthshire area resulted in improvements between Newport and Chepstow, including a new route via Magor and Portskewett.

1925

Barry Urban District Council, no doubt slighted at the 1922 surrender of SWCM's licences in the town, had refused the company's application for new licences from Barry to both Penarth and Bonvilston in 1924, but fierce competition among the large number of operators in the Barry area had become a problem in the town. Swords drawn, SWCM was determined to return.

In January the Cardiff to Penarth service was extended to Lower Penarth, but saw competition from White's — firstly over this new section of route, then by April over its whole length. Tickets weren't interchangeable and it is said the service resembled a gala race meeting at Brooklands, with racing regularly taking place between SWCM's Leyland Lion and White's AEC Renown. They could often be seen neck and neck speeding up Windsor Road past Penarth Police Station!

Frank Winniatt started bus driving in 1925 when the vehicles were mostly solid-tyred and the speed limit was 12 mph. He was once fined for travelling at 16mph along the main street in Neath although it is difficult to imagine how, in those days, his speed could have been calculated so accurately. It was certainly a money-making day at the local magistrates court as no fewer than five conductors were fined for overloading their buses.

At the end of May, Cardiff Corporation Tramways (CCT) joined the melee by running to Penarth. The answer to passenger enquiries about which bus left first was usually: "The others, but we'll get there first!" Following several stormy sessions with the police, SWCM said they would agree a joint timetable with CCT but not with White's — their aim was obviously to run the latter company off the road. It would however, be 1933 before Tom White began negotiations with Western Welsh to sell out, but it wasn't until 1936 that White's was finally taken over.

Despite the fight with White's and the early bus wars, the most profitable service by far was that between Cardiff and Penarth, followed by the Cardiff to Bridgend, Bridgend to Pontypridd, and Bridgend to Maesteg routes. Elsewhere there were route changes. By February, some Newport to Chepstow journeys were running via Magor and Caldicot.

The fleet totalled around 35 vehicles by the end of the year. However, the cost of operation, and therefore the fares charged, were comparatively high. The Commers were particularly thirsty vehicles, and petrol costs dominated the balance sheet. Nevertheless, the modern Leyland Lions and Lancia saloons, with their pneumatic tyres, soon helped to reduce operating costs bringing fare reductions and cheap day returns on certain routes.

An agency to supply Leyland vehicles was authorised in May, adding to the portfolio of SWCM interests and further strengthening its business.

This was the year that roofs first appeared on double-deckers and saloon heaters soon followed. Both were an indication that awareness of passenger comfort was growing and as a result improvements to buses were being made. Vehicles in use after the First World War generally carried between 28 and 30 passengers seated in rows, each with its own door. And what buses they must have been with their solid tyres and formidable steps to negotiate before gaining the relative comfort of a slatted seat. A canvas roof provided some protection for passengers, but this was often far from waterproof. One tale recounts a Lancia bus operating during a particularly fierce thunderstorm and describes how its solitary passenger, an old woman, sat patiently with an umbrella over her head while the rain poured into the bus! Before long however the safety and comfort of passengers would increase enormously.

The first direct parcels service began with the purchase of two Trojan 10 cwt vans. Prior to this, parcels had been

This Lancia was new to SWCM as No. 9 (BO 3081) in 1922 and used on the Cardiff to Penarth service. It served the company well, before passing to Western Welsh where it operated until 1931. The number 42 on the cab door is not a fleet number, but a licence plate to show the vehicle conformed with specifications laid down by Cardiff Corporation, before the 1930 Road Traffic Act. *Viv Corbin*

carried aboard the buses themselves, and handling agents were used for delivery and collection. Now parcels could be conveyed direct from door to door. With the exception of a downturn during the Second World War, the modest parcels service remained a constant source of revenue until the final days of the Western Welsh company.

1926

By now, motor buses had become an accepted part of everyday life, but the operators, like most businesses at the time, were hit by the Depression. This was the year of the General Strike. It saw the company's Bridgend-based crews and buses being pressed into service on routes within Cardiff and postage stamps being accepted as payment for fares.

The South Wales Commercial Motors company was holding its own during these troubled times, and in a typically benevolent move the company contributed to the distress funds set up in those districts through which its buses operated.

The competitor on the Cardiff to Cowbridge service, Maddox of Cowbridge, was taken over along with two buses, for £1,400. A garage was purchased at Kenfig Hill and further land leased in Brackla Street, Bridgend. The town's bus station had already become too small to deal

with the volume of traffic it was handling. Interestingly a County Court judge insisted that the buses should start from the front of the town hall on court days even though it was just a stone's throw from the bus station. It would be 1930 before land was finally obtained for further expansion in Bridgend.

On November 1, a service began from Bridgend to Barry via Bonvilston, finally returning SWCM buses to the streets of Barry. On Thursday, February 25 the Penarth Times carried a story headlined: 'A Luxurious Bus' and proclaimed: 'The South Wales Commercial Motor Company are living up to the wonderful enterprise which they have exhibited in the past in the provision of motor buses on the Penarth to Cardiff Road. Their latest acquisition is a Leyland Lion, a 32-seater saloon bus, which incorporates many new improvements, and is the last word in comfort and easy running. The bus is upholstered in red leather and has aluminium fittings throughout. It is built on the railway coach principle, with side racks for light parcels. It has a 29hp engine, and its tyres are pumped up by its engine. It is a most delightful and comfortable bus: in fact it rides like a luxurious motor car.'

However, it was a lowly Commer 3P saloon that made the news in the summer when it operated an extended tour of Britain — a first for a Welsh operator. The 14-day itinerary had been meticulously planned by Klewer Williams of Caerleon, and embraced some of the most beautiful scenery in the country. Williams had

The garage and workshops of Lewis & James (Western Valleys) at Crosskeys in the 1920s.

approached SWCM for a vehicle and driver. The Commer provided had its 28 seats removed and replaced by dining chairs and a table which were all screwed to the floor enabling Williams's party of eight to enjoy a meal where and when they wished. In the fortnight they were on the road the party and their bus covered 1,200 miles at a maximum speed of just 20mph!

An overall profit of £16,583 was announced for the first six years of the company's existence. However, profits had been hit by the failure of some customers to honour their hire purchase payments for vehicles bought through SWCM's dealership. Consequently, at the year end the company's books showed a shortfall of nearly £4,000. This was a sorry situation. As often happens it came at the wrong time as Hancock's were looking for the finance to purchase another brewery.

Barrett's Eastern Valleys company, associated with South Wales Commercial Motors, operated this all-Leyland Lion (WO 900) from new in 1927. It passed to Western Welsh in 1933 as fleet No. 19 and is seen at The Bulwark, Brecon, following takeover. *AB Cross (J Higham collection)*

1927

The improving economic situation at the end of 1926 no doubt influenced the National Electric Construction Company (NECC), which was connected with Rhondda Tramways, in its purchase of shares in SWCM. Within two years this single act was to have a crucial bearing on the formation of Western Welsh. The NECC's original board of directors resigned and WB Cownie was appointed chairman and managing director. Cownie was also the managing director of Rhondda Tramways, a fact which the press mistakenly equated to a takeover of SWCM by that company. Albert Gray remained general manager with an annual salary of £750. Understandably, business policy was to expand the bus services and scale down the vehicle sales side. By November, the share capital had increased from £20,000 to £80,000. Cownie resigned as chairman and was replaced by the redoubtable Harley C Drayton.

In April, speculating to accumulate, the business of Lewis & James Ltd, Newbridge, a well-respected company trading as Western Valley Motor Services, was bought for £25,250. The name survived until 1933. Conversely, low receipts and high operating costs resulted in the Newport services being sold to a new operator, the South Monmouthshire Motor company, in 1928.

In December, Barry UDC again refused the company licences for the Cardiff services via both Dinas Powis and Sycamore Cross. Undaunted — and much to the

Crews and vehicles on the SWCM Barry to Beddau and Bridgend to Cardiff services connect at Sycamore Cross, near Bonvilston. On the left is a Leyland SGII 36-seater from 1925 (BT 8432), while on the right is a Commer 3P 28-seater from 1926 (UH 1462). *Viv Corbin*

annoyance of the council — the company used the practice of carrying passengers on the Barry to Bridgend service, and changing them onto their Cardiff bus from Sycamore Cross.

At the end of the financial year the company's shortfall had worsened and it reported a loss of £5,046.

1928

The share issue was once again raised, this time to £150,000. In February the business of Barrett Bros, Pontypool, trading as Eastern Valley Motor Services, was purchased for £41,000. The name was retained and as a result the SWCM company now consisted of a group of three fleets. Following this, the company's earlier, abandoned interest in Port Talbot was revived with the opening of a garage in the town's Croft Street, just behind the bottleneck Maypole Corner at the junction of Water Street and High Street. In the meantime, services from Beddau to Barry and from Cowbridge to Llantwit Major, were also started.

In August, another small operator fell prey to the take-over quest of SWCM. This time it was the operation of Josh Jones who traded as Garw & Ogmore Transport. The business, based at Maesteg was bought for £4,500 and with the acquisition came five buses.

Running receipts for SWCM were 10.1 pence per mile (in £sd); for Western Valleys, 11.81 pence per mile and Eastern Valleys 9.19 pence per mile. The group's fleet total stood at 119. A meagre profit of £3,102 was returned for the year.

Company's routes to the future

Negotiations began in 1928 for the purchase of SWCM by the National Electric Construction Company. At this time 13 services appeared in the timetable. They were:

Penarth – Cardiff – Cowbridge – Bridgend – Porthcawl

Penarth – Cardiff – Cowbridge – Llantwit Major – Southerndown – Ogmore by Sea

Bridgend – Ogmore by Sea – Southerndown (summer only)

Cardiff – Sycamore Cross – Barry Island

Bridgend – Sycamore Cross – Barry Island

Bridgend – Maesteg – Caerau

Bridgend – Aberkenfig – Kenfig Hill

Bridgend – Blaengarw

Bridgend – Ogmore Vale

Bridgend – Talbot Green – Pontypridd

Newport – Caerwent – Chepstow

Beddau – Pendoylan – Barry Island

Bonvilston – Llancarfan (Saturdays only)

On track for a revolution

Railway signalled start of bus boom

WALES'S railway network was virtually complete by the turn of the 20th Century, and with rail travel paramount, buses were rarely seen. Most communities were less than 10 miles from a station, and where a town was unlucky enough not to be served by the railway, the companies had cleverly sought a way of connecting it to the system. This created a meaningful opening for bus services. The Great Western Railway quickly recognised the potential of the feeder bus idea and in its heyday, in answer to requests from local authorities, ran more buses than all of the bus companies put together.

The first such route in Wales used a Milnes-Daimler double-decker and began operating between Abergavenny and Brecon via Crickhowell in July 1905, a distance of some 20 miles. A second service linking Lampeter and Aberystwyth began in October 1906, using two vehicles garaged at the Feathers Hotel, Aberaeron, where the road staff were brought in from England and lived in a tent! The following year an approach was made to the GWR to provide a service between Swansea and the Gower peninsula, but it was declined as all authorised vehicles were fully allocated. Had the GWR seized the opportunity at Swansea and gained the support of the council, the later near-monopoly of bus services in and around the city by the South Wales Transport bus company might never have happened.

In following years, GWR bus routes sprung up along the country roads of Pembrokeshire and Cardiganshire, linking Haverfordwest to St David's, Fishguard and New Quay. Further services developed around Brecon and Neath. In 1913 a new depot was opened just outside Neath, where some of the early coal-gas powered Milnes-Daimlers began running from the town to Pontardawe. This service was soon extended to Brynaman, while another ran to Ammanford.

The Great Western Railway took delivery of this 1929 Vickers bodied Maudslay ML3B only weeks before transferring its Welsh bus operations to the newly created Western Welsh company. Bus No. 332 (UU 4815) stands at Brecon on one of the railway services. It was GWR car No. 1588.
A B Cross (J Higham collection)

Devon and Cornwall aside, West Wales saw the largest area of bus operations by the Great Western Railway and these services were well established by the onset of the First World War. Although they were then curtailed until 1918, most services saw rapid development as soon as bus production was resumed, and within 10 years 154 services were operating across GWR territory.

Post-war developments in Wales included a depot in Cardigan for services to nearby Newport and Goodwick station, and to Newcastle Emlyn. The Ammanford service was extended to Carmarthen, while a new service linked Neath with Pontneathvaughan. New AEC saloons arrived in the area and enabled a through service to be run between Carmarthen and Neath. This saw serious competition from James of Ammanford, but was resolved in 1927 when the service reverted to two separate portions, one from Carmarthen to Ammanford and the other from Ammanford to Neath. Additional services in the Fishguard area came in 1923, while the following year the GWR competed with South Wales Transport (SWT) in the Dulais Valley and Vale of Neath. Developments in the Abergavenny and Brecon areas continued, then in 1925 a depot opened in Pontypool for services to New Inn, Griffithstown and Panteg. By now, the foundations were firmly laid for the growth of the Western Welsh company.

Further services were introduced in West Wales in 1926, including a circuitous route which served villages between St David's and Mathry Road station. In 1927 a service began between Cymmer Afan and Glyncorrwg which enabled a considerable reduction in the railway service which ran up the uninhabited side of the Corrwg valley. New Maudslays and Guys began replacing the older AECs and led to further expansion in the Neath area, including a service to Porthcawl which later became a joint venture with SWT.

The GWR referred to their buses as 'cars' and the skill and ingenuity of the men involved with the vehicles has to be saluted. Often the driver was exposed to the elements, and had to negotiate his solid-tyred vehicle over badly rutted roads. The conductor, too, had his problems, for apart from fare collection there was always a considerable amount of luggage, goods and parcels to contend with. As with the SWCM, these men

Station Square, Neath in 1928, showing a variety of Guys and Thornycrofts operated by the Great Western Railway on their services to Porthcawl via Aberavon and Ammanford via Pontardawe. The Western Welsh offices were later built on the right, behind the advertising hoardings. *Stewart Williams*

36

This early bus, 424 (XY 7444) was one of several Thornycroft A1s with Vickers 19-seat bodywork new to the GWR in 1925. It came to Western Welsh at the very beginning, in 1929 and was used at Pontypool until being withdrawn in 1935.
RF Mack

took a tremendous pride in the appearance of their car, polishing the brasses and attending to the oil lamps in addition to their more orthodox duties. There is little doubt that these pioneering operations had a great bearing on the development of the bus industry in South and West Wales and led indirectly to the formation of Western Welsh.

1929

Railway involvement in bus operations was transformed in the period between 1928 and 1930, but the bus boom of the mid-1920s had clearly ended. Many operators found they had too many vehicles carrying too few passengers. Because the legal powers of railway companies to run bus services were unclear, each sought legislation from Parliament to obtain clarity.

In 1927 the Great Western Railway had promoted a Bill seeking to confirm their bus operating powers and allowing them to take a share in bus companies operating within their territory. The GWR, with its experience in bus operation, was also far-sighted enough to lay plans for this eventuality and even before the Bill became law had approached many of these operators with a view to buying their businesses. It also made joint running agreements with the more respectable private bus companies. NECC's interests were not only connected to SWCM but included operations outside Wales, namely Oxford and Torquay, and so was of considerable interest. The GWR had started talks with SWCM (and by implication Lewis & James and Barretts) in 1928 and, although nothing could be achieved until the Bill received Royal Assent, it was decided to form a jointly owned company. The name suggested for the new company was the Great Western Welsh Omnibus Company. A variety of other options included Great Gwalia.

It wasn't long before the name Great Western Welsh was shortened to just Western Welsh, which explains the rather odd name of a company whose greatest mileage lay in south-east Wales. Royal Assent for the 1928 GWR (Road Transport) Bill had been given in August of that year. As part of this the railways had agreed to refrain from taking a controlling interest in bus undertakings. This resulted in partnerships with the bus companies.

An agreement was signed on March 27, 1929, in which the GWR and SWCM united and the Western Welsh Omnibus Company was born on April 1. The GWR acted as agents for Western Welsh until the new public company came into being on June 12, with Albert Gray as its general manager.

At the same time as the GWR's final new bus route began, from Carmarthen to Pontyberem, the railway company's small garage at Abergavenny was transferred to SWCM in readiness for the launch of Western Welsh in June. More than 90 vehicles were transferred in the months that followed.

Bus services operated by the GWR in South and West Wales ceased after July 31, and from August 1, the board of Western Welsh took control of all bus services. With this came a greatly increased sphere of influence. The GWR injected a 50 per cent shareholding interest in the new company, the effect of which soon led to the acquisition of Cridlands and Tresillian Motors. Both had competed on the Cardiff to Pontypridd and Barry routes. Cridlands had also run into the Afan Valley from Port Talbot since 1921 and bequeathed Western Welsh a small depot in the town. The price paid for Cridlands with 21 vehicles was £33,000; Tresillian's cost £6,500 with 10 vehicles, seven of which were taken into stock.

While all this was going on, the small company of Paskin of Brecon, who ran buses from there to Lampeter, was also acquired. The Western Valleys (Lewis & James) and Eastern Valleys (Barrett's) fleets continued to be operated at arms' length by Western Welsh and were not absorbed fully until 1933. Elsewhere, the British Electric

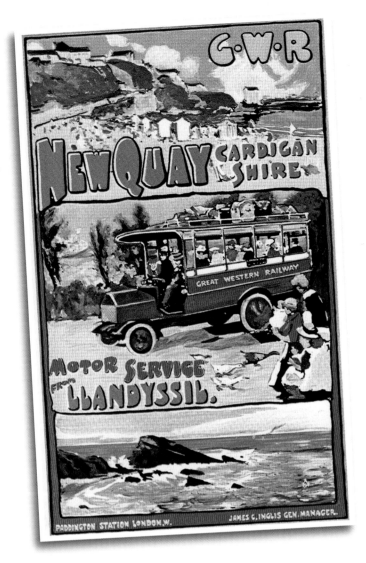

wilful misrepresentation or suppression of facts in a verbal or written report, for failing to report irregularities or accidents, for incivility or want of proper courtesy or attention to passengers or other members of the public. For any of these the fine was 2/6d. If there was a repetition of any of the above offences it was doubled.

Heavier penalties of up to £1 were imposed for negligence or misconduct. No doubt as a precautionary measure, Rule 54 stated: 'Ladies must not be allowed to ride on drivers' seats on double-deck cars, and should, as far as possible, be discouraged from riding beside the driver on single-deck cars.'

The rules relating to speed appear amusing now: 'When two or more cars are running on the same road there must be no racing or attempt at racing. The speed approaching and over railway level crossings must not exceed 4 mph. On hills all cars must stop dead and brakes tested before beginning descent and on no part of the descent must the speed exceed 6 mph.'

Hills were indeed somewhere that crews needed to exercise extreme care. A vital piece of equipment carried on early buses was a kind of wooden chock called a Scotch. When climbing hills conductors were told to hold the scotch in readiness so that they could, if needed chock the wheels to stop the vehicle rolling backwards.

A conductor's duties were many and varied. They were required to clean the interiors and the brass and metalwork of their cars during the day. They were also held responsible for seeing that their cars were properly equipped with waterproof aprons for passengers, and after use they were required to "fold and replace the aprons in their proper position."

In all 96 vehicles were transferred to Western Welsh from the GWR. These comprised 42 Maudslay, 23 Guy, 21 Thornycroft, three Lancia, two Graham Dodge, two AEC, two Morris and one International. There were also two Milnes-Daimlers used for goods and luggage. Guys, Maudslays and Thornycrofts were known to have featured in the early Western Welsh fleet, as well as a few other 'odds and ends'. On many of these early vehicles it was customary to remove a complete pane of glass from each side of the vehicle for ventilation during the summer months. There was also an extra charge of 3d per passenger to sit by the driver, but for this pleasure he was also expected to operate the sump pump.

The services of Dare Valley Motors had been taken over by the GWR in 1928 and were quickly integrated with those of the fast growing Western Welsh company.

In the Vale of Glamorgan it was intended to operate the Barry to Bridgend service every three hours, from October. The two vehicles licensed for the service were to be replaced by two single-entrance Leyland Lions (UH 607 and UH 577), but Barry UDC declined to approve the vehicles and they were refused a licence. This was an

Traction Company, which had a long-standing and complex history of common interests with a number of tramway ownership groups, reorganised its interests with one such group, Thomas Tilling, and formed Tilling & British Automobile Traction (BAT). Their aim was to compete against the large-scale railway purchases that were taking place.

The GWR staff who transferred to Western Welsh retained their National Union of Railwaymen membership and became known as GWR Loaned Staff. They were issued with a rule book for the guidance of the staff working the Road Motor Car Services. Dating from 1907, this was in all probability the first rule book issued for any road transport staff. The 71-page publication was packed with instructions that stated: 'Every servant must make himself thoroughly acquainted with.' Among many other things it contained a scale of fines for non-compliance which must have been very unpopular.

These fines were for such misdemeanours as absence from duty without leave, coming late on duty, leaving duty before proper time or before being relieved, coming on duty without proper rest or otherwise unfit for duty, permitting relief by men unauthorised or unfit for duty, for insubordination or non-observance of the lawful orders of a superior officer or for the use of abusive or offensive language while on duty. Others included the

In 1930 the pride of the fleet was Leyland Lion coach No. 59 (UH 8213). The vehicle was painted in a light blue and cream livery, and was popular with private hire organisers. Gaily festooned from top to bottom, it was about to take part in the local carnival when photographed in Station Yard, Aberdare. *Stewart Williams*

inconsistent decision considering the vehicles that had been approved and used previously. Penarth UDC had a more enlightened policy, UH 607 having been licensed there since March 1926. In the Barry Council meeting of November 6, Councillor CB Griffiths led the attack on the new buses: "They may have been passed by Scotland Yard, they may conform with Ministry of Transport regulations, but we won't have them. Suppose one of these vehicles was going up Holton Road and a small vehicle coming out from a side street hit the side where the petrol tank is. Every person sitting in front of the petrol tank has no proper means of escape. They are caught like rats in a trap, and the only means of getting out is through the windows," he said.

Councillor Griffiths was asked if he had known of a similar accident to the one he had vividly described, and he replied: "There are dozens of them taking place." Councillor EB Smith-Jones said he thought the MOT had certain regulations, and that the council had no power or control over the construction of buses. All they had to do was conduct and manage the buses licensed by the committee. Councillor Griffiths replied: "I am sorry I don't agree. It is our duty to see

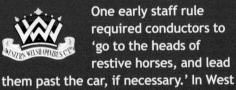

One early staff rule required conductors to 'go to the heads of restive horses, and lead them past the car, if necessary.' In West Wales, it also fell upon the poor conductor to win the constant battle with the badly rutted cart tracks that formed the route ahead. On the New Quay to Talgarreg route, for instance, pot holes had to be filled with small stones before the bus could proceed.

that the vehicles are in a safe condition." Councillor Smith-Jones was correct, and in any event the powers that were bestowed on officials such as Councillor Griffiths would soon be swept away altogether with the advent of the all important 1930 Road Traffic Act.

A total of 59 vehicles were transferred to Western Welsh from SWCM. They comprised 21 Leyland, 26 Commer, seven Lancia, three Thornycroft, one Fiat and one AEC. However, no account is taken of the Western Valleys fleet of 10 ADCs, at least seven of which received WW fleet numbers (213-9). Leyland Lion PLSC3 saloons formed the backbone of the SWCM fleet. There were 25 in service in 1929/30, 12 of which were ex-Eastern Valleys and four ex-Western Valleys. Bodies were by Leyland, Short Bros and Hall Lewis, and varied in seating capacity from 31 to 36. Prior to the new company's formation, the final share value of SWCM in May had increased to £500,000. A profit of £6,466 was recorded for the year.

The first vehicle orders from the new company were placed. They called for 20 large saloons and six small Leyland LT2 buses for delivery in 1930.

1930

Probably the most significant piece of legislation ever to affect passenger transport until the deregulation and privatisation of the industry towards the end of the 20th Century was the Road Traffic Act of 1930. It meant that companies were required to hold licences to operate every journey where they carried fare-paying passengers. The free-for-all days, when any operator went more or less anywhere as long as the local councils let them in, were over. The Act would, through the setting up of Traffic Commissioners, regulate drivers and conductors to ensure they were of good character; require vehicles to be inspected for roadworthiness and introduce compulsory third-party insurance. It was a system that would work well, and was for the most part fair. A deadline of February 9, 1931 was set for the Act to reach the statute books, although it was April of that year before it finally came into effect. This was a vital and important milestone in the history of bus and coach operation, and it had a significant impact on the operation of the new Western Welsh company.

When the company was formed, services to the west terminated at Port Talbot and began again at Neath. However, Albert Gray was quick to see the desirability of a link-up in order to provide through services. This resulted in an hourly limited stop service between Cardiff and Neath and also served to counter competition from the newly-formed Neath & Cardiff Luxury Coaches (N&C). A through service to Swansea, jointly with SWT, was to have followed but found no favour with the newly created Traffic Commissioners, who judged N&C as having a better claim to this traffic. Instead, the Cardiff service was extended beyond Neath to Pontardawe, Gwaun-cae-Gurwen and Ammanford.

With all GWR road services taken over, the opportunity arose to extend routes further west with linked services, through ticketing and better vehicles in the shape of Leyland Lions and Tigers.

One former GWR bus route linked Port Talbot with Abergwynfi in the Afan Valley — the company's trains only ran into the head of the valley from Caerau — and extended at weekends over the new Bwlch-y-Clawdd mountain road to Treorchy in the Rhondda. At this time the Afan Valley was a depressed area and the service wasn't profitable. It was suspended during the Second World War and not restored until 1946.

In January eight acres of land for new workshops and offices at Ely was purchased for £2,300. A further £21,500 was spent on the premises and equipment. This was a massive investment at the time, but the planned expansion didn't stop there. Land was assigned for new offices in Neath, while at Bridgend additional land was acquired in the town centre for an enlarged bus station. Several local passenger carrying businesses in the Carmarthen area were purchased. These were

Edwards Brothers who operated the Narberth route; All Blue (AB) Express, whose Llandeilo service led to through services operating from Carmarthen via Llandovery to Brecon; Thomas Brothers, who ran the Llanstephan route abandoned by the GWR during the First World War; Pontyberem Transport and Cox's Buses which operated the Newcastle Emlyn route. In Brecon, the business of G Paskin, which had a route to Trecastle, was purchased, but no vehicles were absorbed in this transaction.

The advent of the new arterial road at Wenvoe led to serious competition between the railways and the bus companies that shared the route between Cardiff and Penarth. It was rumoured in January that White's Motors were to amalgamate with Western Welsh from April, and that a sum of £100,000 was involved. However, Mr White was quoted as saying that there was no foundation in the rumour. A spokesman for Western Welsh said the same. Nevertheless it was a fact that the White's company books had only a short while before been looked at by WB Cownie, then managing director of SWCM, acting on a request from Albert Gray as to the prospects of acquiring the business.

The Barry to Bridgend service was once again subject to interference from Barry UDC, when the new 20-seater Thornycroft saloon was refused a licence, as it was regarded as a one-man bus. Barry recommended at least two nearside doors on public service vehicles although Western Welsh and Thomas of Barry were allowed to operate single door vehicles.

Developments in the Carmarthen area in November saw the inauguration of a Cardiff service, with Carmarthen staff working through to Sycamore Cross. This service came to be regarded as the backbone of Western Welsh.

A flashback to 1930 and the Westgate Street, Cardiff, terminus of the Cardiff to Porthcawl service. The former SWCM Commer is No. 46 (XB 9920) and the driver was Colston Tipples from Bridgend depot, who later left the company to manage a chain of cinemas in the Midlands. *Stewart Williams*

One of two Park Royal-bodied AEC Regents which entered the fleet in 1931, 174 (KG 313) was put to good use on the Cardiff to Porthcawl service.

realised that autocratic local authorities were no longer to be involved in such matters.

The new arrangements applied not only to bus and coach services, but also to excursions and tours. They brought with them three types of Road Service Licence: one to cover bus services (stage carriage licences); another to cover longer services where a compulsory minimum fare applied in order to discourage short journeys which were rightfully the preserve of the bus services (short stage express carriage licences) and a third to cover pre-bookable long-distance coach services for which tickets would not be issued on the vehicles (express service licences).

Companies wishing to operate services applied to the appropriate Traffic Commissioner and had to support their applications with details of proposed timetables, fares and the location of bus stops. The applications were published, and provision made for other operators, railways, police, local authorities and other interested parties, to object to the proposals. An appeal could be made to the Minister against the decision of the Traffic Commissioner, who was a full-time civil servant, sitting with one or perhaps two lay members. The only operation not covered by the act was

Another long-distance route, that linking Carmarthen and Brecon, also began at about this time. During the year Western Welsh buses travelled a staggering nine million miles and carried more than 16 million passengers. While trading figures for the financial year showed a loss of £1,760, this was carefully calculated and in line with the 'pain before gain' ethos that prevailed as the company found its feet.

1931

Less than two years after the company's inception, all bus services — and therefore competition — were controlled by the 1930 Road Traffic Act, which came into effect in April. The new Act empowered Traffic Commissioners to regulate the competition of regular bus services and oversee provision of co-ordinated timetables, fare tables and ticket inter-availability. Public service vehicles required individual licensing and were subject to inspection to ensure that they complied with construction and maintenance regulations that came into force at the same time. Co-operation, which already existed on some of the company's routes, was encouraged.

The introduction of the Act was described by the Minister of Transport as 'a charter for the ordered use of the King's highway.' The licensing of buses and charabancs had often been subject to the dictates of local authority members such as Councillor Griffiths at Barry in 1929. Depots must have echoed to sighs of relief when it was

A fitter stands proudly in front of a vehicle he has been working on at the company's Cadoxton Road, Neath depot during the mid-1930s.

that of private hire, where it was deemed that one person or organisation when chartering a vehicle would not be charging individual fares. This system operated, with only relatively minor adjustments, until October 1980, although services during the 1939-45 war were operated under permits issued by groups of temporary Regional Transport Commissioners.

In catering for the registration of drivers and conductors, the Transport Act continued to provide for the wearing of a numbered badge so they could be readily identified. This had originated, in London at least, as a result of discourteous attitudes, and a requirement under an earlier Act of Parliament for all PSV drivers and conductors to wear them. Not until an April 1, 1991 amendment to the 1988 Road Traffic Act was this brought to an end when, under EEC regulations, the Public Service Vehicle or PSV classification was changed to Passenger Carrying Vehicles or PCVs.

A further important feature of the 1930 Road Traffic Act was the establishment of regulated hours for drivers which limited the number of hours that could be spent behind the wheel and stipulated the minimum number of hours of rest in the working week. These were to apply with few changes until the introduction of new EEC Regulations in the 1970s.

At the beginning of the year Western Welsh became part of BET when it took over NECC although this organisation was retained as a holding company. The GWR retained a significant 50 per cent shareholding of Western Welsh which continued to run largely from railway premises.

The new garage and workshops at Ely opened in February. Built by Knox and Wells Ltd, they covered around 54,000 square feet, in addition to which there was an additional 16,000 square feet of concrete hard-standing and roadways. The interior provided sufficient accommodation for 100 vehicles, and together with the offices must have been a conspicuous landmark in the district. The Chief Engineer at Ely Works was Jack H Lewis, formerly of the Western Valleys company. Two new posts, those of assistant engineer and assistant traffic manager, were established at this time, and were filled by Albert Gray's eldest son, Leslie and TG Davies respectively. In a special feature published in the Western Mail & South Wales News of Thursday, April 9, the eight-acre site — a large portion of which was utilised as recreation grounds for the employees — was described as: 'a fine monument to the spirit of private enterprise in the Principality, and being among the largest of their kind in the Kingdom.'

The suitably impressed journalist continued his report with: "Walking around the various departments I was amazed at the pains which are taken by the experts in every section to ensure the safety of the travelling public. Buses, I was informed, are completely overhauled after every 50,000 miles. This does not mean merely attending to superficial defects, but the whole of the

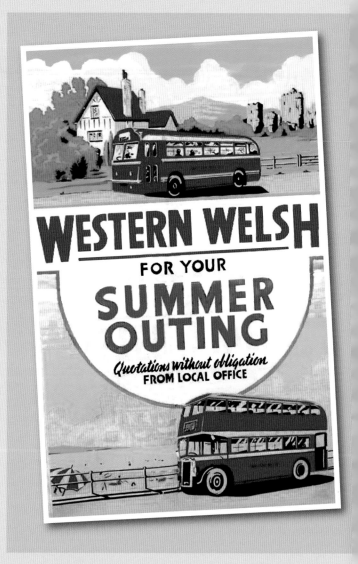

vehicle is dismantled and stripped to the chassis. Every nut and bolt is removed, and any part that shows the slightest sign of wear is replaced by a new component. I was particularly interested in a device for the detection of flaws in the vital parts of an engine, particularly in the mechanism of the steering gear. Mr Jack Lewis, the chief engineer, showed me a steering rod which, as far as the naked eye could see, was in perfect condition. Then he coated it with a solution and placed it on two highly magnetised steel pins. Immediately a crack in the metal became visible, a flaw which might have spelt disaster to many lives. Such precautions as these are exercised in every detail and in every department."

Repair and overhaul of the fleet had previously been carried out around several depots. Chief engineer Jack Lewis felt such a situation was far from satisfactory. He felt that the establishment of a large and up-to-date central works where the whole fleet could be overhauled was of paramount importance.

It was at this time that the company announced its first order for new double deck buses with four vehicles costing around £1,450 each.

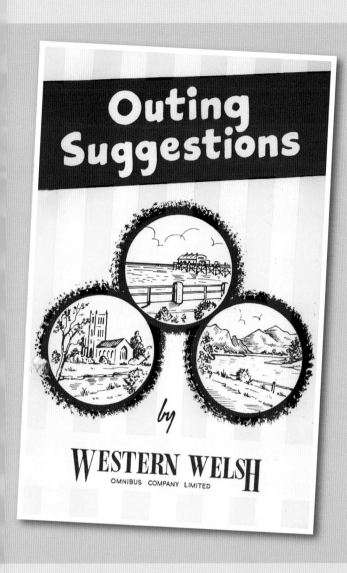

The latter's business was actually offered for sale to the company in July, but wasn't purchased until 1936.

In November the Abergavenny office transferred to a shared facility with Red & White. In the same month a new service began between Barry and Talbot Green, with a running time of 70 minutes and a two-and-a-half hour frequency.

The business of Griffiths & Davies of Newbridge was taken over through Western Valleys and with it came four more Thornycroft saloons.

The end-of-year trading balance showed another overall loss for the company, of £3,004. However, it appears that the company had been thinking ahead and spent a considerable sum on building Ely Works.

1932

The company opened smart new offices at Station Square in Neath, adjacent to the town's GWR station.

The March timetable made mention of 14 jointly operated routes, plus ticket inter-availability and connecting services with many more. It also included full details of the services of Lewis & James (Western Valleys) and Barretts (Eastern Valleys), which had been acquired by SWCM in 1928, but had initially retained their own identities. Arterial services increased with the hourly Cardiff to Ammanford service being extended to two-hourly to Carmarthen, with some services continuing to Lampeter and Aberystwyth. A connection was provided at Sycamore Cross for Barry, with an available through fare from Barry to Carmarthen of seven shillings. A two-hourly Cardiff to Monmouth service also began, as did an hourly service from Cardiff to Abergavenny and Brecon via Newport, Pontypool and Usk, with alternative buses continuing all the way to Carmarthen, a long six-hour run. Most of the network prospered, but a summer service from Cardiff via Newport, Abergavenny, Brecon and Builth Wells to Llandrindod Wells was abandoned.

A serious matter arose in September when the Traffic Commissioners revoked a number of licences because of operating irregularities. It appeared that a senior manager at Western Welsh had unfortunately failed to master all of the new regulations. As a result, traffic manager RAJ Williams was demoted to western area manager and replaced by WT James.

A young coach trimmer by the name of Charlie Bravey began working at Ely Works in the early 1930s. He moved into a house in Caerau Park Road which backed on to the works and his son Graham recalls his father coming home for lunch through a hole in the fence. Charlie had been in the Royal Army Medical Corps in the First World War but by 1940 he was considered too old to be called up again, and instead became a fire watcher at the Cowbridge Road offices. Most of his younger colleagues were called up, and so Charlie became the foreman

An advertisement in the Western Mail and South Wales News in April proclaimed: 'When the man in the street goes motoring, he is assured of comfortable trips at the lowest possible fares in Thornycroft buses and coaches.' John Thornycroft had a sales and service depot at East Canal Wharf in Cardiff, and had supplied vehicles to both the fledgling Western Welsh company and Cardiff Corporation. The manufacturers claimed they offered a high degree of comfort and reliability.

In another newspaper advertisement, Leyland Motors boasted of having supplied 62 vehicles to Western Welsh, while AEC claimed that 20 of its Regal buses were being operated by the company.

Still in April, applications for the continuation of the licences held for Cardiff to Penarth via Cogan; Barry Dock to Pontyclun via Pendoylan and Hensol, and Cowbridge to Llantwit Major via Nash Manor, were granted. The joint Cardiff to Barry Island via Dinas Powis service was also allowed to continue and ran at a 15-minute frequency taking 47 minutes from Tresillian Terrace. Western Welsh and Whites' both provided two vehicles while Reliance Motors, Thomas Motors and CJ Vincent each provided one.

New in 1933, AEC Renown 186 (KG 2202) was one of four fitted with high-specification Weymann 56-seat bodies. The batch was painted in the lavender blue and cream, Western Valleys livery. These petrol engined vehicles were heavy on fuel and as a result exchanged for diesel-engined Regents in 1934. However, they returned to Western Welsh with the White's fleet, and later received diesel engines. The simplified company logo which was used post-1963 wasn't a new design. This picture from some 30 years earlier, proves that it had been used before!

coach trimmer and supervised the training of the replacement female staff who were drafted in to help. He held the post of secretary of the Western Welsh branch of the National Union of Vehicle Builders for some time, and his RAMC background led to him becoming the registered first aider at the works. Graham has fond childhood memories of time spent with friends playing in the adjoining field. He also spent time exploring the works themselves, playing in old buses parked there awaiting repair or scrapping — until he was chased out by the night watchman! Charlie remained at Ely Works until his retirement in 1963.

December brought with it the death of managing director WB Cownie. His name had long been associated with SWCM and latterly Western Welsh. It was perpetuated by the Cownie Cup, an award eagerly fought for by bus company football teams for many years after. A profit of £12,624 was recorded for the year.

Driver EC Williams of Aberdare depot was a prominent first-aider, captaining a team to the finals of the GWR competition at Paddington. He was awarded a Bronze Medal after administering assistance to two motorcyclists and their pillion riders after they were involved in a collision at Nottage, Porthcawl. He spent all his working life, with the exception of the war years, working on the buses in the Cynon Valley town.

Another West Wales operator — JR Adams, of New Quay, who had pioneered the New Quay to Aberaeron route — was bought though no vehicles appear to have been included in the February acquisition.

In March the company agreed to pay Cardiff Corporation £100 a year to gain access for its vehicles to a proposed new bus station in the city centre. However, it was a further 21 years before the central bus station finally opened!

The annual timetable book showed a Pontypool to Aberystwyth service with connections from Cardiff, Neath, Abergavenny and Brecon. By 1935 Newport was the starting point of this service. However, there is evidence that the real service began at Ammanford with the rest consisting of connecting services starting at Cardiff. Also at Newport the GWR had leased its Cambrian Place office to Western Welsh.

In July some of the far-flung routes in the Brecon, Builth Wells and Llandrindod Wells areas were given up, and taken over by FG Jones of the Erwood Inn. It is said that Mr Jones promised a crate of beer in return for the takeover, but he died before he could fulfill his part of the deal. Two small firms in Porthcawl were also taken over in the summer — Morgan Weeks and Francis Motors. Rhondda Transport agreed to pay £400 of the £2,250 cost of the latter and as a result its buses ran into the town.

Notable changes occurred in the Monmouthshire valleys in the autumn, when subsidiary companies Lewis &

1933

Heavy oil engines, later to become more commonly known as diesel engines were first produced in 1933 and gradually replaced their petrol equivalents though it was to be a year before they made their first appearance with Western Welsh. Apart from many operational advantages, the new engines considerably reduced the risk of fire.

James (Western Valleys) and Barretts (Eastern Valleys) were voluntarily wound up and formally merged with Western Welsh. This resulted in a reduction of wages of the former companies in line with staff in the Cardiff and Bridgend areas, something which brought savings of £1,950 a year.

The Eastern and Western Valleys businesses took Western Welsh into the heart of the Monmouthshire coalfield, and while competition existed with well-established operators such as Ralph's and Griffin, there was a degree of inherited co-operation. Further west, in the Taff and Cynon valleys, two large independent competitors, Imperial of Abercynon and Gough's of Mountain Ash, were absorbed by Red & White. This resulted in the surrender to the Western Welsh company of a complex group of Cardiff to Aberystwyth holiday services, and led to the appearance of the company's coaches in Swansea, albeit infrequently.

The year was brought to a close with news of a further drop in profits. This time they had dropped to £8,290.

A new bus station at Bridgend was completed in 1934. It was closely followed by the garage, left. Later expansion included Star Yard (out of shot, left) and the town's cattle market in the background. It remained in use until 1992. *Chris Taylor*

1934

Bridgend's original bus station had rapidly been outgrown in the immediate post-SWCM years, and a new one was opened on the site of the old cattle market, at a cost of £10,493, in April. The occasion was marked by a lunch at the Dunraven Arms Hotel, given by Bridgend UDC. It was a celebration which area manager EG Burgoyne described as providing: "A pleasant memory indeed in these days of shortage."

With BET holding a common interest, Western Welsh and South Wales Transport considered a plan for joint acquisition of its competitors in the Swansea and Neath areas. Talks took place, but no agreement was reached. Nevertheless it was enough to rattle the opposition and as a result United Welsh Services Ltd was formed by the Red & White group in 1938.

Western Welsh announced that a new office and waiting room planned for Bethany Square, Port Talbot, was to be shared with SWT.

The part-exchange agreement of 1934 led to Renowns 185-8 being exchanged for Regents 257-60, which had punchy 8.8 litre diesel engines and 48-seat bodies by Weymann. The two-tier fleet name was unique and appeared on the nearside only, to avoid obstruction from the sliding door. *Chris Taylor*

45

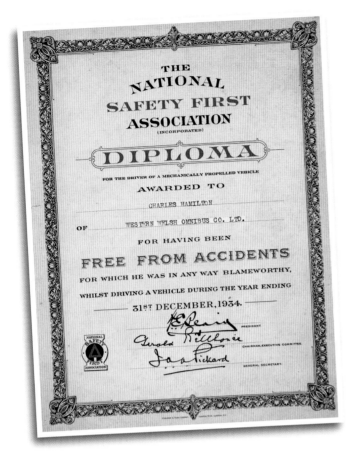

Attempts were made to buy several lucrative companies across South Wales. Rees & Williams and West Wales Motors of Ammanford, Ebsworth Bros of Carmarthen, Green's Motors of Haverfordwest, Caerphilly UDC's transport undertaking, and Pencoed Motors, were all approached. Interestingly perhaps, none was tempted at the time, but Ebsworth's eventually joined the fold 20 years later, with Green's following in 1955. One business that did succumb in October however, was that of Thomas Bros of Llanstephan. Along with two of its vehicles the business was bought for £1,850.

In July Western Welsh became a member of British Electrical Federation Ltd (BEF), a trade association.

Meanwhile as talks began with Thos. White & Co (Cardiff & Barry) Ltd about a possible takeover, the goodwill of William Peter, Carmarthen (in liquidation), was bought through Daniel Jones for £125, heralding an agreement on the Carmarthen to Llandeilo route.

Better news on the financial front saw a turnaround in profits which increased to £13,425 for the year.

1935

Western Welsh's first programme of extended tours began in earnest. Charabancs had been a familiar sight on the roads of South Wales even before the passing of the 1930 Road Traffic Act, and it was from such beginnings that the company realised the potential that properly organised tours could offer. Four itineraries were organised with 12 departures using new Leyland TS7

coaches fitted with 21 green moquette armchairs. These luxurious seats were retained for visitors to head office for many years.

Accelerated services were announced in April for routes between Cardiff and Neath; Porthcawl via Port Talbot to Neath and between Carmarthen and Ammanford via Cross Hands. The journey time between Cardiff and Bridgend was a minute under the hour, and it took a further 52 minutes to reach Neath. This was no doubt in answer to increasing competition from the N&C express service over the shared route. By comparison, N&C coaches reached Bridgend in 45 minutes and went on to reach Neath in a further 45. Expansion continued with acquisition of the business of FJ John, of Nantyfyllon. This included 11 vehicles and property for which £11,500 was paid. Then in June, WT Jones (Express Motors), of Bryncethin, was taken over. Their garage and 12 vehicles were bought for £15,000. Only four of John's vehicles and nine of Jones' were operated. Next came Danygraig Omnibus Services of Risca, with two vehicles, for £6,000. For reasons unknown, but perhaps due to local passenger affiliation, the Danygraig company wasn't wound up until 1941 and so in theory Western Welsh vehicles were hired in.

In Barry, the name of White had been synonymous with passenger transport for many years. Thomas White, founder of White's Motors (Cardiff and Barry) Ltd, took his first bold steps in the business in 1908 when he opened a garage behind his home at 105 Broad Street — directly opposite the later Western Welsh garage.

In the 1920s, White's had obtained a licence to operate from Barry Island via Dinas Powis to Tresillian Terrace, Cardiff. A further application to operate a circular service via Barry – Sully – Penarth – Cardiff – Wenvoe was also granted with the exception of the section from Cardiff to Culverhouse. At the time Cardiff's Lord Mayor proclaimed: "We will not allow or tolerate animated ironmongery running over our roads." However, an appeal to the Minister of Transport allowed the licence to be granted, and the service began in 1925 with a half-hourly winter schedule, and a 10 minute frequency

A fitter stands alongside an AEC bus he had been working on at the company's Cadoxton Road, Neath, depot, mid-1930s.

Service van 1, a Leyland SG11, seen at Pentyrch in 1933 at a time when the company owned 242 vehicles and this was the only breakdown van! From the left are: Leslie A Gray, then assistant engineer; fitters 'Pip' Price, Maldwyn Thomas and Ivor Thomas, and Percy Pidgeon, later works foreman. The van had an interesting history. Its body was the lower saloon of bus No. 351, a former Tresillian Motors' Dennis double-decker. It was grafted on to the chassis of former bus No. 5 and converted for departmental use. It ended its days at the works as an engine testing facility. *Stewart Williams*

during the summer. During August this increased to every five minutes. White's new Penarth Road depot was completed around this time with half the service operating from there. With the introduction of the 1930 Traffic Act, local operators in Barry were co-ordinated to reduce unnecessary duplication and from then on White's gradually began to absorb local operators.

With failing health, White had for some time been negotiating a takeover by Western Welsh. Sadly, as talks proceeded, he died. As a result, it was late in 1936 before his company was finally absorbed. Together with its coaching subsidiary, CJ Vincent (Cardiff) Ltd, a hiring agreement commenced on July 1, 1935 involving 72 vehicles, for a consideration of £85,000. White's was eventually liquidated at a value of £34,233, and Vincent's at £239, in December 1936. Western Welsh now had a commanding position in Barry, although once again the local council wasn't happy. It had always regarded continued competition as being in the best interests of bus users in the town. Fred Pengelly, a conductor with White's, joined Western Welsh at the takeover and enjoyed a long career which culminated in him occupying the post of traffic manager.

A bid was made to take over the bus services of Newport Corporation, but it refused to hold discussions with the company. Negotiations for joint purchase with SWT of James & Son of Ammanford also failed as did a buy-out of James Hughes & Sons of Trimsaran. The successful purchase of the nearby J Jones & Co (Pontyberem Transport) and their associated companies enabled a Carmarthen to Llanelly route to operate with vehicles based at Jones's Pontyberem garage. This eventually became an outstation to Carmarthen. In later years, as the country prepared for war, there was an increase in military activity and land was purchased for a new depot which at its busiest accommodated around 100 vehicles.

Of the many facilities that were introduced by Western Welsh from time to time, none were more eagerly accepted and appreciated than the combined Bus and Boat Ticket. This allowed passengers to travel from their local boarding point to a P&A Campbell steamer berth to sail to a range of destinations, without having to re-book. This exclusive arrangement between the company and Campbell's resulted in many instances of reduced through fares and proved beneficial to organisers of outings. A special pamphlet was produced which included fare tables for all the Bristol Channel resorts, including

Smiles for the camera while preparing
for the road at Ammanford depot, 1937.
Stewart Williams

They were more robust, allowing longer periods between overhauls; they were easier to start, particularly in cold weather and, most importantly, fuel consumption was about half that of petrol engines. Another advantage, albeit a temporary one, was that petrol tax did not apply to 'oilers' which meant that not only did operators have the benefit of double mileage per gallon, they were also paying approximately half the price for diesel when compared with petrol.

The stage service of Bert Langley, Abersychan, was taken over in February, for £1,500. Meanwhile services began between Cowbridge and St Athan, via St Mary Church and Eglwys Brewis as well as between Penarth Esplanade and Sully Hospital. A workmen's service also operated between Cadoxton and RAF St Athan. An application to take over Rhondda Transport's route between Pontypridd and Barry Island via Talbot Green and Cowbridge was refused. Rhondda continued to operate to Barry Island, but only between May 30 and September 19.

The Red & White group's express licences for Cardiff to Aberystwyth were taken over in July for the sum of £7,000, along with three vehicles previously operated by Gough's Welsh Motorways of Mountain Ash. Gough's was already owned by the R&W group, but an existing agreement with Western Welsh meant that R&W could not operate these services. Now, under Western Welsh, there was a sound base for a network of express services from the company's entire operating area to the Cardigan Bay coast. Aberystwyth remained a major seasonal destination for the company throughout its existence.

New garages were completed at New Quay and Carmarthen during this year, and land was acquired for an office and waiting room at Blue Street, Carmarthen. The business of Francis's Motors of Porthcawl was taken over in October, followed in December by the formal takeover of White's which had been in caretaker management for the previous year. It was agreed that the White's name would remain on vehicles for a period of three years, and Thomas White's two sons were to be given employment.

The acquisition of White's allowed a revised joint service to be put into operation on the Cardiff to Lower Penarth route which had previously been operated by Western Welsh, White's and Cardiff Corporation. Albert Gray had studied the working of the route as far back as 1930, and found that despite regular rail competition, it was the most profitable in the area. Gray's findings were that the acquisition of White's would enable the company to speed up the service and maintain the original frequency with fewer vehicles. He felt that the 10-minute frequency could be maintained with four vehicles instead of the original six which would increase the average speed from nine to approximately 14 mph. This in turn would reduce the wages to 2.2d per mile compared with 3.3d. While admitting that the arrangement would necessitate splitting the service with Cardiff Corporation,

Bristol itself. Travel via Cardiff Pier Head was available from the Bridgend valleys and Vale of Glamorgan routes as well as from the Pontypridd, Penarth and Barry areas. Day trips were also available via Porthcawl from Pontypridd, Cardiff and the Bridgend valleys. In Cardiff, the means of transit between bus terminus and Pier Head was by Cardiff Corporation trams Nos. 2 or 3, the fare for which was not included in the deal. Bus-Boat tickets provided a cheap and pleasant method of travel between places served by the company's buses and resorts such as Weston, Clevedon, Minehead and Ilfracombe.

Profit for the year again showed a healthy increase, amounting to £26,958.

1936

By now there were 328 single and 26 double deck vehicles in the Western Welsh fleet. The annual distance they covered amounted to 11,838,275 miles, over which 28,273,576 passengers were carried. Diesel-engined vehicles were the order of the day, as evidenced by the year's new vehicle intake. These engines had several operational advantages.

A major event at Greyfriars Road, Cardiff, in 1935, led to a mammoth private hire contract for Western Welsh. The result was an impressive line up of the company's Lions and Tigers, something that did not go unnoticed by Leyland's publicity department. *Stewart Williams*

he felt that an arrangement was possible where an adjustment could be made to compensate Western Welsh for relinquishing to the Corporation a full sixth of the service. Gray's suggestion, all these years later, could finally be put into practice, and with this came a welcome reduction to both WW and CCT in tolls paid for the use of Penarth Road. The service was to continue in this form into the 1990s.

During the year 45 vehicles, including 11 originating from White's, were authorised for scrapping. The year ended on a high note with a more than useful rise in profits to £45,172.

1937

Services for military personnel and civilian workers at the Vale of Glamorgan establishments were stepped up at this time of increasing unrest in Europe. A new route between Cowbridge and Boverton Aerodrome was approved, but subject to a restriction to 20 seaters, while applications to serve St Athan Camp included daily services from Cardiff, via both Penarth, Dinas Powis and Wenvoe; from Llantwit Major to Main Site and West Orchard, and from Porthcawl via Bridgend and Wick. In addition, an extra journey on the Barry Dock to Llantwit Major joint service was timed to run two minutes behind the Cadoxton to St Athan bus. A Barry UDC survey reported that 510 workmen travelled daily from Barry to St Athan camp in nine Western Welsh and six Hill's buses. The Traffic

Commissioners, in granting short-term licences to both companies, were mindful of a Western Welsh claim that Hill's did not have enough available buses to cope with demand. In defence of this Hill's lawyer claimed that the larger company was trying to take over his client's business. Within less than a year this is precisely what happened.

Leyland Cub 107 (KG 5601) was fitted with a 20-seat Park Royal body, one of two new in February 1935. Four more followed in 1936, but all six were delicensed at the outbreak of the Second World War. Some were used for wartime duties at establishments such as the Royal Ordnance factory at Bridgend. *Stewart Williams*

About to leave Newport for Garndiffaith on July 17, 1936, this 1934 Weymann-bodied AEC Regal I 562 (KG 3606) had recently been re-numbered from 262. It survived until the mid-1950s. *AB Cross (J Higham collection)*

The extended tours programme had proved an immediate success, so much so that in 1937 two new destinations were introduced, increasing the number of departures from 12 to 20. This side of the company's operations was to witness spectacular growth year on year, and by 1939, 65 departures were being offered. Unfortunately the war years brought with them a necessary curtailment of this lucrative part of the company's business.

Extensions to the garages at Penarth Road and Bridgend began while a new garage was proposed on GWR land at

Barry. These were healthy times which brought a wage increase that allowed drivers to earn up to 1s 4¼d an hour, and conductors 1s 2d. Profit for the year amounted to £61,874, another significant year on year increase.

The business of Phipps of Glynneath was purchased, removing a competitor on the Neath to Aberdare and Merthyr route. A total of 10 vehicles were included for the price of £15,000. Next came the acquisition of Green & White Services of Bridgend with 17 vehicles and a garage for £13,025, then Pencoed Motor Co Ltd for £10,000 and finally, the goodwill of Osborne Services, Neath, whose service to Banwen was purchased through SWT for £11,000.

To mark the Coronation of King George VI, at least two Leyland saloons were festooned with flags and bunting. In what was probably a depot-led initiative, 198 (KG 7046) was decorated by staff of Brecon, while a decorative arch was created at the entrance to the depot. Former Jones coach 487 (KG 5745) also received special treatment, possibly for a Royal visit to Newport.

The year ended with the lease of the Cowbridge garage being surrendered in November, the property returning to its owner AS Evans. In December, an agreement was reached with

Four AEC Renowns were bought by Western Welsh in 1933, but found to be unsuitable and exchanged for AEC Regents. They returned to the company on the takeover of White's in 1936, along with five other models of similar vintage. One of these was 599 (KG 2176), seen shortly before withdrawal. *A B Cross (Allen T Smith Collection)*

Straight out of the box! In the days before Eastern Coachworks built bodies for chassis other than Bristol, Western Welsh regarded its products highly, and in the early post-war years a considerable number found their way into the fleet. This splendid example of ECW's lowbridge bodywork is on AEC Regent II 617 (CKG 797) of 1946, seen at Lowestoft ready for collection. The patriotic propaganda on the side of the vehicle was in vogue at that time. *George Wedlake*

were usually donated to Cardiff Royal Infirmary. In what was possibly the final act of enemy action, a repeat of the 1940 blitz on Cardiff severely disrupted both road and rail services in the city. By this date an employee assistance fund was in place to help those workers rendered homeless by enemy action.

The Regional Transport Commissioners immediately became known as the Licensing Authorities, before reverting to their original title of Traffic Commissioners in 1956. Mr IL Gray returned from war service to his post as area manager at Cardiff and Barry. Meanwhile FH Pengelly was appointed assistant transport manager.

The company's Garndiffaith garage, formerly the property of Eastern Valleys, was advertised as being available to rent. Meanwhile Ammanford's new garage opened to much celebrating by the staff. Leading fitter Horace Tout had started his apprenticeship there in 1943 and could recall a wide stream running through the middle and occasions when one end of it would be under five feet of floodwater. The company recorded a profit of £32,658 for the year.

The crew take a break as 841 (CUH 841) their Leyland PS1, single deck vehicle waits at Wood Street, Cardiff, before heading off for Dinas Powis and Barry Island, in 1949.

The Danish Busmen's group, Sporvejenes Engelsk Klub Copenhagen, visited Cardiff in the late 1940s, at the invitation of Western Welsh. It was the start of a long and happy relationship with exchange visits perpetuating in the years that followed. The initial party, along with their hosts from the company's Educational Club, are gathered at Penarth Road depot before boarding the specially decorated Tiger for a day's sightseeing. *Christine Davies*

1946

As was the case after the First World War, many people were now keen to take advantage of their regained freedom. As a result, demand for coach holidays increased enormously. Like many similar operators, Western Welsh faced difficulties in satisfactorily meeting this as new vehicles were impossible to obtain quickly because of shortages of materials. Despite the company making every effort to gear up for the reintroduction of its extended tours in 1947, it was to be several years before they could meet the heavy demand.

Maintenance of the fleet had not been up to the usual standard during the war years, but now the company was at last able to order 60 replacement 35-seat saloon bodies from Willowbrook as replacements on its 10-year-old Leyland TS7s and TS8s. The year end brought news of a £35,889 profit.

The highering of the school leaving age raised a question regarding the issue of half-rate tickets, and all staff were instructed that there was to be no change in the method of issuing them. The existing regulations which confined issue of half tickets to passengers up to 14 years of age would be maintained.

1947

Severe weather early in the year caused major disruption to the whole of Britain. Bus services in particular, and those of Western Welsh among them often ground to a halt. The country was held in the grip of blizzards and sub-zero temperatures for almost three months. From January 22 to March 17, snow fell every day somewhere in the UK. South Wales was hit badly on March 4 and 5, when strong winds quickly whipped the snow into deep drifts. When warmer air eventually reached the area and brought a thaw, many rivers, heavy with meltwater, burst their banks causing flooding. All in all, on top of lingering fuel and food shortages it meant a miserable time for most people.

There was some good news however — the extended tours programme, halted during wartime, resumed with

The story of Western Welsh wouldn't be complete without mention of this cartoon, drawn by troops on 757 (CBO 526), a TS8 requisitioned during the Second World War. It is thought to be linked with insignia worn by personnel leaving the military with an honorary discharge. It showed the military police that the troops were in transit and not absent without leave. The badge depicted an eagle, but was thought by troops to resemble a duck. 'Took off like a ruptured duck' meant they were going home. The bus returned to the company in 1946 and retained the mural during the rest of its working life. The panel it was painted on was removed and stored, eventually being thrown out for scrap during the final clear-out of Ely Works.
AB Cross (Allen T Smith Collection)

A dozen handsome Duple-bodied AEC Regals came from Grey Cars (Devon) in 1948/49, and provided a solution to Western Welsh's difficulties in sourcing coaches in the early post-war years. One of the batch was 534 (JOD 621) seen at Duffryn Gardens in the Vale of Glamorgan.
Viv Corbin

a modest six departures. Despite the use of barely-disguised pre-war TS8 saloons which lost four of their seats but gained a lick of ivory paint, the tours enjoyed a steady growth in popularity. By 1950 there were 86 departures, and by 1951 there were 95, with a total of 1,983 holidaymakers carried to a range of destinations.

In August the first issue of the fondly remembered Staff Bulletin, the company's monthly magazine, was published. The traffic department seized upon the opportunity of using this newly-found media for issuing instructions to driving staff on various matters.

As a result of design improvements and other refinements a 12-year life-span could be expected for all oil-engined buses, but only, it seems, if they were left alone! The bulletin carried the following instructions: "The attention of the driving staff is called to the fact that the setting of fuel pumps on compression ignition engines must in no circumstances be tampered with. These pumps are set by skilled staff in the garage and having been set they should be sealed. They are set with the object of giving the maximum amount of power consistent with economy. If the setting is interfered with it will not necessarily result in more power being given and it will certainly upset the economy of running." It appeared that several cases had been discovered where the seals had been broken and the settings interfered with which resulted in poor performance.

The article went on to suggest that if drivers had reason to think that their engines were not behaving normally in

Newcastle Emlyn bus driver Ann Rees wrote in a magazine article in 1954: "One night I was driving munitions workers to a factory. There was no moon, it was very dark, and the headlamps were masked, due to wartime restrictions. Suddenly the bus hit a very large object, though I couldn't see anything. I pulled up and, with some of my passengers, went to investigate. To our amazement, we found we had run into an elephant which was continuing its journey as if nothing had happened. It left my bus with a slightly buckled wing and me with a sprained wrist! We were told later that a travelling circus was making an overnight move to the next town, which accounted for my unexpected encounter. I shall never forget that my one and only collision was with an elephant!"

any way they should report the matter to their garage foreman who would sort the matter out. A final sentence warned: "Under no circumstances, are drivers permitted to touch the setting of the pump."

The Carmarthen to Cardigan service became hourly, and elsewhere in the west there were route expansions, bucking the trend in other rural areas where for some time passenger numbers had been falling. The supply of new vehicles was a continuing problem, however, and in the heart of Monmouthsire, the Traffic Commissioners granted Jones of Aberbeeg a new licence for a Newport to Ebbw Vale service purely because the larger operators — Western Welsh and Red & White — did not have sufficient buses. This was a decision which the company's general manager blamed squarely on the export drive being promoted by the Government to reduce Britain's post war balance of payments deficit.

The Welfare Club at Ely Works drew a capacity crowd to its November social evening, with the works canteen filled to capacity for the screening of two films. One of these was titled Western Welsh 1947, which contained shots of the latest children's field day, and salvage operations undertaken by the breakdown gang at Ely. This was very much appreciated, as was the premiere of a film about the visit of Princess Elizabeth to Carmarthen. Before long of course she would be Queen.

Best news of the year for the company and its shareholders was the announcement that it had made a record profit of £131,243.

Queuing for new buses

Long wait heralds first fares increase

If wartime had brought Western Welsh some interesting times, and with them many testing challenges, then the years that followed didn't disappoint either. With the quest to return to normality of paramount importance the company began to focus on the future, in particular launching a campaign to refresh its fleet. If it needed something to focus on while patiently waiting for its share of the few new vehicles filtering through as the country struggled to rebuild, it came in 1948 with nationalisation of the railways.

This brought into public hands the substantial railway shareholdings of the Thomas Tilling and BET companies. Tilling immediately decided to diversify its portfolio to a willing government that had formed the British Transport Commission (BTC), and as a result 253,550 Western Welsh shares held by the GWR were transferred to this new organisation. Unlike Tilling, BET had fought nationalisation and retained majority control over its companies. Many bus operators felt that voluntary sale to the BTC might bring a better price than probable compulsory purchase later. Some Tilling firms that were sold ran alongside BET companies and this came to be regarded as a threat to area agreements that had previously existed between the two groups.

At this time, general manager RT Ebury made a proud appeal to employees in an edition of the Staff Bulletin: "We should all feel that the Western Welsh crest means something more than a decoration on a bus. The words underneath have been earned by your efforts, and with continued co-operation between management and staff we can provide even better facilities for the travelling public." Those words were reliability, comfort, courtesy and efficiency.

WESTERN WELSH
OMNIBUS COMPANY LIMITED
(In association with the British Electric Traction Co. Ltd., and British Railways)

New Quay & Llangranog

WINTER SERVICE

Commencing Tuesday, 28th September, 1948

TUESDAYS, THURSDAYS and SATURDAYS ONLY

			am	pm			
NEW QUAY (Commercial Hotel)	..	dep.	9 40	5 20	..	..
Maenygroes	..	"	9 45	5 25	..	..
Nanternis (Chapel)	..	"	9 52	5 32	..	..
Llwyndafydd (Post Office)	..	"	9 55	5 35	..	..
Penybont	..	"	9 59	5 39	..	..
Blaencelyn (Post Office)	..	"	10 01	5 41	..	..
Capel-Y-Wig	..	"	10 03	5 43	..	..
Pant	..	"	10 08	5 48	..	..
Pontgarreg	..	"		5 52	..	..
Pant	..	"		5 56	..	..
LLANGRANOG	..	arr.	10 12	6 00	..	..

			am	pm			
LLANGRANOG	..	dep.	10 20	6 00	..	..
Pant	..	"	10 24	6 04	..	..
Pontgarreg	..	"	10 28	6 08	..	..
Pant	..	"	10 32	6 12	..	..
Capel-y-Wig	..	"	10 37	6 17	..	..
Blaencelyn (Post Office)	..	"	10 39	6 19	..	..
Penybont	..	"	10 41	6 21	..	..
Llwyndafydd (Post Office)	..	"	10 45	6 25	..	..
Nanternis (Chapel)	..	"	10 48	6 28	..	..
Maenygroes	..	"	10 55	6 35	..	..
NEW QUAY (Commercial Hotel)	..	arr.	11 00	6 40	..	..

Issued subject to the Regulations and Conditions published in the Company's Time-Tables, Bills and Notices. Such Regulations and Conditions may be inspected free of charge at any of the Company's Offices.

HEAD OFFICE—
ELY, CARDIFF.
September, 1948.

————T.2641.————
D. Brown and Sons, Ltd., *Printers*, Cowbridge.

REGD. T. EBREY,
General Manager.

The tiny village of Llangranog on the Cardiganshire coast enjoyed this modest service to New Quay in the winter of 1948. *Stewart Williams*

1948

A group of youngsters had a hair-raising experience on their way to school one wintry morning. One of them was Viv Corbin, who clearly recalls sitting on one of the long seats on the top deck of AEC Renown 601 (KG 2700) on his way to Barry County School. As it turned the steep corner with an adverse camber from Park Avenue into St Nicholas Road, the driver missed a gear. There were screams from all the children as the bus began sliding backwards towards the edge of a railway embankment alongside. The cries of the pupils quickly turned to cheers however, as the driver's second attempt to climb the hill proved successful.

In March, a one-way traffic system was inaugurated in Bridgend town centre while the following month saw several new routes open up. In West Wales, town services in Carmarthen and Fishguard began, as did a rural service linking New Quay and Llangranog. In the Cardiff area new services ran to St Lythan's, Duffryn Cross, St Andrew's, Dinas Powis Square and Michaelston-le-Pit, followed in May by an express service to Aberystwyth.

The month also saw a burglary at Penarth Road depot which resulted in the day's takings of £760 being stolen.

By July, the company broke its fleet record when it recorded 605 vehicles in stock. A sound year's trading resulted in yet another record-breaking profit, this time of £281,942.

Between duties in Newport in 1955 is 176 (KG 7024), one of the last surviving TS7s from 1936. *Geoff Morant*

Western Welsh provided an important link for many rural communities as this busy 1950 scene at Aberayron, with all-Leyland TS7 163 (KG 7011) awaiting its next turn of duty, shows. *A B Cross*

1949

A new garage at Newcastle Emlyn opened in April with considerable local celebration. Set in beautiful surroundings, it held eight vehicles and cost £7,540. The comfort provided to both passengers and staff was in sharp contrast to the previous tin shed in the town's Cawdor Yard with its problems of rats and damp.

A letter, purporting to be written by a passenger living in Cardiff, was published in the April Staff Bulletin comparing employee behaviour aboard a 5.05pm Cardiff to Porthcawl bus with that of 'another public transport that I make use of daily'. The writer began: "My attention was drawn to the conductor dealing with two, 'nuisance' passengers. His courtesy and endless patience was to be admired. Later, from the top deck, I watched the manner in which the driver did his duty. His meticulous care in starting off and pulling up, overtaking traffic and rounding bends, etc, gave one a real sense of security."

The letter went on to say that, when its writer lived in West Wales and was a regular user of the company's buses, such things were taken for granted. "It was only now, having tasted others, that I realise what a splendid service your company provides." it added.

This could well have been an early attempt to undermine Cardiff Corporation at this time. Perhaps it was a snipe as a result of a falling-out or, more likely, an attempt by management to unsettle the corporation. It's purely speculative, but it may have been the start of a campaign of attrition which culminated in the attempted takeover of the city's bus fleet in 1951.

Staff at Barry responded promptly to a request from the divisional superintendent at British Railways Western Region on July 28, following a derailment on the causeway between the town and Barry Island, when both lines were fouled. Between 11am and 12.30pm around 1,300 passengers were conveyed between the two stations aboard five buses. A letter of appreciation arrived the very next day.

In September, a visit to Wales by 27 delegates of the Sporvejenes Engelsk Klub of Copenhagen took place. It was the first exchange visit by the Danish busmen's group and led to a close bond with Western Welsh's Educational Club during the 1950s. They arrived at Cardiff General station on September 3, and over the following nine days were escorted around Taff Merthyr Colliery, St Fagan's Castle, Cardiff Castle, Cold Knap and Barry Island, Llandarcy Oil Refinery, the Cow & Gate Creamery near Carmarthen, Hancock's Brewery, Ebbw Vale, Caerphilly Castle, Cardiff Arms Park and City Hall, the Gwyn Hall at Neath and the Wye Valley. They also visited the depots at Penarth Road, Crosskeys, Neath and Carmarthen as well as Ely Works. Their departure on September 12 was by coach, from Ely direct to London.

A healthy £191,356 profit was reported for the year with the fleet total rising to 620 vehicles in October.

Office staff at Pontypool depot, late 1940s. From the left are, back: Joan Gibbs and Jeanne Gough. Front: Ruth Kendall, Elaine Powell and Iris Gregory. *Tony Jenkins*

1950

As the supply of petrol began to ease people were eager to resume travelling, either by bus as they had done before the war, or, preferably, by private car. General manager RT Ebury was keen to alert staff to the fear that the roads would suddenly be 'cluttered with ancient chariots', out for the first time in many years, and driven by 'rusty' drivers.

Meanwhile, the government, seizing the opportunity, started to raise fuel tax at an alarming rate. In April it was doubled, much to the company's consternation, particularly as the increase in cost was completely beyond their control.

Quietly and unobtrusively, with scant ceremony, a new chapter in the history of Western Welsh began on Saturday May 27, when the company's first eight-foot wide vehicles were driven out from Cardiff's Fitzalan Road terminus as they began operating on the Aberystwyth express service. The newly-permitted 8ft wide coaches presented a major headache for the company's traffic department which had to prepare an enormous number of applications to the Ministry of Transport. Every route had to be submitted in detail along with street names and details of local councils. It was a lot to ask as, even at this time, the company's extended tours covered most of the country. At the same time, new dual-purpose double-deckers, built to the wider dimensions, were introduced on the Cardiff to Carmarthen route.

In 1950, if you travelled in the mid-Glamorgan area and the conductor of your bus suddenly burst into song, you could be fairly sure you were listening to one of Bridgend depot's Singing Busmen. They were a group of employees who sang, barber-shop style, and in their spare time were kept busy entertaining audiences and helping many charities. Their conductor — the one with the baton, not the ticket machine! — was TH Davies, a well known Garw Valley musician. Eventually, having enjoyed a successful season which included a concert at the Llanharan Eisteddfod, they announced their busy winter programme and a change of name to The Western Welsh Glee Party.

A fleet survey in November revealed that out of 610 vehicles operated by the company, 255 were of post-war construction. This accounted for 34 per cent of all single-deckers and 78 per cent of double-deckers.

Western Welsh considered itself fortunate in having only 22 vehicles built to wartime 'utility' specification, a low figure considering the size of the fleet. Of these, eight were Bedford 32-seaters, which were the only remaining petrol vehicles owned by the company. The 1946-47 re-bodying programme made the situation more favourable still, with the number of post-war bodies standing at 315, or 51.6 per cent of the fleet. The oldest vehicles in operation in 1950 were a few veterans of 1934-35 which were still providing excellent service. With the anticipated arrival of further new vehicles, an extensive scrapping programme resulted in a considerable reduction in the number of pre-war vehicles.

At this time only the coaching stock fell short of expectations. Western Welsh had no option but to accept that the smaller operators possessed more attractive fleets and as a result, were able to drum up more business. It was reasoned that companies like themselves had to prioritise modernisation of their service fleets at the end of the war. The smaller operators on the other hand could immediately order new coaches. However, having taken delivery of its 8ft wide Windovers, the company was already on the way to boasting a modern coach fleet.

Western Welsh driving accidents in 1950

Depot name	No. of vehicles	Annual mileage	Passengers carried	ACCIDENT CATEGORY				Total Accidents	Total per 1,000 ms
				Passenger	Staff	Pedestrian	Property		
Barry	60	2,318,003	12,246,548	19	37	3	105	164	.07
Brecon	20	821,569	1,733,597	1	2	–	20	23	.03
Bridgend	127	5,475,921	23,349,358	35	76	13	321	445	.08
Cardiff	68	2,691,265	9,977,917	21	54	3	129	207	.08
Carmarthen	65	2,045,222	4,770,044	2	15	3	108	128	.06
Crosskeys	75	3,492,965	14,358,779	16	28	2	132	178	.05
Neath	83	3,758,531	10,148,009	16	30	5	141	192	.05
Pontypool	64	2,617,753	14,227,832	7	24	6	92	129	.05
Total	562	23,221,226	90,812,084	117	266	35	1,048	1,466	.06

Carmarthen depot plays host to all-Leyland PD1/2 975 (FKG 975) and Weymann-bodied Albion Nimbus 42 (WKG 42) in 1963. *Peter Keating*

In November, the BET Group took control of James of Ammanford and Western Welsh became responsible for administering its fleet, with heavy overhauls and the commissioning of new vehicles undertaken at Ely. The subsequent absorption of the James fleet into the South Wales Transport operation in 1962 came as a surprise, particularly as most of the fleet was of Leyland manufacture and familiar to Western Welsh, as opposed to the mainly AEC fleet of SWT.

After many years sterling service, Brecon's leading driver Bill Rhodes retired. He had joined the GWR in 1889 and transferred to its road transport department in 1903. Meanwhile, another popular face was missed at Bridgend. It was that of Mrs Hinton, long-time tenant of the company's bus station café, who died after illness. For a time it had been managed by her son, who only survived her by a few days.

In December, the South Wales Echo newspaper reported favourably on the efforts of the company's road staff during a cold spell. It seems that passengers on Western Welsh buses throughout mid Glamorgan had been full of praise and admiration for the efforts of drivers and conductors who collected ashes in buckets and sacks from houses alongside the icy roads. When they came to dangerous spots, they pulled up and laid the ashes.

Two brothers who drove for Western Welsh became something akin to 'have-a-go' heroes when they helped bring a villain to justice. They were travelling home to Barry on the top deck of a bus after their duty at Cardiff, when they noticed a man sitting opposite emptying the contents of a lady's handbag beside him and pocketing its

Lowbridge Weymann-bodied AEC Regent III No. 652 (EUH 652) was 10 years old when seen at the Brewery Field, Bridgend in 1960. *Paul Redmond*

The narrow streets of Bridgend town centre were a bottleneck even in the 1950s. In this busy scene at Wyndham Street, 611 (CKG 791), on its way to Porthcawl, picks its way through a gap between a United Welsh Bedford OB and a Ford Popular single-handedly responsible for the congestion! *George Wedlake*

contents. Suspicions aroused, they decided to try and contact a policeman before the bus reached Thompson Street, Barry, where the man intended to get off. The brothers went downstairs at St Andrews Cross to give the impression they were leaving the bus, but on arriving at Colcot they felt that if one of them attempted to call at the policeman's house there, the man might see him and be alerted to their intention. When the bus reached Romilly Schools one of them got off, phoned the police then ran down a short cut to the Barry Hotel stop where he got back on board. His brother confirmed that the apparent villain was still aboard. On arrival at the Thompson Street stop, the man got off with the bag concealed beneath his coat. Three policemen were waiting at the stop and surrounded him. Taken by surprise, he was promptly arrested and taken to the nearest police station. But for the action of the off-duty drivers, he would have got clean away.

A profit of £214,191 was reported, a recovery on the results of 1949 that had followed the all-time high of a year earlier.

1951

The company boldly offered Cardiff Corporation £350,000 for its motor bus fleet in January, but it was turned down. The Corporation's last trams had run in 1950 and its modern trolleybus fleet had only just been expanded. It is interesting to consider how the city's transport system might have developed had the deal gone ahead.

In contrast to what followed it is incredible that until 1950 Western Welsh had never sought to raise its fares. In April 1951, a further fuel tax rise changed that. The tax rise cost the company a staggering £118,000 a year, led to the first ever fares increase, and hit passengers badly.

Concerned at how passengers would react to the fares increase, general manager RT Ebrey put pen to paper in the Staff Bulletin. "We have all experienced increases in the price of everything we use — clothing, coal, electricity, gas, rates, food, beer and even railway travel without all this fuss and bother. Until the present time, bus fares have been the only everyday commodity available at pre-war prices. It is not politics, tell your passengers," he told staff.

The fare rise proved unpopular with passengers, but unfortunately it was just the first of many that followed in subsequent years. How different it might have been if governments in the 1950s had realised the importance of buses and eased or even removed fuel tax altogether.

Many tales of the good old days were recounted in the March Staff Bulletin. One told of meths drinkers at Penarth Road who made their home in a former Vincent's Daimler bus. Every few weeks they would throw a party and smash all the office windows before being bundled off in police vans. Another story featured the Cardiff strong man who used to pull buses along with a rope gripped between his teeth, until one of the old company stalwarts jacked a back wheel up, causing the show-off to tug, jerk and nearly pull his head off!

The first 44-seat, underfloor-engined saloons entered service at Crosskeys and Pontypool during May. While such vehicles were here to stay, it didn't stop serious evaluation of other options.

It is thought that the provision of semi-coach type seats in the 1951 delivery of PD2s was the result of a chance encounter between general manager RT Ebrey and driver Eynon Williams of Neath depot. Williams told the general manager that he thought the company's prestige on the 74-mile Cardiff to Carmarthen route had been dented by the replacement of coaches with Leyland PD2 double deckers. It had allowed N&C to become the market leader on the Cardiff to Neath section of the route. Williams felt Western Welsh was losing money as a result. Mr Ebrey pointed out that with the constantly rising fuel and wage bills, cost cutting was vital. The double-deckers also reduced the need for extra vehicles at busy times. However, the new vehicles were not only better appointed, with better seating, heaters on both decks and platform doors, but three of the original PD2s were also upgraded for use as back-up.

The Railway Correspondence and Travel Society wrote to thank the company for the service provided by a driver on their trip to visit locomotive depots in the Cardiff area. They said that they had a first-rate driver who didn't require any assistance from maps or their shed directory, during the visit.

Another, slightly lower profit of £110,131 was reported.

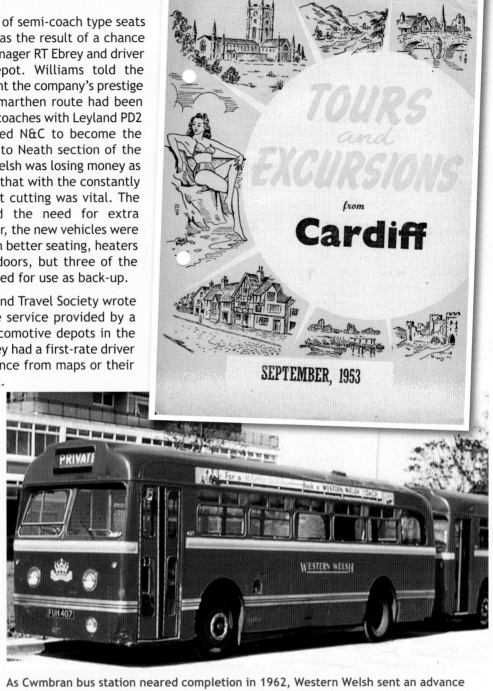

1952

The company's registered office was relocated from 88 Kingsway to Stratton House, Piccadilly, London, in March, but in October was transferred again, this time closer to home at its head office, 253 Cowbridge Road West, Ely, Cardiff. Despite this, directors continued to meet at Stratton House. The company switched its banking services from Barclays to Lloyds, with whom they continued to bank for the rest of its existence.

As Cwmbran bus station neared completion in 1962, Western Welsh sent an advance party to test its facilities and used Olympic 407 (FUH 407) then nearing the end of its days, for manoeuvrability trials. *Tony Warrener*

The sudden death of RT Ebrey occurred in April after a short illness. He had been a well-regarded and popular general manager who was respected throughout the industry. To fill the vacancy created, TG Davies returned from Rhondda as the new general manager, with transport manager T Strange replacing him there. Fred Pengelly was appointed the new traffic manager to complete the loop, while in December Leslie Gray was appointed to the new position of assistant chief engineer.

In March an experimental terminus for Monmouthshire's Eastern Valley services was set up at Newport's central car park to replace the previous Factory Road terminus.

A decade after it was created as a wartime Spitfire training base for the RAF, the civil and commercial potential of the airfield at Rhoose was recognised. Airline company Aer Lingus started a public service to Dublin on Friday, June 13. Flights to Belfast, Cork and France followed and a new terminal block was built. Western Welsh proudly announced they had won the contract to provide a bus link between Cardiff General station and the airport. It all marked the forging of another link between Western Welsh and other forms of transport. The company already enjoyed co-ordination with the Western Region of British Railways, which dated back to the road services operated by the GWR. There had also been a revival the previous year of pre-war arrangements with P&A Campbell's White Funnel Fleet.

The new general manager TG Davies wrote an interesting leader in the September Staff Bulletin. His words stressed the importance of correctly displaying the destination of all operational buses. Quite rightly, he maintained that wrong destination indicators not only misled passengers but inevitably caused loss of custom. He reckoned that the word 'Relief' didn't convey much to an intending passenger, particularly on a section of route where a number of services ran, and this word should only be used in an emergency, such as when the correct destination didn't appear on the blind.

His article concluded with the words: "The road staff are the company's salesmen and I am sure we would not think much of a salesman who refused to show the customers what goods he was selling." It would be interesting to discover TG's view on today's ever popular 'Sorry, not in service.'

The acquisition of 12 AEC Regal coaches from Grey Cars, the touring arm of Devon General, in November was a desperate measure to maintain acceptable standards in the coach fleet. The post-war renewal, with the exception of Regals 500-11 in 1950, had failed to gain momentum because of continuing manufacturing shortages. While the company had readily admitted that its bread and butter fleet had to take priority, it seemed that many local operators were able to renew their fleets with comparative ease, and the company was sufficiently concerned to select a number of Tiger saloons to be upgraded for private hire work. Further concerned that its reputation would suffer, instructions were given that the term 'coach' be omitted altogether when quoting for private hire. However, suffer it did. Despite pressing 12, full-fronted, Windover-bodied Regals into service on the day that 8ft wide vehicles became legal, Western Welsh soon gained an unfortunate reputation for using saloons on inappropriate duties. Some clients, on being faced with glorified pre-war saloons for prestige work, never used the company again.

One of the latest Royal Tiger saloons took on a starring role in a film produced by the Cardiff Amateur Cine Society. The group, which boasted a senior member of head office and Ely Works staff among its members, completed a colour film in which a visitor to Cardiff took on a quest that led him around the area's beauty spots. Use of a Western Welsh vehicle in the opening and closing sequences was an obvious choice, particularly when its arrival and departure was staged outside City Hall. The production topped the bill at a film festival in the city's Reardon-Smith Theatre during October. The senior official referred to was of course, none other than avid film-maker Leslie Gray.

A letter of appreciation was received from the grateful parent of a boy involved in an accident with a bus on Blaengarw Road: "I don't know the driver's name, but my wife and I wish to thank him for the wonderful way he handled the bus to avoid hitting my son. If it wasn't for his presence of mind, my son would have died. As it is, he is very good, and is about playing today, so please will you thank him for us both and we hope he is all right himself."

Capital increased from £600,000 to £1,268,750, while the profit for the year was £143,840.

1953

BET interests in the area continued to grow with the purchase in April of two leading operators, Thomas Bros of Port Talbot, and Neath & Cardiff Luxury Coaches. Thomas Bros had become well-established in Port Talbot, having absorbed a number of local operators.

A 10 shilling note blew out of the hand of the conductress of a bus running through Blackmill and fluttered into the roadway. All 43 passengers not only assisted in the search but, when it proved fruitless, many contributed a few pennies each to make up the deficiency. It was just another example of the relationship between passengers and crews in those distant days.

'Okay, okay, so we missed the plane, now let's forget it!' *Stewart Williams*

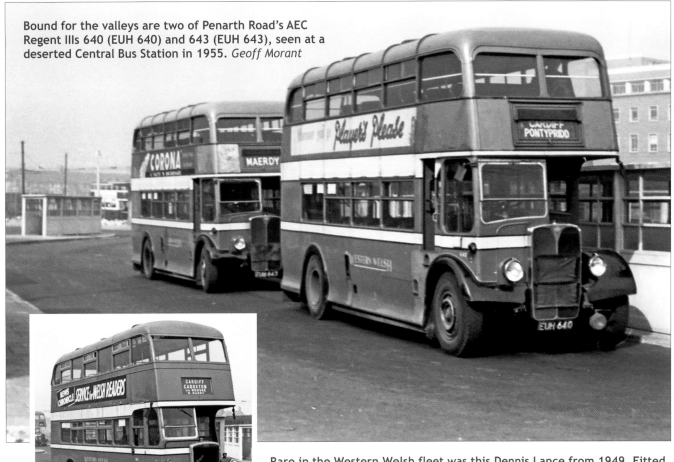

Bound for the valleys are two of Penarth Road's AEC Regent IIIs 640 (EUH 640) and 643 (EUH 643), seen at a deserted Central Bus Station in 1955. *Geoff Morant*

Rare in the Western Welsh fleet was this Dennis Lance from 1949. Fitted with a Davies 56-seat body and acquired from Ebsworth of Laugharne in 1954 No. 983 (FBX 35) had a highbridge body so was deemed suitable for the Cardiff to Barry service, on which it is seen at the city's recently opened central bus station in 1955. *Geoff Morant*

Under BET control they continued to expand and by 1963 had gained a number of Western Welsh routes. The N&C fleet was virtually replaced within three years with new and re-bodied coaches. From this point six N&C vehicles were garaged at Penarth Road, Cardiff.

In November, Western Welsh drivers and conductors at Bridgend were given a pat on the back for their safety record. A letter from the Chief Constable, on behalf of Glamorgan County Council's Road Safety Committee, revealed that Bridgend shared with Penarth the honour of having the lowest accident record — one slight accident in each case.

"I was instructed to write, congratulating you and the men under your charge on this satisfactory state of affairs," said the Chief Constable. "It reflects greatly on the efficiency, care and consideration of the Western Welsh drivers and conductors, who so admirably discharge their duties in the congested streets of Bridgend.

"Their skill in manoeuvring vehicles, and the general high standard of achievements undoubtedly helped, in no small measure, to make the roads of Bridgend safer for those who use them."

A new booking and enquiry office, managed by JC Lewis & Sons on behalf of the company, opened in Albany Road, Cardiff. The Greenline service of AH Jones, between Kenfig and Porthcawl, was bought for £2,000 in February, though no vehicles were included.

On April 14, Mr and Mrs Albert Gray celebrated their Golden Wedding at their Ogmore-by-Sea home, where they had lived for several years. Mrs Gray was an active member of the parish church, while her husband looked after his garden and tropical fish. Celebrations were held in August when their daughter and three sons, who all held positions in the transport industry, assembled with all 10 grandchildren for a family party.

The courage of an Ely works employee in rescuing a boy who, with his brother, had become marooned on a rock 45 yards from the shore at Bendricks Bay, Barry, was recognised at a presentation held in the works canteen in May. Electrician EH Hills was presented with a wallet of notes by the general manager, TG Davies. Mr Hills, who was not in the best of health, was able to bring the younger boy to within five yards of the shore before collapsing himself, but regrettably the older boy panicked and his would-be rescuer was unable to hold him. At the

Two fascinating views of how in the early 1950s buses were an important part of life at the sprawling post-war Steel Company of Wales Abbey Works, Port Talbot. Vehicles came from miles around carrying workers employed in many of the plant's departments. The works was officially opened in 1952, the year the top picture was taken. At shift change times scores of buses would be lined up. There are many AECs in the picture including Western Welsh lowbridge Regent III 638 from Bridgend. Other buses were from Jones Pantdu and South Wales Transport along with one of the Dennis vehicles operated by the steel company for staff transport. In the 1955 picture alongside, a solitary Western Welsh Tiger occupies the foreground, its crew chatting while they wait for their work-weary passengers. Lined up beyond is a range of Thomas Bros and South Wales Transport vehicles, the odd independent and a SCoW staff bus.
George Wedlake

inquest the deputy divisional coroner and the police paid tribute to Mr Hills' courage. Later in the year he was presented with a Royal Humane Society testimonial by the Mayor of Barry.

Fine weather over the August Bank Holiday resulted in 40 buses being used on the Aberystwyth express service on the Saturday. The traffic manager witnessed a convoy of 18 vehicles at Lampeter and was impressed by the high standard of driving shown. There was praise too for the efficient way the buses were despatched from Aberystwyth for the return journey. Meanwhile, September brought the signing of two significant agreements. Firstly arrangements were made with Newport Corporation for continued use of the town's central car park for bus services, and at Cardiff the company entered into an agreement to part-lease the proposed new central bus station.

As the festive season approached, it was widely reported that the company had been granted licences to operate express services to the pantomimes at Cardiff and Newport, from various centres in South Wales. The traffic manager was very keen that all members of staff should spread the word about this provision.

The fleet total rose slightly during the year to 634 in October. Profit for the year was £103,599.

Driving his bus on the road from St David's to Haverfordwest, WT Whelton spotted a fire in a roadside cottage. He stopped, ran in and saw a stove on fire. Ignoring the risk of personal injury, he threw it out of the window. The cottage was empty as the owner was outside in the garden. After all the excitement, driver Whelton calmly continued on his way with his driving duty, probably to the cheers of his passengers.

1954

A new era of expansion began for Western Welsh with the acquisition of Cardiff coach operators Streamways of Penarth in June, and just a month later the surviving coach business of Cridlands. The object of this was to secure dominance of the private hire market in the capital. Excursion and tour licences, four vehicles and a freehold garage for eight vehicles came with Streamways for £20,000. Similar licences, a further 10 coaches and a new AEC chassis came with Cridlands, for £15,000.

Expansion of services in West Wales followed, with the acquisition of Ebsworth's of Laugharne, a stake in which was held by the Cardiff financier Julian Hodge. Ebsworth held the lucrative routes from Carmarthen to Tenby via both Pendine and St Clears, together with other stage and E&T licences. A £27,500 deal was struck for these, along with 11 vehicles. With Ebsworth's being a Leyland devotee this fitted in nicely with Western Welsh. However, no premises were included, and despite talks of a new depot, vehicles were kept in a yard on the edge of the town.

Elsewhere extensions to Ely works were announced and land was acquired for a small bus station at Varteg, near Pontypool, at a site some 1,080 feet above sea level. It was reasoned that the costs involved in building and maintaining the bus station would be less than those of the vehicles continuing a further half a mile to an existing turning point. Meanwhile, much further west, work was well under way on a new garage at St David's. It opened during December, the same month that Cardiff's new central bus station finally opened. The huge block of associated offices, now demolished, followed in 1957.

In March, a special souvenir edition of the Staff Bulletin marked the company's silver anniversary. As TG Davies pointed out in that month's Staff Bulletin, the first 25 years had been an eventful chapter for the company, one

The Newport to Monmouth route was a principal one, consisting of an hourly service via Usk. However, in 1955 it was handed over to Red & White in exchange for their Cardiff to Barry 'lower road' service. Here 407 (FUH 407) has a healthy load for the journey south from Monmouth in 1954.
Tony Jenkins

A summer exodus

Sun, sea and sand-blasted sandwiches!

In the 1950s and 1960s, before most families had a car, Sunday bus trips from valley communities to the seaside were extremely popular. Sunday schools, workingmen's clubs, institutes and societies of all kinds organised outings for their members to the Glamorganshire coastal resorts of Barry Island, Porthcawl and Aberavon Beach.

The statistics were impressive, with thousands of people on the move for a day at the beach and the funfair, and no doubt a few pubs and cafes for good measure. Western Welsh operations, while never on the scale of the mass Rhondda Transport exodus, whose vast fleet of dark red AECs (and borrowed buses in the many colours of the various municipalities) ran in long convoys to the coast every summer weekend, were nevertheless impressive.

Dozens of saloons ran down to Barry from the Monmouthshire valleys, while the mid Glamorganshire communities piled aboard a fair number of Bridgend's double deckers for the shorter journey to Porthcawl or Aberavon. Buses stretched from one end of the street to the other and

Coast to coast: 284 (WKG 284) at Aberavon Beach, operating the 237 summertime route from Porthcawl. *John Jones*

quickly filled up as excited children, with half-a-crown spending money and a bottle of Tizer, piled aboard. Each vehicle carried a label with the bus number, often reaching the 30s and 40s. If your memory was good you remembered the number and avoided the risk of ending up at perhaps Croesyceiliog instead of Blackwood or Bargoed.

Once under way, the buses weaved their way down the valleys, sometimes on roads that were not used by regular services. Collisions with over-hanging branches of trees could be a nasty experience, and on more than one occasion a journey was tragically curtailed by an unexpected low bridge. Youths would gather at the back of the

A lazy Sunday at Barry Island for 1316 (ABO 316B) while the party of small faces it had brought from Cwmbran and Pontypool enjoy themselves on the nearby sands in 1966. *Peter Keating*

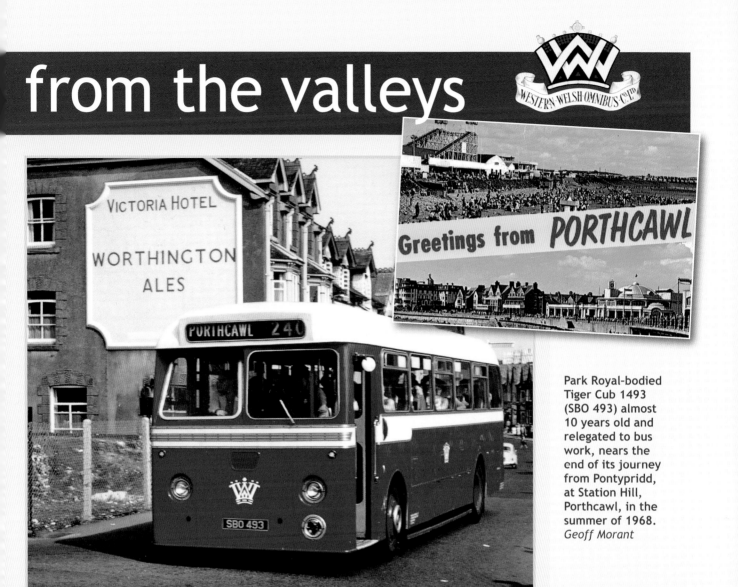

Park Royal-bodied Tiger Cub 1493 (SBO 493) almost 10 years old and relegated to bus work, nears the end of its journey from Pontypridd, at Station Hill, Porthcawl, in the summer of 1968.
Geoff Morant

upper deck, where the emergency rear window was dropped open for air — and for whistling at the girls as they passed!

Eventually the first cry went out from the top deck: 'I can see the sea!' But then, just as the journey seemed over, the queues began, with so many buses trying to get into the town to park up for the day — at Barry Island behind the railway station; in Porthcawl the Salt Lake park near the miniature railway and in Aberavon the buses rested in sand-filled parks along the length of the seafront, where the Afan Belle open-top double decker would convey you along to Miami Beach funfair.

At the end of the day the game of Hunt the Bus would be played out, then, having climbed aboard there

would be sticky handrails from candy floss covered fingers. The trek home saw the last of the sand-blasted sandwiches distributed, as lobster-coloured legs stuck to the seats and faces matched the colour of the bus. Usually the return home coincided

nicely with the opening of the 'workies' club, where weary dads took shelter until Mam had bathed the kids and put them to bed, and all returned to normal at the end of a memorable day out by bus. They were fun-filled happy days.

Bridgend's 1138 (MUH 138) is awaiting work at Porthcawl's station approach ahead of a Rhondda Regent in 1967.
Howard Roberts

that in his words had been "scarred by a world war which brought in its wake a changed outlook on most things."

He pondered over what the following quarter of a century might bring, but concluded on a positive note. His view was one of confidence that the company could overcome the greatest of obstacles providing it always kept in mind its four aims — reliability, efficiency, comfort and courtesy. This was a mission statement which wouldn't go amiss in modern times.

Leslie Gray, in an article in the same anniversary edition of the bulletin considered the changes the early years had brought. These ranged from advances in the design of both chassis and body, the replacement of the petrol engine with the oil engine, and the change of driving position from behind the engine to beside it. In addition there had been a move from timber to all metal body construction and not least the increase of vehicle dimensions. With the tribulations of wartime operation and its restrictions and shortage of skilled staff still fresh in his mind, he concluded by congratulating all staff for their efficiency and care of vehicles and equipment .

The Leyland Tiger Cub along with AEC's Reliance was developed in response to demands for a lighter, more economical vehicle to the PSU1 Royal Tiger and Regal IV.

Driver reaction to the new Tiger Cubs was extremely favourable, and on a visit to Crosskeys depot by a Leyland Journal representative, special praise was given to both their brakes and steering. In the hilly territory covered by the majority of services, great importance was attached to good braking and there is no doubt that they scored highly in every respect. "She steers like a car," was a frequent observation by drivers after a spell of duty at the wheel of a Tiger Cub. It was an important factor when considering bus operation in the South Wales valleys, with their countless steep gradients, sharp bends, narrow roads, and profusion of level crossings and low bridges. The terrain offered as grim a test as could be devised. Examples of the kind of gradients to be negotiated were those at Bancffosfelen and Crwbin on the Carmarthen to Llanelly route. Both were approximately a mile in length, with a general gradient of 1 in 10 or 11, with steeper portions at 1 in 7 and 1 in 8. Despite these difficulties the Tiger Cubs maintained the tight schedules that were imposed without the slightest difficulty. As a precaution, the first vehicles were docked for full inspection at 25,000 miles. When asked about the outcome, chief engineer FA Mason commented that although the Tiger Cubs had a higher-revving engine, in the light of the excellent condition of

Principal Western Welsh bus services in 1953

From	To	Via	Frequency	Journey time
Ammanford	Aberystwyth	Lampeter, Aberayron	3 daily	3 hours
Ammanford	Lampeter	Llandilo	7 daily	1 hr 30 mins
Brecon	Hay-on-Wye	Talgarth	8 daily	50 mins
Carmarthen	Brecon	Llandilo, Llandovery	4 daily	2 hrs 35 mins
Newport	Brecon	Pontypool, Abergavenny	7 daily	2 hrs 25 mins
Newport	Monmouth	Usk	Hourly	1 hr 20 mins
Newport	Tredegar	Crosskeys, Blackwood	15 mins	1 hr 15 mins
Newport	Ebbw Vale	Crosskeys, Crumlin	30 mins	1 hr 20 mins
Cardiff	Garndiffaith	Newport, Pontypool	Hourly	1 hr 35 mins
Cardiff	Ebbw Vale	Crosskeys, Crumlin	Hourly	1 hr 45 mins
Cardiff	Porthcawl	Cowbridge, Bridgend	Hourly	1 hr 30 mins
Penarth	Bridgend	Barry, Llantwit Major	Hourly	1 hr 25 mins
Pontypridd	Porthcawl	Talbot Green, Bridgend	Hourly	1 hr 40 mins
Neath	Porthcawl	Port Talbot	30 mins	55 mins
Aberdare	Porthcawl	Neath, Port Talbot	Hourly	1 hr 15 mins
Merthyr	Porthcawl	Neath, Port Talbot	Hourly	1 hr 20 mins
Neath	Merthyr	Glyn Neath, Hirwaun	Hourly	1 hr 15 mins
Carmarthen	Cardigan	Newcastle Emlyn	Hourly	1 hr 50 mins
Carmarthen	Aberayron	Llandysul, New Quay	2 hourly	2 hrs 15 mins
Carmarthen	Tenby	Whitland, Narberth (Summer only)	4 daily	1 hr 45 mins
Carmarthen	Haverfordwest	Whitland, Narberth	6 daily	1 hr 45 mins
Cardigan	Goodwick	Fishguard	9 daily	1 hr 20 mins

The company's third Tiger Cub, 1003 (HUH 3) is at its home depot of Newcastle Emlyn shortly after delivery in October 1953. The position of the front number plate on the first few buses was lower than the rest, as seen here, and looked out of place. *Howard Roberts*

the first six engines examined, it was not anticipated that any departure from the company's existing 30,000 mile docking interval would be necessary.

The first production vehicles returned a saving of at least two miles per gallon compared with earlier types. However, by the time these vehicles became available, interest had already turned to the production of a chassis-less vehicle where the body and chassis were built as a single unit, with the mechanical components suspended from the underside. Using this technique Leyland and Weymann joined forces to develop the Olympian, which incorporated Tiger Cub mechanical units. A prototype had been built in 1953, for demonstration purposes, but it was nearly a year later that the second vehicle was built and delivered to Western Welsh for evaluation under service conditions in the form of 469, which later became 1469.

As far back as 1897 the council at Cardiff was considering the options for future development of the Wood Street area, known in those days as Temperance Town. It was not until the 1930s, however, that the squalid houses were demolished to clear the way for the planners. A swimming pool, ballrooms, skating rink, hotel and bus station were all pencilled in as possibilities, but only the latter remained a consistent favourite, and along with a telephone exchange fringing the site, the bus station was the first project to be completed. By this time, the building of the Empire Pool, needed for use in the 1958 British Empire Games, had reached an advanced stage.

In June, service revisions in the Vale of Glamorgan removed the need for the Penarth – Barry – Bridgend service to be split at Llantwit Major and vehicles turned. Through working enabled passengers from Penarth and Barry to visit Southerndown and Ogmore-by-Sea without the need for a change of bus, although in practice the need to balance drivers, if not vehicles, often led to a short layover at Llantwit.

Special Sunday excursions operated from Glyncorrwg to Porthcawl throughout the summer months, and on certain weekdays during July.

The interior of one of the 1953 Willowbrook-bodied coaches was probably more comfortable than the armchairs in the homes of its passengers. *George Wedlake*

An amusing incident occurred at Ammanford's College Street stand one day. A buxom elderly lady had made three or four futile attempts to board a bus before standing back with a look of dismay on her face. Sensing her predicament, the conductor said: "Just a moment, lady, please," and rapidly turned the handle of the destination blind. "There," he said, "I've lowered the step quite a few inches, you'll find it easier now." Surprisingly enough, the step was negotiated without further difficulty and the old lady, with a smile of gratitude, took her seat and remarked: "Aren't they clever these days?"

A cause of great concern to the bus industry in general and Western Welsh in particular, arose from a ruling by a London magistrate that an intending passenger had the right, at his own risk, to board a stationary bus, even if it had stopped at traffic lights.

"Conduct of this kind is certainly not conducive to road safety and could defeat the object of queuing," wrote TG Davies in the September Staff Bulletin. "Drivers and conductors should, therefore, discourage it and they will be fully supported by me in any reasonable action which they take to that end."

There had, in fact, been a number of accidents in Cardiff resulting from passengers attempting to board vehicles as they were leaving the bus station. Notices had been posted at depots reminding staff to ensure that the doors of their vehicles were closed before they pulled away from the stand. Nevertheless, the general manager took the opportunity to remind staff that: "A passenger wanting to leave a bus may do so at any point where the vehicle is stationary. At points other than at authorised stopping places, passengers wishing to alight should be warned that they do so at their own risk."

Passengers and neighbours of the Upper Cock Inn bus stop in Croesyceiliog, had often noticed bus crews giving a

Only the second Leyland Olympian to be built, 1469 (JUH 469) was delivered to Western Welsh (as 469) for trials under service conditions in 1954. For a prototype, a remarkably long life followed, with many years based at Barry, Pontypool and Bridgend before it was withdrawn in 1971. The Weymann bodywork was something of a prototype too, being identifiable by its shallower windows when compared to the later Tiger Cubs and Olympians. *John Jones*

The early Tiger Cubs were put to work on the hilly Carmarthen to Llanelli route through Pontyberem. Here 1001 (HUH 1) is seen climbing one of the tortuous gradients along the route. *Howard Roberts*

toot on the horn and cheery wave as they passed the home of Jean Spanswick. Although confined to bed with heart problems, Jean always returned the salute. Eventually she recovered and the Pontypool depot's sports committee invited her to their gala dance hoping it would be an extra tonic. Jean accepted and, after the event said she had been absolutely thrilled by the unofficial prescription!

Parcels Manager Albert E Smith, who had been with the company throughout its existence, retired in April.

Western Welsh management was censured over the deal with Streamways for allowing the latter to default on trading debts, and dispose of one coach which had cost Western Welsh £3,000. Streamways was later wound up without assets. Nevertheless, Western Welsh doubled its profits for the year to £211,330, a figure undoubtedly the result of the superb fuel economy being achieved by the new Tiger Cubs. Capital increased from £1,268,750 to £1,624,000. NECC held 323,296 shares, BET 409,000, and BTC 811,700.

1955

An increase in road casualty figures had led to the publication in April of a new Highway Code with all road users being encouraged to familiarise themselves with it. Staff were encouraged to read and digest the new guide.

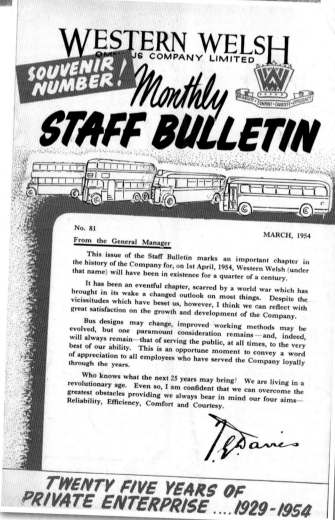

WESTERN WELSH
OMNIBUS COMPANY LIMITED

SOUVENIR NUMBER!

Monthly
STAFF BULLETIN

No. 81   MARCH, 1954

From the General Manager

This issue of the Staff Bulletin marks an important chapter in the history of the Company for, on 1st April, 1954, Western Welsh (under that name) will have been in existence for a quarter of a century.

It has been an eventful chapter, scarred by a world war which has brought in its wake a changed outlook on most things. Despite the vicissitudes which have beset us, however, I think we can reflect with great satisfaction on the growth and development of the Company.

Bus designs may change, improved working methods may be evolved, but one paramount consideration remains—and, indeed, will always remain—that of serving the public, at all times, to the very best of our ability. This is an opportune moment to convey a word of appreciation to all employees who have served the Company loyally through the years.

Who knows what the next 25 years may bring? We are living in a revolutionary age. Even so, I am confident that we can overcome the greatest obstacles providing we always bear in mind our four aims—Reliability, Efficiency, Comfort and Courtesy.

T. G. Davies

TWENTY FIVE YEARS OF PRIVATE ENTERPRISE 1929-1954

The special souvenir edition of the Staff Bulletin produced in 1954 to salute 25 years of Western Welsh.

Touting for day trippers perhaps? Coach 539 (KUH 539), peeps out of the former Streamways garage, Penarth. It was unique as its AEC Regal IV chassis was originally delivered to Cridland's in 1952. When Western Welsh took over in 1954 it was still unbodied and it was 1955 before it had a Willowbrook body identical to their own batch from 1953. *Viv Corbin*

This is the Courtesy Code...

★ **DRIVERS**
Drive safely and smoothly.
Respect the rights of pedestrians and drivers of other vehicles.
Give signals clearly and in good time.
Pull up and start without jolting.
Make sure that all passengers have entered the bus before starting.
Look out for passengers at Request Stops, and any who are hurrying towards them.
SMILE.

★ **CONDUCTORS**
Treat your passengers as your guests.
Be civil, cheerful, considerate, and tactful.
Be helpful, especially to the elderly and infirm, to mothers with small children, and to shoppers loaded with parcels.
Make sure that all passengers are on board before ringing the bell.
Remember that, particularly in rush hours, passengers may have had long waits in queues.
Be firm with queue-jumpers — but not abusive. Make allowances for frayed tempers.
If anything needs explaining, explain it.
Bid them a cheerful " good morning " or whatever it is.
SMILE.

The Royal Society for the Prevention of Accidents (RoSPA) had for many years spearheaded the National Safe Driving Competition, which the public service vehicle industry had fully supported. However, in 1954 a rift occurred. RoSPA introduced a 'disqualification for speeding' rule, the effect of which was to prevent a driver convicted of speeding from gaining a safety award. Western Welsh, along with road transport associations, held the view that, while safe driving was their aim at all times, they could not contend that exceeding the speed limit would necessarily involve unsafe driving. Meetings to resolve matters proved abortive and Western Welsh pledged to assist the industry to establish a safe driving competition of its own, based on similar principles to the original RoSPA scheme.

Three luxury coaches conveyed supporters to Dinas Field, Porth, in March, for the final of the Cownie Cup football competition. "I can only remind our friends at Rhondda Transport that since becoming a general manager I have never been on the losing side in a Cownie Cup game," said TG Davies. Alas Rhondda beat Western Welsh 3-0.

Proposals for a new bus station at Newport were announced along with a bus station and garage at Cwmbran New Town. A freehold garage at Fishguard to replace the town's leased premises was also proposed.

From the air, all looks spick and span at Cardiff's new central bus station in 1957/58. The office block is complete and appears to be occupied. The bus station itself had been operational since the start of 1954. The newly completed Empire Pool is on the left, with Cardiff Arms Park beyond. *George Wedlake*

An exchange of routes involving a hand-over of the Newport – Usk - Monmouth service to Red & White in exchange for its Cardiff to Barry 'lower road' service, was agreed, starting from September 11. The Monmouth route required one vehicle from Crosskeys depot and involved considerable light mileage, but had a human story of excellent relations built up over 25 years of reliable service. The Barry service was operated by R&W as successors to Reliance Motors, which operated three vehicles on this joint route, along with one from Thomas Motors of Barry. Company owner Russell Thomas refused an attempt by Western Welsh to buy him out and so remained the sole competitor on the Dinas Powis route.

'We'll miss you' was the sentiment expressed in a number of appreciative letters received from regular patrons of the Monmouth to Newport route, when operation by Western Welsh ended.

"I would like to convey my appreciation of the many kindnesses shown by your conductors, both male and female, and your drivers on these journeys," wrote a lady from Raglan, "I am a teacher and it has been my

Driver Glyn Harding and conductress Margaret Stanton alongside one of the vehicles they crewed in 1955. They were typical of the people who helped make Western Welsh the proud company it was. *Gail Sydenham*

happy experience to convey many children to and from school on a Western Welsh bus and our days have often been cheered by words and laughter from Mrs Shepherd and her driver Mr Thomas, and Mrs Vaughan and her husband. We could entrust the children at any time to their safe-keeping. I can only bid them farewell with sorrow in my heart." Another passenger wrote: "The drivers and conductors of these buses have all been held in high esteem by the majority of people along this route and I and my family will miss their kindness and courtesy very much indeed."

The decision was taken to replace the company's ATM ticket machines with Setright machines. Bell Punch then Willibrew machines had been in use before the ATMs.

An accident involving a BRS lorry occurred near Crumlin on June 7. In all, 17 people were injured including the conductress, Ada Meredith, and conductor J Wallace who had been travelling to work. They were all taken to the Royal Gwent Hospital. Driver Ray Newman escaped unhurt.

A total of 17 coaches were needed to convey the 379-strong Salt Lake Mormon Tabernacle Choir when it gave a concert at Sophia Gardens Pavilion in Cardiff during August. Things were just as hectic in the west with staff at St David's having a very busy summer with a Royal visit, the Royal Welsh Show, which was at Haverfordwest, and the annual Brawdy Air Day.

In Neath, Monday July 18 brought the worst floods in the town's memory. Days of heavy rain resulted in torrents of muddy water overflowing from the Gnoll Brook, submerging many streets, delaying traffic for hours and

This mixed line-up of coaches was used to transport the Salt Lake Mormon Tabernacle Choir to a concert in Sophia Gardens Pavilion when they visited Cardiff in August 1955 *George Wedlake*

causing untold damage in the town. Members of staff had to wade waist deep in water to reach their homes just a few hundred yards from Neath station, and in some cases properties were under six feet of water. The Mayor of Neath launched a relief fund on behalf of the victims, two of whom were company employees.

It seemed that many retired Western Welsh staff, having served the public in the bus industry, went on to serve them from behind a bar at their local. The list from the Bridgend area included TJ Richards, Coach & Horses,

Waiting at St David's, Pembrokeshire, the remotest terminus in the Western Welsh empire on a warm summer day in 1955 are 449 (GUH 449) and 451 (GUH 451). *Geoff Morant*

Bridgend; W Islip, White Horse, Coychurch; Ray Baker, King's Head, Pencoed; Tom David, Railway Hotel, Pencoed and Dudley Browning, who at one time kept the Fox & Hounds in St Bride's Major.

A report in the Port Talbot Guardian told of the unusual experience of Sidney Jones who, while driving his bus along Margam Road towards Port Talbot, suddenly became aware of a twin-engined plane swooping down along the road towards his bus, giving every indication that the pilot intended to land. He jammed on the brakes and leapt out of his cab. With the conductor and four passengers, he jumped over a wall and waited for the crash. The plane, however, roared on over the bus and they watched as it made a landing approach over a nearby field, but at the last minute it soared up and away in the direction of Kenfig Hill. Mr Jones, shaken but not stirred, continued on his way, too!

Albert Gray, who had remained a consultant to the company after retiring, albeit at an early age in 1938, finally took to full retirement at the age of 75.

The honour of being the first public service vehicle to cross the newly completed Neath River bridge at Briton Ferry, at its time the biggest post-war civil engineering project in Britain, went to none other than a Western Welsh luxury coach driven by Cecil Davies of Neath. It carried a party of local government officials to the opening ceremony on October 31.

 There were times when the banking operation at Bridgend could be little more than quaint. Even in later years, a depot saloon would be commandeered along with every available conductor for the five minutes it took to drive around the block to Wyndham Street, where, with a box in each hand, the conductors would dart off the bus and through the doors of the bank. There was no CCTV, no armour-plated van or security officers, just a Tiger Cub blocking the street for as long as it took to deposit the cash. Then, just as quickly as it had begun, it was back to normal duties.

Every year at Christmas it was the custom for the company chairman to send a message of goodwill and appreciation to the readers of the Staff Bulletin. In his 1955 message, chairman JS Wills remarked: "There is much talk today of taking steps to improve what are called 'human relations' in industry. In our company we need no prompting from outside. Friendly relations have long been the order of the day, not only between staff and management, but what is at least of equal importance, between staff and passengers. We on the management side are well aware that it is not possible to keep a passenger transport service going unless those who run and look after the vehicles regard themselves as members of a team whose job is to serve the public. I believe that Western Welsh does possess that team spirit and takes a pride in its good name. That alone means a great deal."

An elderly man who was a regular passenger in the Aberdare area became extremely annoyed with anyone heard to drop their aitches. A certain conductor, knowing this, found the old gent on his bus and when nearing Hirwaun, kept repeating: "Next stop 'irwaun!" This was too much for the passenger who gruffly remarked, "Man, you've dropped something," to which the conductor replied, "I'll pick it up at Haberdare!"

Once again the company recorded a healthy operating profit for the year of £161,720 .

Chasing the rivals again

Big two bagged, but cars fuel fear

In its very earliest incarnation as South Wales Commercial Motors and then under the banner of Western Welsh, the story of the company through thick and thin had very much been one of almost continual expansion. From the first vehicle of Albert Gray's embryonic company and the earliest single route, from Cardiff to Penarth, operations had gathered momentum at quite a pace, something that had been hindered only by the restrictions brought about by the onset of the Second World War.

For Western Welsh, as with most other enterprises, the post-war period was a time of attempting to get back to normal as quickly as possible, something that the company appeared to handle with consummate ease. The company was never one to stand still, and talk in the boardroom once again focused on the acquisition and absorption of competitors. This time, however, it was not the

minnows of the passenger transport world in South Wales that attracted the interest of the directors. Instead, they eyed up the business of two long-established and well-respected operators. One of these would enhance their growing coaching operations, the other would provide a major foothold in Pembrokeshire. It was a move that significantly changed the map of the territory covered by the company and resulted in an increase in business not just in normal traffic, but also contract hire to satisfy the transport demands of the huge oil refineries that would soon be unveiled in one of Wales' prettiest areas.

It would appear that everything was rosy, but this wasn't the case, and with more private cars than ever taking to the road, passenger numbers began to dwindle and the profitability of certain routes soon became a cause for concern.

When Green's of Haverfordwest was acquired in 1956, its double-deckers were well suited to Western Welsh. Green's vehicles didn't stray far from home, as evidenced by all-Leyland 991 (LDE 603) here. It was hard to spot the differences between these and the Western Welsh examples. The split white/red diamond, introduced when Green's was bought, denotes its Pembrokeshire home. *Paul Redmond*

1956

In April the coach business of ER Forse of Cardiff came into the fold, followed in December by that of Green's Motors of Haverfordwest.

Forse's was a long established and well-respected family business in Cardiff, and with it came excursion and tour licences, a freehold garage at Blackweir, and 21 coaches, at a cost of £75,000. Green's, who needed to sell in order to settle death duties, was bought for £55,000. Before the deal Western Welsh had just four buses in Haverfordwest. With Green's 44 vehicles and 100 staff it had gained a major foothold in the area. Additional property in the town was bought for £14,000.

The acquisition of Forse's and its mixed, but reasonably modern, fleet was seen as an opportunity to significantly strengthen Western Welsh's tour and private hire business in the city. Although the company had now gained large premises at Blackweir, they refused to give permission to Cardiff Corporation to build a new police and fire station on its land at Ely.

Although the acquisition of Green's meant that Haverfordwest now featured prominently on the company's route map, elsewhere in rural West Wales, expansion was the last word on many people's minds as abandonment of the poorest routes started. With the purchase and takeover of services from January 1,1957, Green's was the most significant independent operator acquired post-war, and with it came the only reported profitable services in the area. However, management from Cardiff, nearly 100 miles away, could not have been without its difficulties. Meanwhile, the Ministry of Transport, acting upon the recommendation of the London & Home Counties Traffic Advisory Committee, raised the speed limit on 60 roads in Greater London from 30mph to 40mph for a trial period. This was regarded by Western Welsh, among other operators, as a step in the right direction and seen as a measure likely to ease

Swinging into Charles Street from Queen Street, Cardiff, a manoeuvre no longer possible, is one of the roaring Regents, 670 (LKG 670), travelling light to Penarth Road depot. This was one of the highbridge batch from 1956 which were fitted with smaller engines than their lighter lowbridge sisters. Despite this they sounded powerful, and roared, rasped and reverberated as only AEC470 verticals could! *George Wedlake*

traffic congestion. However, it was noted that the reactions of local authorities across South and West Wales had not been too favourable. The 30mph-restricted PSV still remained a problem.

In April, the Cardiff to Garndiffaith and Newport to Garndiffaith services, along with a number of workmen's services, were extended to Varteg, north of Pontypool to serve a large new housing estate. A new bus station was opened there, but the location proved troublesome in icy conditions. However, bus crews would always strive to reach the terminus as the canteen provided the best bacon rolls and tea for miles. Return journeys could be delayed until road conditions improved!

While it must surely have always been a pleasant duty to give praise where it was due, sometimes the reverse applied when cases of poor service were brought to the notice of the general manager.

On a number of occasions in the 1956 summer season, 'inexcusable lapses on the part of road and office staff'

resulted in delays for the Cardiff to Aberystwyth express services. General manager TG Davies told staff: "I avoid giving specific instances, but obviously these irritating mistakes must be avoided in future. Care must be taken to see that we give maximum efficiency to the travelling public. They pay for it — and they deserve it."

The picture was, of course, not all gloom and doom. The number of bouquets received far outweighed the brickbats. For instance, the headmaster of Greenhill Open Air School in Rhiwbina was full of praise for the Cardiff drivers who had made a collection for the handicapped children there. The drivers conveyed them to the school from the suburbs of Cardiff and having been impressed with their good behaviour, had a collection to help towards the school's Christmas party. "It was a most unexpected gesture of goodwill from your drivers to our children," wrote the headmaster, "While I appreciate most sincerely the money which was so kindly collected, I am more than pleased that your drivers think so highly of the children of my school."

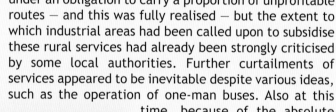

The log book for 1135 (MUH 135) shows the date of first registration, September 27, 1956 and the subsequent disposal to Peake's of Pontypool on August 13, 1971. *Tony Jenkins*

An extension to Crosskeys garage was finally completed, having being delayed by the war. The area had the third largest fleet allocation after Bridgend and Neath, operating 73 vehicles, of which 23 were double-deckers. Crosskeys ran an extensive number of stage carriage and works services that included six large collieries, the GKN steelworks in Cardiff, and the vast National Aluminium Company plant at Rogerstone.

After an absence of seven years, a return visit to Wales by members of the Sporvejenes Engelsk Klub was made in September, and for five days the visitors were the guests of the Western Welsh educational club. They were given a civic reception and series of visits followed, including a tour of Ely Works.

The economic situation brought about by rising costs and declining passenger traffic necessitated a survey of services where the receipts were much lower than the costs. Consequently, in October, the Traffic Commissioners and local authorities were informed of the company's intention to surrender the licences for the Barry Dock to Llantrisant, Cardiff to Gwaelod-y-Garth, Brecon to Hay-on-Wye via Llyswen and Clyro, and New Quay to Llangranog routes.

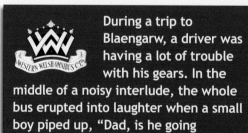

During a trip to Blaengarw, a driver was having a lot of trouble with his gears. In the middle of a noisy interlude, the whole bus erupted into laughter when a small boy piped up, "Dad, is he going through the sound barrier?"

The general manager considered that the company was under an obligation to carry a proportion of unprofitable routes — and this was fully realised — but the extent to which industrial areas had been called upon to subsidise these rural services had already been strongly criticised by some local authorities. Further curtailments of services appeared to be inevitable despite various ideas, such as the operation of one-man buses. Also at this time, because of the absolute dependence on fuel oil, the industry was becoming concerned with mounting problems in the Middle East. The blockade of the Suez Canal meant that fuel rationing had to be introduced in December, and as public transport was materially affected by the restriction, it was obvious that everything possible had to be done to conserve fuel. Western Welsh's vehicles used well over two million gallons of fuel in a year. An emergency fuel tax of one shilling per gallon was introduced in December, so there was double the pressure to reduce certain operations. In addition to cutting out the deadwood, it was necessary to reduce certain services, particularly duplications. Fortunately, in the new year the fuel situation eased as suddenly as it had begun, and rationing ended in the spring of 1957.

The company donated a staircase from the rear of an old double-decker to the Orthopaedic Clinic at St David's Hospital, Cardiff, 'in order to assist in the re-education of children in walking, climbing and redeveloping the use of their legs'.

At a time when membership of various Western Welsh staff groups was at its height, G Langrish who worked at Bridgend depot, started a budgerigar club for fellow fanciers. His efforts led to the formation of the company's Cage Bird Society in February. Presumably the title allowed for an expansion in the range of feathered friends that the group catered for.

In a letter to the company from the assistant chief constable of Monmouthshire, driver Thomas Lewis of Abergavenny was praised for his prompt action in reporting that he had seen a youth, suspected of the murder of a Gilwern woman, at Abergavenny bus station. As a result of the information, police officers were able to arrest the youth almost immediately.

A head-on collision between a Western Welsh bus and a Red & White vehicle at Llantarnam resulted in the driver being detained in hospital. Driver WC Scourfield, from Pontypool depot, had only recently been promoted to driving grade. His conductress, G Barnes, suffered fractured ribs in the accident.

Writing in the April Staff Bulletin, the chief engineer proudly announced that delivery of the large 1956

Glyn and Peter Davies from Barry depot, happy at work with their Leyland PS1 in 1956. *Viv Corbin*

A trades union event at Swansea in 1956 resulted in a fleet of Western Welsh coaches conveying the delegates. Vehicles old and new are seen outside the Guildhall approach. This logistical headache for the coaching unit, was as usual carried out to the satisfaction of all concerned. *George Wedlake*

vehicle order had begun, and that many more were on their way. Staff and observers, who may have had concerns about the stagnant position of the fleet in 1955 would no doubt have had their minds put at ease by his message: "During the next few months the make-up of the fleet will be drastically changed. The process has already started with the introduction of eight new AEC Regent Mk V 59-seat double-deck vehicles and 10 Leyland Olympian underfloor engined, 44-seat saloons.

"There are several new features about these latest deliveries. The Regent Mk V has electrically controlled rear doors which can be operated by the conductor or the driver, or in an emergency by the passenger. The advantages are that they reduce draughts and are invaluable in times of inclement weather. Heaters have been provided in upper and lower saloons. The vehicle can be easily identified by its new-look front. A further 15 of these, with 61 seats, are on order and should be delivered in the near future."

There was further news about deliveries. One of the most popular vehicles in the fleet was the 44-seat underfloor-engined Tiger Cub saloon. These vehicles had been so successful since their introduction in 1953 that follow up orders were placed. The 10 newly arrived Olympian saloons were of integral construction similar to the Olympic already in service, but much lighter. The doors were manually operated and gave a much more positive seal against the weather. Another feature was the improved seating over the wheel arches. Altogether 40 Olympians had been ordered.

Delivery was also expected of 12 semi-coach type 41-seat saloons for use on the company's Cardiff-Aberystwyth express services. With the arrival of this rolling stock, the company could claim a wholly post-war fleet of nearly 700 vehicles. Indeed, 63 per cent of them had been purchased since January 1950.

1957

During February and March the Western Welsh fleet stood at its largest ever with 735 vehicles, having just increased its strength by 65 vehicles that came from Forse's and Green's. The chief engineer's allocation list of rolling stock for March 1, 1957, shows the position clearly. As the summer season had yet to begin the majority of the coach fleet is shown as delicensed and would have been in store at Blackweir.

Green's main service had been a route running half-hourly between Haverfordwest and Milford Haven, with seven or eight buses a day branching off to the old packet port of Neyland and connecting with the ferry to Pembroke Dock at Hobb's Point. Their second trunk route was from Haverfordwest to Fishguard, with a branch to Ambleston. There was also a service to Tenby and Saundersfoot, and one twice weekly to Pembroke Dock. Neyland and Milford Haven were connected by an hourly service, with town services at each end. A circular town service operated in Haverfordwest. The acquisition of this company gave Western Welsh a monopoly west of the Haverfordwest to Fishguard road. This in turn led to a

Cardiff City Hall provides a splendid backdrop for this publicity shot of Olympian 1217 (LKG 217). The photograph was used by Western Welsh on the cover of its 1957 and 1958 timetables. *Stewart Williams*

This East Lancs-bodied Royal Tiger came from Green's of Haverfordwest in 1956. As Western Welsh 484 (PDE 390) it is seen at Laugharne shortly after the take-over.

strengthening of their position in Tenby and Saundersfoot, and gave them a foothold in Pembroke Dock. More significantly, the deep waters and natural harbour of Milford Haven were attracting the large scale shippers of oil, and with plans for the building of a new specially designed jetty, the largest tankers in the world would be able to berth and discharge their precious cargo. The company planned a bus station and maintenance depot in the county town of Haverfordwest so that, as and when the need arose, facilities would be available for new and extended services.

With the situation in the Middle East having eased considerably, pre-emergency frequencies, with one or two exceptions, were restored on stage carriage services on April 15. A reduction in fares was certainly not something that happened every day, but as a result of the ending of the one shilling a gallon fuel surcharge imposed in December 1956, revised fares involving some reductions were introduced on April 24.

The transfer of head office from Ely to the newly completed office block at Cardiff's central bus station took place in June. The first floor was occupied by the traffic department, including the tours and publicity department while the offices of the general manager and claims manager were located on the top floor.

It was around this time that Western Welsh lodged an objection to staff who had been seconded from the GWR receiving enhanced sick pay under the British Railways scheme. Evidence of railway interest within the company had remained for a long time, particularly with regard to

Depot vehicle allocation in 1957

Depot	Coaches	Saloons	D/deckers	Total
Cardiff	6	27	28	61
Barry	1	28	24	53
Crosskeys	1	48	20	69
Pontypool	1	79	0	80
Brecon	0	19	0	19
Bridgend	0	99	16	115
Port Talbot	0	20	0	20
Neath	0	29	6	35
Ammanford	0	10	4	14
Aberdare	0	20	4	24
Carmarthen	0	31	3	34
N/castle Emlyn	0	5	2	7
New Quay	0	7	0	7
Haverfordwest	2	29	16	39
Fishguard	0	5	0	5
St David's	0	7	4	11
Licensed	11	455	127	593
Delicensed	62	72	8	142
Total:	73	527	135	735

One of 10 Willowbrook-bodied Tiger Cubs ordered for the Aberystwyth express service in 1956, this was 473 (MKG 473) . They made a welcome change from the ubiquitous Weymanns. The ivory roof was added after delivery and together with the wine red became the standard dual purpose livery. *Gerald Truran*

'loaned staff', former GWR employees who had transferred to Western Welsh with the road service operations. Many staff employed at Abergavenny, Brecon, Carmarthen, Neath, Newcastle Emlyn, New Quay, St David's and Fishguard continued to enjoy the advantages of railway employment such as free rail travel and enhanced sick pay. These men, members of the National Union of Railwaymen, were causing increasing concern at the depots where drivers and conductors who weren't of a railway background and who were members of other trade unions, had to work alongside each other under different working conditions. However, it seems that this arrangement didn't generally lead to any difficulties in practice.

The managing director, WT James, officially opened the new Neath garage, and in a speech at the event, criticised the road system in general and the A48 bottleneck at Port Talbot in particular. Referring no doubt to the recently opened Briton Ferry bridge,

The low floor concept is not new! In 1958 AEC recognised the disadvantages of the sunken gangway and bench seating of the traditional lowbridge double-decker and came up with the Bridgemaster. Western Welsh took 20, the first of which, 683 (PBO 683) was exhibited at the 1956 Commercial Motor Show before finding its way to Cardiff two years later. The rest, 684 – 702, came in 1959. *George Wedlake*

About to leave Cardiff's central bus station for the Western Highlands on an extended tour in July 1957, 500 (EUH 500) comes under close scrutiny from Western Welsh bus crews. They were taking part in a provincial busmen's strike in support of a pay claim. *Ken Swallow*

he said he thought the powers-that-be were 'putting the cart before the horse' when they embarked on new road building works while the trouble at Port Talbot remained.

By 1957, Western Welsh's coach touring operations were big business. The acquisition of Forse's in 1956 had clearly indicated the aim of consolidation in this field, and in the autumn an order for 18 AEC Reliance coaches with Harrington bodies was announced. With it came the idea to bestow a 'class name' on the new vehicles.

Staff were always very interested in new additions to the fleet and were invited to submit suggestions for naming these new arrivals. Around 80 different names were received from around the depots in answer to an appeal in the Staff Bulletin. The successful name was announced in December, and two people, inspectors WP Phillips of Port Talbot and DK Williams of Cardiff central bus station each received cheques for their winning suggestion of Ambassador Class. Mention of the result was made in the trade press and congratulating the winners, the chairman of ACV Sales Ltd sent a souvenir gift in recognition of their success. "On behalf of the company," he wrote, "I hope that wherever they go, they will always carry out their duties as such to the advantage of all concerned."

Western Welsh's own 'Touring Britain' film show, which travelled around the area early in the year, included a new colour film specially made by Leslie Gray. It was shot during

a tour to Edinburgh and The Trossachs and featured all the major places of interest that the tour visited, together with numerous 'run-pasts' of the Windover coach used for the tour, not forgetting shots of passengers enjoying their holiday. Mr Gray not only made the film, but also created a lasting memento of the heyday of coach travel as well as an historical archive of Britain at a time of post-war optimism. The film shows a fascinating contrast between sparsely-populated trunk roads and congested town centres through which the coach passed sedately on its way.

Around 100,000 provincial British busmen went on strike in July, in support of a claim for a £1 per week pay rise. The employers' highest offer had been three shillings which they felt more than compensated for the rise in the cost of living since the last rise of five shillings in November. Initially car sharing and employer-provided coaches meant the strike had little impact. The railways also provided extra services. On July 23 violent scenes erupted

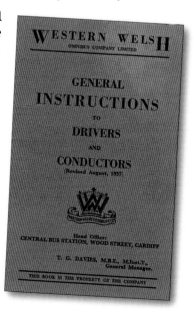

Roads with only buses on them! Not a juggernaut in sight as Royal Tiger 441 (GUH 441) skirts Fishguard Harbour on the run from Cardigan to Goodwick in 1955. *Geoff Morant*

around Britain as the dispute entered its fourth day. Strike-breaking drivers were attacked and vehicles vandalised, including some with passengers on board.

Although support for the strike was high, Western Welsh managed to avoid major confrontation. Most services were suspended, although the extended tours programme, with some curtailed itineraries, went ahead under close scrutiny. The following day, the Minister of Transport referred matters to the Industrial Disputes Tribunal for arbitration, and on July 26 it awarded the provincial busmen an increase of 11 shillings — just over half the amount originally demanded — and the strike ended. A week later the municipal drivers, who hadn't been officially on strike, accepted the same amount.

A month later trouble of a different kind was spotlighted at Barry Magistrates Court. It followed an incident on a Western Welsh double decker in May, during which women screamed, cried and one even hid under the seat when five youths used what the Barry & District News reported as 'riotous conduct and generally behaved in a disorderly manner' as the bus travelled from the Marine Hotel to Cadoxton. During the case, the outcome of which was not recorded, the company's prosecuting solicitor, Derek Howells, warned that if hooliganism and intimidation continued, it would threaten the future of late night bus services. "Bus

Driver EC White of Bridgend met his bride, Gillian Barrow of Barry Island, by sheer chance — his seat being next to hers when taking a late holiday tour following a lengthy period in hospital. Driver/courier Ted Lloyd from Cardiff depot tactfully helped the nervous couple's friendship to blossom, and his actions soon led to a wedding. The happy couple's honeymoon was a sentimental journey back to the English Lakes and Scotland by Western Welsh - and the driver? None other than Ted Lloyd, of course!.

crews would become reluctant to work late at night because of the growth of unruly behaviour," he added.

A fire occurred in the plastics shop at Ely, on November 27. Fortunately, it was quickly brought under control by acting relief watchman J Greedy who heard an explosion in the works, discovered the cause, dialed 999, and with a fire extinguisher had things under control by the time the fire brigade arrived.

The company faced more strike action as a troublesome year drew to a close. Unofficial strikes took place at Ammanford depot on November 14 and 15, while Bridgend and Port Talbot were hit on December 30 and 31. However, these incidents were dealt with promptly by an official of the union concerned.

Bryn Calvin Thomas was a native of Pembrokeshire who had joined Western Welsh when it took over Green's Motors of Haverfordwest. He lamented the passing of Green's — a company that was a much-loved local passenger transport servant — in the Staff Bulletin saying: "Through the years many smaller companies have been absorbed by Western Welsh," he wrote, "But the acquisition of most interest to me is that of Green's Motors of Haverfordwest. "The reason is that I was familiar with Green's buses, long before there was a Western Welsh Omnibus Company. I can remember the excitement when the first Green's bus came through from Haverfordwest to Narberth where we lived.

"As the services grew, we knew all the drivers and conductors personally. What's more, Idwal Jones and 'Tom the Bus' knew us too. On market day we'd watch the red monster struggling up Cox Hill with its load of farmers and their wives, not to mention butter, eggs and chickens. Then we'd race back to the High Street to see it disgorge its load outside Noot's the jeweller.

"On a cold winter's day a very nervous lad stood on bleak Kingsmoor Common waiting for the Haverfordwest bus. Two came along together and in his nervousness the lad stopped the one destined for Pembroke Dock.

"The driver realising the situation told that lad not to worry, turned off his route and gave chase, caught the Haverfordwest bus and transferred the bewildered youngster. Such a considerate act made a great impression on that boy – I know, because it was me!

"It is true to say, I suppose, that the bigger the concern the more impersonal it becomes, and I expect there have been mixed feelings among the old employees of Green's, as with other small companies, at being taken over by Western Welsh. In mixing with people from other depots, as I do, I am inclined to think that Ely is considered to be some cold, unfriendly place peopled by automatons. How untrue this is. Perhaps we are called upon to specialise more, but we are all individuals and just as fallible with hands, heads, hearts and habits as others in the outposts of the organisation.

"How much more important it is that we in the larger concern should maintain a friendly, co-operative personal spirit so that from the general manager to the tea boy at St David's we can work in harmony to our own peace of mind and for the good of the company."

Forse's tours, operated by Western Welsh, did good business despite the poor summer weather, but elsewhere, although revenue increased, the number of passengers fell. Wages and salaries were up on 1956 by £67,000, largely because of two wage awards in November 1955 and 1956, and with the cost of fuel rising by £24,000 during the Suez crisis, the fuel bill was higher than ever. Practically all other expenditure, including the maintenance of the fleet, tyres, rent and rates, was up considerably on the previous year and took a correspondingly higher proportion of the income. The shareholder dividend remained the same but as a proportion of the total income, dropped by one halfpenny in the pound. However, on an optimistic note, great things were expected as soon as the major refinery developments at Milford Haven came to fruition.

Taking all of the year's events into account the company returned a useful profit of £169,019.

A busy scene in the centre of Haverfordwest in the mid-1950s. Prominent is 974 (FKG 974) on its way to St David's. Two sister vehicles are awaiting passengers at the nearby bus stops. *Andrew Porter*

The Andy Capp Club helped protect the income of employees who had lost pay through illness. There were no rules and no meetings, but they did have an annual outing – always to the Symonds Yat Hotel, seen here in 1961. *Graham Bravey*

1958

A major redevelopment plan for Bridgend bus station and depot was announced in February, with an estimated cost of £75,000. Meanwhile, at Newport the cost of a new bus station was projected at £32,000 with Red & White agreeing to pay 40 per cent.

The serious decline in passenger receipts and the failure of the Chancellor of the Exchequer to grant any fuel tax relief in his budget, demanded economies. Much thought was given as to how to address this issue before two main measures were agreed. Firstly, reductions in the frequency and possible abandonment of a number of stage carriage services was proposed and secondly, the introduction of one-man buses in selected areas.

The company's announcement of these steps in July, would have come as no surprise to road staff, for whom the sight of a mere handful of passengers at off-peak times was by this time all too familiar. To them, the outcome was inevitable. One-man buses had been the means of reprieving services elsewhere in the country and there was surely no reason why they should not prove equally effective to Western Welsh. Not only was the company feeling the pinch, but the need to address these issues was becoming increasingly important within the bus industry on a national level. Mr J Spencer Willis, chairman of BET Omnibuses, cut to the chase in his address at its 16th Annual General Meeting in July.

"I need not tell you that the British bus industry is going through difficult times," he told the auspicious gathering. "The past year has been a critical one; your directors view with some concern the present position of the industry as a whole. In the post-war years, expansion helped by economies, enabled bus companies to absorb almost a fourfold increase in costs. Three or four years ago, however, it seemed that the peak was being reached. In 1956, for the first time in many years, there was a slight fall in the number of passengers carried, and this persisted in 1957. Our associated companies are still

About to depart for Aberporth, Leyland TS8 745, (CBO 524) is seen at Newcastle Emlyn in 1955. *Geoff Morant*

One of the 1949 consignment of 38 Crossleys, 939 (DKG 939), is parked up at Haverfordwest, alongside recently downgraded Windover 505 (EUH 505), in the summer of 1961. *Paul Redmond*

carrying many more passengers than they carried before the last war, but there are signs that the tide is on the turn and we do not know how far it may recede. Sweeping changes in social habits have come upon us with unprecedented swiftness. The influence of TV discourages people from travelling, private cars, scooters and mopeds are cheap to buy and have made many people self-sufficient in the matter of transport. An inadequate road system, congestion and obsolete speed restrictions for public service vehicles make it more difficult to maintain regular and speedy services. The bus industry bears a burden of direct taxation on the fuel it uses at a rate which is higher than the tax on many luxuries, yet the industry endeavours to maintain a high proportion of services which, even under the most favourable of conditions, could never be self-supporting. This is the picture which causes your directors concern. One thing is certain and that is that further contraction of unremunerative services has become inevitable.

"You will be aware that the Chancellor did not see fit to relieve us of any of the unjust tax of over 200 per cent, which is imposed solely on that fuel used for road transport. Certainly we thought that our case for abolition of the tax was overwhelming, and the Budget came as a bitter disappointment. It will, I fear, be small comfort to country dwellers that the taxes on port and sherry, fur coats and jewellery, have been considerably reduced while country bus services, surely of a more essential nature than the other commodities mentioned, have received no tax relief whatever."

It was a message that sent a chill through the entire industry, though there would have been few companies

which by then would have needed prompting about the problems and the reasons for them.

Wages formed the biggest item in costs, accounting for nearly 70 per cent of working expenses. The previous year's increase of 11 shillings a week had been preceded by a nine-day strike which caused serious losses in both revenue and goodwill. Additionally, increases in fares granted by the Traffic Commissioners after the usual and unfair time-lag due to statutory procedure, denied the operators the right to apply for interim adjustments, a right enjoyed by the railways and by London Transport. This was manifestly unjust and could have resulted in a fatal blow to financial stability.

It was the view of the BET chairman that the issue of wages in the bus industry and its very future was in the hands of those who worked in it. This may seem a harsh statement, but he made it plain that he didn't want to see significant redundancy occurring.

BET's stark message was reiterated at the 38th annual general meeting of Western Welsh with particular emphasis given to the company's individual position. Passenger journeys had fallen by 8.7 per cent and receipts had declined by £26,000 during the year in review, even with the fare increases of April and October. The routes taken over from Green's in 1956 earned £76,000 more than in the previous financial year, but expenses were £56,000 higher. The company was making a loss on 58 per cent of its routes and 41 per cent of its mileage. On the positive side, the new Tiger Cub and Olympian buses continued to achieve outstanding fuel economy, which helped generate a saving of £30,000 on the previous year.

Another tight squeeze at Corbett's Bridge, Cogan, Penarth, a notorious traffic bottleneck and accident blackspot, that remained until the road was widened in July 1961. *Stewart Williams*

Journalists representing 15 Welsh newspapers sampled the comfort of the new AEC Reliance 'Ambassador Class' coaches when they were treated to a demonstration run in February. The party headed for Abergavenny and lunched at the Skirrid Mountain Inn at Crucorney. Comments received included: "I was most impressed with the high standards of comfort. The footrests and blinds are good ideas," wrote George Halliday of the South Wales Argus. "Exploring Britain in a coach like this must be very pleasurable. I particularly like the individual seating arrangement and the attractive daffodil design," added the Barry Herald's John O'Sullivan. "This coach is all you claim it to be. I found it a most relaxing ride" said Will Hopkin writing for the West Wales Observer. Meanwhile Ralph Slater from the Aberdare Leader thought that the idea of giving the vehicles class names like Ambassador and Capital was first rate and would appeal to passengers, while in The Free Press of Monmouthshire, Jack Slater wrote that externally the coach had a very pleasing appearance. It seems that for once the press were right and the Harrington-bodied coach went on to win an award at the Brighton Coach Rally in April as if to prove it.

Fares on the Cardiff to Newport service were reduced in March to bring them into line with those charged by Cardiff and Newport Corporations.

Western Welsh turned the tables on their friendly rivals and cup holders Rhondda Transport in the same month, with a resounding 5 - 1 win in the final of the Cownie Cup held at Jenner Park, Barry. After the game and over afternoon tea at the Cadoxton Conservative Club, Rhondda general manager, IL Gray, said jocularly that they had decided beforehand to let Western Welsh win as the insurance contributions on the cup were too high!

Good news for users of the Cardiff to Penarth road was the announcement that it was to be widened and re-aligned. The £150,000 scheme was designed to by-pass the notorious Corbett's Bridge, a long-time bottleneck and accident blackspot, with its narrow roadway, lack of pavements and restricted visibility because of the high stone walls of its approach.

Work on a new Esso oil refinery at Milford Haven began in July, and as it progressed, hundreds of specialist workers were transported to the site from distant hotels by Western Welsh buses under contract hire. Adding to the

season's feel-good factor, the British Empire and Commonwealth Games were held in Cardiff in the summer. The high-profile event brought with it an upsurge in passengers. Cardiff was a blaze of colour. Flags on the roof of its central bus station fluttered in the breeze, while on the ground below inspectors worked flat out to ensure smooth running of coaches used to transfer the many teams of athletes to the Games Village at St Athan.

One of the most prestigious private hire jobs undertaken by the company during the games was the transportation of members of the Royal Household from Cardiff General Station to the Royal Yacht Britannia which was moored in Roath Basin.

With so much happening around the area during the summer, it was decided to build a mobile enquiry office for use in an emergency, and for agricultural shows, exhibitions, and as required during alterations and

Windover coaches 508 (EUH 508) and 511 (EUH 511) have received a fresh coat of red paint after being downgraded to dual purpose duties at Haverfordwest in 1961.
Paul Redmond

When Cardiff hosted the British Empire and Commonwealth Games in 1958, Western Welsh proudly conveyed members of the Royal Household from Cardiff General Station to the Royal Yacht Britannia. Plaxton-bodied Daimler 587 (HBO 699), despite dating from 1953, was entrusted with the work and is seen at Roath Basin. This site became the aptly-named Britannia Quay.
George Wedlake

redecoration of existing premises. Designed and constructed by the engineering department at Ely, the exterior colour scheme was identical to the latest Ambassador Class coaches. Inside, it was fitted with settees, an enquiry counter and literature racks. It was also equipped with a sink unit and tea-making facilities.

The number of motoring offences in England and Wales during the previous year was the highest on record. Among large proportional increases in convictions were those of speeding in built-up areas and driving or being in charge of a motor vehicle under the influence of drink or drugs.

It appears that management, having noted the figures, were keen to dissociate busmen with the statistics and concerned about the issue of staff entering licensed premises and drinking while on duty. The general manager reminded them in no uncertain terms that a certain code of conduct was expected of all Western Welsh staff and contravention of the company's instructions in this matter would be seen to undermine the confidence of customers.

"I must repeat that there can be no leniency for offenders. Upon an offence being proved, employees will instantly be dismissed from the company's service," was his stern message to employees in the Staff Bulletin.

Another safety-related message came from traffic manager Fred Pengelly in the November edition:

A wet, bedraggled pigeon strayed into Penarth Road garage one Saturday in August. Remembering his neighbour's pigeon loft, Inspector SJ Reynolds took it home with him to Ely, where it was fed. The owner, it was discovered, lived in Lancaster and the following Saturday, driver Len Morgan, going north on the Western Highlands extended tour, was prevailed upon to take the bird with him. The VIP (very important pigeon) quickly made friends with the passengers and was, in due course, returned to an overjoyed owner. A happy sequel to this heart warming story is that Inspector Reynolds received three tablecloths and a thank you letter from the owner. He gave one cloth to driver Morgan, one to his next door neighbour and retained the third — deservedly so for a very kind act!

"Although we have notices on most of our 44-seater saloons forbidding any person from speaking to the driver, I hear that there are still conductors and conductresses who break this rule. They are very much in the minority, I am sure, but in the interests of safety we must do all in our power to stamp out this dangerous practice. Staff disregarding this rule will, upon conviction, be dealt with most severely."

A vehicle construction committee was formed following suggestions from Trade Unions representing depot staff. Its aim was to discuss various matters relating to the rolling stock. The committee was chaired by the chief engineer and consisted of the traffic manager and staff from all the area depots. Several important features were soon accepted by the company, but technical or financial reasons prevented others from being implemented.

The journalists came back in November — to a press conference at Porthcawl, where the subjects under discussion included the Bridgemaster double-decker, the one-man bus, and the company's proposals to meet the recent pay award. Journeying down from Cardiff on one of the Bridgemasters, the unanimous verdict of the press was that it provided a very comfortable ride. A stop was made at Ely Works, to inspect a one-man bus. Both vehicles were widely reported on BBC Wales TV.

Craig-y-Parc School, Pentyrch was the grateful recipient from Western Welsh in the spring of a withdrawn double-decker, former Ebsworth's Dennis Lance 983. Buses always had an attraction for children, but in this case the vehicle provided more than enjoyment. It helped disabled pupils strengthen muscles and give them the confidence to overcome everyday obstacles.

The death was announced, aged 92, of WJ Barrett, founder of Barretts (Eastern Valleys).

The Cardiff-based steamer firm of P&A Campbell owed Western Welsh £1,400 for unpaid hire of vehicles. Campbell's White Funnel Fleet had incurred serious debts following an extremely wet summer. They had already suffered a significant decline in excursion traffic which, together with increasing operating costs, had led to a gradual reduction of its fleet.

St David's own 449 (GUH 449) waits for custom in the centre of Britain's smallest city, 1955. *Geoff Morant*

New Ambassador class Harrington-bodied AEC Reliance 101 (OUH 101) at Llandaff Cathedral. Those on board were head office staff enjoying a break from normal duties. Western Welsh had 18 of these coaches which heralded a new era for the extended tours department. They had individual seats, upholstered in Western Welsh daffodil-design moquette. Sister vehicle 106 won a well-deserved Concours D'Elegance award at the 1958 Brighton Coach Rally. *George Wedlake*

1959

A receiver was appointed for P&A Campbell who had got into financial difficulties the previous year. However, Campbell's chairman, Clifton Smith Cox, brokered a deal with George Nott Industries, parent of the Townsend Ferries group which was significantly expanding its cross-channel car ferry business. The Townsend company bought the Campbell business in order to offset tax losses elsewhere. In December 1959, it surprised everyone by announcing that paddle steamers in the Bristol Channel would continue, albeit with a reduced fleet of two operational steamers — Cardiff Queen and Glen Usk — and one, Bristol Queen, laid up for the 1960 season. As a result, Western Welsh continued to be associated with the Campbell's company.

Another two West Wales companies were taken over in the form of TJ Harries & Sons of Milford Haven, and Prendergast Motors of Haverfordwest. The two firms were in common ownership, and no vehicles were included in the purchase price of £20,000. Western Welsh obviously had high hopes for expansion in this part of Pembrokeshire, as the rapidly growing oil industry was

bringing a significant economic upturn to the area. This would surely help offset the cost of maintaining services in the surrounding rural areas. With this optimistic view of better times lying ahead, land was purchased at Milford Haven and Haverfordwest for new bus stations.

In January it was announced that one-man operation was to be introduced on many rural routes where receipts were very much below the cost of operation. The first of these economy measures began with services operated from Fishguard. It was anticipated that there would be a certain amount of initial apprehension among staff, but many drivers reported how much they appreciated the new-found contact with their passengers. It was also feared that single manning would lead to large-scale redundancies, but the company keenly emphasised that this fear was entirely without foundation, natural wastage was occurring through the departure of many veteran conductors. With as many as 64 rural services converted to one man operation a sizeable order was placed for Albion Nimbus 30-seater saloons.

At the opening ceremony of the new Fishguard garage in August, TG Davies disclosed that the company's services in the area were losing around £6,000 a year, but the building of the garage was evidence that it had no

A sad scene at Ely's 'graveyard' in 1960, as Crossley 916 (DKG 916) left, and Leyland PS1 859 (CUH 859) await their fate. *P Yeoman*

intention of abandoning the area. "We recognise our obligation to run some unremunerative routes, and the new garage should help things in Fishguard by increasing efficiency," he said. Unfortunately, despite the coming of the refineries, not only would the profitable services remain many miles further east, but the Albions were to prove no more effective in the battle to save costs than the vehicles they had replaced.

In a debate in the House of Commons on the Finance Bill, 17 members from both sides urged the necessity of fuel tax relief if rural bus services

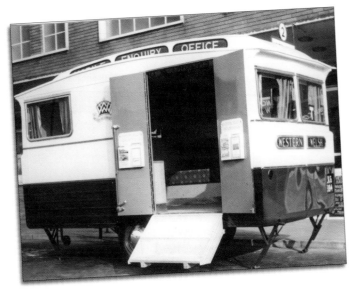

were to be saved. It was rare to find the House so united on any subject, but still the Chancellor wouldn't budge. One small concession did come about with the 1959 budget — road tax was cut, saving the company around £30,000 a year. However, this only nullified an increase in profit tax from three per cent to 10 per cent that was contained in the previous year's budget.

The Ministry of Transport announced that £522,000 would be spent during the following 12 months on the Neath by-pass project between Earlswood and Lonlas. This expenditure was the largest of the year's trunk road projects, and had already kicked off in 1956 with £350,000 allotted to the work, with a further £231,000 required to complete the job. Briton Ferry River Bridge, which had opened in October 1955, had not exactly brought relief to Neath, as the new bridge only fed into Swansea. This scheme was designed to ease traffic flow in the Briton Ferry – Neath – Skewen corridor. A further major problem, at Port Talbot, would remain until the construction of the M4 around the town.

This mobile enquiry office was built at Ely Works in 1958 and found use during reconstruction work at bus stations, and at major events and shows. It received coach colours and despite its clerestory roof, the similarity to contemporary coachwork may be noted. *Stewart Williams*

Time was up for the unpopular Crossleys by 1962 and most, like these, ended up in the 'graveyard' at Ely Works. *CTPG*

The field alongside Ely Works, where withdrawn vehicles were dumped pending disposal. This was the view from the main road in 1960.
Stewart Williams

Western Welsh helped to shuttle more than 28,000 people to the Metal Box Company's factory at Neath, during Canned Foods Week which ran from April 27 to May 2. Visitors were shown the latest high-speed machinery. In May, the Neath Town and District tour, the brainchild of area manager WJ Jones, was launched by the Mayor and Mayoress of Neath, who travelled on the inaugural journey. It operated daily through the summer and ran via Tonna, Cadoxton, Caewern, Duffryn Church and Longford to Neath Abbey where there was a short stop. It went from there to Baglan Estate before returning via Llansawel Church, Giants Grave and Cimla. The fare was two shillings and sixpence.

The South Wales Echo newspaper ran a story headed 'The Cupid Special', based on service 718 from Varteg Hill, Pontypool, to Cardiff. Four people had met, fallen in love and proposed aboard the 7.15am bus. They were members of a group of regular passengers who had formed The Pontypool Bus Friends group. Organiser, AL Davies, said: "The idea came to me about five years ago, when I noticed the same people were using the bus each morning. Gradually we got to know each other."

Western Welsh was the name retained on the Cownie Cup after a second meeting with Rhondda Transport in the final, played at Lysaght's Sports Ground, Newport, on March 24. Although the semi-final resulted in a narrow win over Devon General, the final was far more decisive, with a 7-0 victory by the holders.

The new bus station at Newport, shared with Red & White Services, opened for business on July 24 at a final cost of £33,292.

For every pound received in 1959, 11/7¼d (58p) went on wages and salaries; 2/9¾d (14p) on maintenance of rolling stock, machinery, buildings, tyres, lubricants,

The Mayor and Mayoress of Neath, with Western Welsh officials — including general manager, TG Davies — and guests before setting off on the inaugural Neath town tour, in May, 1959. The coaches are Harrington-bodied Reliances, then barely a year old.

uniforms, etc; 2/4¾d (12p) on taxation (1/9¾d on fuel tax alone); 1/10d (9p) on depreciation and provision for renewals; 9d (4p) on fuel, and 7¼d (3p) on dividend.

The 39th AGM was held on July 22, with new chairman J Spencer Wills presiding. In his address to the shareholders he said: "While results for the year were better than those of the previous year, they were still not satisfactory, especially when it is remembered that the year included a nine-day strike at the peak traffic period. This lost your company over £70,000 in revenue and had serious side-effects."

The record year for the number of passengers carried by Western Welsh had been 1955/56. This year's figures were 17 per cent lower. However, traffic receipts were

Their days of serious coach work over, the attractive full-fronted Willowbrook AEC Regals from 1953 were distributed around the depots for express service and day touring by 1960. About to be pressed into local service at a busy period, 520 (GUH 520) is ready and waiting at Bridgend bus station. *AB Cross*

Without a cloud in the sky, even before the conductor has set the blind it was a case of all aboard for Barry Island as Bridgemaster 683 (PBO 683) waits at its stand at Cardiff central bus station in 1959. *RL Wilson/Online Transport Archive*

£100,000 higher than in the previous year and were, in fact, a record. Part of this increase was attributable to extended tours, day and half-day tours — up £5,500 on 1958; contracts for the conveyance of workpeople and schoolchildren was up £9,500 and hire of coaches by private parties, £13,100. Extended tour bookings for the year once again exceeded all records, despite intense competition in both this field and with private hire. It appeared that Western Welsh's touring clientele simply returned year after year. Increased operating and maintenance costs, national insurance and taxation left a net profit of just £113,583. The directors recommended an unchanged final dividend of three per cent.

"I am taking the liberty of writing to express my views about the Western Welsh service," began a letter to managing director WT James from Sir Robert Webber, JP. "I don't often use it, but during the past month my chauffeur has been on holiday, so that I have to travel to Porthcawl several times a week by bus or train. I want to tell you that I think yours is an excellent service in every way, and would like to congratulate you and your staff both at the terminus and en-route. Your drivers seem to me to be very careful though they don't waste any time, and I cannot speak too highly of your conductors and what they do for the passengers, especially the old and infirm. Yesterday, for instance, the conductor on the 3.35pm to Porthcawl — his number was 14447 — was an excellent fellow in every possible way." The conductor

who had attracted such high praise was Reginald Collins from Cardiff depot.

The company entered 913 drivers for the Safe Drivers competition under the auspices of the Road Operators Safety Council and 354 of them were successful in obtaining awards. It was reported that during 1959, Western Welsh vehicles were involved in 1,678 accidents. As this equates to at least two accidents for every vehicle in the fleet, it is probable that non-damage incidents such as passenger 'slips and trips' were included in these figures. One person was killed and 285 were injured. The cost of third party claims was £11,358 14s 4d, and the cost of repairs £5,446 9s 5d.

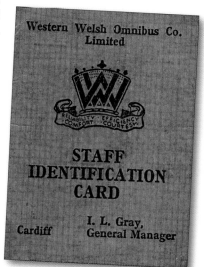

A staff pass such as those issued to employees around the mid-1960s.

Space race didn't help

Services slowed by traffic congestion

By the 1960s Britain was considering a space programme, making it feasible that hundreds of millions of pounds could be spent to allow a person to travel at 18,000 mph, 125 miles away from the surface of the earth.

These facts may have been impressive, but they cut no ice in South Wales, least of all with those at Western Welsh responsible for the smooth operation of its many routes and perhaps more importantly keeping the buses running on time.

Success in any far-reaching space race would provide no consolation for the bus driver, or passenger, who was unlucky enough to achieve progress of no more than three miles an hour through the centre of Port Talbot, nor the tens of thousands of drivers nationally, bogged down by a road system that was 30 years out of date.

But while traffic congestion may have been abundantly visible to most Western Welsh passengers, other problems that faced the company at this time wouldn't perhaps have been so obvious. Among these was the constant battle it faced to combat rising fuel costs, something which saw it continually and vigourously campaining for the removal of the 200 per cent tax on fuel oil, a point that was seldom far from the chairman's report.

A further problem was the continued operation of an ever increasing number of loss making rural routes. One-man operated buses did ease the situation, but it remained such a problem nationally that it was eventually examined in detail by a government-led committee.

There was no doubt the situation was becoming serious for Western Welsh and though the company carried around 81 million passengers a year at the dawn of the 1960s, this was markedly down on the peak years of the previous decade.

1960

In the New Years Honours List, an OBE was bestowed on general manager TG Davies, for his service to the National Savings movement. Unfortunately he began to suffer ill health during the following months, and he retired early at the end of 1961. In September chief engineer FA Mason was appointed assistant general manager, and Ken Allender made a welcome return to the company to oversee the growing tours business.

Leyland's efforts to dispense with the unsatisfactory lowbridge arrangement of double-deck design resulted in the Atlantean, a revolutionary vehicle featuring a transverse rear-mounted engine, front entrance and step-less access to the lower saloon. Drive was through a pneumo-cyclic gearbox, then an angle drive to the rear axle. The need for a clutch pedal was eliminated, the engagement and disengagement of gears being automatic once selection was made. The prototype was exhibited at the 1958 Commercial Motor Show and with the maximum dimensions for PSVs recently increased to 30ft by 8ft, was undoubtedly the star. Western Welsh was suitably impressed and ordered an initial batch of 12. As soon as they were delivered in January, a demonstration run from Cardiff to Porthcawl attracted media coverage from press and TV. The run went very smoothly and although the day was cold and foggy, the bus was warm and comfortable, a fact which was commented upon by the party. Excellent coverage followed, and a film shot outside the Seabank Hotel, was shown on BBC TV.

Press comments showered the vehicle with praise. Graham George of the Barry & District News wrote: "My verdict — the best double-decker I have travelled on, a smooth performer, comfortable seats and warm."

When Driver Bill Salmon of Crosskeys was asked for his opinion of the new Atlantean, he replied that it was the best double-decker he had ever driven, a view shared by his colleagues at the depot, where several of the new vehicles were in service.

The conversion of many routes to one-man operation continued as the unions agreed to co-operate in the introduction of this form of operation. While of immediate benefit to rural areas, the long-term future sustainability of many of their services remained uncertain. The company was eagerly awaiting a report from a government-sponsored committee chaired by Professor DT Jack, that had been tasked with finding a practical and effective solution to the difficulties of rural bus operation.

The Vale of Glamorgan was an early recipient of one-man operation. Many Tiger Cubs were fitted with a bracket and slotted plate to hold a Setright ticket machine, a cash tray on the top of the cab gate, and a removable 'pay here' board.

Leyland's Atlantean was a popular vehicle with staff and passengers, although the engineers were faced with problems that took time to solve, and which brought about several modifications. Western Welsh ordered 66 of the vehicles for delivery between 1960 and 1962, but it was 1969 before the much refined Atlantean was re-ordered. These views show the layout of both upper and lower saloons, and illustrate the split-level seating arrangement which was necessary to keep height to a minimum. There was a lack of moquette on upper deck seating. Workmen and smokers were not allowed to enjoy the plusher upholstery down below! *George Wedlake*

Western Welsh outstationed a number of buses in rural areas. The driver usually lived in the village where it spent the night, and in contrast to today's practice, uneconomic dead mileage was avoided. Railway stations often hosted the bus as seen at Lampeter in 1961, where a Tiger Cub rests until morning. *Stewart Williams*

By 1960, single manning was the norm in the area and while working the Bridgend to Llantwit Major service it wasn't unusual for a driver to be met at Wick by the landlady of the Lamb & Flag Inn. She would ask him to bring a package back from Llantwit Major. There, a local butcher would meet the bus with a parcel of sausages or steaks for the pub. At the end of the week the driver would usually be handed a packet of cigarettes for his trouble.

Early in the year, The Green at Bridgend was cordoned off and temporary traffic arrangements introduced to assist with the major redevelopment of the company's largest depot and bus station. The site remained operational throughout, although many buses were stabled in Bridgend RFC's car park at the Brewery Field.

Construction of the new oil refineries around Milford Haven resulted in a demand for contract vehicles that was met by the purchase of second-hand AECs from sister BET companies, Devon General and South Wales Transport.

The price of diesel had reached 3s/9d per gallon and was continuing to cause concern. Something else that was raising eyebrows led to a warning from Fred Pengelly, the traffic manager. It had been brought to his attention that vehicles engaged on duplicating services or over common routes, but serving different destinations, were 'leap-frogging' bus stops, to the annoyance of passengers. Mr Pengelly felt this was detrimental to the company and losing it not only goodwill, but vital revenue. "Will staff please note that vehicles in convoy must pull up at all recognised stopping places," he warned staff in the Staff Bulletin's March edition.

Four coaches were needed for the inaugural Port Talbot Town & District Tour on June 2. Guests were the Mayors of Port Talbot and Neath, the chairman of Neath Rural District Council and chief officers of the authorities. The route covered Cimla, Pontrhydyfen, Cwmavon, Penycae, Margam, Sandfields and Aberavon. It cost 2s 6d and operated every Wednesday at 6.15pm and on Sunday afternoons, allowing time to attend a service at Margam Abbey at 5.45pm.

James of Ammanford, which operated jointly with Western Welsh on the Ammanford to Llanelly service, handed over its share of the journeys to the company. However, joint operation of the service to Aberystwyth continued as before.

In his address at the 40th annual general meeting of the company in July, the chairman referred to the fact that representations had been made to the Ministry with regard to the overall dimensions permitted for PSVs. The limit at the time was 30ft by 8ft, but operators and manufacturers groups were pressing for this to be increased to 36ft by 8ft 2in to conform with the maximum permitted in most other European countries. It was felt that saloons of the dimensions suggested would be useful in the industrial valleys of South Wales where low bridges often prevented use of double-deckers.

The issue of increasing fares in line with wages, which dated back to October 1958, was thought to have been resolved in December 1959 following a fresh fares application to the Traffic Commissioners. However local authorities had appealed against the application and though this caused a delay it was eventually over-ruled and fare increases went ahead. A further wage increase for employees was secured in May, including a reduction in the standard working week from 44 to 42 hours without loss of pay. In the case of road staff at most depots it resulted in an increased rate per hour and the payment of two hours overtime, as there was not enough labour available to enable working hours to be cut. As the cost to the company was almost £200,000 a year, the submission of yet another fare increase application followed.

The problem of loss making rural services, while it was eased by progressive one-man operation, remained a major concern, and was examined in detail by the government-led 'Jack' committee. The feeling remained strong that the solution lay in the removal of the 200 per cent tax on fuel oil, a point once again hammered home in the chairman's report. The company had anticipated that the Budget would have brought a considerable reduction in the tax, but this didn't happen.

"The fact that we are more than carrying our obligation to run unremunerative services will be apparent when I tell you that during the year under review, 55 per cent of our routes representing 37 per cent of our mileage were run for revenue lower than our average cost of operation. I do not believe the public and the press have any idea of the magnitude of these figures, which are far from uncommon throughout the bus industry," he said.

Taking the rough with the smooth had long been a tradition of the industry, where a comparatively small number of 'fat' routes always supported a much larger list

> Driver Bill Davies, who worked for many years at Bridgend depot, remembered that many of the stops he served were given amusing but irreverent nicknames by the staff. For instance, Happy Valley Caravan Park near Porthcawl was called 'Tally Valley', and Glanrhyd Hospital was referred to as 'Butlins'! They were happy days.

of 'lean' ones. This had been possible largely due to the licensing system set up by the 1930 Traffic Act. Prior to that, unrestricted competition for the 'fat' routes did not allow responsible operators margin enough to subsidise the 'lean' routes, and so maintain a comprehensive pattern of services over a wider area.

The term 'marketing' meant far more to Western Welsh's tours and private hire department than it did to many of its rivals, who, in their rush to undercut prices, regarded the term as meaning little more than fixing a paper sticker to a windscreen. The company knew that attractively designed and presented advertising was essential in selling luxury travel. As a result, a new Ford Thames stores department van took to the road featuring brightly coloured artwork by the company's own apprentices, David Peterson and Peter Mitchell, of Ely Works. A small printing and poster department was set up at Penarth Road depot, and the company's printing requirements were met by W Thompson, who came from Pergrif Studios in Cardiff.

Since its formation in 1958, the vehicle construction committee, which met twice yearly, had proved its usefulness and resulted in improvements in performance, comfort and safety. It was a good example of constructive co-operation between management and staff at a time when the industry, beset with many problems of maintaining its economic stability, needed all the help it could get.

In September, Leyland Motors Ltd sought to buy land at Ely from Western Welsh for a distribution depot. The company was still fiercely guarding its assets and

Devon General's Weymann-bodied Regent III JUO 565 was one of 10 acquired in 1960 to allow Western Welsh lowbridge double deckers to head off to West Wales, where they were needed for use on the Milford Haven oil terminal contract. They cost a mere £175 each, and were needed for only a few months, so they retained the original owner's livery but did receive fleet numbers, in this case 1565, which came closest to matching the registration number without clashing with existing stock. *Gerald Truran*

Smartly turned out during a North Wales tour on July 3, 1965, is Weymann-bodied AEC Reliance 129 (WKG 129).
RL Wilson/Online Transport Archive

demanded in excess of £20,000 for two acres. Leyland refused and the plan was quietly dropped.

Erroneous speculation appeared in the September Staff Bulletin, under the heading New Vehicle Registration System. It announced that soon, many licensing authorities would have exhausted the current registration series and so a new system had been devised. The article suggested that all licensing authorities would introduce the new system on January 1, 1961, irrespective of whether existing registrations were exhausted. The article continued: "The new system will provide for the use of four letters preceding up to three numbers. The first letter will indicate the year of registration, for example: A-1961, B-1962, C-1963. The second letter will be a progressional one, while the third and fourth letters will be the well known marks which indicate the issuing authority, as at present. For example, Cardiff will start on January 1, 1961 with registrations AABO 1-999, then AAKG 1-999. These will be followed by ABBO 1-999 and so on. In 1962 registrations will start with BABO 1-999, BAKG and so forth."

It later proved to be speculative nonsense, coming at a time when 'reversed' registrations where numbers rather than letters appeared first on a registration plate had only recently begun to be issued by the busiest licensing authorities. How different Western Welsh number plates would have looked had this method been implemented!

"Would you please express my very grateful thanks to the conductor on the Pontypridd to Cardiff bus which stops at

Hollybush at 1.10pm, for paying my daughter's fare to school today, after she had lost her money, and for giving her the bus fare to travel home, out of his own pocket," wrote Mrs C Davies of Whitchurch, Cardiff. These actions of conductor WJ Bates of Cardiff depot were duly acknowledged by the traffic manager.

Driver Denis O'Neill, of Cardiff depot, drove TUH 2, one of the new Albion Nimbus vehicles, at the Brighton Coach Rally, and gained first prize in his class in the Road Section and Driving Test. He also received an award for being the smartest driver.

For Fred Trawford, his job as night watchman at Crosskeys depot usually passed without incident, but while on duty one night, a masked man entered the garage and pointed a Winchester rifle at him. Fred threw a hammer at the man and he ran away. But Fred recognised his hat and his manner of running and phoned the police at Abercarn telling them to watch a certain house. They did this and saw the man go in, followed him and discovered the rifle and mask. Later Fred went to the police station and the Superintendent said: "Lucky for you the hammer on the gun was bent, it only struck the inside of the bullet and not the cap." Night life at Crosskeys was not always as exciting!

Driver DM Parry of Brecon depot died in November, as a result of head injuries sustained in a collision with a van carrying newspapers.

This was also the month that the new Esso refinery at Milford Haven was opened by the Duke of Edinburgh. The rapid build up of transport needs had resulted in a peak daily vehicle requirement of 32 buses. On the opening day 24 coaches were required, all of which were fitted with public address systems at Ely Works. The weather on the day was a major concern because part of the tour was to feature a drive down the long jetty at the Haven, then a reversal, under the control of an inspector before returning. All went well however and the 24 coaches returned to their normal duties the next day.

As November drew to a close, a period of heavy rain battered Glamorgan. Following this in the early hours of Sunday December 4, the normally placid River Ogmore burst its banks and flooded Bridgend town centre. The alarm was raised by the cleaning staff on duty in the early hours. They quickly became aware of the seriousness of the rising waters and raised the alarm. Even so, within 20 minutes of the calamity, 39 buses were submerged to a depth above the tops of their wheels.

More than 40 buses were damaged at the depot, and many more were towed through the floods to the safety of the temporary base at the Brewery Field. Leslie Gray arranged for Matador No.1 from Ely Works and No.2 from Neath to be rushed to Bridgend, and by lunchtime the following day all the submerged vehicles had been towed to safety. Some remained at Bridgend but many were towed to Neath and Ely for the replacement of contaminated lubricants and the drying out of all electrical units. To cover the loss of rolling stock, vehicles were loaned from Barry, Cardiff and Neath depots.

The scale of operations for entertaining children of staff around the depots during a 1960s Christmas was amazing. Pontypool depot provided nine 44-seaters to convey children to Newport's Lyceum Theatre to see Little Miss Muffet. At Crosskeys, St Margaret's Church Hall was the venue for a visit from Father Christmas. Families of the staff at Ely trooped to Glanely Church Institute where they were treated to a film show by Leslie Gray.

Another 125 children were entertained at the Old Pioneers Hall in Barry; 100 at the Central Club in Neath; 160 at Haverfordwest's Drill Hall; and last, but not least, 60 children went along to the Dyfed Café in St David's. No doubt there would have been plenty of smiling faces at all of those events.

It wasn't a happy time for driver Cliff Miles of Bridgend depot however. He had an unfortunate accident after finishing duty on Christmas Eve. His motorcycle skidded and he received cuts and abrasions which required hospital treatment. However, he was soon well on the way to recovery.

Chairman John Spencer Wills reported that results for the year ended March 31, 1960 were better than in the previous two years, but still not entirely satisfactory. A recorded profit of £151,918 was split equally between general reserve and dividend. The summer had been good; traffic receipts from express services increased by £40,414; tours and contracts by £22,887. However the figures were still regarded as disappointing. The marked increase in private cars and the congestion they caused had impaired running efficiency and it was suggested that local authorities did all that they could to encourage people to use buses instead of cars in congested areas.

Passenger journeys during the year, at 81 million, were 15.6 per cent down on the peak year of 1955/6, although 1.3 million or 1.7 per cent up on the previous year.

It had been a year of change, with Atlanteans and Nimbuses arriving in large numbers. Leyland worked hard with Western Welsh to overcome the many mechanical problems with the Atlanteans, and eventually they gained a reasonable reputation. The same couldn't be said for the Albions, however. Viewed as the saviours of rural routes they were prone to frequent breakdown and were even known to backfire. Most would be withdrawn after only a few years service, and in many cases the routes they were intended to save went with them.

A major private hire contract was undertaken by the company when the Esso oil refinery opened at Milford Haven in November 1960. It required 24 AEC Reliance coaches, all but three of which were assembled for this impressive line-up which includes six of the very latest from Weymann. *George Wedlake*

A varied collection of rolling stock at Crosskeys garage in 1962. All-Leyland 962 (EUH 962) dating from 1950 attracts the gaze of the onlookers. It was still on front line work at the ripe old age of 12! *John Jones*

1961

Results for the year to March 31 were not good. The net profit at £142,109 was around £10,000 less than the modest total achieved in the previous year. It was necessary to set aside from taxed profits a sum sufficient to meet the difference between the depreciation written off against assets such as life-expired vehicles, and the amount that would be required to meet the cost of their replacement. In the circumstances it was recommended that £60,000 should be transferred to the General Reserve, and as a result, payment of the same dividend as the previous year was recommended. Revenue from stage carriage services had increased by £71,000 due to higher fares introduced in the winter of 1959/60, and a

further rise in July 1960. The yield from the increased fares fell seriously short of expectations for a number of reasons: severe weather during the second half of 1960 brought floods in South Wales in October and again in December; traffic during the busy Christmas period had been disrupted by a strike at most depots on December 27 the previous year, and a serious 'flu epidemic in February and March had caused further loss. On the brighter side, express service revenue improved, and extended tours hit a new record. The wage bill for staff had seen a substantial increase from the middle of the previous year, with the increase in the hourly rate

Western Welsh's two AEC Matador recovery vehicles were rarely seen together. They were former Government vehicles converted at Ely Works in 1959 and put into service there and at Neath depot. They found themselves side by side in this view from summer 1966, when the Neath vehicle, right, was called to Ely for a repaint. *Stewart Williams*

amounting to around £200,000 in a full year. It was hoped that a period of stability would follow, but within three months further demands were made by the trade unions. These were rejected by the companies but were eventually referred to an arbitration tribunal which awarded a general increase from May 1961, of 11 shillings on the basic week. There were also some additional concessions for Saturday afternoon working and regular turns starting before 5am or finishing after midnight. This award cost the company a further £120,000 over a full year, and so the process of yet another application to increase fares began all over again.

One of the unfortunate features of the industry was the necessity to apply wage awards promptly and then go through the cumbersome licensing procedure to recoup the cost. In the situation now faced by the company, the application needed to be heard promptly, otherwise fares could not be adjusted until the autumn, in which event the financial prospects for the current year would be very grim indeed. Gone forever were the days of stability in bus fares.

Competition from private transport continued to intensify due to constantly increasing car ownership. This led to further congestion, which, to the company,

On one occasion the area manager at Bridgend found himself assisting police with their enquiries! A double-decker was driven to the town's police HQ where photographs were taken to illustrate contraventions of the Road Traffic Act. The crew was driver FV Taylor and his brother, conductor TG Taylor. In one shot the area manager was being ordered off the bus by a constable and in another having his details taken by the conductor. Others showed staff smoking, being rude to a passenger, and the driver turning and talking to a passenger. The pictures were made into film strips and issued to police training colleges throughout Britain and the Commonwealth. It was probably the only time the company's staff behaved that way aboard a bus!

meant added delays and increased maintenance and fuel costs. It reckoned that one of the ways of easing congestion lay with the prohibition of parking on main streets of many town centres. There could be no reason why vehicles left for many hours on end should not be required to use a car park at a reasonable fee, thereby freeing the highways for the purpose for which they were intended. As for the problems in rural areas, the government committee set up by Professor Jack to consider the plight of bus services, made its report in March and recommended that rural services should be maintained by direct subsidies through county councils, a solution which, for many reasons, the whole industry deplored. Western Welsh thought that the idea was unworkable. They cited as an example the 205 route linking Cowbridge and St Athan, which earned just one shilling a mile or half the cost of operation, even with a Nimbus. The company insisted the only solution was the reduction or abolition of fuel tax for buses, and continued to bang the drum for this, but no-one listened. The tax remained at 2/6d a gallon, more than 250 per cent on the cost of the fuel. Furthermore, a further 2d per gallon increase had been levied in the latest budget.

Newly-introduced Nimbus 14 (TUH14) at Abergavenny in 1960. Service 732 ran two-hourly, between Brecon and Abergavenny via Llangynidr and Talybont. The journey took two hours and required two buses to operate. It alternated with the 731 via Bwlch and enjoyed a 30 minute layover at its destination. *Tony Warrener*

The accident statistics for 1960 were released early this year and showed a worsening situation. As far as the company's vehicles were concerned, although there were fewer collisions, they were of a more serious nature and resulted in six fatalities, against one in 1959 and 290 injured, an increase of five on that same year.

But the general manager had faith in the safety awareness of his staff. "I am reluctant to believe that there has been a marked relaxation in the degree of care exercised by our drivers," he wrote in the Staff Bulletin, continuing "Indeed, in many instances the fault was not ours. However, with the busy months ahead and a consequent increase in the volume of traffic, this is an opportune time to remind you to go carefully and keep clear of trouble."

The statistics showed that the company's vehicles were involved in 1,743 accidents. There was one fewer fatality and injuries fell to 278. Nevertheless, the cost of third party claims amounted to more than £14,095, and the cost of repairs to 1,206 incidents of vehicle damage to £8,213. Around 800 days of availability was lost while vehicles awaited or received attention.

In May, new workshops and a canteen opened at Bridgend as the initial part of redevelopment of the bus station there. The block featured four vehicle maintenance pits with a sunken workshop area and foreman's office, with a paying-in room and cash office above. The canteen had been constructed over the workshop area and had a kitchen, committee room, games room and toilets, the whole of which had a concrete barrel-vault roof.

A passengers-eye view of the cab and entrance of 124 (TUH 124), one of the initial batch of Weymann coaches built to Western Welsh design and new in 1960. Outward vision was unparalleled as a result of the reduced number of window pillars and the distinctive, curvaceous front windscreens which soon gained the coaches the nickname Sabrinas. *George Wedlake*

Carefree touring on quiet roads. Harrington-bodied AEC Reliance sisters 114 (OUH 114) and 118 (OUH 118) during an afternoon tour at Coity, near Bridgend, in 1958. *George Wedlake*

When this old Western Welsh AEC Regent turned up at Ysgol Erw'r Delyn in Penarth in 1961, it brought smiles to the faces of the handicapped children at the special school. The vehicle was donated following a request from the local authority. It was intended that the children could use the staircase to strengthen their leg muscles.

A Bridgend and District tour was inaugurated in May, when members and officers of Bridgend Urban District Council, Penybont Rural District Council, Glamorgan Constabulary, Glamorgan County Highways Department and company officials toured Coity Castle, Bridgend Trading Estate, Ewenny Pottery, Ogmore Castle, Ogmore-by-Sea and St Bride's Major. Afterwards, the party adjourned to the Dunraven Hotel for a buffet supper and refreshments provided by the company.

In May's Staff Bulletin, a message from general manager TG Davies reminded staff of the need to comply with the company's rule book. It seems that only a technicality in police evidence prevented a West Wales employee from being fined for failing to display his PSV badge.

"I regret to say that these offences are by no means confined to one area," wrote TG. "I believe that some staff are unfamiliar with the rule book. Another breach involves the occasional conversations between conductors and drivers on front entrance saloons and Atlantean double-deckers. This, too, is definitely against the rules and could well be the cause of a serious accident." Compliance with these regulations was not only required by the company, but also the Ministry of Transport under the Road Traffic Acts.

In another move typical of the benevolent nature of the company and its staff, a retired double-decker was given to Ysgol Erw'r Delyn, Penarth, in May to encourage its handicapped pupils to play using the staircase which aided their rehabilitation.

While on the subject of old double-deckers, bus No.626 was retired from active service and converted for the essential duty of tree lopping. The roofs and ventilators of most of the double-deck fleet had at some time

This glorious image of one of the Western Welsh extended tours to Scotland appeared on the cover of the company's brochure in the early 1960s.

suffered damage caused by low branches, and it was hoped that this would in future be considerably reduced. The vehicle, equipped with suitable tools, spent periods in various operating areas and staff were encouraged to report any trees which required attention.

Britain's Buses was the name of a new body formed in May, dedicated to the task of convincing the authorities of the important part played by the bus industry in the life of the community. The BET Group, London Transport, the Tilling Group and the Scottish Omnibus Group united to form it with the support of the Passenger Vehicle Operators' Association, the Municipal Passenger Transport Association, the Public Transport Association, and the Scottish Road Passenger Transport Association.

Commonwealth Training Week in Wales reached its climax at Cardiff's City Hall on June 2, with a two mile parade of marching apprentices and a mobile pageant of industry. The event was attended by the Duke of Edinburgh — the inspiration behind the idea of the event — along with Henry Brooke, Minister for Welsh Affairs; Lord Brecon, Minister of State; the Lord Lieutenant of Glamorgan and the Lord Mayor of Cardiff. Two Western Welsh entries — a Cambrian Class luxury coach and an AEC Matador recovery vehicle — took part in the transport section. Western Welsh Youth was represented by eight apprentices, four on each vehicle. During the week, Ely Works was visited by two parties of RAF boy entrants and their instructors. In addition, parties from Headlands School, Penarth; Cadoxton Secondary Modern School,

Cyntwell Secondary Modern School and Viriamu Jones County Secondary School were shown the various skills employed in maintaining the fleet.

Traffic manager Fred Pengelly caused a stir in July when he announced a ban on the indiscriminate use of transistor radios on the company's vehicles. The ban was widely reported in the press as well as on radio and TV. In addition to Britain's national dailies, the story also appeared in the San Francisco Chronicle. This may well have been the only time that Western Welsh made international headlines.

Picnic tours were introduced early in the season, and the traffic manager was quick to explain the idea to the press. He said that the company had discovered that many people on day trips found meals in restaurants or hotels too expensive. They didn't want to be bothered with taking their own food so it was thought that picnic trips would provide the answer. The picnic baskets cost passengers between 2/6d and 5/- each, according to individual tastes and requirements.

Most operators serving rural areas outstationed a number of buses away from their home depot each night. The vehicles would be parked in a yard or small garage instead of returning to town, saving the cost of running an empty bus for many miles, then reversing the process in the early morning. Western Welsh outstationed 36 vehicles out of a total fleet of around 700. This was one of the oldest practices in the bus industry and dictated purely by economics. Usually, the driver of the bus would live in the village. Against this saving in dead mileage, there were, however, certain disadvantages. A driver would need to sweep his bus out at night. The vehicle would then normally need to visit its depot for refuelling and thorough cleaning during the day.

An altercation with a farmer's Land Rover in the Vale of Glamorgan resulted in Nimbus 20 (TUH 20) being forced off the road and dented. The village Bobby appears to have matters under control. *Tony Jenkins*

This congestion at Port Talbot was typical in the 1950s, when the A48 route through the centre of town was hindered by this level crossing and the narrowness of the streets behind the cameraman. One of the 1953 Royal Tigers, 442 (GUH 442), passes a Thomas Bros, Saunders Roe-bodied Tiger Cub, in 1957. *Gerald Truran*

Minor maintenance could be a problem too, as there were no night staff to attend to any small adjustments which might be necessary for the bus to continue in service the following day. Problems could also arise in winter, particularly if the bus had to be left in the open. If it failed to start on a cold morning, there was no help at hand, and no hope of providing a substitute bus within a reasonable time. Equally, if the driver went sick, there was no spare man at hand and no way of finding a substitute in time to begin the service. Against this, the financial saving by outstationing buses could be considerable. A typical example was the vehicle outstationed at Aberystwyth. If it hadn't been possible to do this, operating the timetabled service would involve between 100 and 120 dead miles of operation each day. Another example was at Lampeter, where 80 dead miles were saved every day. Similar cases arose with other outstationed vehicles, though the mileage and cost involved weren't always so great. The Aberystwyth bus was luckier than many as it was garaged under cover, courtesy of Crosville Motor Services. Most of the others were kept in the open, usually in the secluded environment of a railway station yard or goods depot.

The award of annual contracts by the Ministry of Aviation for services to the Royal Armament Establishment at Aberporth, and also the Proof and Experimental

Establishment at Pendine, had led to ill-feeling among local operators Lewis Williams, Richards Bros and Midway Motors, and brought recurring problems for the traffic commissioners. The Ministry had awarded the contracts based on individual quotations without considering the existing operators of such services, or established stage services in the area. To cope with licensing regulations Western Welsh and Crosville operated vehicles on hire to one another, against which the local operators felt unable to compete.

A new Road Traffic Bill, concluded in the autumn parliamentary session, contained provisions which the industry supported. These included raising the speed limit for buses and coaches to 40 mph, and increasing PSV dimensions to 36ft x 8ft 2½ inches.

An anomaly, regarded with dismay by all professional drivers, was a list of offences, conviction for which on three occasions in as many years would involve automatic licence suspension.

It was felt that some of these offences could be regarded as technicalities and didn't necessarily involve danger, such as exceeding the speed limit. If a good professional driver lost his licence, he would automatically lose his job, which in some circumstances could be unfair.

In the days before service areas on motorways, 129 (WKG 129) has pulled in at the roadside to allow its passengers a 'comfort break' on an extended tour in 1962. *AB Cross*

It was also a mystery as to why well-maintained and expertly driven vehicles such as buses, which required regular official inspection, should have their speed limited to the advantage of the private car.

A new garage and bus station at Manchester Square, Milford Haven, opened in November while attention was then given to the opposite end of the company's territory when a contract was placed for the construction of offices and garage accommodation in Cwmbran New Town, for completion in 1963.

The Cownie Cup returned to the grateful hands of the Western Welsh team in a closely fought final with City of Oxford Motor Services, played at Cheltenham on November 23. The team scored the all-important second goal in extra time to regain the prize. The general manager, whose retirement had been announced, had been something of a lucky mascot, first to Rhondda Transport, and then Western Welsh in post-war Cownie Cup encounters, and this was a fitting finale to a man whose support over the years had been unfailing.

The last of the handsome Harrington Wayfarer coaches 118 (OUH 118) with its guests at Ewenny Pottery during the inaugural Bridgend and district tour in May, 1961. *George Wedlake*

The various yards that comprised Haverfordwest depot usually emptied during mid-afternoon as large numbers of double-deckers left for the school run. The crew are about to join the rush in this lovely study of 960 (EUH 960) in 1965. *Peter Keating*

Severe weather conditions were experienced during the last week of December and over the New Year which caused considerable disruption of services, particularly in West Wales, where Haverfordwest depot was closed completely for several days.

Driver Jack Fox of Barry became the first 40-year service holder with the company. At the end of the year TG Davies, OBE retired. His replacement bore a familiar name — IL Gray, son of the first general manager, who now returned to the fold from Rhondda Transport.

1962

In April, the new bus station at Bridgend was completed after two and a half years of redevelopment. The result transformed the appearance of the biggest of the company's garages and Wales's second largest bus station. The site now boasted covered head-on passenger boarding bays in two areas, a new workshop and canteen. The work was carried out in three phases. The first was the workshop and canteen on former gas company land, a subsidiary boarding area and paving. The second, the main boarding area including seating, advertising, vending facilities, an enlarged enquiry office and improvements to the waiting room and toilets. The final phase involved partitioning of the pits in the existing garage and construction of fuel and washing bays, the latter being accessed through an opening in the end wall. Costing a little over £100,000, the result proved an asset not only to the company, but also to the people of

Bridgend and district who were handed a considerably improved facility. It was a far cry from the distant days when passengers had to wander across the hardstanding to find their bus. The work itself met with its fair share of problems. Difficulties were experienced due to the one-way system operating in Bridgend, the small ground area of just two acres available for development and the fact that the bus station and depot had to be kept operational while the work progressed. An added complication was that this building work had to be adjusted to allow for the introduction of newly-permitted 36ft long vehicles, considered essential for the Bridgend valleys.

The pleasure of a holiday by Western Welsh coach was the feature of local ITV company TWW's advertising magazine programme Ticket to Sunshine, which was broadcast on five consecutive Sundays at the start of the year. The popularity of the company's extended tours had increased, except during wartime, year on year since they began in 1935, and each year the programme was extended accordingly. In 1962, the modern fleet of 39 AEC Reliances made 190 departures and carried 5,978 happy passengers to all corners of Great Britain. Although many tours retained the same title over many years, route and accommodation changes were made as

The main departure bays at Bridgend's impressive new bus station shortly after opening in 1962.

required. The planning of the tours was an evolutionary process which always ensured the best choice could be offered. Paradoxically, 1962 was one of the few years that saw no new coaches delivered to the company.

The old Streamways garage in Penarth was sold in March, and in June, a major £60,000 upgrade of Ely Works was announced. Included in this was a new coach garage to replace the former Forse's premises at Blackweir. Spare land was available at Ely, and so despite the Blackweir premises being a modern, purpose-built building, it was declared surplus to requirements and advertised for sale. However, restrictive covenants on the use of the land meant there were lengthy legal hurdles to overcome before it was eventually sold.

In the spring, Seaway Parade, a new link road between Baglan and Sandfields, opened and by May it was revealed that almost 1,000 vehicles an hour had been using the road at peak periods. While no Western Welsh routes used the new road, it was acknowledged that it played an important part in easing the congestion in Port Talbot. The town had long been a notorious bottleneck, one of the most badly congested areas in South Wales.

With spring came an outbreak of smallpox in Bridgend and the Rhondda Valley. The epidemic was soon brought under control, but it had a serious effect on the company's revenue for many months. As a result, staff were urged to encourage and look after their passengers if they wished to avoid curtailment of certain services that were now losing money.

Since the early 1950s the company had worked closely with the Development Corporation and local authorities to plan the future of public transport in the Cwmbran New Town area. Building work was well advanced and the company was establishing a strategy of increased routes to serve the expanding area. New and revised stage

carriage services began in March and operated on roads built to a width and strength suitable for the operation of the maximum permitted size of bus. Three new cross-town services formed the basis of the transport system and replaced the old town services in operation since the late 1950s. The new services, using 44-seat saloons, were 709, Upper Cwmbran to Pontnewydd; 713, Croesyceiliog to Oakfield and 737, Upper Cwmbran to Llanyravon. An abundance of low bridges in the eastern valleys prohibited the use of double-deckers, although it was thought that when the company's new garage at Cwmbran was opened, and pending an anticipated upturn in traffic, certain services would switch to double-decker operation. The company reluctantly acknowledged the losses incurred at Cwmbran during the previous four years, but was optimistic that with the improved facilities it would begin to reap some benefit.

If the Weymann-bodied Atlanteans could be described as smart, then perhaps this pair illustrates the point. They were quiet, smooth and customer-friendly. What fun it was to sit side-saddle near the door and watch the driver clicking his way through the pre-selector and waiting for the jolt that followed! Standing by at the newly expanded Bridgend bus station in 1962 are 314 (VKG 314) and 335 (XUH 335). *Howard Roberts*

Elsewhere, as many rural railways closed, even before the fall of the Beeching axe, British Railways-subsidised bus replacement services began. Passenger rail services were withdrawn between Brecon and Hereford, and Brecon and Newtown at the end of the year, and two replacement bus services began. These were 738, Brecon - Talgarth - Builth Wells - Newtown and 739, Brecon - Talgarth - Hay on Wye - Hereford. There were two return journeys daily, except Sundays, intended for Nimbus operation. Service 738 was operated jointly with Crosville, and provided a connection at Talgarth for the Hereford service. This was new territory for the company as far as stage carriage operation was concerned.

Loss-making rural services were highlighted in the general manager's message in a spring Staff Bulletin. He commented on the way in which councils were increasing rates, along with pay for policemen and teachers. It seemed that, despite opposition to fare increases some councils were supporting the abolition of fuel tax in country areas.

In the six weeks up to March 24, 83 cases of seat slashing were repaired at Ely Works. Despite the widespread publicity given to this senseless vandalism, it persisted on a serious scale. Bridgend depot suffered most, with 28 incidents. Carmarthen and Crosskeys, at the other end of the scale, recorded four each.

The staff canteen at Bridgend afforded a grandstand view of all that was going on in the bus station. In this everyday scene from 1962 a solitary Albion Nimbus picks its way through its bigger cousins while in the background is a lone Coity Motors Tiger Cub. *George Wedlake*

Fronting Market Street, Bridgend, were the express service and tours bays of the town's bus station, where Willowbrook coach 520 (GUH 520) waits alongside a dual-purpose Tiger Cub on the Carmarthen to Cardiff service. Hurrying off to Swansea is one of the stalwart Guys of the N&C 'Brown Bombers' fleet. *George Wedlake*

A note from the chief engineer in May's Staff Bulletin warned that more stringent action against the emission of black exhaust smoke from diesel vehicles had been issued by the Ministry of Transport. "Although we are by no means the worst offenders in this area, it is quite apparent that in future the use of smoke meters will enable the police to prosecute if a vehicle exhaust is found to be denser than specified," he said.

Reference was made to the company's small-engined buses — the Tiger Cub and Nimbus — that worked close to their full power output. Any slight defect in the fuel injection equipment of these vehicle types could cause their engines to smoke badly. It was easy to combat this by allowing a larger safety margin and reduce the maximum fuel settings. Unfortunately this increased fuel consumption because more gear work was necessary when driving, and this in turn brought greater driver fatigue.

"If you notice your bus smoking, or indeed any other Western Welsh bus, report it in the defects book at your depot. This procedure will also help in the event of the company and the driver of the bus concerned being prosecuted for black smoke, since we would be able to show that we were doing all within our power to prevent such an occurrence."

It was all a long way from ultra low sulphur, EEC dictates and 'nil defect' reporting, but nevertheless it was an environmental issue acknowledged and dealt with responsibly by the company and to the best of its ability. The chief engineer also reminded drivers that the company's new Atlanteans and Leopards, together with the Bridgemaster fleet, required a particular engine-starting procedure. Once the engine had started, it had to be allowed to tick over for a while, as considerable damage could result from revving a cold engine with dry

The first 36ft long vehicle in the fleet was Willowbrook-bodied Leyland Leopard 601 (601 BBO), seen at Bridgend bus station in 1973. The rear overhang must have come as a shock to some of the drivers faced with negotiating the town's narrow streets, and it is said that the design of the bus station had to be modified to accommodate these vehicles. Of the 18 ordered 12 were based at Bridgend, and gave years of sterling service on the valley routes. The original livery has weathered favourably as this was well into the NBC era, but only the grey wheels give a clue to this. *Mike Street*

With its destination blind set for a mystery tour 509 (EUH 509) stands at Bethany Square, Port Talbot in July 1961.
Paul Redmond

cylinder bores and thick oil in the sump. Rocket science it wasn't, but these tips were vital to enable trouble-free and economic operation.

The excellent working relationship that the company enjoyed with other road transport companies, P&A Campbell Ltd and British Railways Western Region was once again acknowledged in the chairman's review at the annual general meeting on July 17. Ever closer co-operation was a natural outcome of the various closure proposals then under consideration for parts of south and central Wales by the infamous Dr Beeching, then chairman of the British Railways Board. Also, not to be underestimated was the escalation in holiday charter business from Rhoose Airport, which resulted in passenger numbers there exceeding 100,000. In addition to its regular link between Cardiff and Rhoose, Western Welsh was always mindful of the potential for private hire bookings to and from the airport.

The meeting was informed of another reduced profit. This time it was down to £70,004, the lowest since 1945-46. The stage carriage revenue for the year fell £124,000 short of the anticipated total. Factors that had adversely affected receipts included severe weather conditions at the start of the year, the smallpox outbreak at Bridgend, short-time working at Hirwaun Industrial Estate, and a drop in attendances at Cardiff City and Newport County football grounds. Two applications were made for fare increases, and the company was mindful that this was not going to help matters. Continuing economies of operation and the vigorous promotion of other sources of revenue such as tours and private hire helped an otherwise bleak situation. Despite all of this, it was yet another record year for extended tour operation, with a healthy 12 per cent year on year increase.

Management invited suggestions for a new company crest but despite many being submitted, all the designs were deemed uninspiring or over-detailed and the company dismissed them on the basis that unless a design was an improvement on the existing badge, there was no point in adopting it. "What is wrong with the present badge?" commented one conductor. "It's like changing the Union Jack. It just isn't done. Whoever designed the present crest did a first-class job, and whoever designed the cap badge finished the job to perfection."

At the end of 1962 a blizzard brought 18 feet deep snowdrifts to parts of South Wales. Villages were cut off, some for several days, with roads and railways blocked and telephone wires brought down. The snow brought cancellation of a visit to the Cardiff pantomime by Pontypool staff arranged for New Year's day. In the weeks that followed, the country was continuously under snow, and conditions in Wales were the coldest since 1740. Tribute was paid to busmen by hundreds of motorists who wouldn't risk their own vehicles on the icy roads, but were happy to travel by bus. They were certainly not let down by the road staff of Western Welsh.

All change for the future

Old enemies still cause problems

Changing lifestyles meant that the Western Welsh company was approaching what many would consider in later years to be a turning point in its fortunes. Three old chestnuts would continue to haunt senior management. These were of course increasing private car usage, the chaos and congestion this was causing on a seriously outdated road network and finally the effects on the business of a crippling fuel tax that seemed to be constantly rising. Added together they would become three insurmountable foes.

The general manager quoted a speech by Minister of Transport Ernest Marples in the Staff Bulletin of March 1963, the words of which he considered vitally important to the future well-being of the bus industry. Marples had said: "Our large cities cannot survive on the basis of 'one man, one car' commuting; the answer must be public transport in one form or another. In present circumstances we are in no position to ignore the benefits which an efficient bus system can give in tackling the urban traffic problem."

Marples and the general manager were not alone in recognising the difficulties the transport industry in particular and the country in general were facing.

So what of the future? That was the question asked in a presidential address to the Omnibus Society by Western Welsh chairman EL Taylor.

It was indeed the question of the hour and one which hindsight has revealed had no real, definitive answer. Taylor tried to be positive and expressed the belief that despite everything that was being thrown at it, the bus industry in its many different forms was one that would survive. He envisaged that it would still be around in 50 years even though vehicles and techniques would evolve. He was of course right.

Atlantean 340 (XUH 340) faithfully served Barry from its arrival in 1962 until 1967 when it moved to Crosskeys. It is seen here on September 2, 1962, before setting off on route 303 from Cardiff central bus station to Cadoxton via Wenvoe. *RL Wilson / Online Transport Archive*

1963

In sharp contrast to the way London ground to a halt in the snow of February 2009, the community was certainly not let down by the drivers, conductors and clippies of South Wales during the winter — the worst since records began. There may have been unavoidable delays, diversions and cancellations on many routes, but by battling through the arctic-like conditions, they succeeded in providing an essential service for

Pontypool depot didn't have an allocation of double deckers for a good reason. Its operating area was peppered with low railway bridges like this one at Old Cwmbran. It wasn't until Beeching axed many rail routes that Western Welsh could relax, by which time operations had transferred to Cwmbran. Olympian 1235 (LKG 235) is on a Varteg to Cardiff service in 1962. *Tony Jenkins*

thousands. And all this in vehicles where anti-lock braking systems, individual traction control, and all the paraphernalia associated with 21st Century safety technology hadn't even been dreamed of! Ironically, many of the crews operating the buses had to walk to and from work themselves because the roads in their particular district were impassable. Despite this, there was never a shortage of volunteers to work overtime to ensure that office, shop and factory workers reached home before the ever threatening blizzards and icy conditions forced the buses to stop running. Passengers, with their usual quota of moans and groans, rarely offered praise, but in difficult times camaraderie was evident between one and all. Many letters of thanks poured in from appreciative passengers, headmasters, factory owners and local councils. The busmen could be congratulated in scoring a resounding victory in the 1963 battle of the snow. An article penned by John O'Sullivan, a South Wales Echo reporter who had worked for four months as a conductor at Barry depot in 1955 before entering journalism, praised the road staff for their efforts at this stressful time. "They do not appear in the New Year's honours list, they are never thought of when we praise famous men, but at the same time, honour should be paid to the men and women who are keeping the wheels — of buses, trains and essential road transport — turning. Only those who have had to footslog through deep drifts to bus stops, know what thankfulness the sight of a bus approaching along the main road is greeted with. The bus crews have a thankless and difficult job and they have been discharging it with skill and determination, not to speak of amazing cheerfulness. The thanks of the community should go out to them."

The year began with the replacement of the state-owned British Transport Commission (BTC) by the Transport Holding Company Ltd (THC). The significant 50 per cent shareholding that had originated with the GWR and which had transferred to the BTC in the 1948 nationalisation now passed to the new umbrella company.

New offices were proposed at Ely for which £31,000 was earmarked from the £35,000 accepted for the sale of spare land elsewhere on the site which was to be developed for housing. At Cardiff central bus station, plans were announced to convert the public waiting room into a booking and enquiry office.

In a press conference held at the Barley Mow pub, Penlline, on St David's Day, general manager IL Gray and traffic manager, FH Pengelly, answered many questions from reporters, who were naturally transported to the venue by one of the latest coaches. The subjects discussed included fuel tax, the company's 1963 Luxury Holiday Tours programme, Holiday Runabout tickets, the newly-introduced special 12-guinea, seven day tour to Newquay, Cornwall, and the new express service to Saundersfoot and Tenby.

In 1963 the company's services made a total of 102,149 departures from Cardiff's central bus station, second only to Cardiff Corporation Transport. A total of 13 operators used the bus station, and there were 395,719 scheduled departures annually.

The 1962 Leyland Leopards had extra-wide entrances and were delivered in plain red. They were handsome vehicles and soon gained popularity in the Bridgend Valleys and on Cardiff to Barry services. *George Wedlake*

In sharp contrast were the services, often in single figures, which originated from GWR days and operated from various stations. The vehicles needed for these services were often outstationed at railway station yards, and were by no means confined to rural areas. The replacement of the BTC by the THC brought with it an air of change and talks were held in August 1963 between general manager IL Gray and RC Hilton, divisional manager of BR's Western Region at Cardiff. It was accepted that revised charges needed to be brought about, both for housing the company's vehicles on railway premises, and the basing of services on station premises. The revised charges introduced in September resulted in an unwelcome rise in costs to Western Welsh. In total, the annual fee rose from just over £135 to £455. This led IL Gray to write to the rail boss: "There are certain instances where our stage carriage services have been extended to operate to and from stations at your special request and we now have to consider whether the number of passengers conveyed are sufficient to justify the additional expenditure that is involved in this form of operation. For this purpose, it is proposed to take a census at the various points and dependent upon the result of this, it may well be that we will communicate with you with a view to consideration of some form of modification to the existing arrangements." In a way it does seem that BR was biting the hand that fed them. In any event, Mr Gray's response appears to have been a polite way of calling their bluff.

The only profitable services operated in West Wales were those in the Haverfordwest and Milford Haven areas. The absence of regular headways, which characterised many of the former Green's services, was still apparent in the area. It was a problem that would never adequately be resolved.

A new express service was introduced, from June to September, running on Saturdays only, from Cardiff to Saundersfoot and Tenby. This ran via Bridgend, Neath, Ammanford and Carmarthen. A Holiday Runabout ticket was introduced which allowed passengers unlimited travel on the railway and most bus routes west of Carmarthen. The adult tickets were just under £2 and a child's just under half that and were available for seven consecutive days.

An AEC Regent III (633) was based at Pontypool depot as a driver familiarisation vehicle pending the intended introduction of double-deckers to the area. Pontypool's allocation had previously consisted of single-deckers only.

One of the first batch of 180 Tiger Cubs to enter service between 1954 and 1957, 1010 (HUH 10) was new to Neath depot and remained in the area until 1959. A year at Brecon followed, then Haverfordwest became home. Seen there a little worse for wear in July 1961, 1010 eventually returned to Neath in 1966 to live out its remaining days. *Paul Redmond*

Thomas Bros (Port Talbot) took over Western Welsh services in the Baglan area, and at the same time Western Welsh introduced regular summer services from Bridgend via Port Talbot to Aberavon Beach. Meanwhile, in a joint move with Crosville, the goodwill of the Newtown to Cardiff service of Mid-Wales Motorways was bought for £2,000.

The special football express services, which had traditionally been run from Bridgend and the Newport valleys to Cardiff's Ninian Park ground, were discontinued due to a considerable downturn in revenue. In an attempt to economise, the suggestion was put to the Branch Trades Union officials that the services should become one-man operated, but this proved unacceptable to them. As a result the licences held for the services were surrendered and returned to the Traffic Commissioners. While on the sporting theme, Rhondda Transport killed Western Welsh hopes of lifting the Cownie Cup, by winning 5-2 at Porth in the semi-final in October. It was an enjoyable game, but, as often happens in local derbies, an amount of needle crept in which resulted in one of the company's players being sent off.

In what was to be Western Welsh's penultimate new depot, Cwmbran, opened in October. The steel framed garage had a 100ft roof span and housed up to 38 vehicles. A segregated workshop and four bay pit area occupied one end, while outside there was a covered fuelling bay, washing facilities and room for a further 19 vehicles. A two-storey office block ran the full length of one side of the garage and contained an enquiry office, paying-in facilities, cleaner's mess room and foreman's office on the ground floor. The first floor housed the area manager's offices and general mess room. Cwmbran had

now become the administrative control centre for the company's eastern area, replacing Pontnewynydd. The new facilities had cost £76,664. However, a hint of hard times ahead saw the introduction of a number of services run jointly with Red & White and the consequent pooling of revenues.

Western Welsh may well have a claim to fame for inventing the executive coach. Ely Works staff fitted a Leyland Leopard Alpine Continental coach with a purpose-built cocktail bar for a four-day private hire by the British Iron and Steel Federation. The coach was needed at short notice to convey 23 technicians drawn from 15 countries, many from South America and the Orient, on a plant inspection tour of various steelworks. Described as an 'inter-regional symposium', the hire took place from November 18-21 and included visits to Llanwern, Wolverhampton and Sheffield. On board the coach to dispense refreshments was Mrs Winnie Preece, a member of Cardiff central bus station's enquiry staff. She described the task as an exciting experience and one which she enjoyed to the full. The tour was filmed by an overseas TV unit for transmission in South America. After the tour, the bar was removed and the coach restored to its full seating capacity, but not before a small party of company executives sampled its contents on a pre-Christmas jaunt.

Western Welsh played hosts to The Omnibus Society on the occasion of its Presidential Weekend based at the Angel Hotel in Cardiff. This began with a visit to head office and the city's central bus station, followed by a tour of the Ely Works and offices. Two coaches took the party to Bridgend for an afternoon, where they were shown over the bus station, garage and workshops.

Willowbrook-bodied AEC Reliance 281 (WKG 281) adds an extra splash of colour to the bunting-clad streets of Fishguard during a day tour in 1967. *Howard Roberts*

They returned east through the Vale of Glamorgan to Barry, where once again a depot visit was laid on, then returned to Cardiff in time for the society's annual dinner and speeches. A special edition of the Omnibus Magazine to mark the weekend was distributed at dinner and contained a detailed account of the company by Lyndon Rees, and another on coach touring by George Wedlake, both of whom were employed in the traffic department at head office. On the Sunday morning, a number of coaches conveyed the members to Merthyr Tydfil, where they visited the municipal bus undertaking, before

heading for Brecon and lunch. In the afternoon the party continued via Talgarth, Crickhowell and Pontypool to Cwmbran for yet another garage visit. The weekend finished at Newport, where members dispersed by rail to their various destinations.

During his presidential address to the Omnibus Society, Western Welsh chairman EL Taylor asked: "So, what of the future? The story I have tried to tell covers more than 50 years. Apart from the interruptions of war, and the lesser effect of economic stress, it is a story of constant

A delivery of 10 attractive AEC Regents with Northern Counties highbridge bodies arrived in 1963 and were so highly regarded by Penarth Road and Barry depots that they were never allowed to escape. At Cardiff City Hall shortly after delivery, 709 (709 CUH) was one of Barry's treasured examples. It is said they were easier to drive than a family car. *Viv Corbin*

expansion. Human nature changes, if at all, so slowly as to be almost imperceptible; the 'call of the road' seems to persist as a survival from the dim past when much of mankind was nomadic. So it seems likely to me that in another 50 years, however vehicles and techniques may evolve, coach tours will still be operating, to more faraway places than ever, giving the same kind of joy they undoubtedly give now."

AEC Regal semi-coach 518 was extensively damaged in a serious accident while on the Cardiff to Carmarthen express service. Meanwhile, this was also the year that Jack H Lewis, former chief engineer and co-founder of Lewis & James Ltd, died aged 74.

In common with bus undertakings throughout Britain, Western Welsh was still campaigning for the abolition of duties levied on fuel oil used by buses and coaches. Fuel tax cost the company a staggering £270,000 a year at a time when bus companies everywhere were losing passengers and struggling to maintain loss-making services. Even so, there was a slight improvement in company profit for the year 1962-63 which was recorded as £74,915.

Touring by coach was exciting at times like this. At Torpoint in August 1967, 154 (DBO 154C) carefully boards the ferry for Plymouth. Most of the party have embarked on a river cruise to the Tamar bridges and Devonport from where 154 will collect them to complete the short hop to Plymouth's Duke of Cornwall hotel for the night.

1964

In April, as the new coach garage at Ely was completed, Forse's Blackweir coach depot was sold to Harold Leigh Ltd (Kardov). Improvements as part of the overall scheme for Ely Works included the provision of five new docking pits and a new entrance from Caerau Lane. The new facilities enabled the increasing fleet of 36ft long vehicles to be catered for, while a special cut-out at the back of one of the new pits was provided for the rear-engined Atlantean double-deckers. Other improvements to the workshops included the resiting of the paint shop and reorganisation of the machine and body shop areas.

At Cardiff central bus station, work was completed on the conversion of the waiting room into a spacious new enquiry office for tours and express services. The original enquiry office was converted into offices for the Tours Department.

Partly as a result of the various mid-Wales rail closures, Western Welsh applied jointly with Crosville Motor Services for permission to operate an express service between Cardiff and Liverpool via Pontypridd, Brecon, Builth Wells, Newtown, Oswestry, Wrexham, Chester and Birkenhead. It began in July and was to become the first through north-south service in the Principality. Connections were provided at Newtown with the

Winter drawers on! Another touring season is over and except for vehicles employed on private hire, the coach fleet is mothballed for the winter months. This Harrington Grenadier is less than a year old, but has been thoroughly checked over at Ely and spruced up in readiness for the following season. Cleaner Tommy Lee is enveloping the coach in polythene sheeting which would keep it snug until spring.
Stewart Williams

Think of it in today's terms as a stretched limo. Cardiff's 680 (MUH 680) was unique to Western Welsh in so many ways. It was one of the first 30ft long Regents to be built and the first with a fully automatic gearbox. *Viv Corbin*

Associated Motorways Cheltenham to Bangor and Aberystwyth routes, effectively opening up mid-Wales. Journey time was eight hours 20 minutes inclusive of refreshment halts en-route. Onward connections from Liverpool enabled the Lake District, Scotland and the North-East to be reached.

A handful of the 1961 AEC Reliance coaches were painted in a distinctive new blue and ivory livery and dedicated to this service. The general manager reported that the company felt pleased at having forged this important new link between north and south, especially as there was a tendency in some quarters to regard the bus industry as being rather unenterprising. By this time there was no doubt that the industry's post-war expansion had ceased, largely due to the increasing availability and affordability of the car.

Another step, taken jointly with Rhondda Transport, to attract more passengers came in March with the introduction of a new limited-stop service between Maesteg and Cardiff. This immediately showed considerable promise and proved a boon to the local community when the railway stations at Pencoed and Llanharan were closed.

In April 1964 the general manager must have struggled to avoid sounding politically motivated in his Staff Bulletin message: "Another disappointing budget for the bus industry, with no relief from the burden of fuel tax. Indeed it is whispered in some quarters that the Chancellor gave consideration to increasing the tax. This alarming prospect may lead one to assume that the Government neither knows nor cares about our difficulties."

"As a user of the Baglan Estate bus service at Port Talbot, which has recently terminated, I should like to pay tribute to the drivers and conductors who served us so faithfully throughout the years," wrote a resident of Albion Road along which the service passed, "I am sure I speak for many when I say it was with regret we saw this bus service come to an end. We had come to rely on your buses, by which we could almost set our clocks, and travelling on them we found the courtesy of the drivers and conductors was unfailing. Thank you one and all."

In a way, this frustration could be understood. It was three years since the Jack Committee emphasised the urgency of solving the problem of loss-making rural bus services and still nothing tangible had been done.

Meanwhile, a further example of the benevolent nature of Western Welsh within the community was demonstrated with the provision of two specially adapted coaches, based on AEC Regal chassis. The first was adapted during the summer and equipped with a ramp and locking devices to accommodate wheelchairs. Its initial purpose was to convey multiple sclerosis victims to Rhyl for a week's holiday. It was the first holiday for several members of the MS Society whose well-known champion Major Harold Blondell, had approached the company for help. The coach remained in the operational fleet for the conveyance of incapacitated people to places that would otherwise have been beyond their reach. Painted in the new dual-purpose livery, coach 522 was also available to convey small parties and sporting organisations. In a letter of appreciation to the company, the secretary of the Barry branch of the Multiple Sclerosis Society wrote: "Many of our disabled members had misgivings in travelling so far, but with the facilities provided, fears were forgotten. They travelled in comfort, thoroughly enjoyed their holiday, and all commented on the cheerful and willing help given by your staff."

The second vehicle was presented to the Danybryn Cheshire Home at Radyr for the use of the residents and was made possible by the generosity of former managing director WT James and members of the management and

Most of Cardiff had ground to a halt by the time this bus returned to base at the city's central bus station in the severe winter weather of early 1963. Beneath the snow lies Park Royal bodied AEC Regent V 665 (LKG 665). *Arnold Richardson / Photobus*

Approaching its destination after heavy snow is Bridgend's 1133 (MUH 133). Vehicles such as this played a vital part in keeping services running during the harsh winter of 1963. *Stewart Williams*

Ely Works staff who gave freely of their time to make it possible. Local traders had also responded and supplied materials free of charge as their contribution to the project. A volunteer driver was always available when required. This heart-warming story came about after an approach by Mrs Elliot Seager, one of the home's trustees. In a letter of thanks to Ivor Gray, she wrote: "Everyone at Danybryn truly appreciates the wonderful work done to bring a modicum of happiness and love into the lives of these courageous people for whom there is no hope of a cure. Their bodies may be stricken, but many of them have alert minds and human desires and longings, and it has been frustrating for us that it was not possible to provide more contact with the outside world. Now we can do this, thanks to our delightful coach." By coincidence the livery of the coach was light blue, the colour of the old Lewis & James fleet, which 'WT' had good reason to nostalgically comment upon!

The 1963 wage award had added £80,000 to the company's annual costs and led to a fares increase at the end of May. Further pay claims lodged in January resulted in a negotiated settlement of increases on the basic week of 14/- for drivers and skilled maintenance men, and 10s 6d for conductors, semi-skilled and unskilled grades, together with three days additional annual leave for staff with five years' service. This became effective in March, further increasing the company's costs by £130,000 in a full year.

The 44th annual general meeting of the company was held on July 14. Despite a net profit of £105,473 being recorded for the financial year 1963-64, the results were again regarded as disappointing. There was an increase in profit of £30,000 over the previous year's figures, even after providing £20,528 in taxation. A sum of £25,000 was added to the general reserve fund as a contribution towards the continually increasing cost of vehicle replacements. Gross revenue at £3,051,000 was some £100,000 below the figure anticipated, and was blamed on competition from the car, motorcycle and moped along with an increase in the operation of illegal minibuses. The traffic recession was aggravated by poor summer weather.

Despite this, Western Welsh's extended holiday tours enjoyed another record breaking season, with a 15 per cent increase in customers over the previous year. Particularly successful were the 'off-peak' tours offered early and late in the holiday season at very reasonable

Enjoying a day at the seaside in Tenby during July 1964 is 512 (GUH 512). Even the driver appears to have gone for an ice cream. The 'no parking' sign is bigger than the coach, but this was Western Welsh, and some rules for ordinary motorists simply didn't apply! *Malcolm Jones*

prices, helped by favourable rates negotiated with the hotels during their quietest period.

In the annual general meeting, it was once again reported that the company's relationships with neighbouring bus companies, British Railways (Western Region) and P&A Campbell Ltd, with whom co-ordinated arrangements were in operation, continued to be what was described as 'most cordial'.

An article on the picturesque Route 802 — Haverfordwest – Brawdy – Solva – St David's — was featured in the July Staff Bulletin. "For sheer breathtaking beauty it would be hard to find a bus journey to equal the 16 mile run between Haverfordwest and St David's which passes some of the loveliest scenery in the whole of Pembrokeshire," it read.

"We are in sight of the sea for much of the journey but before glimpsing the magnificent sweep of St Bride's Bay at Newgale we cover some attractive country, the quaint old

stone bridge at Pelcomb, and Roch where we see briefly the 13th Century castle. Newgale has a two mile stretch of sand and at certain times of the year when tides are low, tree stumps drowned in post-glacial times are revealed. A little more than a mile away is Brawdy Royal Naval Air Station. Next we see the village of Solva, considered by many to be the gem of the Pembrokeshire coast. In the days of schooners the harbour was busy; now it is a

Climbing out of Newgale on the coastal run to St David's, 974 is about to leave the A487 to proceed to the village of Llandeloy. It was a useful diversion and also served Brawdy Royal Naval Air Station. *AB Cross (RF Mack collection)*

The improved rear design of 1961 Weymann coaches over the 1960 model, right, is shown to good effect at Cardiff central bus station in 1969. Now in ivory and blue, 134 (WKG 134) awaits its next duty. Being June 26, a Thursday, this could well have been an afternoon tour to Slimbridge or Symond's Yat. *Mike Street*

Driver/Courier Ray Thomas took this happy party of holidaymakers on tour in 1964. *Ray Thomas*

holidaymaker's paradise offering bathing, flowers, bird life, antiquities, fishing and boats. Another four miles of beautiful country and with the sea sparkling and blue on our left we reach the city of St David's. The 14th century cathedral is the largest and finest in Wales. Most cathedrals are visible from afar but at St David's, its appearance is a surprise. The modern pilgrim must enter the unpretentious village and actually search for the great church."

Ordinary bus services provided 90 per cent of the company's revenue, but the mounting problem of traffic congestion was causing upset to schedules, frustrating passengers and seriously increasing operating expenses. The Buchanan Report underlined the fact that public transport had a big part to play in relieving traffic congestion and was by far the most economical user of road space. In short, the report concluded that if public transport was to function effectively, particularly in towns and cities, certain priorities such as reserved lanes for buses and stricter control of kerbside parking was essential. Furthermore it highlighted that the problem should be tackled quickly.

A protracted conflict had taken place between the company and Daniel Jones and Sons of Carmarthen, over contract services from Carmarthen to Pendine. A second appeal by Daniel Jones was upheld by the Minister of Transport, who ruled that the licences should be granted to that operator. It was made clear by Western Welsh when the applications were heard in the traffic court that the loss of the contracts would have a serious effect on stage services in Carmarthenshire, as such contracts were playing a vital part in helping to maintain services in what had become an extremely unremunerative area. Daniel Jones had been awarded three contracts — one was previously held jointly by Western Welsh and Tudor Williams of Laugharne, the other two by Western Welsh.

Following the loss of these contracts, the company found itself unable to continue the little-used 613 service between Ammanford and Carmarthen via Tycroes and Capel Dewi. This presented a very gloomy picture for staff at Carmarthen and Ammanford depots, who feared that any further contract loss would lead to job cuts.

AEC Reliance 148 (ABO 148B), with stylish Harrington Grenadier bodywork, at St Andrew's in the Vale of Glamorgan in 1964. It is fortunate that two out of the six operated by Western Welsh remain active in preservation. *George Wedlake*

A serious accident involving an Atlantean bus and a lorry occurred in Neville Street, Cardiff, and resulted in driver George Ramsey being trapped by his legs, and having to be freed from the wreckage of his cab by police and firemen. He fractured his right knee, but made a full recovery in nearby St David's Hospital.

The death of Albert Gray, founder of SWCM and the first general manager of Western Welsh, occurred in August. He was 85 and had been living at his daughter's home in Pendoylan. Many of his former colleagues, including WT James and TG Davies, together with officials and staff, attended his funeral at Thornhill Crematorium.

A typical good news story from the summer illustrates how times had changed, and not perhaps for the better. A magistrate travelling from Maesteg had occasion to write to LA Smith, area manager at Bridgend: "Sir, May I draw your attention to the kind and efficient way in which two of your employees dealt with an incident on one of your buses on Saturday March 21. I travelled from Maesteg on bus No. 616 and during the journey a little

boy tendered 3d to the conductor and requested a ticket to Bridgend. As the boy sat in the front seat of the bus and the conductor was taking fares from the back, it was of necessity some time before he got to the boy. I boarded the bus at Heolfaen and the conductor was worried about his passenger. I overheard him discuss it with his driver, and being a magistrate I suggested they might drop him at the nearest police station. This they decided to do. They stopped at Cwmfelin Police Station and a sergeant came over and talked to the boy. On police advice your staff stopped a passing Maesteg bus, put the boy in the care of the conductor and the police arranged to meet the boy in Maesteg. Now, Sir, that would seem to be normal procedure, but I would like you to compliment your staff on the kindly way in which they carried out their duties. The boy was not in any way frightened and went confidently with your conductor. If there were more people of this nature in public service I am convinced there would be a reduction in the tragedies that often occur as the result of some mishandlings and misunderstandings."

scenes were shot in Brecon and also at Cardiff bus station. Entitled The People's Man, the 60-minute play was about a busman who was in revolt against the laxity of his colleagues who paid no heed to timetables and ran the service to suit themselves. Things reached boiling point when, to oblige a couple of soldiers who were anxious to catch a train in Cardiff, he left on time — without his conductor who was still enjoying a cuppa. Dismissal followed and then the men walked out in sympathy. The Western Welsh vehicles were unmistakable despite being labelled South Western.

A total of 11 men completed 40 years combined service while 20 completed 25 years. This brought the total with 25 years or more service to 405, a figure which the company regarded as a fine achievement in loyalty. Company chairman RC Hilton, in summing up his report at the AGM, stated: "Loyalty is indeed a heart-warming virtue, and with that in mind I will conclude by expressing the hearty thanks and appreciation of the directors to the whole staff of the company, who have, under the able leadership of the general manager, Ivor Gray, worked hard and well to provide that high quality of service all at Western Welsh are determined to maintain and enhance."

Company directors and chief officers made a tour of inspection in late September. They arrived at Porthcawl on a Tuesday evening, and on the Wednesday morning left their hotel in the latest Harrington Grenadier coach for the first stage of a visit which took them to Port Talbot, Neath, Ammanford, Carmarthen, Haverfordwest, St David's, Neyland and Milford Haven, where they spent the night. On Thursday the party visited Fishguard, New Quay and Newcastle Emlyn, from where they travelled to Swansea to catch the Paddington train.

A complimentary letter was received from Glamorgan County Council's divisional surveyor, which expressed appreciation at the courtesy and care taken by drivers while negotiating the lengthy road works at Kenfig Golf Course and Sarn Hill. The surveyor wrote: "With road works of this nature a certain amount of delay and obstruction is unavoidable, and throughout the whole course of these works your drivers have shown considerable patience and consideration to employees of my staff engaged there, and by their action have materially assisted in maintaining good relations."

A BBC TV play starring Glyn Houston in the role of a busman was screened late in the year. Western Welsh vehicles were used for the route sequences, and terminal

1965

The economies already implemented in West Wales had resulted in service reductions and staff redundancies in the Newcastle Emlyn area. This was followed by announcement of the proposed closure of Ammanford depot. It had been an uneconomic unit for some time, with the number of staff employed and vehicles allocated being disproportionate to the volume of work carried out. Moreover, the losses that had been incurred in rural traffic were now spreading to urban routes. Principal cause was declining reliability due to traffic congestion and staff shortages. In many parts of urban South Wales, BET and Tilling interests existed side by side. There was already a good working relationship between Western Welsh and Red & White with co-ordinated timetables over shared routes. Declining viability resulted in area co-ordinating agreements being set up as wider measures became necessary.

Bridgemaster 701 (PBO 701) near Broad Haven, on the Prendergast to Little Haven route in 1965. The service survived longer than most as Pembrokeshire routes were pruned, and was absorbed into South Wales Transport in March 1972. *John Jones*

Head Office staff returned to enlarged offices at Ely after eight years at the central bus station, vacating the first and second floors there. Construction costs of the new offices, together with improvements at Ely Works, including the new coach garage, totalled £105,119. As a result of the reorganisation, the entire administrative operation was centralised at Ely. The office extension virtually doubled the size of the existing building on Cowbridge Road West. It had two main floors and covered parking bays in the basement. Also vacating the central

bus station at the same time, Cardiff's clerical staff returned to Penarth Road after an absence of eight years. The Penarth Road offices, which already housed the area manager, chief clerk and the Express Service office, was completely redecorated and fitted with improved lighting and telephones.

In keeping with all major operators of bus and coach services in Britain, the 24 hour clock was adopted on all timetables and publicity, and came into effect with the

In 1964 a new limited-stop service was introduced, jointly with Rhondda Transport, between Maesteg and Cardiff. It served Pencoed and Llanharan, whose railway stations had recently closed under the Beeching cuts. One of 14 MCW-bodied, dual-purpose Tiger Cubs from 1960/1, 1268 (UKG 268), awaits departure at Maesteg's bus station which doubled up as the fire station yard, in 1965. *John Jones*

annual timetable, publication of which from this year changed to May 1. The new timetable booklets featured a breakaway cover design and conversion to the new specification presented the traffic department, and D Brown & Sons of Cowbridge, the company's printers, with an enormous task. Two staff members had been fully occupied for over six months on the preparation. Before the printers could begin their work, all 181 tables had to be written out in manuscript form, in addition to an Express Service section which was to become a standard feature of all future issues.

Following the successful launch of a South Wales to Merseyside express service in 1964, through bookings to Scotland were announced, utilising links with Ribble Motor Services and the Scottish Omnibus Group. The return fare from Cardiff to Glasgow was only 91s 5d (approximately £4.57) and was a good example of co-ordination between bus companies working to the advantage of the travelling public. Passenger numbers on this service soon exceeded all expectations, and at peak periods as many as six vehicles were operating in each direction. On summer Saturdays, Bishop's Meadow Café on the outskirts of Brecon became a 'mini-Cheltenham', where services connected for Newport, West Wales, Aberystwyth and Swansea. Portable bus stop signs and a tannoy system were used to ensure passengers boarded the correct coach.

Conductress Winnie James of Haverfordwest depot was a 'Personality of the Week' in the Western Telegraph newspaper which proclaimed: 'This slight, quick-witted and capable girl is known to thousands who go by bus. Winnie was one of the early conductresses of Green's Motors, and continues with Western Welsh. The elderly passengers, especially the women, regard her with affection and gratitude for her consideration and kindness. The younger with delight for her repartee and deft answers, and those who show a little too much liveliness on the late buses are handled with firmness and dexterity. Winnie certainly conducts her bus.'

To suddenly be confronted with a life-threatening situation while at the wheel has always been the fear of every busman. Sooner or later, most drivers face that moment when there is little that can be done to avoid disaster and everything that happens before them is in the lap of the gods. For driver Ray Thomas, a busy summer Saturday and the opportunity of a few hours overtime at the end of a hard week was too good to miss, but it was a day that he would never forget. "It was Saturday lunchtime, and I was making my way to the car to drive home, when the station inspector called me and asked if I wanted some overtime. Actually, it wasn't overtime, it was 'IA', which stands for In Addition. I don't know if it was the same in other depots, but that's how it was in Cardiff. I didn't really want to work on. It had been a long, hard week, and I would have liked to have finished there and then. But I needed the money, so I accepted his offer. He asked me to take a semi-coach and follow the Cardiff – Liverpool service, but only as far as Brecon, as it wouldn't pick up many more passengers. So I set off, following the Liverpool coach. When we reached Brecon I spoke to the other driver, and he agreed to go on alone, although he must have had at least 10 standing! He would only be dropping off from there, so I gladly turned round and headed for home, but it wasn't going to be such a straightforward journey as I had expected.

"With Brecon behind me, I was climbing the A470 towards the Beacons and although the road wasn't wide, two coaches could just about pass each other. It is a continuous uphill slog for many miles, and despite

A serious accident which led to its early withdrawal befell Tiger Cub 1093 (JBO 93) while on service near Neath in 1964.
Stewart Williams

Deep in Rhondda Transport territory in 1964 was highbridge Regent 667 (LKG 667), keeping company with a Rhondda vehicle. How the valley must have echoed with the sound of AECs plying their trade, day in, day out.
Viv Corbin

some serious IA! After about an hour, they phoned me back, took all my details and then said I could go. It was an awful experience and I never found out what happened to the driver."

Four new express services were introduced for the summer season. The most far-reaching provided a fast holiday service from Newport to Tenby and Saundersfoot, and a service ran on Saturdays via both the eastern and western valleys then through Tredegar, Merthyr, Ystradgynlais and Ammanford. These routes saved the through traveller from several changes of vehicle and also opened up opportunities for travel between intermediate points which had hitherto been poorly served by public transport.

The second new service ran from Brecon to Tenby via Llandeilo, Carmarthen and Haverfordwest, and connected at Bishop's Meadow with the X71 Liverpool service. It was anticipated that Tenby would prove a popular destination to Merseysiders wishing to visit beautiful West Wales for their holidays. Encouragingly, towards the end of the season it became necessary to introduce an extra trip, starting from Cardiff, to Aberystwyth via Newport, Crosskeys and Pontypool. The third new 'X' service was between Neyland and Aberystwyth, via Haverfordwest and serving the Pembrokeshire coast and Cardigan Bay resorts. It also proved a boon to passengers heading for Butlin's at Pwllheli, and for Liverpool, Birmingham and Manchester via connections at Aberystwyth. Finally came a service heading out of Wales, from Port Talbot to Minehead, picking up at Bridgend, Cardiff and Newport. With the opening of the Severn Bridge still a year off, the journey via Gloucester must have seemed endless and it is perhaps no surprise that this service, which always encountered considerable traffic congestion, was to prove the least remunerative of the four.

Despite the serious recessions in traffic carried overall, it can be seen from the above enterprises that every

wanting to get home I wasn't driving fast — I was on overtime, remember! The road ahead entered a left hand bend about 200 yards in front, from where a large car came into sight, driving towards me at what appeared to be a very fast speed. Just as it came around the bend the car hit the bank on its nearside, swerved across the road, then, still moving at an incredibly fast speed, hit the kerb on its offside. It did this a few times from one side of the road to the other, obviously out of control, and heading towards me. It then overturned and continued on its side, still heading my way. It was somersaulting very quickly towards me, and about 30 yards from the front of the coach, it hit the bank again, flipped around the other way and continued towards me, now rolling end to end, not side to side. By this time I had stopped, put on the handbrake and fled down the aisle, waiting for the crash. At the last moment it crashed down on to its roof and stopped, wheels turning, alongside the coach.

"I couldn't believe my luck. You can imagine how I felt. I was shaking. People were getting out of the cars that had stopped behind me. I told one of them I was going for help. I was also aware that I was blocking the road, being stopped directly alongside the wreck. I drove about half a mile to an AA box and phoned the police. They told me to wait there for a return call. This was turning into

The Tiger Cubs were still arriving in 1966 when Marshall-bodied 1388 (HBO 388D) was spotted new at Station Square, Neath on October 23 that year.
RL Wilson/Online Transport Archive

147

A coachbuilder puts the finishing touches to the latest Plaxton Panorama coach at Ely in 1966. *Stewart Williams*

Could things get any better than this? The Plaxton Panorama became coach of choice between 1965 and 1968, and it's easy to see why. How sumptuous were those seats, and how stylish the fittings. From floor to ceiling, the vehicles simply oozed quality that is only now being surpassed by 21st Century coachwork. *George Wedlake*

effort was being made to win back a proportion of lost custom. The smart new blue and ivory Tiger Cubs were employed on these services and it can now be seen that the company, in exploiting these new avenues of revenue, enjoyed something of a renaissance in their express services at this time.

For two weeks in May, 11 vehicles — three Harrington coaches, two Weymann coaches and six Willowbrook saloons — were converted into mobile showrooms for Bridgend-based furniture manufacturers, Christie-Tyler Ltd. Driven by Bridgend staff, the vehicles were sent around the country advertising the company's products and together covered 12,700 miles.

In the September Staff Bulletin, IL Gray's message consisted of a plea to drivers to react positively towards the ever-increasing need for economy. In citing that during the first eight months of the year there had been 311 known cases of 'own damage' to buses, the message was for extra care to be taken.

The figure was 92 more than that of the similar period the previous year and the cost to the company through repairs and loss of use was certain to amount to several thousand pounds.

He said that this was an opportunity for drivers to do something positive to help the company's economy. "Please be extra careful. Carelessness costs money," he told them.

The company's profit for the year 1964-65 was £84,130, described by company chairman AFR Carling, as

Bishops Meadow, near Brecon was the Welsh version of Cheltenham for the interchange of express services. During the heady years of the early 1960s, three dual-purpose saloons are en-route to Aberystwyth. The driver of 1494 (SBO 494) has had the sense to place the windscreen stickers away from his line of vision! *J Jones/CW Rowth*

disappointing, being £21,000 less than the previous year's result, which in itself was not a particularly good year. Gross revenue was £3,123,324, about £160,000 below expectation due to the disappointing yield from increased fares following the March wage increase. Cost-of-living related pay increases were rejected by the unions together with an offer to refer the difference to arbitration. Eventually, against a background of unofficial sporadic strikes, the Minister of Labour appointed a Committee of Inquiry which sat for four days in April. Known as The Wilson Report, its conclusions were announced in May with the result that wage increases more costly than those of 1964 were applied immediately. With changes in busmen's conditions of employment due the following year, all this added further to operating costs. Overall, the economies in stage-carriage mileage of some 180,000 miles a year should be viewed against 120,000 miles of new operations serving new housing estates or in substitution for withdrawn rail services. In addition the new summer express services added 70,000 miles. Meanwhile, extended holiday tours continued to go from strength to strength with a 27 per cent increase in bookings over the previous year. The low-cost spring and autumn tours in particular were proving extremely popular. Many customers were regular patrons who returned time after time to meet up with old friends and visit familiar places, often with a driver/courier that they had come to know as a friend. With the tours market buoyant, completion of the Severn Bridge was very much in the mind of the tours department.

EXPRESS SERVICE

FRIDAYS/
SATURDAYS,
SUNDAYS/
MONDAYS

9th JULY
to
6th SEPTEMBER

CARDIFF/NEWPORT
CROSSKEYS · PONTYPOOL · BISHOP'S MEADOW

ABERYSTWYTH

with connections for
LIVERPOOL · CAERNARVON · BANGOR

1966

The year began with the closure of Ammanford depot in January, some 21 years after the 'new' garage there had been opened. It was a sad time for those who knew something of the long and interesting background to bus operation in the town stretching back to the early days of the GWR.

The BET group was watching the political scene closely. A white paper from transport minister Barbara Castle proposed 'conurbation transport authorities' which were really Passenger Transport Authorities by another name. In South Wales, the large number of bus companies and operations may have seemed ideal for control by such an authority, so BET was sufficiently worried to mount an anti-nationalisation campaign. However, it wasn't to happen. Nevertheless, BET's view was that to sell at a good price was the only option.

Western Welsh orders for 1965 concluded late in the year with delivery of a batch of 14 Park Royal-bodied Tiger Cubs, 1361-1374. The first four to enter service did so before the registration suffix changed to D at the start of 1966, but the vehicles were numerically random. Vehicles 1361/3/5, seen at Ely, along with 1367, had a C suffix. They were attractive vehicles that didn't skimp on frontal treatment like the later Marshall bodies. They featured automatic heating and ventilation which accounted for the large roof vents. The new extension to Ely's head office accommodation can be seen in the background. *Stewart Williams*

Bridgend's 1474 (MKG 474) rests at Lias Road, Porthcawl on a sunny afternoon in 1968. The destination blind showing Kenfig Hill station reflects a bygone era. Western Welsh buses were undoubtedly the best shade of red. *Geoff Morant*

A further stage in the modernisation of Ely Works was reached with the opening of a new 46ft by 16ft paint-spraying bay. Such a feature had become an essential requirement, because the latest coaches were finished in cellulose which, due to its fast drying properties, could only be successfully applied by spraying. The fully enclosed bay was fitted with two air lines, one to each wall, for the operation of the spray guns. Two large extractor fans enabled a complete change of air every two minutes during spraying. While the bay initially only catered for coaches already finished in cellulose, it was anticipated that in time its operation would extend to other vehicles.

In the 1960s, in keeping with a long-held tradition, Western Welsh painted its vehicles once every two years on average, although its coaches were often re-painted annually. This meant that the Ely paint shop turned out about 24 repaints a month. It took four days to repaint a double-decker, and one gallon of paint was used for each coat. Single-deck vehicles took approximately three quarters of a gallon.

On older buses where the interior also had to be painted, the job usually took about a week. If the condition of the old paintwork was sound, vehicles were only given one coat after rubbing down and touching in, otherwise an undercoat was first applied.

By this time the job of the painters had been simplified by the use of an all-over red livery, and the signwriters' painstaking work of lining-out the black edging to the cream relief was a thing of the past.

In March an unsuccessful attempt was made to purchase the goodwill of Peakes of Pontypool for £7,500. The month also saw the death of Harry Barrett, the remaining co-founder of Eastern Valley Motors, aged 72.

A graphic reminder to road staff of the more gruesome side of bus operation appeared in the centrefold of the March Staff Bulletin.

The loneliness of the long-distance runner is temporarily relieved at Lammas Street, Carmarthen, where everybody, including the driver of brand-new dual-purpose Tiger Cub 1341 (DBO 341C), seems to have adjourned for a cuppa. These vehicles were capable of a nifty performance and the limited-stop run would have been accomplished very much with cuppa time built in!

Heading along Orchard Street, Neath in the summer of 1965, on the 301 Carmarthen to Cardiff service, Park Royal dual purpose bodied 1340 (DBO 340C) had only been delivered new a month or so before.

Illustrating the mangled remains of four of the company's buses which had met with serious accidents, readers were requested to 'spend a few minutes studying the photographs — they are surely more eloquent than words.' The photographs showed the results of three head-on collisions and an overturned Bridgemaster alongside a slain telegraph pole.

Statistics showed that most bus drivers, at some time, would be involved in an accident regardless of whether or not they were to blame. This was worrying, particularly as the increase in traffic was outpacing all efforts to modernise the country's inadequate road system. Figures revealed that during 1965, four people were killed and 275 were injured while travelling on the company's vehicles. There were 1,542 accidents resulting in 1,294 instances of damage and a repair bill of £10,290. The vehicles were out of action for a staggering 3,247 days. They were not pleasant facts, and the photographs didn't make pleasant viewing either, but if their publication resulted in drivers exercising 'an extra degree of caution' then they served their purpose.

The intention to forge a closer management link between Western Welsh and Rhondda Transport was the subject of the general manager's headline message in the April-May Staff Bulletin. It was suggested that such a move between the two companies was to be welcomed. "In order to dispel unfounded rumour I would like to emphasise that the arrangement does not amount to a take-over and that Rhondda will retain its individual identity," he added.

The 46th annual general meeting of the Western Welsh company was held on July 19, with chairman Carling presiding. Financial results had again been disappointing

Only two years old, and with two winters safely tucked up at Ely, Grenadier 147 (ABO 147B) is receiving its first repaint — into ivory and blue — in 1966. It was regarded as essential to have coaches looking as good as new for each season. As a result of this care, the vehicles continued to provide many years of service after being sold on by Western Welsh. Happily coaches 145 and 147 survive in active preservation.
Stewart Williams

showing a profit of only £68,509. The biggest new burden facing the company resulted from the wage award, the first and immediate effect of the previous year's Wilson Committee of Inquiry. That alone had increased costs to the tune of £140,000 a year. In addition, there were increases in National Insurance contributions, local rates and various other items of expenditure. They all added to the problem of recovering costs. The inevitable application to increase fares had been submitted in May 1965. Six weeks elapsed before this was brought to public hearing, and a further month before a decision was announced. The increase was granted, but only in part, and in August, cross-appeals to the Minister of Transport were lodged by objecting local authorities. These were heard in December, and in July, 14 months after the increase in costs, the company still awaited the final decision. Further consequences of the Wilson Report meant that the cost of its recommended sick pay scheme had to be

A telegraph pole on the Milford road seems to have halted the progress of Bridgemaster 699 (PBO 699) in this mid-1960s accident. Despite the damage. The bus returned to service after repair.

met, and from April, at even greater expense, came the cost of reducing the basic working week from 42 to 40 hours without loss of pay. Over a full year £144,000 had to be found, and even assuming the fares increase would be approved and introduced by August, there remained around £50,000 that would never be recovered. It was the true turning point of the company's fortunes, as profits were now falling steadily and this trend was to continue over the remaining years of the decade.

The British system of road service licensing and control of fares, with the due right of local authorities to object by appeal to the Minister, while fair and reasonable, had its pitfalls. It could be argued that if local authorities wished to be unscrupulous, they could delay the hearing of one application and, as a result, delay that which followed. Appeals could – and did – become routine and the recovery of bus operators' increased costs, a process already safeguarded in the public interest, could be

frustrated almost indefinitely. The chairman's message at the AGM called for reasonable expedition by the Ministry of Transport in dealing with both applications and appeals, as not to do so would result in an unfairness, not to the bus operators alone, but to their demoralised and unmotivated staff, who would witness the running-down of the undertaking until it could only offer a second-class service worked with shabby equipment from unkempt bases.

On the positive side, the chairman went on to mention the continuing success of the new express services for holiday traffic. In particular, the new Coast and Country limited-stop service between Brecon and Haverfordwest via Carmarthen and Tenby. This was very successfully worked by the latest coaches in the new blue and ivory livery. He also reported that extended tours continued to gain in popularity. In 1965 there were 282 separate departures to various parts of Britain.

It appears that a thoroughly patched-up 1065 (JBO 65) had been pressed into service at Bridgend on this occasion. It was rare to see a Western Welsh bus in service in such an unkempt condition.

Proudly waiting at Brecon under the eagle eye of the Duke of Wellington, Park Royal bodied Tiger Cub 1337 (DBO 337C) is about to set off for the seaside in 1965. It was one of 15 such vehicles to join the fleet in the new blue and ivory dual purpose livery that year. *Andrew Mann*

In terms of fixed assets, 29 new buses and 21 new coaches or semi-coaches had been introduced in the 1965/66 accounting year. In addition came improvements at Ely Works and Crosskeys depot. Concluding his AGM report, Mr Carling said: "As soon as we are helped to maintain a reasonable level of net revenue, I hope we shall be able to allocate the resources necessary to provide better working conditions for our staff at Penarth Road, and at Haverfordwest."

A new staff canteen was opened at Crosskeys depot in August, and the chairman seized the opportunity at the opening to warn of 'dire danger' ahead. He told staff that despite a fares freeze and continued economies, costs were rising — in particular due to the introduction of the

40 hour week which, without loss of pay amounted to a rise in earnings of between six and seven per cent. The £6,000 cost of the canteen came first from fares and later from what was described in the accounts as 'profits' — that part of the profit which was ploughed back into the company and not given to shareholders. "The same was true," he said, "of the money needed to bring any other depot, workshop or offices up to standard. Our accounts have to balance in the end."

Mr Carling appealed to those present to impress on anyone interested in Western Welsh, considered to be the biggest and best company in the whole of South Wales, "that it is in danger of being pushed downhill, through no fault of its own."

A rare view of a Western Welsh bus in Radnorshire. Service 738 was a rail replacement route operated jointly with Crosville's S23 with four journeys on weekdays between Rhayader and Newtown, and two extending to/from Brecon via Builth Wells. Brecon's 1261 (SBO 261) forms the 0900 departure from Rhayader in the summer of 1965. *J Jones/CL Caddy*

On a relief from its Brecon base in the summer of 1965, 1322 (ABO 322B) will return the crowds home later in the day. Service 750 was a marathon route of 95 miles which ran through to Haverfordwest, and assuming it left at 16.00 hrs it wouldn't arrive home until 19.45 hrs. *Arnold Richardson/Photobus*

Smiling faces all round, despite the misfortune of breaking down near the Severn Bridge on a trip to Weston-super-Mare at Easter 1968. With luck, 278 (WKG 278) wasn't last in the convoy and help was soon at hand. The passengers' happy demeanour is much in evidence, suggesting this was on the way back! *Mike Street*

The chairman's words were reiterated by the general manager in the July-August Staff Bulletin. "I commend his words to you. We are in a most difficult position and the future has never looked more uncertain. Perhaps the only glimmer of hope is that we have faced crises in the past and overcome them."

In August the maximum permitted speed for PSVs was increased to 50 mph. They had, of course, along with other vehicles, been unrestricted on the growing motorway network. The first Severn Bridge, construction of which had begun in 1961, was opened by the Queen and Duke of Edinburgh on September 8. General manager IL Gray accompanied by Mrs Gray were among guests invited to the opening, and no doubt they were very much aware of the opportunities the bridge would make available to the more forward-thinking coach operator. Western Welsh immediately explored the far greater range of destinations for day tours and excursions that were now within reach. Express services to resorts on the English side of the Bristol Channel were revised in time for the 1967 holiday season. Congestion on the A48 corridor to Gloucester and the Cotswolds was now non-existent. This provided the company with new and improved tour opportunities to the Midlands, and all within the scope of existing driver hours.

On the day of the opening of the bridge, two coaches from Neath depot were among the first vehicles to cross. Their drivers were Jim Moses and Lynn Whitney. The event did not go unnoticed by members of the company's educational club, who made a number of visits both by day and night, and were most impressed, particularly by the general illumination of the bridge and approach roads. Refreshment stops were made at Aust Services which offered an excellent view of the bridge.

Western Welsh and Red & White announced the integration of all their services within the Newport – Caerphilly – Tredegar – Abergavenny area. In setting up a traffic pool, it was envisaged that a better service would be provided using fewer vehicles. This scheme also involved Jones of Aberbeeg, together with Bedwas & Machen and Gelligaer UDCs, and once fully integrated, would lead to the closure of several depots. While fewer single-deck vehicles were needed, a significant expansion of the Western Welsh double-decker fleet in the area was needed, but company engineers decreed that the AEC

Bridgemasters then being used were not suited to the valleys, and so were banished to West Wales to enjoy a quieter life. It had originally been intended to send Atlanteans to West Wales to bring about much-needed one-man operation, but as a result of the Monmouthshire scheme, this never happened. Instead West Wales received the Bridgemaster vehicles together with the second batch of Renowns. Sadly their lack of one man facilities was responsible for hastening the eventual loss of the entire area. With hindsight, perhaps the situation could have been saved had the one-man operation proposals been handled differently.

Another improvement was the result of greater co-operation with neighbouring bus companies and British Railways. This led to more comprehensive timetables. That for the Swansea area, a virtual 'no-go' zone throughout the life of Western Welsh, now at least carried detailed information about connecting bus and train services.

In October, the mid-Glamorgan area saw cut-backs with the closures of the Port Talbot garage, together with its outstations at Kenfig Hill and Glyncorrwg. The cumulative effects of the economic squeeze and the refusal of the company's fare increase application were to blame, and while alternative employment at Bridgend and Neath depots was offered, there were few takers. The closures resulted in 50 redundancies.

November 21 is a date firmly etched on the minds of many aged over 60 in South Wales. It was a day when 144 people, 116 of them children, were killed when a colliery tip slid onto Aberfan's village school. The tragedy has been well documented, but little has been reported of the part Western Welsh played in providing practical assistance during the disaster. Drivers from Cardiff depot volunteered to do several jobs without pay, as explained by area manager Ivor Day: "We were called upon at short notice to provide drivers on a Saturday evening and without hesitation at least six volunteered. Since then we have been requested to supply further vehicles and again we have not had the least difficulty in obtaining the free services of the staff."

An article in the Christmas edition of the Staff Bulletin payed tribute to driver Percy Coles from Crosskeys depot. Percy was born in 1917 and left school at 14 to work as an assistant at a local grocery. Bus work offered the sort of security Percy needed and by sheer perseverance he eventually persuaded area manager Danny Williams to give him a start as a conductor at Crosskeys. He worked the Newport – Caerphilly – Bargoed service and recalled the friendly relationships between passengers and staff. "It was not unusual to receive bottles of wine and boxes of cigarettes at Christmas and when I got married I was given several presents." he said.

After wartime service with the RAF, in which he drove through Europe and sailed to Australia and the Far East, Percy was promoted to the driving grade in 1946 and for many later years was one of the hand-picked team of extended tour driver/couriers.

A lovely study of Northern Counties bodied AEC Renown 726 (BKG726C) at Newport in 1968.
Tony Jenkins

Before and after: Olympian 1487 (OUH 487) left, has arrived at Ely in 1966 for a visit to the paint shop, where it will emerge in bus livery identical to 1489, right. These vehicles officially saw out their final years on stage services. In practice they had already been demoted to this work for some time, and only received repaints at their standard two-yearly recall. *Stewart Williams*

1967

In January, it was announced that a road widening scheme and new river bridge at Penarth Road in Cardiff would necessitate the demolition of part of the company's offices.

Buses it seems were being demolished too! Not for the first time did a decapitated Leyland Atlantean double-decker limp into Ely Works for repair. Bus 329 needed works attention in 1966, and now a year later 308 suffered identical damage when it hit a low railway bridge in Monmouthshire. Fortunately, no serious injuries were recorded in the incident.

Work had been going on behind the scenes for two years to streamline the operations of Western Welsh and R&W

services in the Monmouthshire valleys. Dubbed 'C' Day, the Monmouthshire Co-ordination Scheme took effect on Sunday, June 4 and was in line with the views expressed by the area's local authorities. The Minister of Transport had called for voluntary co-ordination measures. These were necessary for survival and enabled vital savings to be made for both companies. The operators now participated in a traffic pool on the basis of a 50/50 share of revenue and mileage. Against this background the two companies set about the task of streamlining their operations.

Many of the area's bus routes had outlived their usefulness, were no longer ideal to the travelling public and were ripe for revision in one way or another. Many of the towns in the upper reaches of the valleys had experienced a population drift southwards as the

More than 30 Western Welsh vehicles were hired by Gulf Oil for the opening of its Milford Haven refinery by the Queen in August 1968. At the height of the summer season the entire coach fleet, except those on tour, gathered at the Royal Naval Air Station, Brawdy, to collect passengers from incoming aircraft. They had a police escort to the Haven. *Stewart Williams*

The cream and the black have gone, but there's still a touch of Gray. All-Leyland 979 (FKG 979) is at Broad Haven in 1967, smartly turned out in its final guise. *John Jones*

traditional industries had been run down, a situation accentuated by the development of the new town at Cwmbran. The measures that resulted were expected to reduce overall mileage in the area by 10 per cent, bring about a saving of between 20 and 30 buses and yet avoid any large scale service reductions. Indeed many service frequencies were increased, mainly in Cwmbran, where a complete reorganisation of routes was planned to provide for its needs.

Much thought and careful consideration had been given to the scheme, and it was decided that Pontypool's Pontnewynydd depot had to close, along with the R&W garages at Abertillery and Blackwood. The Western Welsh outstation at Abergavenny was also reduced in status and its allocation of five single-deckers cut to one. In an attempt to avoid undue infringement, discussions with the other main operators in the area took place with the result that Jones of Aberbeeg were brought into the pool immediately, along with Bedwas & Machen UDC, who participated jointly in the Newport to Caerphilly service with Western Welsh, their buses operating through to Bargoed. This was followed by Gelligaer UDC shortly afterwards, which resulted in their vehicles running into Newport. Following the reorganisation of services, Pontypool depot closed in April. Most of its staff transferred to Cwmbran.

The scheme brought even-interval services to joint WW/R&W routes, new limited-stop services down the valleys to Cardiff and Newport, and enabled more through services together with through ticketing. A total of 66 new licences were approved for the company and

a further 27 existing licences were varied. Red & White gained 62 new licences, and varied a further 21. In all, Western Welsh surrendered 31 licences, and R&W 23. The Monmouthshire Co-ordination Scheme was viewed by all as an example of what could be done within the industry to improve not only efficiency, but also the image of public transport.

An unusual overtime turn for Ray Thomas was a run from Cardiff prison to Newport law courts with a 30-seat Albion Nimbus. "I drove into the prison courtyard after the security checks and saw lots of prisoners there. I waited for around 10 minutes with the Nimbus doors firmly closed! Then I saw about 10 prisoners and the same number of prison officers approaching the bus. They all piled in, the gate swung open and off we went to Newport.

"As we arrived at the courts, one of the prison officers directed me to the back entrance. As we got nearer, I could see a large garage with several police cars parked inside. I was instructed to drive right in, and head for a door in the corner which led to the court. This I did, but as we were about to draw up, there was an almighty crash! I was the first one out of the bus, and quickly looked around to see what I had collided with. Meanwhile, all my passengers disappeared into court. I couldn't see anything obvious, but then noticed the roof vent had become jammed under a concrete beam which ran across the ceiling of the garage. Because all the passengers had got off and there was no longer their weight on the suspension, the Nimbus was well and truly stuck under the beam. I asked someone working in the

Bodywork by Park Royal was chosen for Tiger Cubs ordered by Western Welsh in 1965. These attractive vehicles were split between C and D registrations as most didn't enter service until early 1966. Negotiating the one-way system at Water Street, Port Talbot, is 1362 (FUH 362D) plying its trade on the 602 Porthcawl to Merthyr service. *RF Mack*

garage if there was a way I could get the prison officers back on the bus so I could reverse out. He told me they would be in the canteen, and basically I would have to manage without them. I spotted an air line, and thought I might let the front tyres of the bus down, free the bus from under the beam, then pump them back up again. But my luck wasn't in as the air line wouldn't reach the front tyres, and so I couldn't use it. I let them down gradually and evenly, until I could edge the Nimbus out from under the beam.

"Then I drove back to Penarth Road with very heavy steering. When I got back, the tyre fitter checked the pressure, and said both front tyres were about 80psi. I think they should have been 120psi," he said.

At the 47th Annual General Meeting in July, a resolution was passed that 50 per cent of the company's directors would in future be from the THC. The chairman, AFR Carling, in his address to the shareholders, commented on the results of another difficult year's trading as being thoroughly unsatisfactory, profit had dropped further to just £48,027.

"When one considers that we have the largest road passenger undertaking in South Wales, and one which is basically healthy — last year it still carried 47 per cent more passengers than in the year before the war — it will be realised that there is something seriously out of adjustment," he said.

The action of the Traffic Commissioners and Minister of Transport, by keeping fares low, had created a disproportionate and unreasonable effect upon the company. In short the company wasn't allowed to generate enough extra revenue to offset the general increase in wages and decisions on the appeals that followed were not made known for over a year — on the day after the Prime Minister had announced a price freeze. The cost of the new sick pay scheme and 40-hour week, both further findings of the Wilson Report, were also taking their toll. Thus, when the Commissioners eventually did hear the application, the 'standstill' had become decisive and, despite other bus companies being allowed their retrospective revenue, Western Welsh's was refused. Further anomalies became apparent when fresh applications were invited. Once again, in December, these were turned down by the commissioners. Despite an appeal in February and a recommendation by the inspector that it be allowed in March, transport minister Barbara Castle announced her rejection of it on June 29. In the circumstances, had it not been for the strenuous efforts of the management to economise, the company's financial position would have been much worse than it actually was.

During the summer it was found necessary for the chief engineer to warn about the problem of overheating vehicles, caused by drivers allowing engines to labour in too high a gear while climbing hills. It appears that the 1300 series of Tiger Cub saloons and semi-coaches were

A second batch of dual purpose vehicles — 1375-1384 — arrived in time for the 1966 summer season, this time with bodywork by Marshall. A further 10 service buses completed the order. Heading out of Cardiff along Cowbridge Road West, is 1379 (HBO 379D) while hot on its heels is one of the N&C's 'Brown Bombers' heading for Swansea. *RF Mack*

particularly susceptible. Their cooling fan speed was proportionate to engine revs and too high a gear on hills, coupled with low road speed meant low engine speed which restricted the flow of air through radiators and caused inefficient cooling. In truth, the Leyland 400 engines were underpowered compared to AEC's 470 or 505, and on hilly routes the drivers had their work cut out maintaining engine revs.

In November, the first section of Cardiff's latest one-way traffic scheme came into operation, aimed at relieving congestion in the crowded Central Square and Wood Street area. The latter now carried two lanes of traffic travelling west, with eastbound vehicles following a new route via Scott Road, Park Street and Westgate Street. From this point vehicles leaving the central bus station would only have two one-way lanes of traffic to cross Wood Street, instead of four.

Further to BET's fears for the future, in November the whole of its empire in England and Wales in which the state already held the former railway companies' shares, was sold to THC, the successor to the BTC of 1948, for £35m. From then on, all associated operating companies came under common ownership. All that remained to be done was the formal setting-up of the nation's government-owned bus company. A despondent Mr Gray was quoted as saying: "Whatever the outcome of plans to reshape the road

passenger transport system in this country, the same essential ingredients will be required to make it work efficiently, These are loyalty, integrity and enthusiasm. I have always considered our staff to be above average where these qualities are concerned and I hope they will continue to foster them in the future."

Leaving Forse's garage, Kingsway, Cardiff, with a private party is 1328 (ABO 328B), one of six Willowbrook Tiger Cubs, delivered in an ivory and red scheme. Fitted with luggage boots and used on express services they were a stop-gap measure pending arrival of the smart blue and ivory Park Royal semi-coaches in 1965. *J Jones/M Hodges*

159

Dawning of the decline

Takeover leads to sad end of an era

Following the sale of the BET companies, the Transport Act of 1968 allowed for the setting up of the National Bus Company to control both the Tilling and BET interests. Under the Act, local authorities were permitted to make grants to operators to retain rural services. Most major operators were reluctant to go down this road, preferring instead to cross-subsidise from their better routes. However, it soon became evident that this was not going to provide a workable solution. They realised that it was no longer possible to run certain services without such local authority grants.

The decline in the number of Western Welsh passengers year on year in the late 1960s tells the story in very stark terms. Few who consider the declining figures that the years ahead would bring would fail to see just how significant the problem really was. Initially the annual percentage drop could be measured in single figures, but by the end of the decade they were into double digits and while passengers declined, the percentages climbed ever higher. In 1967 there was a 7.5 per cent drop which by 1968 had increased significantly to 9.5 per cent. Sadly, the downward trend finally hit double figures in 1969 with a 10 per cent drop, and this continued unabated into the 1970s with the decade starting at an unprecedented 11.6 per cent fall.

When the National Bus Company formally came into being in January 1969, it took over the bus interests of the THC, that is to say it brought all the former BET, Tilling and BTC companies together under one umbrella.

Initially, few changes were visible following the NBC's formation, but within a few years things were to alter beyond all recognition.

To mark the centenary of Solomon Andrews, the pioneer of horse bus operations in Cardiff, a surviving horse bus was restored by the Andrews company in 1968 and paraded through the city. Western Welsh and Cardiff Corporation staff were invited to the event and are seen here at the launch. Among Western Welsh employees present and standing in front of the horse bus are Stewart Williams, second from left; Leslie Gray, third from left; Fred Pengelly, second from right and EGA Singleton, far right. *Christine Davies*

1968

In March, plans were announced for the replacement of Haverfordwest depot at a projected cost of £70,000. The premises inherited from Green's was just a collection of ramshackle buildings that lacked the standard of facilities expected by both passengers and employees.

To mark the centenary of the Cardiff transport business of Solomon Andrews, pioneer of horse buses in the city, an exhibition and parade was held to which Western Welsh and Cardiff Corporation staff were invited. An original horse bus, restored to perfection by the present day Andrews' firm, was used in the parade, and was respectfully followed by one of the latest Western Welsh AEC/Plaxton coaches.

Members of the Educational Club enjoyed a busy season, visiting Powis Castle in July, and Creigiau Potteries in August. In October they travelled to Blackpool for the Illuminations, and enjoyed a show by the much loved comedian Tommy Cooper.

The £30 million Gulf Oil Refinery at Milford Haven was opened by The Queen on August 10. An important requirement for the Gulf Corporation was the movement of guests, and to meet this they hired a fleet of Western Welsh vehicles in the form of 25 coaches, two semi-coaches and four double-deckers. The coaches were drawn from 10 different depots and all equipped with public address systems for use by Gulf couriers in describing the installation to guests when touring the refinery. The West Wales drivers were smartly turned out for the event, in white shirts and black ties, which added an extra touch to the occasion.

In the morning, nine coaches proceeded under police escort to the Royal Navy Air Base at Brawdy to meet guests who had flown in from Pennsylvania on two Corvair aircraft, and an Eagle Britannia from Glasgow, Edinburgh and Manchester. The remaining 16 coaches met special trains at Milford Haven station. Later a party of 300 children was conveyed to a special viewing area where they were able to see the Royal party arrive at the jetty to board a tender for the Royal yacht Britannia.

Mr IL Gray joined the board of directors, while at the same time the company chairman AFR Carling was elected President of the Institute of Transport.

Time recording clocks, a once familiar feature on many of the company's routes, particularly in the eastern and western valleys of Monmouthshire, had all but disappeared by 1968, rendered surplus to operational needs by the introduction of pooling schemes. However two clocks remained in operation on the 240 and 244 routes, where in addition to the joint operation by Western Welsh and Rhondda, the Beddau to Pontypridd section of route was supplemented by the Amalgamated Bus Services (ABS) of Messrs Bebb, Edwards and Maisey. These services, although co-ordinated with inter-availability of tickets, didn't benefit from the sophistication of a pooling scheme.

The clocks were located at the Three Horse Shoes, Tonteg and at East Glamorgan Hospital. To safeguard against unfair poaching, the system required that, as each bus reached the timing point, the conductor recorded the time of departure by inserting a key in the clock which then registered the time on a tape. The tapes were analysed weekly at the offices of ABS, where a representative was present to agree the imposition of fines: two shillings per minute for being up to five minutes late, or 10/- for being more than five minutes late or if he had failed to clock. There was no fine for early running.

A particularly nasty road accident occurred at Leckwith Hill, Cardiff, in August. One of Barry's Leyland Leopards, 610, came into contact with a car at the bottom of the hill, ploughed through a bridge parapet and came to rest hanging perilously over a 30ft drop. As a result, 24 passengers returning from Barry Island were treated in hospital and the bus driver, Stan Glover from Barry, suffered minor back injuries. The car driver was killed, and a child at play below the bridge narrowly escaped being hit by falling masonry.

It was reported that, on average, four accidents involving Western Welsh vehicles took place every day of the week. "This may seem an alarming figure," wrote Leslie Gray in April, "but to view matters in their correct perspective it should be explained that in round figures we have in service 560 vehicles operating something like 20 million miles annually." Yet again, his underlying message was of the need to take extra care as the ever-increasing cost of repairs was an unwelcome burden. "We must regret every accident, but those that worry me are the ones that could be avoided." he added.

The final 11-month period under BET control, from April 1967 to February, 1968 returned a profit of £49,677. With the final month of the 1967/68 financial year included in the first calendar year's figures under THC, the profit was recorded as £77,842.

Taking a party on extended tour was the highlight of many a driver's career with Western Welsh, particularly as they could choose the work if they felt they were suitable, having gained a degree of seniority in the ranks. It was an enjoyable and rewarding job for those cut out for it, as Ray Thomas recollects: "I can think of lots of amusing incidents that happened in the time I occupied such a role. One I will never forget came about on a 'Grange-over-Sands and Lake District' tour. We were enjoying lunch at the usual hotel in Penrith when one of the waiters called me to the phone. I went into the office, picked up the phone, and to my surprise it was the foreman fitter at Ely Works. He asked me to confirm the number of my coach, which I did, and then he said he wanted me to have the vehicle checked out at the Ribble depot in Grange-over-Sands as soon as possible. He asked

Express route to summer

Express Services which operated during the 1968 season were as follows:

X11   Cardiff – Aberystwyth via Llandrindod Wells

X12   Cardiff – Aberystwyth via Lampeter

X13   Cilfynydd – Aberystwyth via Aberdare

X14   Bridgend – Aberystwyth via Neath

X15   Neath – Aberystwyth via Swansea

X18   Neyland – Aberystwyth via Cardigan

These Aberystwyth express services ran on Saturdays only from May 18 to September 28 and upon arrival provided connections for the resorts on the Lleyn peninsula (including the Butlin's Holiday Camp at Pwllheli), Caernarvon and Llandudno; also to Wolverhampton, Birmingham and the East Midlands; and to the Manchester area.

X20   **Cardiff – New Quay via Cardigan**

This ran on Saturdays only from June 29 to September 7 and consisted of one return journey.

X30   **Cardiff – Tenby via Neath**

X31   **Newport – Tenby via Eastern Valley**

X32   **Newport – Tenby via Western Valley**

This group of services ran on Saturdays only from June 1 to September 14.

X71   **Cardiff – Liverpool via Mid Wales**

This ran daily from May 25 to October 14 with the 1315 Cardiff – Liverpool and 0800 Liverpool – Cardiff, and extended from and to Butlin's Holiday Camp at Barry Island on summer Saturdays. Connections were provided at Newtown to and from Caernarvon, Bangor and Holyhead. On Friday nights from June 1 to September 21, an overnight journey operated from Liverpool to Butlin's, Barry Island, returning to Liverpool on the Saturday.

X80   **Neath – Minehead via Severn Bridge**

This service operated on Saturdays only from May 11 to October 5.

X81   **Neath – Liverpool via Merthyr and Mid-Wales**

This was a new feeder service and ran on Fridays, Saturdays and Mondays from 5th April, connecting with the X71 service at Merthyr.

At first glance this could be your average Albion Nimbus in Ely Works for overhaul. However, all is not what it seems. No. 27's Weymann body has been mounted on the unique Bristol LHS6L chassis that became No 1 (MBO 1F) in April 1968. The bodywork has been altered to allow for the Bristol's longer wheelbase, resulting in a smaller boot space. The 'new' vehicle was fitted with blue tartan moquette seats and finished in blue and ivory livery. It was also the first vehicle in the fleet to be fitted with reflective number plates. It was very fast, but did not possess the braking capability to match! *Viv Corbin*

me to write down the following and then read it back to him. I wrote: 'Please check the hose between the unloader valve and the compressor. One has broken up on a similar coach.'

"We set off after lunch, and it wasn't until I was driving over the very steep Kirkstone Pass that I started wondering what the message meant. Bearing in mind this was a new coach, I thought it couldn't be anything serious. I eventually convinced myself that this hose breaking up might affect the brakes on the coach. I went all hot and started sweating — it was a hot day anyway. By now I was becoming really worried. I remember thinking that it was a good thing the passengers didn't know. We got back without incident. I had the hose checked at the garage and breathed a sigh of relief when

I was told everything was fine. I discovered later that someone had fitted ordinary water hose instead of air pressure hose, and that was the reason for the phone call. I never really found out if that fault could have caused the brakes to fail, but at the time I was convinced we were all going to die!

"A few weeks later I was taken off the Cardiff to Penarth run and told to report to Ely for training on the new Plaxton coaches. I'd already taken three of them away for a week at a time! The most remarkable thing to come out of that was being told that if ever we were away somewhere and the windscreen shattered, then the rear windscreen was a direct replacement. Very useful but I don't think the passengers would have endured touring without a rear window for long!"

Senior driver/courier Cliff Harley from Bridgend assists his passengers in boarding for the next leg of an extended tour to the south-east of England in 1969. The coach is 176 (OUH 176G) a Plaxton Elite-bodied Leyland Leopard.

1969

A new government bus grant of 25 per cent of the cost of new vehicles was announced. This was broadly welcomed and available on all purchases, subject to certain conditions regarding the equipment to be fitted.

The popular Day-Out tickets, which had been available on Western Welsh buses since 1964, became available over a much wider area thanks to Rhondda Transport and Red & White allowing their routes to be covered by the 12/6d ticket. Known as the Five Counties Day-Out ticket, it could now be used in an area stretching from Swansea to Gloucester and from Hereford and Brecon to the Glamorgan coast. Also, in a measure designed to keep abreast of the increasing trend towards a five-day working week, weekly tickets, traditionally available for six return journeys from Monday to Saturday, were now available for journeys to be made within 28 days of issue, and in effect allowed multi-journey travel at any time and in either direction between the points covered.

Pontyberem depot closed at the end of January, bringing to an end a chapter of Western Welsh history which began in 1935 with the purchase of the Pontyberem and District Transport company. Of the six staff members affected by the closure, only one took up the offer of alternative employment at Carmarthen depot, the remainder accepted redundancy. The traffic manager wrote a deserved letter of congratulation to driver Llew Thomas of the ill-fated depot. He had achieved a worthy record of never having lost a day's work through illness since joining the industry in 1930. He was due to retire in March, but stayed on as caretaker pending sale of the premises. What a poignant period that must have been for him, strolling around an empty depot surrounded by

a lifetime's memories. As Pontyberem closed, the Blue Street office in Carmarthen was put on the market. With the closure of Pontyberem, Western Welsh's share of service 612 Ammanford to Llanelli operated jointly with West Wales Motors was taken over by South Wales Transport. The other service with which Pontyberem had an interest, 401 Carmarthen to Pontyberem and Llanelli, was altered so that operation became the sole responsibility of Carmarthen depot.

Western Welsh as a major rural operator suffered more than most as passenger numbers continued to plummet. Local authority supported services in Brecon and Cardigan saw only minor reductions, but its hold on Carmarthen and Pembroke declined rapidly. Carmarthenshire County Council tended to favour local operators, while Pembrokeshire chose to subsidise none. For this reason, operations at Fishguard and St David's would cease within just two years.

In March, chief officials, area managers, head office staff and friends paid tribute to Lyndon Rees, who was leaving to take up a post with the Ministry of Overseas Development in Hong Kong. Traffic manager Fred Pengelly, presenting him with an inscribed tankard and writing case at his farewell party in Cardiff, said: "It has been a pleasure to see Lyndon make such good progress in the industry. He has worked extremely hard and efficiently with Western Welsh and is an outstanding prospect." He had played a significant part in the setting up of the Monmouthshire Area Co-ordination Scheme and, in a further presentation on behalf of area officials, Crosskeys area manager, IL Phillips also paid tribute to Lyndon's ability and pleasant personality. Representatives from R&W Services and RTC were also in attendance. In his reply, Lyndon thanked everybody for their kindness and stressed how much he appreciated the opportunities he had been given, and the confidence shown in him, which, he said, had been invaluable in helping him to obtain his new post.

Closure of the parcels department came about in March, with the business in the Cardiff and Bridgend areas taken over by National Carriers Ltd, formerly British Rail Sundries Division. This section of the company's activities had begun back in SWCM days, but had been uneconomical for some time. The conveyance of newspapers continued by service bus.

An experimental winter Sunday timetable was tried out on the 825 Tenby local service from mid-April, until the full summer Sunday service began. The two return journeys to Saundersfoot were undertaken by Silcox Motors vehicles on hire to Western Welsh.

The Leyland Atlantean had evolved during the mid-1960s and now returned to the Western Welsh order books. Drop axles now allowed for a lower floor line so that a conventional highbridge seating layout could be achieved within a body built to lowbridge dimensions. These vehicles could operate on routes which had hitherto been out of bounds to double deckers, such as at Newbridge, where there was a clearance of only 13ft 7ins. Special dispensation was granted which enabled the vehicles to qualify for the Government's newly-introduced bus grant. Under the scheme 10 vehicles were bought.

In Cardiff, measures were at last taken to improve traffic congestion which had placed an intolerable strain on the city's roads and hit the bus industry particularly hard. Progress on several schemes was evident by the summer

Marshall-bodied Leopard 635 (PKG 635G) was fitted with extra brightwork in 1970 to gauge official opinion for the body styling of the dual purpose vehicles then on order. Many would agree that 635 was without doubt one of the prettiest buses in the fleet. *Viv Corbin*

including the widening of Penarth Road bridge. The Penarth Road depot itself was threatened with a compulsory purchase order due to the Hook Road scheme. Other major schemes included renewal of Ely and Wood Street bridges, Rumney Hill and the three-level interchange at Gabalfa. In the Vale of Glamorgan, the opening of a new road around Rhoose Airport with the consequent rerouting of the Barry to Llantwit Major service led to some criticism of the dangerous crossing

It probably wouldn't happen today. In December 1969 resurfacing work at the junction of Cardiff's Central Square and Wood Street meant that services couldn't leave the bus station by its only exit. To solve the problem a section of the low perimeter wall was removed and a lorry load of tarmac used to smooth over the kerb. Leaving via this temporary exit is 910 (910 DBO) on its way home to Barry. Standing here In later years, the onlooker would have been faced with at least a dozen Cardiff Buses queuing for several minutes to get through the traffic lights. *Mike Street*

Newly-delivered Atlantean 368 (PKG 368H) shows off its sparkling paintwork at Cardiff's central bus station shortly before setting off on route 303 for Cadoxton in 1969. *RL Wilson/Online Transport Archive*

of the main road near Porthkerry caravan site. As a result Barry staff were issued with a notice that when operating the school bus from Rhoose they should warn the children to be careful when they crossed the road. A letter from the Headmaster of Rhoose County Primary School was received by the Barry area manager which said: "May I express my gratitude for the co-operation of the conductors and drivers of the buses which drop the children at Porthkerry caravan site. I understand that your staff generally ensure that the children have safe conduct across the road at this extremely dangerous spot. It is particularly gratifying to know of the assistance which they have given, outside their normal duties, to safeguard the lives of these children. I hope that my appreciation may be passed on to those concerned."

In July, co-ordinated services began with N & C Luxury Coaches on the Briton Ferry — Cardiff corridor, along which N&C services were retimed to dovetail into a 20 minute headway with Service 301. In addition, the N&C services now observed the 301's stopping places. This was a short-sighted move which affected punctuality on an already tight schedule and was the beginning of the end for the N&C company. The co-ordinated timetable had in fact been under discussion for some time. An application to the Traffic Commissioners was hastened by the bringing together under common ownership of the two companies as subsidiaries of the NBC in January. Western Welsh benefitted from the new arrangement and it was found that 70-seater crew-operated Atlanteans had to be used on certain peak journeys in lieu of the 41-seat semi-coaches. As a result these journeys had to be re-routed via Westgate Street because of a weight restriction on Wood Street bridge.

There were a number of changes to the express service network for the summer season. Service X30 was given a more direct route between Neath and Carmarthen enabling the overall journey time from Cardiff to Tenby to be reduced by half an hour each way. Morriston and Pontardulais, which were no longer included on the X30 route, were transferred to the X31/32 from Newport, which now ran from Glynneath via the Vale of Neath to Morriston and Pontardulais; in doing so this service also resulted in a saving of half an hour each way. The X71 Liverpool service was also speeded-up, and on Saturdays during July and August a new through express service operated from Tenby via Carmarthen, Llandeilo, Brecon and mid-Wales, dispensing with the need to change coaches at Brecon.

Back in 1958, work had been completed around the depots to accommodate the Setright ticket system. It was a system designed to speed up the collection of fares and to economise in clerical labour. Now, little over a decade later, Almex ticket machines were introduced for use by one-man personnel operating from Neath, Aberdare, Cardiff and Crosskeys depots. These machines were hugely inferior and calculated fares in pence only, the often indecipherable ticket being little more than a postage stamp in size.

In October Leslie A Gray retired as assistant chief engineer after 50 years, so ending an association which dated back to just after the First World War when SWCM was formed with his father Albert as general manager. "There are still quite a few members of head office and Ely Works staff with whom I have enjoyed a close and happy relationship for well over 40 years together with road staff," wrote Mr Gray.

"There are supervisors and craftsmen who I remember engaging as apprentices and there are many sons and even grandsons of former associates.

"To these people and to staff everywhere I express my sincere thanks for the friendly co-operation on duty and also on social occasions, which has made the job satisfying at all times. Included in these few words of farewell I must, of course, remember the Educational Club and the Ely Works Welfare Club, the management committees of which have done so much in cementing friendships between all grades of staff within the company."

A letter was received at the traffic manager's office during the first week in December which read: "Dear Sir, On Tuesday December 2, while my daughter was travelling from Cardiff to Port Talbot on the 13.45hrs service, she became ill near Cowbridge. She was eventually admitted to Bridgend General Hospital where her appendix was removed and she is now progressing well. I would like to express my great appreciation of the action of the crew of the bus in arranging for an ambulance to meet her at Bridgend and for all the kindness they showed to her. Perhaps you could pass on to them a father's grateful thanks, since I have no way of knowing who they are and thanking them personally. I have no doubt they will say it was all in a day's work, but I feel deeply in their debt."

The driver of the bus was L A Beaton from Neath depot, and Frank Ringrose of head office also rendered assistance. In his reply, traffic manager FH Pengelly wrote: "To receive such a letter is a refreshing change as almost

During an extended tour in Scotland, a car attempted to squeeze through the narrow gap between a coach and a grass verge in Tomintoul and a slight collision resulted in the trafficator of the coach being damaged. Nothing particularly unusual about that, but driver/courier Ron Vaughan of Cwmbran was surprised to discover that the driver of the car was Queen Elizabeth, the Queen Mother! Royalty of another kind appeared alighting from one of the company's coaches in the Vale of Glamorgan village of Llancarfan during September. Heads turned in disbelief and TV cameras rolled as a King in full military uniform, ermine and crown, stepped down from the vehicle. It was in fact a scene from the company's 10th TV advertisement featuring Welsh actor Hugh Smith-Marriott. Soon after Harlech TV viewers would have been able to see the company's 30 and 60-second adverts on Saturdays around Christmas and early January.

everybody one comes into contact with these days is complaining about something or other. We were glad to be of service."

The total number of passengers carried in 1969 was 51 million. Mileage amounted to 19.7 million. Revenue for the year was £3.2 million and a profit of £50,435 was recorded. General manager IL Gray wrote of the company's mixed fortunes in the autumn Staff Bulletin. He remarked that the company's spring and autumn tours had, in the first week of booking shown an increase of 300 over 1968, which was itself a record year. Things however couldn't have been any more different when it came once again to stage carriage services. While the growth of holiday traffic was a source of satisfaction, it was from the ordinary services that the company got its daily bread. He told the bulletin's readers: "As most of you will be aware, our recent application to increase fares was only partially granted, so we are in the unhappy position of taking less than we require for healthy survival. In addition we must expect to lose more customers if past experience is a guide. This situation is not unique to Western Welsh and the ultimate solution to the problem has yet to be found. What we can do to keep losses to a minimum, however, is offer the public first-class service for their money and see that every fare is collected. Then at least we can console ourselves that we are doing our utmost to keep the company's head above water."

Traffic was light on the A48 at Tumble Hill, Wenvoe and so 287 (WKG 287) should have had no problem keeping time on its journey to Carmarthen in 1964.
Gerald Truran

1970

As passenger numbers continued to fall, staff at Carmarthen depot were told that the town services, which were still fully crew-operated, were no longer viable and that one-man operation must begin immediately. The depot was clearly under serious threat of closure.

With Pembrokeshire County Council's stubborn and possibly illegal refusal to grant-aid its constituents' rural bus services, the Western Welsh hold on Pembroke declined rapidly. Decimation of many life-lines began when services 409, New Quay-Talgarreg-Llandyssul; 803, Haverfordwest – Llandeloy-St David's; 815, Haverfordwest – Bolton Hill - Milford Haven; 817, Haverfordwest – Herbrandston – Milford Haven, and 829, Haverfordwest to Pembroke, were all withdrawn after operation on February 28. Even on trunk routes, Sunday services were withdrawn and weekday frequencies reduced, resulting in a saving of around 700 route miles a week. Services to the Royal Naval Armament Depot at Trecwn were reduced, and with it the need for one bus. Operations at Fishguard and St David's soon ceased entirely. It seems incredible that the lifeblood of so many rural communities was mercilessly sacrificed by individuals democratically elected to serve them.

Ironically, in April, the large new garage and offices in Haverfordwest opened. Transforming a previously derelict area, they consisted of a two-storey administrative office, single-storey workshops and canteen. The building was short-lived as the services that it was intended to manage were curtailed.

A long service dinner was held in February to salute 139 employees who had served the company for 40 years and a further 212 who had notched up a 25-year record. Included among these people was a dwindling band of 'loaned staff' who came over in 1929 to join forces with SWCM to form the basis of Western Welsh. In 1970 they were still technically 'on loan' from the railways and retained membership of the National Union of Railwaymen. All took a deep-rooted pride in their association with the Great Western Railway. Bus workers' wages and conditions had improved slowly during the 1960s, the most notable improvements being in the length of the working day. The National Council for the Omnibus Industry had succeeded in reducing the working week from 44 to 42 hours in the summer of 1960, then five years later a Committee of Inquiry, under the chairmanship of Sir Roy Wilson, QC, recommended the introduction of the 40 hour week, a proposal which was implemented in April 1966. However, overtime payments, Sunday, late-night, early-morning and Bank Holiday working allowances were less generous than those granted to railwaymen.

Also in February, three coaches conveyed 110 members and friends of the Educational Club to Bristol Hippodrome to see the pantomime Aladdin. An extra thrill for some was a backstage meeting after the show with the star Freddie 'Parrot Face' Davies, who turned out to be as pleasant and good humoured off stage as he was on it.

Staff at Bridgend depot became increasingly disillusioned with a number of work issues, in particular agreements for one-man operation of buses, and the introduction of an urban bonus scheme. They had for many years benefitted from the exceptionally stable employment situation at the depot, but now they felt betrayed by alleged 'steam-rollering' from national officers into the acceptance of unpalatable working practices, and so, by September 1970, a large number of branch members had

Coach excursion

The luxury tour that reaches the parts others can't

The blue and ivory coach livery looks good on Leopard 141 (141 DBO), at Merthyr Tydfil in 1970 on a summer express to Tenby.
RL Wilson/Online Transport Archive

Imagine for a moment we have accepted an invitation to join the directors and senior management of Western Welsh on their annual tour of inspection in October, 1962.

It is an offer that brings with it the option of dinner and an overnight stay at the Angel Hotel, Cardiff, followed by a hearty full English breakfast, all accepted — and enjoyed.

A wonderful autumn morning greets our emergence from the hotel to board the waiting luxury coach, a Weymann-bodied 36-seater AEC Reliance, one of just 12 Cambrian Class coaches that entered the fleet only a year before.

This is the directors tour, remember, so everything has to be just right. Once again, there's pride at stake. So as arranged, at precisely 9am sharp, the driver, having checked that everyone is comfortably seated, eases the Reliance into gear and smoothly leaves the hotel behind.

Ahead of us is a 45-minute dash along the A48 to our first port of call, Bridgend bus station and garage, where a major expansion has been completed. Apart from Cardiff, it now boasts the biggest bus station in Wales. It can still, however, lay claim to being the first! From the modern passenger facilities to the new staff canteen and workshops, inspection reveals that everything is spick and span. With much territory to cover, we are soon on our way again, heading for West Wales, as the depots there are the main focus of the tour.

Shortly before 11am we hit the main traffic bottleneck of Port Talbot town centre, a constant headache to services. Escaping lightly we continue through Baglan and cross the impressive A48 Neath River Bridge, and skirt Swansea through Morriston, Llangyfelach and Pontardulais, heading for Ammanford's Tirydail

Lane garage. It's small with a 12 vehicle capacity. After a good run through Cross Hands we reach Carmarthen, and lunch at The Queens Hotel before visiting St David's Street garage. At one time home to nearly 90 buses, its current tally is just 17. At 2.30pm we are once again on the move, continuing west along the A40, through St Clears, Whitland and Haverfordwest, to Milford Haven. Here we are given a tour of the new Esso refinery. All too soon we bid farewell to Esso's directors and engineers, and head for the town's Lord Nelson Hotel, our base for the night.

The cry of gulls heralds the dawn, dispensing with the need for an early morning call. It is a sharp contrast to the previous morning's clatter of

trolleybus booms in Cardiff. A peep through the window reveals a clear sky, and outside our coach awaits. As we breakfast, the driver is busy distributing copies of the Western Mail to each of the coach seats. At 9am we're away, but not far, and within minutes are pulling into the town's new bus station and garage at Manchester Square which we are informed by the accountant cost £2,000 under budget — good news!

Within a short while we are back on board, heading for Haverfordwest, a town where Western Welsh is a relative newcomer. It was only when it took over the operations of Green's in 1956 that the company had a real presence in the town, and that explains why the combined bus station and garage premises at Cambrian Yard

with a difference

and Marsh Yard appear ramshackle. It's not devoid of character, however, and has recently benefitted from £1,500 worth of improvements to create a temporary bus station in its yard. With a site area of nearly 12,000 square yards, Haverfordwest is now the company's largest depot west of Bridgend, and has an allocation of around 75 vehicles.

After half an hour at Haverfordwest, we resume our tour, and as we continue to St David's, we experience the rural nature of some of our services this far west. The 16 miles are covered in 40 minutes with some tricky hills between Newgale and Solva. The route is more profitable than most of its rural contemporaries. In the summer the number of tourists using the service warrants a double-decker, though market days apart, patronage in winter is sparse. We pull into the depot yard at St David's and are greeted by Mr Burley, the supervisor. A welcoming coffee awaits as pleasantries are exchanged, then all too soon we are back aboard the coach for the next leg of the tour, which will take us along the coast to Fishguard. Our stay there is brief, but we cannot fail to be impressed by the ultra-modern garage completed in 1959, replacing that at Goodwick. We continue along the coastal road towards Newport, and climbing out of Fishguard old town, we look down on a British Railways ferry entering the harbour at the end of its morning passage from Cork. Over at the landing stage a train waits patiently to offer passengers a well-timed onward connection for Cardiff and London.

The road diverts inland after Newport, but on reaching Cardigan we turn off and follow the River Teifi to regain the coast once again at Gwbert-on-Sea. Here we have a leisurely lunch, but first there's time for a stroll through the grounds of the hotel to enjoy the invigorating sea air.

In November 1963 one of the new Duple Alpine Continental coaches was fitted out at Ely with a purpose-built cocktail bar for an important four-day private charter. The coach was later restored to its original configuration, but not before senior managers and directors sampled its wares. *Christine Davies*

At 2.15pm we are on the road again, retracing our steps to Cardigan, before turning inland along the twisting road and across the river near the foaming falls at Cenarth.

Here, the River Teifi maintains a long tradition of coracle fishing for the river's legendary salmon. It's a short drive on to Newcastle Emlyn, where a brief break is taken at the company's garage, which dates from 1949. This is a typical post-war rural bus garage and houses eight vehicles, although the history of operations in the town goes back to the days of the GWR, when services were run from a cramped and damp tin shed in Cawdor Road. It is quite an important hub, not only for local services, but as a strategic post on the Aberystwyth express services. After a mere 15-minute call here, our journey continues south towards Carmarthen.

Our driver has handled the coach with ease and skill throughout the tour, and the roads we have encountered in the latest section have been a thorough test for both. We take the undulating 'B' road to Pontyberem, our final depot visit, where we arrive on schedule at 4pm. It's a tortuous route, no wonder the Tiger Cubs were openly

welcomed by Pontyberem staff when the first deliveries entered service here after being tested on this route in 1953. Western Welsh took over the garage here in 1935 along with the Pontyberem & District Motor Services business. Extensions were made to the garage in 1948, and the depot has survived unaltered ever since. The seven vehicle capacity of its collection of sheds could hardly be in greater contrast to the other garages we have visited. The staffing here is unusual too, as we have a 'driver-in-charge', Harry Cook, looking after many things in addition to his regular driving duties.

Once again we have to be on our way very quickly, and as we proceed to Swansea, several members of the party prepare to leave the coach to catch the 5.30pm Paddington train at High Street station. We have visited nine of the company's garages since our tour began. If time had allowed, New Quay and the Neyland outstation would have completed the list as far as West Wales is concerned; never mind, we'll add them to the agenda for the next tour of inspection! It has certainly been an interesting and informative experience.

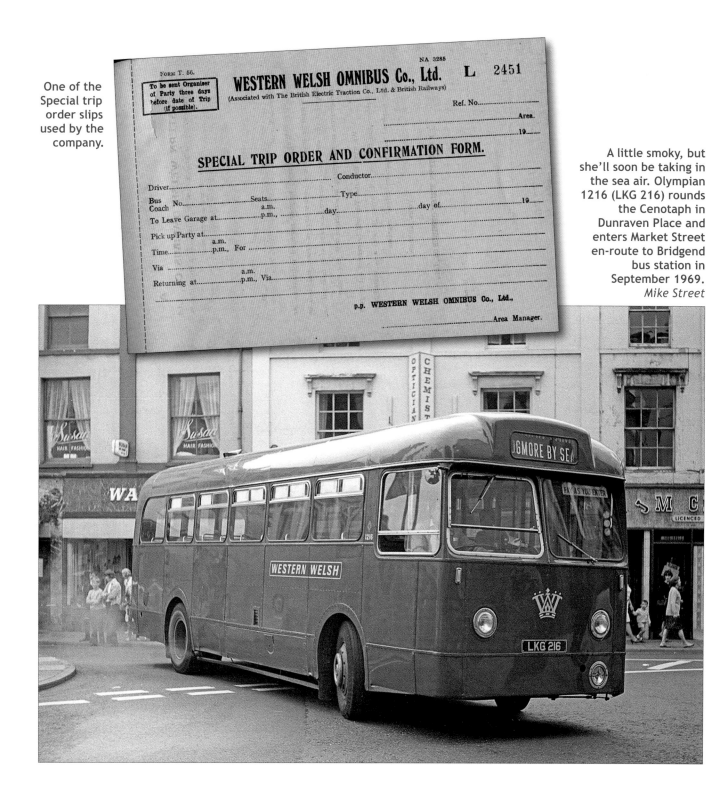

One of the Special trip order slips used by the company.

A little smoky, but she'll soon be taking in the sea air. Olympian 1216 (LKG 216) rounds the Cenotaph in Dunraven Place and enters Market Street en-route to Bridgend bus station in September 1969.
Mike Street

left the NUR and formed the Bridgend Busworkers' Association. This survived until 1971, when its members joined the Transport & General Workers Union (TGWU).

Rookwood Hospital in Cardiff specialised in the rehabilitation of disabled people. No doubt aware of the donation of withdrawn vehicles to similar establishments by Western Welsh in the past, the hospital authorities contacted the company to see whether there were any old buses available. Their idea was to utilise the entrance section to boost patient confidence in tackling difficulties they encountered boarding a bus. There were no suitable vehicles available at the time, but instead, a

mock-up of a vehicle entrance and seating layout was created at Ely Works. A number of employees in the body shop and paint shop volunteered to construct the unit in their own time, and the company and its suppliers donated the materials used. The mock-up was handed over on May 5 at an informal ceremony at Ely.

From July, pensioners and the registered disabled living in the Barry area became eligible for travel concessions on Western Welsh and Thomas Motor Services operating in the borough. This was the first time such a concession, made possible by the 1968 Transport Act, was put into effect in South Wales.

In October, sites were inspected at Crichton Street and Curran Road, Cardiff, as possible replacements for the blighted Penarth Road depot.

The two AEC Matador recovery vehicles were given a facelift to bring them into line with modern day requirements. Several modifications were carried out to the recovery equipment, while improvements to the front, rear and jib lights were incorporated. The dark red and ivory livery of both vehicles was replaced by canary yellow, and the traditional Western Welsh crests gave way to modern lettering.

Rhondda Transport came under the company's control during the year, with the assets officially transferred on January 1, 1971. There were strong views concerning the disappearance of this historic name, so much that a degree of rethinking led to its retention on Porth-based vehicles for a time. However, with a need for further autonomy identified, plans were announced for combined management of all the south-east Wales National Bus Company operators.

The year ended with the first operating loss since the depression years of 1930/31. A massive deficit of £269,565 was recorded, far worse than was feared and no doubt attributable to the cost of reorganising for nationalisation. In comparison, both SWT and Rhondda, despite having endured pre-war records of unprofitability — and some rather lean post-war years — were compact organisations and able to contract relatively painlessly. Western Welsh wasn't, and couldn't. Problems in West Wales had strained the company's resources. Over-staffing and too many services were also taking their toll.

The Monmouthshire scheme of 1969 may have played its part in reducing losses and even improved profitability, but service frequencies remained high, and it was realised that in other areas such co-ordination was no longer a practical option.

The year that followed saw Western Welsh withdraw from Aberdare in favour of Red & White, and by 1972 the Neath and Port Talbot areas would see South Wales Transport take over, reversing that company's step-by-step withdrawal of the 1930s. It was inevitable that Ammanford, then finally the far west, would follow.

1971

The assets of the Rhondda Transport Company were officially transferred on January 1. They comprised the Porth depot and workshops and 158 vehicles, at a book value of £457,174. The Rhondda name remained registered, but as a dormant company. The RTC, with its single depot and network of high-frequency urban services, had a prosperous look about it, and should have been beneficial to Western Welsh. However the merger was not welcomed locally.

The general manager's New Year message regretted the passing of the Rhondda company, whose proud history went back further than that of Western Welsh. Having managed Rhondda and worked among the staff, Mr Gray admitted the inevitable pangs of regret at its passing: "True the name will remain the same yet awhile, but ultimately who knows?" Who could have foreseen that the Rhondda name would again be seen on buses many years after the demise of its appointed guardian!

The NBC took rapid steps to simplify its inheritance in South Wales. On paper, from January 1, United Welsh, Thomas Bros and Neath & Cardiff were absorbed by South

Some might wonder what Western Welsh was thinking when it ordered 20 Bristol RELL6Ls in 1971 in a departure from the company's normal Leyland intake. Only five entered service and those that did soon left to join the rest at South Wales Transport. On its way to Newport 801 (UKG 801J) shudders through Caerphilly when nearly new — perhaps the reason the streets have suddenly emptied! *John Jones*

You won't find this one in the fleet list! Early in 1970 a request was made by Rookwood Hospital in Cardiff to see if there were any life-expired buses available to assist their rehabilitation department in helping patients to gain confidence in boarding a bus. There were none to spare so Western Welsh produced a replica with materials provided free and employees volunteering their services. The result was 'bus' No. 1600 complete with orange diamond! The hand-over ceremony took place at Ely Works in May.

Wales Transport, N&C being split so that Western Welsh had its share. The loss of N&C in particular was sorely felt due to the prestige that existed in the company. It was popular with the passengers and profitable until the end. In such a short time the company was destroyed and delivered into the hands of SWT and Western Welsh. 'Killed by nationalisation and mourned by all,' as the staff rightly claimed in the obituary column of a local newspaper. The N&C staff based at Penarth Road depot transferred to Western Welsh along with six coaches valued at £16,177.

While much appeared to be wasteful in the way services were operated in the area, it is doubtless regretted that the goodwill attached to the lost names and liveries was not retained. This should serve as a meaningful lesson to the major bus industry players of today, some of whom have scant regard for the heritage and local identity of its bus services.

How do you deal with a bus with two fleet numbers? It must have been a nightmare for administrative staff when Rhondda 489 (ETX 489C) was adorned with the system used by Red & White. Another puzzle would have been the use of a Cwmbran White diamond for the Porth garage, just at the time the green diamond became spare. It all made sense to somebody, no doubt.

Bethany Square, Port Talbot, plays host to Leyland Tiger Cub 1177 (MUH 177) in operation on the Aberdare to Porthcawl service in 1967. The grey diamond carried by the vehicle gives a hint that it had recently been transferred to Neath depot from Crosskeys. Soon the diamond would become red.
RL Wilson/Online Transport Archive

Fishguard and St David's garages closed in January and brought about the abandonment of 17 licences. Inevitably there were 52 redundancies — victims of the unyielding pressures which had placed the company in dire financial straits. For years the network of rural services in this area had operated at a loss, but had been subsidised by more profitable services. But the point had been reached where the profitability of even these services was undermined by spiralling costs and declining passenger numbers. If rural services were to survive they would need some form of subsidy. The 1968 Transport Act allowed for local authorities to help out, with any support from the rates to be matched by Government where it was clear that the operator could no longer afford to run the service. Pembrokeshire County Council chose not to do this, and so drastic measures had to be taken. A further 21 staff at Haverfordwest and eight at Carmarthen were made redundant. Brecon might well have suffered a similar fate, but there the local authority agreed to subsidise operations for six months until July, which allowed a reprieve. In Cardiganshire, too, the action of the county council saved New Quay and Newcastle Emlyn depots and their services.

The Carmarthen to Llanelli via Pontyberem route was abandoned in January after Carmarthenshire County Council declined to make a grant. A reduced service, without a grant, was offered by Eynon, Trimsaran, who ironically used a former Western Welsh Olympian to operate it. Carmarthen depot succumbed in May, as the company tried to cut its heavy losses in West Wales. Once again the blame was put squarely on the shoulders of the local authority, who had refused to offer a subsidy towards the cost of running thousands of unremunerative route miles annually. However, a contributory factor was surely the failure of staff to accept the single-manning agreement. The company, unable to introduce the economy measures that were vital for survival, closed its depot on May 1, resulting in 45 redundancies. The only Western Welsh routes that continued to serve the town were operated by vehicles and staff from other depots. The axe fell on the Carmarthen to Haverfordwest and Carmarthen to Cardigan services, while the Carmarthen to Ammanford section of service 301 to Cardiff continued, using Carmarthen as an outstation. The Carmarthen to Pendine service was taken over by Tudor Williams, of Laugharne. Small local operators applied to take over the town services.

The small depot at Aberdare also closed in May and its services transferred to Red & White. Despite 23 staff moving to R&W, there were 14 redundancies. While these were troubled times, there was the occasional good news story. The Prince of Wales visited Haverfordwest on St David's Day. It was a red letter day for Western Welsh, as they were entrusted with the job of conveying the Prince by coach to Milford, from where he boarded a launch for a cruise on the Haven.

Ivor L Gray retired as general manager at the end of April and was replaced by Keith Holmes. Mr FH Pengelly was appointed assistant general manager, and former Rhondda man WF Cooper became traffic manager.

The break up of the Neath & Cardiff company saw several of its coaches transferred, at least on paper, to Cardiff. There was no visible change apart from a white triangle on the front of these vehicles. Certain reshuffling took place before all traces of N&C disappeared. Among these, LTX 828E ended up with South Wales Transport, yet here still retains clues to its immediate past.

In his message to staff Mr Gray wrote: "My life has been so closely intertwined with the affairs of Western Welsh that it is very hard to imagine a different way of life, but retirement inevitably comes to us all and enough is enough, as they say."

Later in the year, following a study undertaken by outside consultants, NBC planned a more coherent express network, under central direction and with just one marketing department.

There was a worrying increase in vandalism to the company's vehicles, something which had become an evergreen problem. This not only resulted in a sharp rise in maintenance costs, but made it difficult to meet vehicle availability commitments at the worst hit depots. Seat slashing, removal of light fittings, and graffiti from felt-tipped pens and aerosol paint featured prominently and the cost of repairs ran into thousands of pounds annually. In the worst of instances, vehicles had to be returned to Ely Works for refurbishing.

Anyone watching the BBC TV programme Tomorrow's World would have seen a double-decker bus lifted high into the air by the world's largest mobile crane owned by Sparrow's of Bath. The bus lift was the centre of attraction at the hire firm's open day, but few would have realised that the vehicle belonged to Western Welsh. This particular private hire did not carry any passengers, and the bus was on the disposal list — just in case of accident!

 One Western Welsh employee special interest group that made a splash was the tropical fish society formed at the Maindy Hotel, Cardiff. Apart from affording the chance for open discussion on any fish topics, the society aimed to build up a library of fish-related publications, show films and slides on fish, and invite speakers to their meetings to pass on their knowledge. There is no record of any refreshments being provided, but perhaps a fish supper was enjoyed by the members on their way home!

In the Second World War, Western Welsh had employed a number of women drivers. Now, nearly 30 years later the company appeared to see women behind the wheel as a way of easing the problem of staff shortages. Bridgend's Margaret Lewis became the first conductress of eight at the depot to pass the PSV test.

From this year's deliveries, every new saloon featured a fault warning indicator panel in the cab. A total of 11 Daimler Fleetlines and 11 Bristol RELL6Ls were ordered, but all were diverted elsewhere within the NBC empire. During the winter months the coach fleet was adorned with a new style fleet name consisting of seven inch high bold capital letters. The edges of each letter had a border in Peacock Blue to enable the same transfer to be used on either a blue or ivory ground.

Once again the end of year financial report was not good and a loss of £163,486 was recorded.

1972

A significant event in the restructuring of the bus industry in South Wales took place on January 1, 1972 when the Neath depot, its staff, services and buses transferred to SWT. Initially, all operations in Glamorgan west of Porthcawl went to SWT along with 35 vehicles. The Western Welsh name was soon to become even less appropriate. The closure of Carmarthen created a large gap between the company's core in Glamorgan and the isolated services in

West Wales. In March, the transfer of operations at Haverfordwest depot followed those at Neath. The 11 services that remained were taken over, along with around 70 staff and a further 22 vehicles. Milford Haven garage and Carmathen garage and office were closed, while property at Port Talbot and land at Cadoxton, Neath, was sold.

While subsidy negotiations continued to drag on in Pembrokeshire and Carmarthenshire, in Cardiganshire, Crosville had been more successful. Accordingly, as a third stage in April, Newcastle Emlyn and New Quay depots, together with the Aberystwyth to Ammanford route were transferred to that company. A further 11 vehicles left Western Welsh, in addition to two already with SWT.

thought that a mere 15 years had elapsed since Western Welsh took over the old-established family firm of Green's of Haverfordwest, and enjoyed a monopoly in that part of Pembrokeshire. Now the company's name had disappeared entirely from all buses west of Bridgend.

The cost to SWT of the Neath and Haverfordwest operations was £200,000, while to Crosville, the operations at Newcastle Emlyn and New Quay amounted to £23,693.

National Travel Ltd was formed in April 1972, and the extended tours operations of Western Welsh, along with all the other subsidiary companies, were brought under this umbrella. A standard, white livery was introduced

These transfers were seen as a logical step in the restructuring of the National Bus Company's interests in South and West Wales. Sentiment apart, they were seen as a way to meet the challenge of the 1970s. It is a sobering

One of Bridgend's 'baby' Leopards, 1515 (TKG 515J), waits at Cosy Corner, Porthcawl — anything but in bad weather — with a Pontypridd service in 1971.
John Jones

The Prince of Wales visited Pembrokeshire on St David's Day in 1971 and Western Welsh had the honour of providing the royal carriage between Haverfordwest and Milford Haven. *Stewart Williams*

Probably the final vehicle to emerge from Ely Works in proper Western Welsh livery. Only the fleet name betrays the 1972 date, as 1345 (DBO 347C) stands at Abergavenny. *Mike Street*

for the 1,500 front line coaches, and individual company names were still shown, but in the corporate style. The ability to market express services under one name — National Express — and operate coaches in one livery was expected to have a greater impact on the public than the 30 or so names and liveries of the individual companies. The National Bus Company aptly named newspaper 'Bus'

reported the setting-up of a Central Activities Group (CAG) whose role was to develop more fully the tours and express side of the business.

As stage carriage traffic had declined steadily, the holiday trade had increased. Despite being responsible for only a small amount of revenue, it was showing promising growth. With the strength and marketing expertise of the new group, Keith Holmes echoed the words of the regional director and confidently looked forward to a larger slice of this lucrative business. He foresaw the need for more coaches, drivers and staff to maintain them, and reassured staff that it was not the intention to take this work away from those concerned but rather to give them more opportunities. The CAG's success would lie in calling on the knowledge, experience and enthusiasm of those running the services. Holmes boldly concluded: "There is an exciting challenge to be

The final saloons ordered by Western Welsh and delivered in 1972 were 1531-44, Marshall-bodied Leopards. At the head of the Garw Valley in 1974 is 1536 (XBO 536K). By this time the entire batch had received NBC livery. Judging by the oil-stained engine panels, standards appeared to be slipping. *Howard Roberts*

Newly unwrapped and immediately put to work on the Porthcawl run in April 1972 is 1522 (XBO 522K) one of 10 Marshall bodied dual purpose Leopards. Their blue trim and tartan moquette reveal that they were originally intended for delivery in blue and ivory livery. *Mike Street*

faced and the prize is a better future for us all." However, many both inside and outside the industry felt the anonymity of the 'National' name would in many respects achieve the opposite of what it set out to do. As far as tours were concerned, it was a retrograde step for a company proud of its heritage and desperate to maintain public loyalty.

Once again staff praise came from a passenger: "Dear Sir, On Tuesday March 14, I caught the 3.45pm bus from Cardiff to Neath and occupied the front seat. About two miles on the Cardiff side of Bridgend I suddenly saw the whole window in front of the driver, for no apparent reason, become like a sheet of pebble frosted glass and it immediately splintered into hundreds of small pieces, a number of the splinters showering all over the driver. He instantly applied the brakes and drove the bus on to the grass verge almost before the passengers in the bus had realised what had happened." So wrote Phyllis James of Briton Ferry, in a letter of appreciation. She continued: "I feel I must record my appreciation of the calm efficiency and great presence of mind of your driver as a very serious accident could easily have occurred because there was a stream of traffic going in both directions at the time." Driver J O'Donoghue of Cardiff depot was duly notified of his passenger's appreciation, along with that of the company.

Fred Pengelly retired in September, 46 years after he had started as a conductor with Whites Motors in 1926.

A new tours and travel enquiry office opened in Cwmbran, conveniently situated near the bus station in Gwent Square. In Barry, £29,000 was allocated for an upgrade of the workshops.

In December, the government grant towards new bus purchases was increased to 50 per cent. Meanwhile, An operating loss of £56,968 was reported for the year.

Service switch

The 11 services operated by Haverfordwest depot and taken over by SWT in March 1972 were:

801	Haverfordwest - Carmarthen
813	Haverfordwest Town Service
814	Haverfordwest - Milford Haven - Hubberston
818	Haverfordwest - Neyland
819	Milford Haven Town Service
823	H'west - Neyland via Sentry Cross
824	H'west - Neyland via Rosemarket
825	Tenby - Saundersfoot - Hill
826	Haverfordwest - Tenby
828	H'west - Llangwm - Burton Ferry
841	Prendergast - Little Haven

The transfer to Crosville of the Cardiganshire depots involved the following services:

404/5	Carmarthen - Cardigan
406	Newcastle Emlyn - Aberporth
407	Newcastle Emlyn - Llangranog
408	Groesffordd - New Quay
410	New Quay - Aberaeron

Times were changing as the range of fleet colours on display at Porth depot in April 1973 shows. By now the Rhondda fleet was well and truly absorbed, as evidenced by 2316 (RTG 316F), a former Rhondda vehicle in Western Welsh blue and ivory, 2393 (393 WTG) in original Rhondda green and ivory, and 2317 (RTG 317F) in the latest red and ivory livery. *Andrew Mann*

Members of the road staff at Bridgend made a collection before Christmas for the children of Cefn Glas Residential School for mentally handicapped children. Western Welsh staff had a fond regard for these unfortunate youngsters, and the feeling must have been mutual because the children sent a Christmas card to the drivers and conductors. A warm letter of thanks was sent from Elizabeth Sharkey, headmistress of the school.

The Christmas edition of the company's own Staff Bulletin marked the end of another era as it was the last issue. The NBC had decided that local magazines would no longer be produced. Instead there would be five issues of the Bus newspaper, which would include a page of local news. The axing of the Staff Bulletin was regrettable, but the production of local company magazines had become increasingly difficult to justify in a shrinking industry. The Staff Bulletin had first appeared in July 1947, and from October 1950 Stewart Williams had been its editor. He 'put to bed' 220 issues during this period, wrote hundreds of accounts of the company's functions and interviewed dozens of colleagues at all levels. In the final edition, he thanked all the contributors past and present, the photographers, and not least printers, D Brown & Sons of Cowbridge, for their interest and support over a quarter of a century.

As part of the restructuring of the National Bus company's interests, South Wales Transport took over the Western Welsh depot at Haverfordwest, along with its 11 remaining services, in March 1972. The varied selection of vehicles received SWT fleet branding including former 1242 (SBO 242). *Peter Keating*

By now in NBC livery, 604 (604 BBO) looks resplendent at Derwen Road, Bridgend in 1973. *Peter Keating*

The final 'proper' Western Welsh vehicle order was for five Leyland Leopards with Duple Dominant coach bodies. Vehicles 191-5 were to Bus Grant specification and arrived early in 1974 carrying the new National all-over white livery, together with R&W's fleet numbering system in advance of its general introduction to the company's fleet. *Viv Corbin*

1973

The National Bus Company announced its intention to use the brand names National Holidays and National Express.

Red & White was largely unaffected by the trials of maintaining rural services that had affected Western Welsh, and in 1969 had bought Jones of Aberbeeg, the largest independent operator in Monmouthshire. There had been close operational links between the two. Control of the Jones company, one of the very few NBC companies to have a blue livery, moved to R&W head office at Chepstow. Similarly, while R&W and Western Welsh retained their separate identities, a single management team for the two was looking likely.

In March, Keith Holmes was appointed general manager of NBC Western Region's South Wales division. He later moved to Midland Red as general manager and JB Hargreaves became the new general manager.

In Cardiff, the threat of compulsory purchase of the Penarth Road depot was removed, as plans for the Hook Road scheme were dropped.

Amazingly, given the huge losses in previous years and the cost of setting up NBC a tiny profit of £1,717 was reported for the year.

1974

The final Western Welsh vehicle orders were completed and four Duple-bodied Leopards entered service bearing the R&W fleet numbering system. The whole former

Western Welsh fleet were soon to be renumbered likewise. The NBC poppy-red livery was very much in evidence by this time.

The company joined the BEST pension scheme, and redundancy payments were increased by 50 per cent. Much later, this move was to play a part in successful pension payment litigation against the receivers of the National Welsh company in 1999.

In August, the company's operating areas were split into three sections. These were South Glamorgan, North Glamorgan, and Gwent and Dean.

As the year ended, the company owned property that had been revalued at a total of £1,751,500. Nevertheless, the year closed with a massive operational loss of £264,989.

WESTERN·WELSH·OMNIBUS·Co·Ltd

The portfolio of property

Workshops, garages, depots and offices

The head office, central workshops and stores, and subsequently the coach garage, of Western Welsh were situated at Ely, Cardiff. Its regional operating bases which consisted of garages, workshops and offices were located at Barry, Brecon, Bridgend, Cardiff, Carmarthen, Crosskeys, Haverfordwest, Neath, Pontypool and later Cwmbran. By far the biggest of the individual garages was Bridgend. At its height in the summer of 1957 there were 127 vehicles allocated there. Next came Pontypool with 81, all of which were saloons, then Crosskeys with 74. Smallest was Brecon with 20. At this time, 691 vehicles were licensed, while 39 coaches were based at Blackweir, Cardiff, for tours. Only six vehicles were delicensed, either withdrawn and awaiting disposal, or otherwise receiving attention at Ely. Most of the main depots had secondary garages. Bridgend's was at

Port Talbot; Carmarthen's were at New Quay, Newcastle Emlyn and Pontyberem; Haverfordwest had Fishguard, Milford Haven, Neyland and St David's; and Neath's were at Aberdare and Ammanford. Cardiff had two garages — Penarth Road, and Blackweir. Coaches from here were transferred to Ely in 1963. Apart from these locations there were 18 strategically located outstations where vehicles from both main and secondary depots camped for the night in a bid to cut dead mileage. Abergavenny and Hay-on-Wye were outstations to Brecon; Glyncorrwg, Kenfig Hill and Porthcawl to Bridgend; Laugharne, Llandyssul and Pendine to Carmarthen; Freystrop, Llangwm, Narberth, Saundersfoot and Tenby to Haverfordwest; Aberystwyth, Lampeter, Llanelly and Porthcawl to Neath; and Varteg Hill to Pontypool. Laugharne was the largest, with

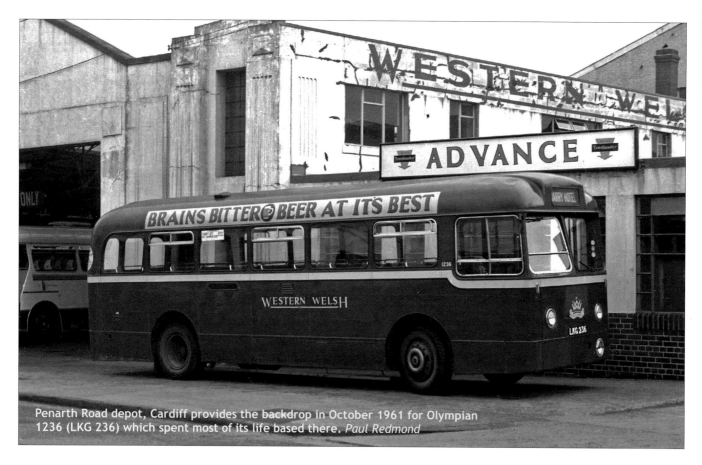

Penarth Road depot, Cardiff provides the backdrop in October 1961 for Olympian 1236 (LKG 236) which spent most of its life based there. *Paul Redmond*

four vehicles based there overnight. With the exception of Kenfig Hill and Lampeter, which hosted two vehicles each, the others had just one. There were effectively two outstations at Porthcawl, one to cater for services to Bridgend, the other to Neath. Aberystwyth, some 80 miles from Neath, was the furthest-flung. Only Barry and Crosskeys depots were completely self-contained, with neither sub-depots nor outstations. Cwmbran came into being in 1963, with operations at Pontypool transferring there in 1967.

The property story started long before this. The first recorded premises of South Wales Commercial Motors consisted of a leased garage at 8/8A Penarth Road in Cardiff, used by SWCM and then Western Welsh from June 1919 to September 1938, when it reverted to the Hancock company. SWCM also took up tenancy of office premises in Tresillian Terrace and a large recreational hall in nearby Crawshay Street.

It was the foresight of Tom White, who started services in Barry in 1910, that an expansion of services to Cardiff in the 1920s led to premises being found close to bus termini at Tresillian Terrace and the general railway station. The ideal site was found at Penarth Road with room for a large front and rear entrance. So favourable was this site that it was decided to make Cardiff the head office, with all operations, maintenance and administration transferring from Barry. The garage was built by direct labour and normal reinforcement was considered insufficient — bus chassis, road springs, axles, wheels, ships' wire hawsers and three-quarter inch steel rods

were placed in the concrete walls. When the workshop was complete, state-of-the-art machinery enabled vehicles to be overhauled, chassis to be lengthened and even a double-decker bus built. When Western Welsh took over White's, administration was switched to Tresillian Terrace while land adjacent to White's garage was bought in November 1936 at a cost of £3,000. This was followed by the purchase of more adjacent land in July 1937 for £9,000, and yet more costing £1,000 in 1939. Staff transferred from Tresillian Terrace to Ely in 1938 after which there is no further record of occupation. The size of the original garage had doubled and work was completed by 1939 at a further cost of £10,800. Contractors took nearly three months to demolish the original garage wall!

The depot was bombed in January 1940, and an unexploded land mine discovered close by, with the result that evacuation became necessary. A bus, rigged up to serve as an emergency office, was parked on Fitzhamon Embankment. Further depot extensions were approved in April 1953 at a cost of £3,150. And this was how it remained until January 1967, when part of the depot's offices was subject to a Compulsory Purchase Order by Cardiff City Council and demolished for a road-widening scheme.

In 1969, the premises were again threatened by compulsory purchase for the Cardiff Hook Road Scheme, however the scheme was dropped in 1973, but not before sites at Crichton Street and Curran Road had been inspected as a possible replacement. The change of mind

184

by Cardiff City Council paved the way for £45,000 to be spent on alterations including a new workshop block, improvements to the canteen, and the rebuilding of the area manager's office. A Swan National car rental office opened on part of the site in December 1973. The depot closed in March 1981 after 58 years of operation. Disposal followed in January 1982.

Turning to Ely, Albert Gray had been busy searching for suitable land on which to build a headquarters for the newly formed Western Welsh company. Close proximity to the Cardiff to Cowbridge road was important, and eventually the ideal site was found – a grazing field situated on the green belt which at that time surrounded the city. Negotiations commenced, and in January 1930, eight acres of land were purchased at Ely for a head office and central workshops.

Excavations began in the summer and work proceeded apace. The resulting offices and works were opened in February 1931 and became the heart of Western Welsh operations throughout the company's existence. The building contractors were Knox and Wells of Cardiff and the steelwork was erected by Braithwaites of Newport. Ely Works consisted of three main departments: Chassis, Electrical and Body, and its emergency electricity generator, powered by an old bus engine, was sufficient to drive the works' machinery and illuminate the entire premises. Modern machinery facilitated every type of vehicle repair, and state of the art detection equipment brought a cost-effective regime of preventative maintenance to the fleet. The main stores ran the length of one side of the works, and the joinery even made its own workbenches, steps and ladders. Extensions were carried out in 1942 at a cost of £6,108, and again in 1954 at a further £8,500. From October 1952 the adjacent office block became the company's registered office. A new coach garage and docking pits was announced in 1962 as part of a £60,000 upgrade of the premises intended to facilitate the closure of Blackweir garage. This was completed by April 1964, by which time a large extension to the office block was underway. Once complete, headquarters staff returned to Ely after an eight-year exile at the central bus station. A final round of improvements to the works was completed early in 1966. After that the site remained unchanged into NBC days. Closure came in May 1981, and it was sold for redevelopment in 1986.

There remained a considerable area of non-operational land at Ely. For many years this was the venue of the company's annual field day, but in May 1963 it was sold for housing development. The graveyard was the name given by many to this undeveloped patch of ground at the works for it was here that redundant vehicles were dumped to await disposal or cannibalisation for parts. The vehicles were sought after by independent operators, contractors, or even for export to under-developed countries where, with the odd door modification, they would be looked upon as first class buses capable of many more years of work. Some even found their way behind the Iron Curtain. Letters were occasionally received from excited Welsh people who had seen a bus, with the Western Welsh name only faintly obliterated, chugging through the mountains of Austria. Most of them, however, spent their retirement less strenuously and less romantically as caravans, mobile shops, canteens or tool sheds. One even became a chicken coop! Cine film of the field day events taken by Leslie Gray show helter-skelters and egg and spoon races, against a backdrop of withdrawn buses in various stages of cannibalisation.

An office at Fitzalan Road, near Queen Street station, was noted as in operation in 1947, but had gone by 1958. A tours and enquiry office at 2 Albany Road opened in February 1953, on an annual lease of £156 from JC Lewis & Sons. The Albany Road office probably replaced that

Ready to rumble. A summer evening scene at Penarth Road garage in 1964 shows one of the new Tiger Cubs in the short-lived ivory livery, alongside more traditional fare. Castle Avenue, a rarely-depicted destination, was the Lower Penarth terminus of one of the town services.
Tony Warrener

The booking office and enquiry bureau at 2 Albany Road, Cardiff, managed for Western Welsh by JC Lewis & Sons *Stewart Williams*

at Fitzalan Road and remained open until around 1963, by which time similar facilities were available at the central bus station. This had opened in December 1954, and tenancy of the offices that followed, agreed as early as September 1953, was taken up in June 1957. Many head office staff transferred from Ely and occupied the first and second floors there until August 1965, when they returned to newly extended premises at Ely and the bus station offices were vacated. The offices at central bus station were light and airy. There was surprisingly little noise considering the proximity of the main street, bus bays and railway station. In May 1963 a booking and enquiry office was opened on the ground floor, converted from a waiting room. The company's registered office remained at 253 Cowbridge Road West.

The former Forse's garage at Blackweir was included in the takeover of that company in April 1956 and used to house the coach fleet. Part of the modern premises was let to the BBC while the remainder was advertised for sale in June 1962, following the transfer of vehicles to the new coach shed at Ely. However, there were problems with disposal of Blackweir due to a restrictive covenant on the land, and it was late in 1964 before it was sold to Harold Leigh Ltd (Kardov) for £65,000.

The company's next need for property was at Bridgend. The importance of the town as a bus centre, situated at the foot of the Llynfi, Ogmore and Garw Valleys, and midway between Cardiff and Swansea, was apparent to the pioneers who opened up services there in 1921. With the extension of the service from Cardiff, a garage off Nolton Street was leased, together with an office at the Wyndham Hotel. A five year tenancy of additional premises in Brackla Street was obtained in October 1921. This was held over upon expiry, and in November 1926 tenancy of additional garages was agreed. In March 1922, land was leased in Market Street for what, a year later, became the first bus station in Wales. It was a long single storey structure forming an island between Market Street and Wyndham Street which was accessed from both sides. A refreshment room run by a Mrs Hinton was included in the facilities. There was also a women's toilet and general waiting room, bookstall, wash and brush-up facilities and a staff mess room.

With the takeover of the Cridlands company in 1929 came the lease of an office at 1 Market Street. This expired in March 1946 and wasn't renewed as additional office accommodation had been obtained above Lloyds Bank in Wyndham Street, overlooking the bus station. Cridlands also had a garage at Brackla Street, but it is

How wonderful it would have been to have worked in those Cardiff central bus station offices and look out at this scene all day long. Western Welsh vehicles predominate, with Rhondda out in force, centre; Red & White and Associated Motorways, right and Neath & Cardiff, top left. *Stewart Williams*

Forse's spacious modern garage at Blackweir, Cardiff. When Western Welsh acquired the business in April 1956, it must have been considered a major asset to the company's coaching arm. It survived in use until 1962, after which the coach fleet transferred to Ely Works. In this view, shortly after acquisition, 532 (JOD 619), 593 (FUH 375) and 580 (FBO 360) can be seen. Just visible is 591 (FBO 850). All but 532 were Forse's vehicles which retained their original livery for their first season with Western Welsh. *Peter Smith*

not known whether this was used by the newly formed Western Welsh company. In 1930 there was a sub-office at Green & White Services, The Green, though Green & White's wasn't absorbed until 1937. Land at the cattle market was bought for £2,241 in September 1930 for a much-needed, enlarged bus station which was completed in April 1934. Meanwhile, the Riverside Garage in Brewery Lane had been transferred from the GWR in January 1931. Following completion of the bus station, the company turned its attention to further land, at The Green with a price tag of £7,500 for a new garage, In 1938 Star Yard was bought for extensions to the workshops, at a cost of £3,035. These were finished by October 1941 at a further cost of £8,539, and the combined premises were regarded as one of the finest in the whole of Wales.

Bridgend suffered lightly at the hands of the Luftwaffe, but in 1945 there was a catastrophe of another making when the roof of the main garage collapsed due to a heavy snowfall. For a year the maintenance staff suffered from not having a roof over their heads. Further expansion at Bridgend continued into the 1950s, with the purchase of the town's gasworks site for £4,250 in May 1957. Developments on the town side of the river rendered the Brewery Lane site surplus to requirements and it was let to Moorwell Motors in April 1956. Three years later Moorwell bought the site for £2,250. Major redevelopment plans were announced in 1958, and piece by piece a new 20-bay bus station was built around existing facilities along with new workshop and staff accommodation. During reconstruction work around 40 buses were kept

overnight as Bridgend's RFC's car park in Tondu Road. The development suffered in the town centre flooding in December 1960, but the project was eventually completed in April 1962.

While Cardiff's multi-leased central bus station was the largest in Wales, Bridgend's was in the ownership of Western Welsh, although it was used by N&C, RTC, R&W, WH John (Coity), and Associated Motorways. It was also by far the largest freehold site. To the people of Bridgend, it seemed unfeasible that their bus station should ever close, but that's exactly what happened in 1992 when a buy-out bid by an employee-led group of the ailing National Welsh company failed. Around 130 redundancies ensued and the whole site was sold in December 1993 to National Car Parks. The dilapidated garages remained at first, but demolition and redevelopment eventually followed.

Having established itself at Bridgend, Western Welsh acquired land at a cost of £309 for its first freehold garage at 'Green Talbot' which is how the company referred to Talbot Green at that time. Building was

The bus station and garage at Bridgend at around 1950. The extended garage on the left occupies the former Star Yard, acquired in 1938, while the gasworks, subsequently purchased in 1957 is in the right background. In the foreground is the original bus station, disused since the 1930s. *Christine Davies*

Bridgend Bus Station in 1962. A Bridgemaster is about to leave for Porthcawl via Kenfig Hill, while an Atlantean is on the end stand of the main block, on a service to Heol y Cyw via Pencoed. A Royal Tiger, two Tiger Cubs and an Olympian await their next call of duty, and the N&C Guy Arab on the right is standing by for relief work to Cardiff. *George Wedlake*

approved in December 1923 and completed in October 1924. The garage was non-operational by the early 1950s, but remained on the company's books until June 1955, when it was sold to its sitting tenant for £900.

Tenancy of a converted barn at Caerwent for use as a garage was agreed in 1921, and renewed in February 1924. Although the company had encountered problems in entering Newport, a garage at Charlotte Street was being rented by 1925, and offices leased from the GWR at Cambrian Place (known variously as 8 and 31 Cambrian Road) from June 1933 until July 1959, when a new bus station and office opened at Dock Street at a cost of £33,292. The land for the bus station was bought by Newport Corporation and before reconstruction could take place, various old cellars and disused brick sewers came to light and had to be dealt with. A cast-iron gas street lamp dating back to around 1870 was found in the mortuary area, but fortunately no bodies! The bus station had been 30 years coming, but had been designed to fit the proverbial quart into a pint pot. The Mayor of

Ready and waiting — Bridgend's new bus station in 1961. The new canteen block, with repair facilities underneath, is in the background, while the furthest stands catered mainly for the visiting services of Associated Motorways, Red & White and Neath & Cardiff. *Stewart Williams*

Newport described it as: "A wonderful bus station and an excellent example of the way in which local authorities and private concerns can co-operate."

In 1924 a 21-year lease was taken for the Armoury Garage, Cowbridge, although the premises were no longer in use by November 1937. By 1925, garages were also situated at Llanharan and Pontycymmer as well as a sub-office at Station Yard, Porthcawl, also referred to as John Street. A garage at High Street, Kenfig Hill was in use from March 1926, although not officially conveyed to the company until May of that year, at a cost of £240. This was used until May 1930, after which the Cridlands garage was used and the earlier one demolished. Freehold land for new premises at Moriah Place was acquired in April 1945, and the Cridlands garage sold. The new garage closed in October 1966 and was sold in March 1969 for £2,500.

The foundations of bus services in Port Talbot were laid by Cridlands Motors, from premises in Croft Street. Then, in 1928 a new garage was built in Margam Terrace, believed at one time to be called the Noll Garage. By this time, SWCM were running on the Kenfig Hill route in direct competition with Cridlands, and there was much bitterness between companies as each attempted to win passengers. The eventual victors were SWCM and the Cridland business succumbed in 1929.

When Western Welsh was formed, services west of Bridgend terminated at Port Talbot, and restarted at Neath. The desire to bridge the gap gave birth to the limited stop service, and for a time Port Talbot depot

Carmarthen depot remains largely unscathed by the passage of time. This 2009 view is just crying out for a few Tiger Cubs and Bridgemasters.

Leyland TS8, 880 (DKG 880) on a town service in the mid-1950s picks up passengers alongside the booking office at Blue Street, Carmarthen. *J Jones/SE Letts*

OFFICIAL OPENING

by

HIS WORSHIP THE MAYOR OF NEWPORT
(COUNCILLOR E. ASTON)

of

BUS STATION at NEWPORT, Mon.

Friday, 24th July, 1959

played a big part in this. Administration of Port Talbot came under Bridgend, but in all other aspects the depot was self-contained, with a sub-office at 9 Station Buildings, Bethany Square, recorded in 1930. An office and waiting room was opened there in June 1934 in a joint venture with SWT. Western Welsh interest in this office ceased in March 1966. The garage in Margam Terrace survived until October 1966, when it was leased. It was sold for £14,500 in 1972 and demolished as part of the town's redevelopment scheme.

The GWR could have claimed to be the pioneers of road passenger services in Carmarthen, having started regular services in August 1903, even before the first motor bus appeared on the streets of London. Some services in the town were abandoned during the First World War when many vehicles found their way to Mons and other war-torn places. Following the war limited development took place, mainly because of the uncertain position of railway companies in the operation of road services. The Act of 1928 encouraged arrangements of the kind which led to the formation of Western Welsh and similar bus companies. GWR buses had been stabled in the open in the town's station yard, but within a year of the formation of Western Welsh, vehicles were kept at the Edwards Bros garage after that company had been absorbed. A move was then made to TP Jones' yard at Towy Garage on the station side of the river. However, this was prone to flooding and the arrangement discontinued, as was the practice of conductors paying in at the railway station. An independent office was opened in St Mary's Street auction mart prior to 1930, then in 1935 a move was made to more suitable premises above the Maypole grocery at 5a Guildhall Square. Building land was acquired in April 1930, but details are sketchy and it

is assumed that the St David's Street site, bought in February 1935 with a garage completed a year later, was the only one used by the company after vehicles were transferred from the riverside garage. During the Second World War, in excess of 100 vehicles were drafted into Carmarthen for Ministry of Supply work, so additional premises may have been used at this time. An office and waiting room at Blue Street is listed for 1930, but additional premises to replace those at Guildhall Square were commissioned in June 1936. Included in the freehold was a first floor office which the company let at £90 a year. Blue Street remained in use until advertised

Port Talbot's garage at Margam Terrace originated with Cridlands Motors and passed to Western Welsh when barely a year old in 1929. It couldn't accommodate double deckers and it was normal to see its allocation of saloons parked outside, as seen here in 1963 with 548 (GUH 548) prominent. *John Jones*

189

Colours shine and

The earliest charabancs of SWCM are said to have been painted brown. The later, covered saloons were painted red with cream roofs, separated by a brown band, sometimes resulting in the appearance of two shades of red. There is photographic evidence to suggest that this livery also featured on the early Western Welsh saloons, but this could merely have been carried over prior to repaint.

The motor vehicles of the GWR were, like their railway carriages, painted brown with cream relief, and again this livery may have perpetuated into Western Welsh days. Lewis & James's Western Valley fleet of ADCs and Leylands had a light blue and cream livery, while the mixed fleet of Barrett's Eastern Valleys was painted red with white roof and buff waistline. The company's early fleet contained examples of all these liveries, at least until overhaul or possibly even until new vehicles entered the fleet in their

own right. The colours soon evolved to just red and cream, and were likely to have been applied in differing shades but widely described as carmine. Also, while some have suggested yellow rather than cream, it is more likely that a rich cream is as yellow as it got. There must have remained a strong hankering for the lavender blue and cream of Western Valleys, as some coaches purchased in 1930/1 were delivered in these colours. The early AEC Renowns which carried White's fleet names were also delivered in

Symbols that tell a story

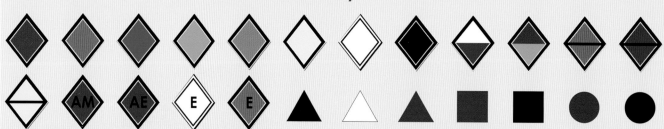

Depot/Sub Depots	Era	Symbol
Cardiff	1945–49	Black triangle
	1945–63	Orange diamond with black bar
	1963–71	Orange diamond
	1970/71	White triangle b
Barry	1945–71	Black diamond
Neath	1945–71	Red diamond
Ammanford	1945–49	Red diamond
	1949–58	Red diamond with letters AM
	1958–71	Red diamond
Aberdare	1945–49	Red diamond
	1949–58	Red diamond with letters AE
	1958–71	Red diamond
Carmarthen/New Quay/ Newcastle Emlyn	1945–49 1949–71	Red square Green diamond
Haverfordwest/ Fishguard/St David's	1945–49 1949–58	Red square Red and white diamond
	1958–63	Red and green diamond a
	1963–71	Green diamond

Depot/Sub Depots	Era	Symbol
Bridgend/Port Talbot	1945–49	Red triangle
	1945–71	Blue diamond
Brecon	1945–49	Red circle
	1949–71	White diamond
Pontypool	1945–49	Black circle
	1949–58	Brown diamond with black bar
	1958–63	Yellow with a black bar
Cwmbran	1963–71	White diamond
Crosskeys	1945–49	Black square
	1949–63	Yellow diamond
	1963–71	Grey diamond
Cwmbran	1963–71	Grey diamond
Porth	1970/71	White diamond
Ely Works	1949–58	White or orange diamond with E c

Key

a Following purchase of Green's of H'west. b Applied to former N&C vehicles upon transfer. c In its heyday Ely Works had an official allocation which was sent around the depots when necessity dictated.

lavender blue and cream, and no doubt looked magnificent. The sheer volume of vehicles from White's, Cridlands, Forse's, Ebsworths and Green's suggests that some vehicles ran in their former company's colours for many months.

A brighter shade of red was introduced for buses after the war following the drab years of austerity grey. The cream relief was lined-out in black, painstakingly applied by hand to every vehicle. BET red then became the norm, with the number of cream bands reducing from three on double deckers to two, then one, as economies dictated by the early 1960s. The position eventually arrived at an all-over red livery for buses. BET red in itself requires defining; memories, photographs and popular opinion describe it as a bright, carmine shade. This becomes especially apparent when compared to the BET dark red, and BET crimson worn at this time by the neighbouring Rhondda and South Wales Transport fleets respectively.

Coaches were ivory with red relief, the shade of red being darker than the buses and described as wine red. Dual-purpose vehicles also featured wine red. From the mid-1960s, peacock blue replaced the red, which, together with the royal ivory, was of extremely pleasing appearance. Rhondda's coach and DP fleet was also freshened-up at this time; dark red gave way to a vibrant Georgian green, the ivory again being retained. Soon after, however, dual purpose vehicles from both fleets began to appear in BET red and ivory and the final batch of DP Leopards (1521-1530) were the first new vehicles delivered in this colour scheme. The handful of Neath & Cardiff coaches absorbed at this time was quickly repainted ivory with large white 'Western Welsh' lettering within a broad blue band — an early attempt at standardisation of the

The 10 Willowbrook-bodied AEC Reliances delivered in 1961 turned out to be one of the most successful vehicles. They were comfortable, reliable and could be turned out for any job. During their working life they ran in a variety of smart liveries all of which can be seen here.

NBC's coach fleet but allowing for retention of an individual second colour in keeping with the former companies' colours. No sooner had this scheme made its appearance than everything changed once again as NBC white became the order of the day from 1971.

The introduction of the NBC corporate livery saw Western Welsh repaint its buses into poppy red (or to give it the official designation, NBC Red. This afforded the welcome return of a contrasting waistband in 'NBC White' which was more of a grey. Dual-purpose vehicles soon appeared in a basically half-and-half white over red scheme.

A miscellany of coloured symbols was brought into use after the war and applied to vehicle cabsides to denote the area in which they were based. The purpose of this is unclear, but

could have been an attempt at instilling depot pride. In 1949 the whole system was simplified by use of coloured diamonds. The initial scheme was over-complicated but, by 1963, had been amended. Coaches and dual-purpose saloons did not carry symbols. The diamond device was a transfer which at first consisted of a double-lined black border only. When it had been fixed to the vehicle the centre colour was added by hand. For a short period, Ely Works was given a diamond, although descriptions vary. Later, the colour contained in the diamond was included in the transfer. Crosskeys' diamond changed to grey in the 1960s as the yellow was being confused with Cardiff's orange. Oddly, the white diamond was extended to cover the Rhondda fleet at Porth in 1971, just as the green diamond had become spare.

Inside the company's Cadoxton Road, Neath depot, mid-1930s.

Built in 1939 the company's depot at Gadlys, Aberdare accommodated 19 vehicles. *Stewart Williams*

Newcastle Emlyn's garage opened in 1949, and awaiting their next turn of duty soon after are 238 (KG 9620) and 797 (CKG 847). *Peter Smith*

for sale in 1969. It was sold in 1972 for £5,750. The St David's Street garage closed in May 1971 and sold in February 1972 for £12,500. The building still stands as a garage and is instantly recognisable.

In Abergavenny, the GWR sold its garage at Swan Meadow to Western Welsh in October 1929 and an office was transferred there, probably from the railway station, in November 1931. The latter was shared by Red & White until December 1940, when Western Welsh moved to The Watton, Brecon. This had been bought by the GWR and completed in January 1941. It replaced their facilities at 4 The Bulwark. Most GWR garages in the area covered by Western Welsh operations were taken over by November 1929 when only the company's outstations at GWR stations at Glyncorrwg, Cardigan, Haverfordwest and Llandysul remained to be assigned. The Glyncorrwg shed (telephone number Glyncorrwg 5!) remained operational until October 1966, then survived for many years as a private garage on long-abandoned railway land. In 1930 the R&W garage in Monmouth was used as an outstation. A later outstation at Hay-on-Wye closed in April 1969, with its share of the 730 Brecon service transferring to the Brecon depot. Brecon garage, in turn, was closed by National Welsh in December 1988.

The history of Neath depot originates in 1912 when the GWR created an improvised garage consisting of two tarpaulin sheets draped between two locomotive tenders. This purpose-built structure housed two Milnes Daimler vehicles which began a service between Neath and Pontardawe. The service extended to Brynamman in 1913, but the Midland Railway objected to GWR vehicles invading their territory and so during the First World War the service was terminated at Gwaun Leision (Gwaun Cae Gurwen). In 1921 the service reached Ammanford, and in 1922 Carmarthen. It was then that the depot moved to another improvised garage, this time at Neath & Brecon Junction. On the formation of Western Welsh and with further expansion planned, the Neath office, which had been at the railway station, moved to a room above an outfitter's shop in Windsor Road. In May 1930, land was assigned for new offices in Station Square which opened in February 1932 at a cost of £2,250. Meanwhile, in 1931 the spacious new Riverside garage was opened in Cadoxton Road. The company obtained further surplus land from the GWR at Cadoxton in March

The 1932-built booking office and staff facilities at Station Square, Neath in 1954.

1939, although it was never built upon. In June 1954, land was purchased for modern facilities at Neath Abbey Road and a new garage opened there in July 1957 to much celebration, including a lunch at Neath's Castle Hotel; the combined cost was £55,155. The new premises, which featured a sawtooth roof to provide northern light, two sets of pits and a sunken workshop, offered covered accommodation for vehicles needing attention while outside, on a concrete apron there was parking for 50 buses. The Cadoxton garage was sold to the BR Property Board for £3,500 in April 1958, while the other land at Cadoxton was apparently sold in 1972 for £13,750. Operations at Neath passed to South Wales Transport in January 1972 and the depot at Neath Abbey Road remained operational until around 1987, when it was taken over by a builders' merchant.

The GWR's garage in High Street, Aberdare, which dated from 1922, was taken over along with the business of JL Rosser's Dare Valley Motors in 1928. By July 1930 it had been rebuilt at a cost of £2,241. When Western Welsh was formed, a reorganisation of services in the area took place and Aberdare became a sub-depot of Neath. Services were cut, and for some reason the previous rapid growth in bus operations was halted. Nevertheless, a new garage in the Gadlys district of Aberdare opened in July 1939, just before the start of the Second World War. It held 19 vehicles and cost £7,123. In June 1956, adjacent property known as Penybryn House was purchased for a depot extension. This was disposed of in November 1961 although part of the site was retained for bus parking. Also adjacent to the Gadlys Road depot was a welfare building, erected by the staff from monies raised in a football tote and with the co-operation of the company. This opened in 1958, the company supplying the land as well as architectural, legal and building advice. The High Street garage passed to the local council, while the Gadlys site was transferred to SWT in May 1971 and closed soon after when operations transferred to the town's Red & White garage. The Gadlys premises was finally sold in February 1972.

The story of Western Welsh at Ammanford is certainly not for the faint-hearted. The first garage, at the GWR station, was known as The Shed and housed six vehicles, but was poorly situated and difficult to approach. Over the years it developed an alarming tendency to become completely electrified! This was due to corrosion when the base of the building developed an abnormally high resistance to earth, and sometimes an inside live wire touched the metal framework with disconcerting results. In 1930 the chief engineer secured the use of a former wholesale fruit store building known as Strick's in College Street. The approach was just as awkward with the pit

Tiger Cubs 1140 and 1165 are standing by at Abergavenny in August 1960 for duties to Newport and Brecon. Alternative journeys on the 733 from Newport were extended to Brecon as service 731, and often required a change to a single deck vehicle here. *Tony Warrener*

having to be built at an angle before buses could access it, which meant that only one vehicle could be accommodated. The situation became even more absurd when the depot moved from 'Strick's' to the 'Old Garage' at Tirydail in November 1934. Incredibly, the garage had a river running through it and was prone to flooding. It was not unknown for the shed driver to wade down to the bottom of the garage and attach a tow chain to an axle well under water. Authorisation was given to provide every man working at the garage with wellington boots! An office and waiting room in College Street was opened in 1937, but had gone by 1962. Things struggled on with the Tirydail garage remaining in use for 13 long and wet years until a new site in the best part of Ammanford was bought for £1,000 in 1944. A new garage, costing £8,000, opened in December 1945. The old

With its 'pay as you enter' sign clearly visible, the penultimate Western Welsh Weymann-bodied Tiger Cub, 1179, awaits its next duty at St David's depot, 1967. *John Heighway*

premises became the Regal Ballroom with enhanced water feature. Closure of the depot occurred in January 1966, with the Ministry of Transport purchasing the premises for use as a vehicle test centre, for £16,000.

The history of a depot at Newcastle Emlyn dates from 1926 and the GWR, who operated a service from the town to Cardigan. This was an extension of the rail service from Pencader and linked up at Cardigan with the branch from Whitland. For many years the garage consisted of a corrugated iron shed in the yard of the Cawdor Hotel. A new eight vehicle garage in New Road with office and waiting room was proposed in December 1947 and opened in April 1949 at a total cost of £13,450. Situated in extremely pleasant surroundings, the careful planning of the opening ceremony was confounded by the

enthusiasm of the townsfolk who made it their day as much as anyone else's! After the chairman of the UDC had cut the tape, a short service with the singing of a hymn took place in the entrance. It is unlikely any other Western Welsh garage witnessed such a family party. A civic lunch followed at the Emlyn Arms, but the real festivities came at the end of the day when the company generously provided dinner for all the depot staff. Full attendance was possible through the kind co-operation of Carmarthen staff who took over the entire working of those who would otherwise have been on duty. The premises was still operational when transferred to Crosville, along with New Quay, in April 1972. It was closed by Crosville Wales in September 1990 and converted for use as a car body shop. The forecourt was used by First Cymru until February 2005.

Two vehicles were outstationed at Jones's Ivy Garage, Bridge Street, Lampeter, in 1930, when a garage at Station Road, Llandovery was also in use. Later, Lampeter railway station became the home of the town's outstation. Llandysul, an outstation to Newcastle Emlyn, housed one vehicle for a short time.

At St David's, the original garage, formerly part of the coach house of the City Hotel, was one of the first road motor depots opened by the GWR and opened in 1912. Two Daimler buses were provided for the rail link to Haverfordwest, a distance of 16 miles, but with a running time of four hours on account of the badly rutted and narrow country roads. When the need for expansion arose, the problem was solved by a runaway bus which demolished the partition wall of the coach house. Consequently, the whole building served as the Western Welsh garage until replaced by a new facility opposite,

The original GWR garage at St David's was the coach house at the City Hotel, seen in the background, as English Electric-bodied 99 (KG 3616), a Leyland LT5a from 1934, lays withdrawn in the yard opposite in 1950. A replacement garage was built here in 1954. *AB Cross*

New Quay's eight-vehicle garage at Park Street. Services in the area were increased following its opening in 1936. The rear yard still serves as an outstation and departure point for Arriva Cymru. *Stewart Williams*

music from a bewhiskered lifeboatman — rounded off a memorable day. Very similar in appearance to that at Newcastle Emlyn, St David's remained in operation until transferred to SWT in January 1971. Its sale took place the following April for £7,000. The building survives today, but in much-altered form as a supermarket.

A garage at New Quay was opened in 1907 and was the first depot of the GWR, the object being to provide a service from New Quay to Llandysul station, just over 15 miles away. Two Daimler buses were provided for the service and at that time the road was so badly rutted that the running time for a single journey was two hours which restricted the service to two round trips a day. A zinc shed housed the vehicles until February 1936, when Western Welsh built an eight vehicle garage in Park Street.

Services greatly increased under the company, and by 1951 there was a two-hourly service to Carmarthen and also to Aberystwyth, connecting with Crosville at Aberaeron. With the forming of the NBC and the redistribution of much reduced West Wales services, the depot was handed over to Crosville in April 1972. Closure followed in 1976, but the forecourt was used by Arriva Cymru as an outstation, the only Western Welsh property in West Wales remaining in bus use. A shop has since been built on the forecourt, but the garage still stands and Arriva Cymru's outstation has moved behind. A shelter at Mathry Cross, was another property bought from the GWR in 1929, for £12.

authorised in June 1953 and opened at a cost of £11,796 in December of the following year. The outbreak of war resulted in considerable military activity in Pembrokeshire, and led to an increase in local services and contract work to the armed forces. Consequently, fleet requirements grew to 16 vehicles, and this figure remained constant for summer periods throughout the 1950s. The opening of the 1954 garage at New Street was witnessed by a number of prominent people including the Dean of St David's, Pembrokeshire's chief constable, councillors, and Colonel Browning, Pembrokeshire's Civil Defence Officer. Lunch followed at the Dyfed Café. In his response to the general manager's speech, the chairman of the county council paid tribute to the excellent service given to the county by the Western Welsh company. In the evening a dinner for the St David's staff was again provided by the company. Spontaneous entertainment — ranging from a Rachmaninov piano solo by the area manager to improvised Russian folk

In Pontypool, the former Eastern Valleys (Barrett's) garage at Pontnewynydd went on to serve the Western Welsh company for many years. The premises were extended in 1939 and again in 1943, as vehicle requirements increased. By 1951 64 vehicles were based there, all single deckers. *Stewart Williams*

Maintenance staff at Crosskeys in the late 1940s. *Viv Corbin*

Crosskeys garage in the late 1940s. In the front is Brush-bodied 316 (BBO 897), a 1939 Leyland TS8. *Peter Smith*

In the Pontypool area, the GWR station yard at Panteg, Griffithstown, was used in the company's formative years. Then in April 1934, Western Welsh acquired the freehold land of the former Eastern Valleys (Barrett's) company at Garndiffaith and Pontnewynydd, together with the former Lewis & James' garage at Newbridge and leasehold L&J land at Risca. The Pontnewynydd premises stood on the site of the Eastern Valley Brewery, purchased by W J Barrett, a hotelier whose sons operated the first bus — a Commer purchased from SWCM — in 1921. The land at Garndiffaith and Risca was presumably disposed of shortly before the outbreak of war. The takeover of Barrett's came in 1928, when their fleet strength stood at 25 vehicles. With Pontypool seeing an ever-increasing network of services, additional land for an extension at Pontnewynydd was obtained in June 1938 at a cost of £10,532. The resulting building was opened in September 1939 after which 60 vehicles could be garaged on site. Further land for parking buses was purchased there in January 1943 for £500, and by 1951, 64 vehicles were needed. The area was unfortunate in being burdened with many low railway bridges and so double-deckers couldn't be allocated there. The site was retained until April 1967, when economies introduced under the Monmouthshire Co-ordination Scheme with Red & White, saw vehicles and staff transfer to Cwmbran. The Pontnewynydd depot was sold to Pontypool UDC.

At Newbridge, land, an old garage and canteen, possibly the one-time headquarters of the Lewis & James Blue Fleet, was sold to Llanover Estates for £5,500 in October

1965. Further premises, owned by L&J, were let to R Tyler in October 1948 and sold in August 1973. The L&J company had built a new garage in 1927 at Risca House Yard, Crosskeys (telephone number: Crosskeys 6!), and included in its equipment was a much-publicised 10,000 gallon fuel tank. A major setback came when a disastrous fire broke out, causing considerable damage and destroying two Daimler vehicles. Had the fire spread to the fuel tank, Crosskeys might not exist today. The L&J headquarters moved to Crosskeys in the 1930s, and soon after a new office block was built. In 1933 the L&J company went into voluntary liquidation and the depot was taken over by Western Welsh. Land for a new garage on the main Crumlin to Newport road was acquired in March 1939. A large main building was completed in 1940 at a cost of £16,638. Further expansion was halted by the war and it was 1956 before the premises was extended at an estimated £23,000 cost. In July 1966 a new £6,000 canteen was completed at the side of the existing garage. The depot was closed by Stagecoach in May 2000.

In the Mid-Glamorgan area, unspecified property was acquired at Nantyffyllon in January 1935 with the business of FJ John. The business of WT Jones (Express

The Pontyberem & District Transport company was taken over in July 1935. With it came this wonderfully rustic garage, complete with lean-to shed and a pair of lean-to fitters! Resting from the rigours of the Carmarthen road are 220 (KG 9602) and 333 (BBO 340). Remarkably, the garage remained in bus use until 1969 and later became a car showroom. *Peter Smith*

Motors) was bought in June 1935 in a deal which included its garage at Bryncethin. It was sold for £400 to Penybont Rural District Council in January 1941, and is unlikely to have been used by Western Welsh which had recently expanded its own premises in Bridgend.

In July 1935, the company took over a garage at Pontyberem along with the Pontyberem & District Transport Company business of J Jones & Co, who had commenced a service to Llanelli in 1922. A second service from Ponthenry to Llanelli via Pontyberem began in 1928. A vehicle was outstationed at Llanelli's railway station from this time until 1969. Western Welsh's hilly route from Carmarthen to Llanelli via Pontyberem and Felinfoel was a hard one to operate, returning poor fuel figures and high maintenance costs. The former GWR Maudslays which were used required continual attention. A lean-to extension was added to the Pontyberem garage in 1948, and part of the main building was altered to provide a foreman's office and small staff room. Altogether these improvements cost £1,169. The depot survived with the company until the end of January 1969, when it was sold for £1,500. It was later used as a car sales showroom.

White's Barry office was situated above King Square, and there was a leasehold garage and canteen at Kendrick Road. Western Welsh's use of the latter premises, together with a leased garage at Penarth, was mainly for the storage of unlicensed vehicles, and the leases were sold in 1958 and 1962 respectively. Kendrick Road was bought by the GPO for £4,000, and sale of St Nicholas Road raised £5,250. The lease of an office at 119 Holton Road, and the rental of a kiosk at Barry Island were also transferred to the company. The latter, at a tourist attraction, was always regarded by the company as a summer gift from the gods! Former Barry Railway company land was acquired from the GWR in September 1937, and more followed in June 1938. The resulting 52-vehicle garage at Broad Street was opened in February 1939 at a cost of £13,983. With both Barry and Cardiff depots firmly established, the staff met every Christmas Day to play inter-depot football at Wenvoe. Buses were supplied free and official support was strong. After the game everyone retired to the Wenvoe Arms and indulged in free drinks on the company.

Further railway land at Barry was bought from British Railways in February 1956, when Holton House together with adjacent land was earmarked for offices, canteen and bus parking. Staff requested that the canteen be licensed as a club, but this was refused! In 1957 The decision was taken to demolish the house and construct the canteen above the existing office at Broad Street. It opened in May 1958 at a cost of £7,000 and replaced the facilities at Kendrick Road. It was necessary to keep weight to a minimum because the existing building was designed as a single storey structure. Upgrading of the workshops took place under the National Bus Company in 1972. Part of the bus parking area was sold to South Glamorgan County Council in 1982 for the Dock View road improvement scheme. The depot building passed to the

The unique design of Fishguard garage is instantly recognisable in this picture which was taken during construction in 1958. *Stewart Williams*

Vale of Glamorgan Council, is now leased to the Cardiff Transport Preservation Group, and is a working bus depot once again.

In Penarth, a garage at Ship Hill, St Nicholas Road, was acquired with the White's business late in 1936, and used by Western Welsh for storage of delicensed buses and coaches. By the late 1950s it was no longer needed and was sold in 1962, and used for light industry until demolition in 1991. The Streamways garage at Albert Road was acquired in April 1954, and ownership continued until 1962. It was used as a coach depot and vehicle store. A booking office was situated within the garage. The sale of the premises raised £9,000. In September 1940, a waiting room was opened at RAF St Athan, replacing withdrawn saloon 378 which had previously served as a temporary waiting room there.

A six vehicle garage at Goodwick station was leased from the GWR in 1944, and 10 years on, at the opening of new facilities at St David's, TG Davies described Goodwick as the only one of which the company was ashamed. "I hope that in the year ahead we can replace the 'duck pond' at Goodwick with a modern garage," he said. It was eventually replaced by an ultra-modern depot at Sailors Yard, Fishguard, proposed in 1955 but not complete until August 1959, at a cost of £11,732. The new depot featured an experimental electric underfloor heating system, which was cheap to install and maintain, and took advantage of off-peak loading so that the floor slab was warmed at night and gave off heat to the adjacent waiting room and offices during the day. The garage housed six vehicles, while a further six could be accommodated outside. Freehold land for a turning point in Lower Town was noted in the 1962 minutes. Fishguard survived until the end of the company's operations in West Wales in January 1971, but was not transferred to SWT, the premises being sold in May of that year for £10,000. The garage is currently in use as an electrical retail store and the waiting room is now a café.

Barry depot, including the booking office with a canteen above it, can be glimpsed behind Atlantean 342 (XUH 342) as it stops for a crew change in 1963. *Gerald Mead*

Land at Varteg Hill, Pontypool was purchased for a bus station in July 1954, and operations commenced from there in 1956. The site was in use until late in 1971, when the land was sold to Pontypool Urban District Council.

Land for a bus station in Cwmbran was announced in 1955, although it was not conveyed to the company until July 1964. Land was also leased for a new garage at St David's Road from February 1960 and completion of the building followed in October 1963. Covered accommodation for 38 vehicles together with maintenance facilities and a large office block were provided at a cost of £76,664. This became the Stagecoach bus company depot in St David's Road. A new tours and enquiry office was opened in the town centre in 1972, replacing the office at the depot. From October 1963 to May 1971 Western Welsh had two St David's Road garages at nearly 100 miles apart.

A proposal for a new garage to house the Ebsworth fleet at St Clears was mooted in 1955, but later shelved. The few buses that would have benefited remained out-stationed at Laugharne.

The former GWR outstation at Haverfordwest wasn't needed after 1956 with the takeover of the Green's garage and office in Marsh Yard. The repair shops were partly sited in the yard, and partly in a converted RAF hangar. Western Welsh now had a significant presence in the town, and with the coming of the oil refineries at Milford Haven, it prepared for expansion of services. Land was bought in June 1959 for a new garage and bus station. Until then, area management was based in a building known as The Bungalow, an adapted and extended small dwelling. In 1968 plans were announced to upgrade the site. Impressive new facilities opened in April 1970, but the glory was to be short lived. In March 1972 operations in Haverfordwest passed to SWT, but the premises were soon swept away by yet another road scheme. Green's garaged three vehicles at Neyland and two at Saundersfoot. The former garage was listed as a freehold asset in 1962 with two vehicles allocated. It was disposed of

The final building project undertaken by Western Welsh was the impressive new garage and offices at Haverfordwest, which opened in April 1970. Within two years it was no longer part of the company's empire, having passed to South Wales Transport with NBC's territorial re-organisations in 1972. It didn't last long and was soon demolished to make way for a new road. *Stewart Williams*

in November 1967. One vehicle was kept at the Saundersfoot premises, and outstations for single vehicles were situated at Narberth, Llangwm and Freystrop.

Land for a new garage and bus station at Manchester Square in Milford Haven was purchased for £3,000 in January 1959. The facilities were completed in November 1961 at a further cost of £28,950. Six lock-up garages were included in the development and let on tenancies at 12/6d per week. The garage, designed to accommodate nine vehicles, featured a portal frame steel structure and low pitch roof. There was room for a further seven vehicles outside. This building also had facilities for fuelling and repair work, including a pit, mess room, staff toilet and store. The bus station with enquiry office and public toilets featured a wide, cantilevered canopy over eight bays. The opening ceremony was performed by Councillor E Aubrey Grove, chairman of Milford Haven UDC, who was presented with an inscribed pair of silver scissors by the company's architect, GS Henman. Afterwards, Councillor Grove thanked the company for providing the town with such a magnificent garage and bus station, and reasoned that it must have every confidence in the prosperity and expansion of the town. At its peak, the bus station saw 853 departures every week. The premises survived in operation until January 1972 and was sold the following January for £26,000. The buildings were demolished and the site used as a supermarket car park. This in turn was vacated in 2007.

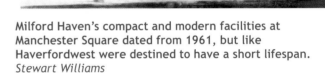

Milford Haven's compact and modern facilities at Manchester Square dated from 1961, but like Haverfordwest were destined to have a short lifespan. *Stewart Williams*

An unusual move saw the company buy a small garage in Treorchy in January 1960, from Rhondda Transport for £3,500. Situated well away from its operating area, it was described by the chairman at that year's AGM as a purchase which would allow Western Welsh to save considerable empty running. There is no evidence however to suggest this building was ever used by the company and it is not surprising to record that the premises were being advertised for sale by 1962.

Tenancy of a kiosk at Aberystwyth Railway Station was also listed in the company directors' report of 1962.

Finally, the assets of Rhondda Transport were taken over at the end of 1970. There were several garages and workshops at Porth, built over the years, the oldest originally housing Rhondda's trams. The site was situated in the narrow valley bottom, astride the Rhondda Fach river and hemmed in by the A4233 road and the railway line to Maerdy. The garages worked their way up from Porth Square where there was a small bus station, and they seemed to go on forever and were always full of perfectly lined-up AEC Regents! The offices were situated in an adjacent elevated position at Hannah Street, on the A4233. The premises were assigned to Western Welsh and continued in use with National Welsh. Later they were divided between the Stagecoach group and the Thomas of Rhondda company.

The new bus station at Varteg was opened in April 1956. It was built in advance of a planned estate of more than 500 houses nearby. *Stewart Williams*

Powered by the people

Team spirit was the name of the game

One of the most fascinating aspects of almost any company formed to serve the public is the people responsible for running it. This doesn't limit itself to the management alone, but often a work culture permeates the entire operation right down to the lowliest employee. If those behind a company take pride then such an ethos will spread and help create an enviable reputation. This is exactly what happened in the case of the Western Welsh Omnibus Company.

It is no exaggeration to say that from its very beginning right up to the last days the vast majority of its staff displayed an enormous pride in the business. Indeed pride was prominent in everything the company did. Everything had to be just right, from the appearance of its buses and coaches, through the conduct of its road staff to the way passengers were dealt with. The original company crest carried four words beneath it —

reliability, efficiency, comfort and courtesy. If there was space then the word pride would have been there too. They all combined in the daily life of Western Welsh.

A number of different sections of the company helped make it tick — the management, office workers, road staff and of course the engineers and fitters who kept the vehicles running. They all played an equally important part. However it was the road staff, the drivers and conductors, who were generally at the sharp end. For it was they that passengers met and encountered on a day to day basis. It was they who were the first point of contact and it was they who got the job done. True, the activities of the boardroom were vital to the company's continued existence, but even the directors and managers knew that their men and women on the road were the very heartbeat of the operation.

All hands to the pump in the Traffic Department in the late 1950s. From left are Dennis Rawlinson, Tom Phipps, George Wedlake and Leslie Smith.
George Wedlake

From the earliest days, road staff figured prominently in the company's dealings with the public. And just as often they were at the centre of stories of bravery, heroism and often simply plain, cold common sense and courtesy that saved the day.

Management was very well aware of this. The reason was that those who witnessed or had been helped by a driver or conductor were never slow to put pen to paper and write to the general manager. They made no secret of the fact that letters of praise poured in and as many letters of thanks were sent in reply. The number of reports of exemplary staff behaviour that appeared in the Staff Bulletin were legion.

Perhaps this bond between passengers and crew was clear evidence that Western Welsh was a company that from the start set out to do it right. That they succeeded is not in doubt. This was something that was not confined to ordinary, everyday services, but also the luxury long distance tours for which the company established a pioneering name. People came back year after year to holiday with Western Welsh and the reason was simple — they were looked after. And royally. During its lifetime, the company experienced good times and bad. That it survived leaner moments is further testament to the quality of the staff at all levels.

Many of these staff were intensely loyal and continued to work for the company for many decades, often until retirement. The number of employees who had worked with Western Welsh for more than 25 years was impressive. The number who stayed with the company for 40-plus years even more so. Much of this is down to the team spirit that existed between departments. Yes, the driver and the conductor were the front line, but back at the depots were the staff who kept them supplied with well-maintained, well-presented vehicles of which they could be proud.

Drivers, conductors and buses of course needed routes to run over and passengers to carry, all of which needed consummate planning. This is where, from the very origins of Western Welsh, the company had many notable personnel who each played a part in taking the company to the next level of success.

South Wales Commercial Motors, the forerunner of Western Welsh, began in 1919 and was first registered as a company in 1920. Among its directors were: Col J Gaskell, chairman; Major J G Gaskell and the renowned Albert Gray, jointly managing and WT Wilks, secretary.

It was Gray of course who, more than anyone else was responsible for the construction of the vehicles that began the very first service of SWCM.

The first directors of the newly formed Western Welsh Omnibus Company Limited, in association with the Great Western Railway, were: JS Austen, chairman; the Rt Hon Lord Glanely, Sir Ralph Cope, FCA Coventry, HC Drayton, Sir James Milne KCVO, FE Stanley and JS Wills.

Lord Glanely was killed in the Second World War, and Austen died in 1942. Drayton became the new chairman, but in 1946 he resigned and was replaced by Wills, who had been managing director. He in turn was replaced by RW Birch.

When SWCM began, Albert Gray was its general manager. He saw that company through its early years and was the natural choice of general manager for the Western Welsh company in 1929. He remained at the reins until his retirement in August 1938, though he was kept on as a consultant, receiving an annual retainer of £700. He kept this link with the company until 1955, when he finally stepped down at the age of 75. He died nine years later in August 1964.

In November 1921, SWCM's first manager at Bridgend, Captain GT Wilcox, was appointed at an annual salary of

£350. He was superseded by E Rees in 1923. Between them they laid the foundation of services in and around the town and fought hard to keep their gains in the unregulated years that led up to the passing of the Road Traffic Act of 1930.

In December 1932, long-serving managing director WB Cownie died. At the start of the following year FE Stanley was appointed as his replacement.

The chief engineer was Jack H Lewis, one of the Western Valleys team along with WT James. In 1933 Lewis resigned, and was replaced by A Dimmack, formerly of Potteries Motor Traction, at an annual salary of £800. Dimmack died in 1944 and the chief engineer's position was filled by FH Kidd from Western National, also at an annual salary of £800.

Leslie A Gray had joined his father's SWCM company as a junior clerk in 1919, and served an apprenticeship in the overhaul and maintenance department. On the formation of Western Welsh he transferred to the Neath area, where he was involved in the amalgamation of the GWR road services. He moved to head office in 1930 and was assistant engineer when FH Kidd arrived as chief engineer. He had a hand in the planning of the central workshops, then in 1951 was given the new post of assistant chief engineer. His tenure remained a long and happy one, and he retired in October 1969 after 50 years of service. He was closely associated with the Ely Welfare Club, Educational Club and Inter-Depot Sports Club, and he maintained links with twin company SEK Copenhagen, organising many exchange visits between the companies.

Leslie's brother Ivor L Gray began his association with the company as area manager, Cardiff in 1939. His career was interrupted by overseas service in the Army, but by 1945 he had returned in that position covering both Cardiff and Barry. He left the company a year later to join Hebble Motor Services as general manager, then went on to Yorkshire Woollen District, South Wales Transport, Jamaica Omnibus Services and Rhondda Transport, in each case as general manager. Turning full circle, he returned to Western Welsh in 1962. His retirement in April 1971 ended a family association with the company that stretched back more than half a century.

Fred Pengelly started as a conductor with White's in 1926 and joined Western Welsh at the takeover in 1935. He was appointed temporary manager at Cardiff and Barry in 1943, at an annual salary of £400, then in 1945 was appointed assistant transport manager. He was promoted to assistant traffic manager in 1948,

and became the new traffic manager in 1952. He became known as Pengelly the Telly for his frequent appearances on TV with the company's annual holiday tours advertising campaign. In 1971 he was appointed assistant general manager, a post he held until his retirement in September 1972.

Having replaced RAJ Williams as traffic manager in 1932, WT James replaced Albert Gray as general manager in 1938, at an annual salary of £1,200, while in turn TG Davies replaced James as transport manager, at a salary of £450. James became managing director in 1947, with Davies promoted to general manager, but the latter resigned to take up an appointment at Rhondda Transport in June 1948 and was replaced by RT Ebrey from East Yorkshire Motor Services.

Ebrey was awarded an OBE in the 1951 New Year Honours, and upon his death in April 1952, Davies returned to his original post at an increased annual salary of £1,800. In turn, TLC Strange came from Ribble to take up the position of traffic manager. In the 1960 New Year Honours, an OBE was bestowed on Davies, who unfortunately suffered ill health over the coming months and retired in 1961.

The company's area managers in 1939 were: IL Gray, Cardiff; AJ White, Barry; E Rees, Bridgend; W Barrett, Pontypool; RAJ Williams, Carmarthen; AC Willett, Neath & Aberdare; A Bridgeford, Brecon and D Williams, Crosskeys. RAJ Williams was a GWR man whose career began in 1912.

Assistant secretary H Goodes was replaced in 1940 by JG De'Ath, who in turn resigned after two years; his post was not replaced. A change in the company's accountant came with DG Philip replacing TH Underhill, who had resigned in 1939. On the retirement of E Rees as Bridgend's area manager in 1943 the post was taken up by AJ White. It seems he was unhappy with his move from

An office outing — travelling by Western Welsh, naturally. In the front row are Stewart Williams, George Wedlake, Don Williams and George Sharpe. The identity of the person behind has been forgotten over time. *George Wedlake*

Barry, as he left within a few months to join Hebble Motor Services, and was replaced by EG Burgoyne, who had been chief clerk at the depot since 1924. White was obviously a high-flyer as he had moved south by 1948 to become general manager of Devon General.

Not everyone in the company was honest it seems. In June 1944, a case of embezzlement was proved against RG Evans, who was assistant to the local accountant. He was sentenced to 18 months of hard labour.

A large number of changes took place in 1946, many as a result of personnel returning from war service. That of IL Gray was short-lived, and when he left for Hebble his replacement as area manager for Cardiff & Barry was SB Stevenson, who came from Devon General. In February, company secretary EA Bond resigned after 18 years and was replaced by AW Groocock. A product of the old family firm of White's, TC White, was appointed chief clerk at Barry depot in March.

Office staff at Pontypool depot, mid-1950s. *Tony Jenkins*

In June 1946, George Alexander, former secretary to the directors, was appointed company accountant, replacing DG Philip who had served through the war. Local accountant for 18 years, SB Norris, was promoted to assistant accountant.

In 1948 CS Richardson, chief clerk at Pontypool, was promoted to area manager at Crosskeys on the retirement of former L&J man, D Williams.

In February 1949, chief engineer FH Kidd resigned and was replaced by Frank A Mason, formerly of City of Oxford, at a salary of £900 a year. Leslie Gray had been overlooked again.

Neath area manager AC Willett, who was ex-GWR, retired in August 1950 with 44 years' service. He was replaced by A Davies. In September, Brecon's leading driver Bill Rhodes retired. He had joined the GWR in 1889 and transferred to the road transport department in 1903.

In 1951, the death was announced of T Arrandale, who had been tours manager for the company since 1933. He was replaced by Ken Allender. In October, Cardiff & Barry area manager SB Stevenson left to take up an appointment at Hants & Sussex. His post was then split, and two new area managerss were appointed: TC White at Cardiff and RC Maunder at Barry. In November, P Wyke-Smith came from Birmingham & Midlands Motor Omnibuses (Midland Red) to take the appointment of assistant engineer, western.

In April 1952, when Fred Pengelly was appointed the new traffic manager, the position of assistant traffic manager went to DGF Rawlinson, formerly of Westcliff-on-Sea Motor Services. Also in October 1952, AW Groocock resigned and George Alexander was appointed company secretary. P Wyke-Smith moved on to East Midlands Motor Services and was replaced by J Walsh. Last, but not least, in December, Leslie Gray was appointed assistant chief engineer, a new post.

CS Richardson left the company in 1953 for a post at Jamaica Omnibus Services with Ivor Gray, and was replaced at Crosskeys by RC Maunder, whose Barry post was filled by TC White moving over from Cardiff. The loop was completed by S Harris's appointment as Cardiff's area manager.

Parcels manager Albert E Smith retired in April 1954. He had been with the company throughout its existence, having joined Wm Hancock & Co in 1911. DGF Rawlinson left for Maidstone & District, and his position as assistant traffic manager was taken up by S Harris. Leslie A Smith, son of Albert, became Cardiff area manager.

When eastern area manager W Barrett retired in 1955, his position was filled by RC Maunder. A 30-year stint at Crosville preceded the arrival of WJ Jones as Neath area manager in October, and his responsibility was extended to the Ammanford area following closure of that depot early in 1965.

Rhondda Transport beckoned for assistant engineer J Walsh in September 1956. He was replaced by WN Williams from British Road Services.

In 1957, T Baker, former traffic manager at Green's, was appointed area manager at Haverfordwest. Company architect E Webster retired aged 78 after a long career, during which time his distinctive yet functional buildings had sprung up across the entire Western Welsh empire. Much of them would now be regarded as classic 20th century industrial architecture.

The traffic superintendent at Haverfordwest, RL Johnson, was found guilty of embezzlement in June 1958. His conviction was a result of CS Richardson returning to the company in January as a trouble-shooter around the depots. In the same year, tours superintendent K Allender moved to Greenslades Tours, Devon. The death was announced of William Barrett, former area manager at Pontypool, aged 65. Within two months the death of his father, WJ Barrett, aged 92, occurred; with his sons William and Harry he had been responsible for establishing Barrett Bros (Eastern Valleys).

Area managers at Haverfordwest and Carmarthen respectively, T Baker and RAJ Williams retired in 1959. The latter had joined the GWR in 1912. As an economy measure control of the Carmarthen area passed to RC Maunder, the new Haverfordwest area manager. CS Richardson's trouble-shooting days were short-lived and he returned as eastern area manager based at Crosskeys.

In 1960, chief engineer FA Mason was appointed assistant general manager. At the end of 1961, TG Davies retired through ill health and his replacement early in the new year bore a familiar name – IL Gray who returned to the fold from Rhondda Transport. Ken Allender also returned to the company, as tours superintendent, in May.

The company secretary and accountant, G Alexander, retired in February 1961 and was replaced by CM Williams, ex-Devon General. Local accountant SB Norris retired in April after 42 years' service, and was replaced by BG Barry. Another retirement was that of EG Burgoyne, area manager at Bridgend, who was replaced by LA Smith. TC White was now assistant manager of a regrouped Cardiff & Barry area.

In January 1962, FA Mason moved to Rhondda to replace IL Gray as general manager. Former South Wales Transport employee PC Wickens was appointed chief engineer. The untimely death of RC Maunder, western area manager, at 52, saw K Allender move from tours to replace him until 1966, when he returned to head office as assistant traffic manager, responsible for all tours, express services and private hire.

Cardiff & Barry area manager TC White left the industry in 1963 after 33 years, and was replaced by Ivor R Day. In August it was announced that Jack H Lewis, former chief engineer and co-founder of Lewis & James Ltd, had died aged 74.

In April 1965, assistant secretary and accountant BG Barry resigned and was replaced by DPG Thomas.

Staff moves in January 1966 saw DP Thomas leaving for Rhondda, and PC Wickens for Maidstone & District. HP Gwyther was appointed assistant secretary and accountant, and DW Cherry (ex-Rhondda) became chief engineer. Harry Barrett, co-founder of Eastern Valleys Motors, died in March, aged 72.

In 1967, the death occurred of S Richardson, by then assistant manager at Cwmbran, aged 62. He was temporarily replaced by DK Williams. Ivor L Phillips was appointed Crosskeys area manager in 1967, while Lyndon Rees was promoted within the traffic department to become chief clerk to the assistant traffic manager, and CR Brown was appointed area manager at Cwmbran in March 1968. Lyndon Rees, who had started his career with Rhondda Transport in 1957, left Western Welsh early in 1969 to take up a position with the Ministry of Overseas Development in Hong Kong. His job there involved setting standards for public transport services and assisting in the running of the colony's two large bus companies. He pursued an illustrious career in Hong Kong, went on to buy the said companies and become a tax exile, for which he readily paid homage to his formative years with Western Welsh.

Company accountant and assistant secretary HP Gwyther resigned in February 1969 and was replaced by RA Dixon. In October, LA Gray retired as its assistant chief engineer after 50 years' service and was replaced by JP Piper. K Allender was appointed Cardiff area manager.

In 1971, Ivor L Gray was succeeded as director and general manager by Keith Holmes who came from Northern Counties Motor & Engineering Co Ltd, at a salary of £5,200 a year.

Office staff gather for the camera outside the company's Cwmbran travel office in the 1960s. *Tony Jenkins*

People, prams, parcels and perishables!

A bus consists of 52 seats, a horn and a rail, all screwed together on top of a lot of wheels. The driver sits in front of these wheels and blows the horn. The conductor stands at the back and shouts 'Hold tight!'

He also goes for walks around the bus and counts the passengers. These are people who sit in the bus and get in the conductor's way. Passengers who stand at bus stops and count the number of buses that don't stop are called the public.

The top of a bus is called the upper deck, and underneath is the lower saloon where they don't serve drinks. The decks are joined together by a stairway, in the middle of which is a mirror. A conductor can look in the mirror and count the passengers being trampled to death on the platform below. Passengers so trampled to death are brushed off onto the roadway. They are called transport statistics and are collected by Corporation vans later on.

Every conductor has a barrel-organ riveted to his chest, and often, when he turns the handle, nothing happens. When it does, he opens the top of the barrel-organ, tears off a ticket and gives it to the nearest passenger or throws it on the floor.

48mph is bad enough, but when he asks for your name and address, and you say Reg T Ebrey, c/o Western Welsh Offices, Ely — well that's asking for trouble!

A cheeky cartoon reflecting the issue of bus speed limits which appeared in the Staff Bulletin.

A bus time-table is simply an official publication which gives passengers a complete list of all the buses they couldn't get on to. For whiling away travelling time, the company provides games in which the passengers can take part. One of these is called "Tickets Please!" In this particular game an inspector boards a bus and sneaks up to the top deck with a pair of pliers. Standing at the back, he suddenly yells 'Tickets, please' Passengers immediately become panic-stricken and begin searching for tickets in their pockets, handbags, books, attaché cases, and under the seats. The passenger who first presents a ticket may be thrown off the bus if the ticket number is wrong.

Another game is 'Guess Where?' This is played between a speechless passenger and the conductor. When the conductor shouts 'Fares, please!' the passenger gives him a shilling and says nothing. "A penny one?" asks the conductor. The passenger shakes his head. "A twopenny?" guesses the conductor. The passenger shakes his

Three members of the road staff smile for the camera, while a fourth looks decidedly furtive at Station Square, Neath, 1957. *Howard Roberts*

Port Talbot's Jack Handford and Dai Austin enjoy the sea air at Porthcawl between journeys in the summer of 1962.

head again. "A first class return with sleeper to Liverpool, maybe?" asks the conductor. 'No,' says the passenger, 'One and a half to The Swan.' The above game is greatly appreciated by conductors with powers of telepathy.

A third game is 'No Standing!' This is played when a conductor suddenly shouts: 'No standing on the top deck!' Upon hearing this, the driver applies his brakes very quickly and everyone standing on the top deck is thrown forward in a heap on the floor. A quick driver can often trap as many as six passengers and lay them flat. Any passenger thrown down the stairway or out into the street is disqualified for cheating. In the event of a passenger considering the

rules unfair, he makes a visit to head office, and pays his respects to the umpire who, after hearing the complaint, gives the conductor 'one day's leave' to rearrange the rules.

The final game is called 'Season Tickets'. This game is only enjoyed by a privileged few who, having paid in advance, take full advantage of the Rules. Unlike the ordinary fare-paying passengers, season ticket holders have a number of signs, which, if read correctly, save the conductor a lot of trouble. The production of a season ticket is purely voluntary. No conductor is expected to insist, as it gives him an unfair advantage. Should this passenger fail to produce his season ticket, the matter is amicably settled

between the passenger and Inspector by an exchange of addresses. The conductor is not invited to take part and is considered the loser.

To add to the fun and games in the life of a busman, there are children, smokers, 'left money at home' passengers, 'under the weather' passengers; not forgetting the perambulators, parcels and perishable goods, and the thousand-and-one oddities that go to make up the day's work.'

'As others see us', an article from the Staff Bulletin, November, 1950.

In August 1972 Holmes was appointed general manager of Red & White Services and Jones Omnibus Services in addition to his existing post at Western Welsh. In March 1973, he was appointed general manager of the National Bus Company's Western Region South Wales division, and later progressed to Midland Red as general manager. Former Rhondda man WF Cooper became traffic manager. Ivor Day was appointed internal auditor in March 1972, and Ken Allender became Cardiff & Barry area manager. Fred Pengelly retired in September after 46 years' service while S Harris retired as assistant traffic manager and was replaced by Sydney B Morgan (ex-Crosville). Chief engineer DW Cherry moved to Northern Counties and was replaced by RO Blatchford, formerly of R&W, as group engineer.

In 1973 JB Hargreaves was appointed general manager while assistant engineer JP Piper resigned and was replaced by Frank Langlois, formerly of Red & White. Following the integration of the R&W management team in 1974, Ron H Nicholls, formerly of Rhondda Transport, was appointed area engineer (West), based at Porth, John Wilkins (Central) and Owen Parry (East).

In 1974, WF Cooper was appointed planning manager while JH Snell (R&W) took on the traffic manager's job for four months. Keith Holmes was followed to the Midland Division by JB Hargreaves and was replaced as general manager by FE Dark (ex-West Riding). RH Brooks was appointed assistant to the general manager, and in September Bert Boys (ex-National Travel NE) transferred to take up the position of traffic manager, completing the NBC joint management team.

In the Western Welsh boardroom the story of its directors is no less complicated. The Earl of Hopetown was appointed a director, but he resigned from the board in May 1947 and was replaced by P Yorke. Possibly as a result of the frequent brevity of tenure, the board authorised removal of directors' names from stationery to save on printing costs. Birch resigned in November, and was replaced by WT James OBE, who came from BET and was co-founder of Lewis & James.

From this point on there seemed to be many comings and goings and the records show that appointments and resignations seemed to follow one another with surprising regularity. Occasionally people would move from one bus company to another. Sometimes they would return in the years that followed. Often those at the top would enjoy directorships of more than one company.

Changes at the board in the autumn of 1960 saw the resignations of JS Wills, chairman; WT James, managing director and KWC Grand. Their replacements were: EL Taylor, chairman; JR Hammond and WM Dravers. However, in an additional move, the post of managing director was dispensed with.

Following a spate of board resignations during 1968, IL Gray was appointed to the board, while continuing as general manager.

The influence of the Gray family

When it comes to the people behind the successful creation and operation of the Western Welsh bus company there can be none more important than the members of the Gray family.

One member of this transport dynasty who remains justifiably proud of her family's importance in the history of road transport in Wales is Christine Davies, daughter of Leslie Gray and granddaughter of company founder Albert Gray.

Christine holds many fascinating memories and mementoes of her family and its multi-generation links to Western Welsh.

She recalls how her grandfather, Albert Gray, was born in 1879 in Birmingham and how he began his engineering career in the Midlands.

"In 1906 he joined Cardiff brewers William Hancock as transport manager and engineer, where he maintained their fleet of delivery lorries," she said.

"During the First World War he worked for the Ministry of Mines. When he returned to Hancock's in 1919, the time was right for the start of a motorbus operation, and so South Wales Commercial Motors began.

"He married my grandmother and they had four children. The first was Leslie, then came Ivor, Bob, and a daughter Dora. Bob didn't join Western Welsh, and Dora, the last survivor, died in March 2007 aged 93. The family's interest in all things mechanical continues to this day, through five generations to my grandson.

"I remember as a child being taken around the various Western Welsh depots in our Austin Seven car. The Gray family home was at Heath Park Avenue, Cardiff, but my parents lived in Butleigh Avenue, Victoria Park, Cardiff, which is where I grew up.

"Because of my father's position, we were one of the few families to have a car and a telephone. He was called out to every accident and breakdown involving company vehicles, and I used to lie awake well into the night waiting for his return home to hear all about it.

"We had a very busy social life. Being part of Western Welsh was like having an extended family. There were big Christmas parties, where Father Christmas appeared with presents for the children. Then in the summer there were field days within the grounds of Ely Works, with sporting events, games and contests for the staff and their families. It was all recorded on film by my father.

"My father was involved with the Education Club, and we frequently had coach outings to all sorts of places. I

The Ely breakdown gang at the works field during the late 1950s.
Christine Davies

Bryn Calvin-Thomas wrote the following appreciation of Leslie Gray in the Staff Bulletin of November 1957:

"Perhaps the letters LAG on memos from the assistant chief engineer are not very significant to younger members of the staff," he wrote, "but older ones will know that they are the initials of a personality with direct and unbroken connections with the very roots of Western Welsh. Leslie Albert Gray is one of the dwindling band of employees who started with South Wales Commercial Motors, the firm from which this, the largest bus company in Wales, has grown. His father, the much respected Mr Albert Gray, happily still in good health and living in retirement at Ogmore-by-Sea, was in at the beginning of SWCM and later became general manager of the new Western Welsh company. Thirty seven years ago his son Leslie started as an apprentice at the time of the introduction of the first bus service between Cardiff and Penarth. After periods of experience of various departments, he was made assistant engineer when the Ely Works site was being developed in 1930. Some 20 years later, in 1952, he was appointed chief assistant engineer, and in 1955 also works superintendent.

"At and away from work, Mr Gray can be described as intensely active. He is keenly interested in all forms of art and music, but his abiding off-duty interest is in film-making, having held all the important offices in the well-known Cardiff Amateur Cine Society.

"This interest has been turned to the advantage of the Western Welsh tours department, for whom he has made successful films for advertising and publicity purposes. The time and energy of this busy person is, however, always freely given for the many good causes who seek him as artist or projectionist.

"The Welfare and Educational Club have always commanded his helpful interest and together with Mrs Gray, and their two children, Christine and Clive, he is always welcomed at various social gatherings."

remember these trips for the singing — everyone on board spent the journey home singing. There was also a Welfare Club, a Sports Club, even an Andy Capp Club; their activities were encouraged by the company, who saw it as an ideal way of getting to know your colleagues at all levels and chatting about the many aspects of the job over a pint or a game of darts.

"We also had exchange visits from our Danish friends. I have vivid memories of these visits, which began in 1948. My father's passion for photography covered these occasions, and he also took his cine camera on many holiday tours. In the big freeze of the winter of 1947 he filmed buses stuck in the snow. Those films made a lasting impression on me as a child."

Many of the Gray family films have not survived the test of time, being found to have disintegrated beyond rescue. Those that were salvageable have now been carefully transferred to video and are kept at the National Library of Wales.

Fleet facts and figures

Vehicles of a true transport legend

THE history of the vehicles operated by Western Welsh, particularly in its early years, is complicated. There was a considerable variety of types and origination, and their details have been difficult to source. It was never expected that this book would contain a comprehensive list of everything, but thanks to the tireless work over many years by Chris Taylor and Viv Corbin along with their kindness in releasing the information, the list that follows is as complete an account as is possible to achieve, and proudly published here for the first time. There may still be omissions during the first 10 years of the company's existence, as it is known that during this period various vehicle identities were exchanged, whether legally or otherwise, at Ely Works. In all probability this was a fairly widespread practice among major bus operators, London being perhaps the prime example. At the risk of upsetting some historians, it is an area

that is best avoided. It is perhaps safest to say that there is photographic evidence of the same, identical, registration marks appearing on a number of different chassis.

The dates 'new' and 'in use' are as precise as possible, given that vehicles were sometimes not registered for up to a month after they had been delivered. In certain cases acquired businesses and vehicles continued to be run as separate companies for many years. Where known, the date is given when Western Welsh no longer listed the vehicle. However, in many cases buses had been withdrawn for a considerable time. A few were stored at Ely's 'Graveyard' for up to three years after the 'out' date before being sold or dismantled. The numbers in the notes column refer to supplementary information which follows the main list and may be of additional interest.

1929

New	Fleet No.	Re-number	Reg No.	Chassis & type	Body & type	In use	Origin	Notes
4/25	903		XY 2095	Thornycroft A1	Vickers B19F	1929 – 1930	GWR	
5/25	913/4		XY 5374/5	Thornycroft A1	Thornycroft B19F	1929 – 1933	GWR	1
5/25	919/22	424/5	XY 7444/7	Thornycroft A1	Vickers B19F	1929 – 5/35	GWR	
5/25	921	423	XY 7446	Thornycroft A1	Vickers B19F	1929 – 10/35	GWR	2
6/25	926/7/9/31/ 2/5/7/8/40		YK 3820/1/3/5/ 6/9/31/2/4	Thornycroft A1	Thornycroft B19F	1929 – 1933	GWR	1
6/25	1149	426	AX 8427	Thornycroft A1	Hall Lewis B20F	1929 – 10/35	GWR	3
10/25	1042		BX 6226	Graham Dodge	GWR B20	1929 – 2/30	GWR	4
10/25	1044		BX 6402	International SL	Strachan B20	1929 – 2/30	GWR	4
12/25	293		NY 9842	AEC 202	GWR B26	1929 – 7/31	GWR	
2/26	291		TX 178	AEC 202	GWR B26R	1929 only	GWR	
3/26	1043		BX 6585	Graham Dodge	GWR B20	1929 – 2/30	GWR	4
4/26	1203	301	YR 6214	Maudslay ML3	Buckingham B32R	1929 – 1/34	GWR	
6/26	1145		UH 1329	Lancia	Hall Lewis B26	1929 – 1/32	GWR	3
6/26	1147		AX 9268	Thornycroft A2	Hall Lewis B20F	1929 – 1933	GWR	3
7/26	1144		UH 1475	Lancia	Hall Lewis B26	1929 – 1933	GWR	3
10/26	1213	302	YR 2663	Maudslay ML3	Buckingham B32R	1929 – 1/34	GWR	
10/26	1214/6/8	303–5	YR 6413/5/7	Maudslay ML3	Buckingham B32R	1929 – 3/34	GWR	
10/26	1219	306	YH 3791	Maudslay ML3	Buckingham C32D	1929 – 5/35	GWR	
2/27	1146		AX 9900	Lancia	Hall Lewis B26	1929 – 1933	GWR	3
2/27	1250–2		YE 7048–50	Guy FBB	Hall Lewis B32R	1929 – 1930	GWR	5
2/27	1253/4		YE 7308/9	Guy FBB	Hall Lewis B32R	1929 – 1930	GWR	5
3/27	1258		YE 9027	Guy FBB	Hall Lewis B32R	1929 – 1930	GWR	5
3/27	1266		YF 712	Guy FBB	Vickers B32R	1929 – 1930	GWR	5
4/27	1262		YF 3916	Guy FBB	Hall Lewis B32R	1929 – 1930	GWR	5
4/27	1278		YF 5746	Guy FBB	Vickers B32R	1929 – 1930	GWR	5
4/27	1272/4		YF 8295/6	Guy FBB	Vickers B32R	1929 – 1930	GWR	5
4/27	1276/7		YF 9507/8	Guy FBB	Vickers B32R	1929 – 1930	GWR	5
5/27	1291/3/5/6		YH 1935/7/9/40	Guy FBB	Vickers B32R	1929 – 1930	GWR	5
5/27	1248		YH 1944	Guy FBB	Hall Lewis B32R	1929 – 1930	GWR	5
6/27	1242–4		YH 6815–7	Guy FBB	Hall Lewis B32R	1929 – 1930	GWR	5
8/27	1148	428	WO 848	Thornycroft A2	Hall Lewis B20F	1929 – 4/35	GWR	3
2/28	1231	307	UC 4238	Maudslay ML3B	Buckingham B32R	1929 – 3/34	GWR	
2/28	1234	308	UC 4862	Maudslay ML3B	Buckingham B32R	1929 – 8/35	GWR	
3/28	1240	309	UC 7507	Maudslay ML3B	Buckingham B32R	1929 – 3/34	GWR	
3/28	1532–4/6	316–19	UC 9099–101/3	Maudslay ML3	Vickers B32R	1929 – 3/28	GWR	
3/28	1513/4	311/2	YV 1107/8	Mausdlay ML3B	Weybridge B32R	1929 – 1934/5	GWR	
4/28	1531	315	YV 1113	Maudslay ML3B	Vickers B32R	1929 – 1935	GWR	
4/28	1538/40	320/2	YV 1114/5	Maudslay ML3B	Vickers B32R	1929 – 8/35	GWR	
4/28	1541	323	YV 1116	Maudslay ML3B	Vickers B32R	1929 – 5/35	GWR	
5/28	1515/6	313/4	YV 1109/10	Mausdlay ML3B	Weybridge B32R	1929 – 1935/4	GWR	
5/28	1539/43/8	321/4/5	YV 7194/5/8	Maudslay ML3B	Vickers B32R	1929 – 8/35	GWR	
6/28	1511	310	YV 8569	Maudslay ML3B	Strachan C32D	1929 – 5/35	GWR	
6/28	1100/3		YW 5364/7	Morris Z2	London Lorries B14	1929 – 1930	GWR	6
8/28	1116/9		UK 5812/5	Guy FBB	Guy B32R	1929 – 1930	GWR	
11/28	1473		XV 5109	Thornycroft A1	Vickers B18F	1929 – 1933	GWR	
2/29	1478		UL 4053	Thornycroft A1	Bartle B18F	1929 – 1933	GWR	1
3/29	1563/4	326/7	UL 8387/8	Maudslay ML3B	Vickers B32R	1929 – 1936/7	GWR	
3/29	1620	336	UL 8390	Maudslay ML3B	Buckingham B32R	1929 – 9/37	GWR	
4/29	1566	328	GU 2927	Maudslay ML3B	Vickers B32R	1929 – 4/37	GWR	
4/29	1622/5	337–8	GU 6354/7	Maudslay ML3B	Buckingham B32R	1929 – 9/37	GWR	
5/29	1626/8–31	339–43	UU 1166/8–71	Maudslay ML3B	Buckingham B32R	1929 – 9/37	GWR	
6/29	1578–80	329–31	UU 3018–20	Maudslay ML3B	Vickers B32R	1929 – 1936/7	GWR	
6/29	1588–90/4	332–5	UU 4815–7/21	Maudslay ML3B	Vickers B32R	1929 – 1936/7	GWR	

Note: Fleet numbers above were those of GWR. Vehicles that survived post October 1933 were re-numbered by WW as shown.

New	Fleet No.	Re-number	Reg No.	Chassis & type	Body & type	In use	Origin	Notes
3/20	32		L 6404	AEC YC	SWCM B26	6/29 – 5/32	SWCM	
5/20	46		XB 9920	Commer 3P	? B29	6/29 – 1/33	SWCM	
5/20	44		XD 8189	Commer 3P	? B28	6/29 – 9/30	SWCM	
7/20	6		L 6471	Commer 3P	SWCM B35R	6/29 – 9/30	SWCM	
1921	2		AT 5732	Commer 3P	SWCM B?	6/29 – 7/31	SWCM	
3/21	54		L 9283	Leyland 36/40	? B32	6/29 – 9/32	SWCM	
7/21	45		XD 4913	Commer 3P	? B28	6/29 – 9/30	SWCM	
7/21	47		XH 2169	Commer 3P	? B29	6/29 – 9/30	SWCM	
1921	16/26		BO 3944/4034	Commer 3P	SWCM C29	6/29 – 3/31	SWCM	
1922	17/8		BO 4271/2	Commer 3P	SWCM B26	6/29 – 1930/2	SWCM	
1/22	3/10		AT 6320/1	Commer 3P	SWCM B26	6/29 – 7/31	SWCM	
2/22	22		BO 4565	Commer 3P	SWCM C29	6/29 – 7/31	SWCM	
2/22	23		BO 4562	Commer 3P	SWCM B29	6/29 – 9/30	SWCM	
3/22	24		BO 4721	Commer 3P	SWCM B25	6/29 – 3/32	SWCM	
6/22	48		XL 2079	Commer 3P	? B26	6/29 – 7/31	SWCM	
9/22	9		BO 3081	Lancia	SWCM B20	6/29 – 9/30	SWCM	
9/22	28		BO 5270	Lancia	SWCM B20	6/29 – 7/31	SWCM	
12/22	57		NY 2303	Lancia	? B20	6/29 – 1/30	SWCM	
6/23	31		NY 3307	Fiat 25hp	SWCM B20	6/29 – 3/30	SWCM	
6/23	29		BO 6078	Lancia	NCME B20	6/29 – 7/31	SWCM	
7/23	34		BX 3748	Lancia	NCME B20	6/29 – 9/30	SWCM	
9/23	30		BO 6539	Lancia	NCME B20	6/29 – 9/30	SWCM	
2/24	53		NY 4755	Leyland A9	Leyland B20	6/29 – 9/30	SWCM	
12/24	36		BO 8794	Commer 3P	SWCM B32	6/29 – 9/30	SWCM	
2/25	35		BO 8666	Commer 3P	? B20	6/29 – 1934	SWCM	
4/25	37/25		BO 9028/9	Commer 3P	SWCM B30	6/29 – 1930/1	SWCM	
5/25	41/3	5/6	BT 8424/32	Leyland SG11	Leyland B36R	6/29 – 8/35	SWCM	7
5/25	42		BT 8429	Leyland SG11	Leyland B36R	6/29 – 4/33	SWCM	
6/25	14	3	KL 7422	Leyland SG11	? B32	6/29 – 8/35	SWCM	
6/25	21		KL 7423	Leyland SG11	? B32	6/29 – 3/32	SWCM	8
6/25	33/20		KL 7961/2	Leyland SG11	SWCM B30	6/29 – 1930/1	SWCM	
8/25	12		NY 9303	Thornycroft A1	Norman B19	6/29 – 5/33	SWCM	
12/25	11		UH 323	Commer 3P	SWCM B26R	6/29 – 5/31	SWCM	
12/25	56		NY 9898	Lancia	? B26	6/29 – 9/30	SWCM	
2/26	5	7	UH 607	Leyland Lion PLSC1	Leyland B32R	6/29 – 8/35	SWCM	
3/26	4/7		UH 818/9	Commer 3P	SWCM B28R	6/29 – 1931/2	SWCM	
5/26	8		UH 1173	Commer 3P	SWCM B?	6/29 – 3/32	SWCM	
6/26	40		UH 1376	Thornycroft A1	? B20	6/29 – 6/33	SWCM	
7/26	27/19		UH 1375/462	Commer 3P	SWCM B26R	6/29 – 1932/30	SWCM	
7/27	1	10	UH 3395	Leyland Lion PLSC1	Leyland B31D	6/29 – 4/35	SWCM	
8/27	38/9	8/9	UH 3396/8	Leyland Lion PLSC1	Leyland B31R	6/29 – 1938/5	SWCM	
8/27	49	11	UH 3397	Leyland Lion PLSC1	Leyland B31R	6/29 – 11/38	SWCM	
12/27	50-2	28–30	UH 3895-7	Leyland PLSC3	Short B31R	6/29 – 11/38	SWCM	
4/28	55	427	TX 5047	Thornycroft A2	Thomas B20	6/29 – 9/35	SWCM	
2/29	58-61	31–4	UH 5776-9	Leyland PLSC3	Leyland B36R	6/29 – 11/39	SWCM	
Note: Fleet numbers above were those of SWCM. Vehicles that survived post–October 1933 were re-numbered by WW as shown.								
10/29	62	37	UH 7048	Leyland Lion LT1	Leyland B30R	10/29 – 4/40	New	
10/29	63/4		UH 7049/50	Leyland Lion LT1	Leyland B31R	10/29 – 1/31	New	8
10/29	65-8	38–41	UH 7061-4	Leyland Lion LT1	Leyland B31R	10/29 – 4/40	New	
11/29	69/70	42/3	UH 7065/6	Leyland Lion LT1	Leyland B31R	11/29 – 5/49	New	
11/29	71/2	51/2	UH 7067/8	Leyland Lion LT1	Leyland B31R	11/29 – 7/30	New	8
11/29	73/4	44/5	UH 7087/8	Leyland Lion LT1	Leyland B31R	11/29 – 3/50	New	9
1921	84		BO 3698	Daimler	? B26	11/29 – 9/30	Cridlands	
1/21	80		HL 593	Daimler CK	? B26	11/29 – 3/33	Cridlands	
2/21	91		B 8977	Daimler CK	? B26	11/29 – 3/33	Cridlands	
2/21	97		DU 9105	Daimler CK	? B25	11/29 – 3/32	Cridlands	
9/21	98		BO 4441	Daimler CK	? B26	11/29 – 3/32	Cridlands	
12/22	85		NY 2247	Daimler CK	? B29	11/29 – 9/30	Cridlands	

Continued overleaf

New	Fleet No.	Re-number	Reg No.	Chassis & type	Body & type	In use	Origin	Notes
1/24	86		BO 6894	Daimler CK	? B26	11/29 – 3/33	Cridlands	
4/24	87		BO 7353	Daimler CK	? B26	11/29 – 3/33	Cridlands	
1924	78		BO 8263	Dennis 4-ton	Dodson O52R	11/29 – 3/34	Cridlands	10
8/25	92		BO 8944	Daimler CK	? B26	11/29 – 3/32	Cridlands	
9/25	79		BO 9957	Daimler CK	? B?	11/29 – 7/31	Cridlands	
11/25	89		UH 337	Daimler CM	? B28	11/29 – 3/33	Cridlands	
5/26	88		UH 1150	Daimler CM	? B26	11/29 – 7/31	Cridlands	
7/26	77		UH 1631	Daimler CM	? B31	11/29 – 7/31	Cridlands	
7/26	90		UH 1632	Daimler CM	? B32	11/29 – 3/33	Cridlands	
3/27	93		TX 2618	Daimler CM	United B32	11/29 – 2/33	Cridlands	
4/27	94/5		TX 2710/2	Daimler CM	United B31	11/29 – 3/32	Cridlands	
6/27	96		TX 3381	Daimler CM	United B31	11/29 – 3/32	Cridlands	
5/28	75/6	35/6	UH 4715/4	Leyland Lion PLSC3	Leyland B31	11/29 – 10/38	Cridlands	11
9/23	110		BO 6589	Guy	? B21F	11/29 – 9/30	Tresillian	
1924	109		BO 6886	Dennis 4 ton	Dodson O54R	11/29 – 9/30	Tresillian	
7/24	106	352	BO 7833	Dennis 4 ton	Dodson O52R	11/29 – 9/35	Tresillian	2
6/26	107		UH 1359	Daimler	? B29D	11/29 – 1930	Tresillian	
10/26	82		UH 1853	AEC 202	? B20	11/29 – 9/30	Tresillian	
10/26	108		UH 1895	AEC 202	? B29D	11/29 – 9/30	Tresillian	
11/26	81		UH 1920	AEC 202	? B26	11/29 – 3/31	Tresillian	
1921	—		BO 4275	Commer	? C?	—	Tresillian	12
1924	—		BO 8202	Commer	? C?	—	Tresillian	12
1927	—		UH 2143	Dennis	? B?	—	Tresillian	12
12/29	83	46	UH 7171	Leyland Lion LT1	Leyland B31	12/29 – 3/50	New	
12/29	100–5	429–34	UH 7187/95/6/201-3	Thornycroft A2	Hall Lewis B20	12/29 – 4/40	New	
			These six vehicles were further re-numbered 386–91 in 1935.					

Notes: Where shown fleet re-numbering occurred in October 1933. 1 913, 938 and 1478 joined the service fleet in 1933. 2 To Barrett's (EVMS) 9/30 – 10/33 and re-numbered upon return. 3 New to Rossers, Usk. 4 New to Cox, Carmarthen. 5 Guys 111-32 (see 1930) were replacements for 1242-4/8/50-4/8/62/6/72/4/6-8/91/3/5/6, which were unsuitable. 1278 came to WW via Western National. 126 was burnt out, 12/34. 6 1100/3 came to WW via Western National. 7 41/3 joined the service fleet in 1935. 8 Transferred to EVMS, 3/32 - 10/33; 9 45 hired out during 1941. 10 78 joined the service fleet, 3/34. 11 35/6 transferred to White's for one month (11/36 – 12/36) for tax purposes 12 Vehicles not operated by WW.

1930

New	Fleet No.	Re-number	Reg No.	Chassis & type	Body & type	In use	Origin	Notes
4/30	133/4	57/8	UH 8211/2	Leyland Lion LT2	NCME C28R	4/30 – 3/50	New	13
4/30	135–8	59–62	UH 8213-6	Leyland Lion LT2	NCME C28R	4/30 – 5/49	New	13
4/30	111-3/6-8/22	401-3/6-8/12	UH 7801-3/6-8/12	Guy Conqueror	Guy B31R	4/30 – 4/36	New	5
5/30	114/5/9-21/5-7	404/5/9-11/5-7	UH 7804/5/9-11/5-7	Guy Conqueror	Guy B31R	5/30 – 4/36	New	5
5/30	123/4	413/4	UH 7813/4	Guy Conqueror	Guy B31R	5/30 – 11/36	New	5
6/30	128–30	418–20	UH 7818-20	Guy Conqueror	Guy B31R	7/30 – 4/36	New	5
7/30	131	421	UH 7821	Guy Conqueror	Guy B31R	7/30 – 4/36	New	5
7/30	71/2	230/1	UH 8360/70	AEC Regal 662	Metcalfe B32R	7/30 – 3/40	New	
			These two vehicles were further re-numbered 551/2 in 1935					
8/30	140–50	232–42	UH 8621-31	AEC Regal 662	Park Royal B30R	8/30 – 1940	New	
			These 11 vehicles, together with 243 below, became 553-64 in 1935.					
8/30	151	243	UH 8632	AEC Regal 662	Park Royal B30R	8/30 – 3/50	New	14
9/30	132	422	UH 7822	Guy Conqueror	Guy B31R	9/30 – 4/36	New	5
12/28	99	441	BX 717	GMC T30	Grose B20	5/30 – 3/34	Edwards Bros, Carmarthen	
1926	139		CX 8268	Karrier	? B?	7/30 – 7/31	A Bowen, Carmarthen	

Notes: Where shown fleet re-numbering occurred in 10/1933. 13 133-38 were part of an order for 12 purpose-built coaches for extended tours. The second batch 152-7 followed in 1931. 153 (as 566) was converted for gas running in 1942, by which time the batch had been downgraded to bus work. 133/4 were hired to the RAF, 1941/2. 14 Hired to Rhondda TC, 1941/2.

1931

New	Fleet No.	Re-number	Reg No.	Chassis & type	Body & type	In use	Origin	Notes
4/31	152–7	244–9	UH 9628–33	AEC Regal 662	NCME C30R	4/31 – 1950	New	13/14
				These six vehicles were further re-numbered 565–70 in 1935.				
7/31	158–70	63–75	UH 9860–72	Leyland Lion LT3	Leyland B36R	7/31 – 1949/50	New	15
10/29	182/3	435/7	WO 3448/50	Thornycroft A6	Thornycroft B24	10/31 – 4/36	Griffiths & Davies, Newbridge	16
				These two vehicles were further re-numbered 392/4 in 1935.				
10/29	—		WO 3449/51	Thornycroft A6	Thornycroft B24	—	G & D Newbridge	12
11/31	171/2	85/6	KG 310/1	Leyland Titan TD1	Leyland L51R	11/31 – 5/49	New	17
11/31	173/4	250/1	KG 312/3	AEC Regent I	Park Royal H52R	11/31 – 11/50	New	17
				These two vehicles were further re-numbered 580/1 in 1935.				

Notes: Where shown fleet re-numbering occurred in October 1933. 15 63/70/3 hired to WBoH, 1/42 - 3/45; 72 hired out during 1941.
16 Not operated by WW but transferred to Lewis & James (WV), then Barrett's (EVMS). 17 The choice of chassis for the four double-deckers was reached by way of a compromise: Albert Gray favoured Leylands, while NECC preferred AECs. 171/2 transferred to Lewis & James (WV), 1/33.

1932

New	Fleet No.	Re-number	Reg No.	Chassis & type	Body & type	In use	Origin	Notes
8/28	177–9	442–4	WO 2030–2	Albion PKA	SWCM C24 (later B26)	4/32 –9/37	Lewis & James (WV)	18
1929	181	255	KG 1005	AEC Regent 1	Short H52R	4/32 – 11/50	Demonstrator	19
				This vehicle was further re-numbered 585 in 1935.				
5/32	175/6	252/3	KG 972/3	AEC Regent 1	Brush L54R	5/32 – 3/50	New	18
				These five vehicles were further re-numbered 582/3 in 1935.				
5/32	184	256	KG 1404	AEC Regent	Short H54R	5/32 – 3/50	New	
				This vehicle was further re-numbered 586 in 1935.				
3/32	180	254	MV 1905	AEC Regent	Short H52R	9/32 – 11/50	Demonstrator	19
				This vehicle was further re-numbered 584 in 1935.				

Notes: Fleet re-numbering occurred in October 1933 & 1935. 18 175-9's petrol engines were replaced with Gardner diesels during the war. 19 180 and 181 were demonstrators taken into stock to supplement the Regents on the Cardiff - Pontypridd route.

1933

New	Fleet No.	Re-number	Reg No.	Chassis & type	Body & type	In use	Origin	Notes
3/33	185–8	257–60	KG 2201–4	AEC Renown	Weymann CH56FD	3/33 – 6/34 7/35 – 3/50	New	20
				These four vehicles became 593–6 in 1935 upon return from White's.				
3/33	189–91	82–4	KG 2205–7	Leyland Lion LT5	Leyland B35F	3/33 – 1949/50	New	
7/24	351		BO 7833	Dennis 4 ton	Dodson B30	10/33 – 5/34	Barrett (EVMS)	21
1/25	1		AX 8434	Leyland GH7	Leyland B30	10/33 – 9/35	Barrett (EVMS)	21
5/25	423		XY 7446	Thornycroft A1	Thornycroft B19	10/33 – 10/35	Barrett (EVMS)	21
6/25	4		KL 7423	Leyland SG9	Leyland B32	10/33 – 8/35	Barrett (EVMS)	21
10/25	426		AX 8427	Thornycroft A1	Thornycroft B19	10/33 – 10/35	Barrett (EVMS)	21
9/26	15		AX 9515	Leyland Lion PLSC1	Leyland B31	10/33 – 8/35	Barrett (EVMS)	21
6/27	16		WO 339	Leyland Lion PLSC1	Leyland B31	10/33 – 11/38	Barrett (EVMS)	21
7/27	17/8		WO 740/1	Leyland Lion PLSC1	Leyland B31	10/33 – 11/38	Barrett (EVMS)	21
9/27	220		WO 921	ADC 416A	Metcalf B32	10/33 – 6/35	Barrett (EVMS)	21
9/27	221		WO 961	ADC 416A	Metcalf B32	10/33 – 10/35	Barrett (EVMS)	21
10/27	19/20		WO 900–1	Leyland Lion PLSC3	Leyland B36	10/33 – 11/38	Barrett (EVMS)	21
10/27	21–24		WO 902–5	Leyland Lion PLSC1	Hall Lewis B31	10/33 – 11/38	Barrett (EVMS)	21
5/28	222–5		WO 1616–9	ADC 416A	NCME B32	10/33 – 1935	Barrett (EVMS)	21
7/28	25/6		WO 1620/1	Leyland Lion PLSC3	Hall Lewis B36	10/33 – 11/38	Barrett (EVMS)	21
10/29	436/8	392/4 (in 1935)	WO 3449/51	Thornycroft A6	Thornycroft B24	10/33 – 4/36	Barrett (EVMS)	21
11/29	47–9		WO 3475–7	Leyland Lion LT1	Leyland B31	10/33 – 5/49	Barrett (EVMS)	21
2/32	352/3		WO 6081/2	Dennis Lancet	Weymann B32R	10/33 – 1946/9	Barrett (EVMS)	21
7/32	354–7		WO 6573–6	Dennis Lancet	Weymann B31	10/33 – 1940	Barrett (EVMS)	21
2/25	2		AX 7102	Leyland SG9	Leyland B40D	10/33 – 3/34	Lewis & James (WV)	21
4/27	201–3		WO 189–91	ADC 416	Short B32	10/33 – 5/34	Lewis & James (WV)	21
6/27	204		WO 436	ADC 416	Short B32	10/33 – 5/34	Lewis & James (WV)	21
7/27	205–7		WO 617/6/5	ADC 416D	Short B32	10/33 – 1934/5	Lewis & James (WV)	21

Continued overleaf

New	Fleet No.	Re-number	Reg No.	Chassis & type	Body & type	In use	Origin	Notes
7/27	208		WO 779	ADC 416D	United B32	10/33 – 5/35	Lewis & James (WV)	21
8/27	209		WO 877	ADC 416	United B32	10/33 – 5/34	Lewis & James (WV)	21
9/27	210/1		WO 878/9	ADC 416	United B32	10/33 – 1934	Lewis & James (WV)	21
10/27	212		WO 880	ADC 416	United B32	10/33 – 10/35	Lewis & James (WV)	21
12/27	12–4		WO 1120–2	Leyland Lion PLSC3	Short B32R	10/33 – 11/38	Lewis & James (WV)	21
5/28	213–9		WO 1670–6	ADC 416A	NCME B32R	10/33 – 1934/5	Lewis & James (WV)	21
7/28	27		WO 1996	Leyland Lion PLSC3	Short B32	10/33 – 11/38	Lewis & James (WV)	21
3/29	445/6		WO 2438/9	Bristol B	Hall Lewis B32	10/33 – 1940/39	Lewis & James (WV)	21
6/29	226–8	543–5 (in 1935)	WO 2933–5	AEC Reliance	Hall Lewis B32	10/33 – 2/40	Lewis & James (WV)	21
6/29	229	546 (in 1935)	WO 4312	AEC Reliance	Dodson 27	10/33 – 2/40	Lewis & James (WV)	21
12/29	54–6		WO 3457–9	Leyland Lion LT1	Leyland B31	10/33 – 5/49	Lewis & James (WV)	21
3/32	76–81		WO 6061–6	Leyland Lion LT5	Leyland B36	10/33 – 1949/50	Lewis & James (WV)	21

Notes: Where shown fleet re-numbering occurred in 10/1933 unless stated as 1935. 20 The AEC Renowns had sliding front doors and received Gardner oil engines during the war, when they gained bus livery and were upseated to 60. 593 was an early casualty suffering fire damage at Rhoose in 11/1941. 21 34 vehicles were transferred from Barrett's (EVMS) in 10/33. 39 vehicles were transferred from Lewis & James (WV) in the same month. 19 and 76-81 retained their Eastern Valleys identity until fully merged with WW in 1933. 76-81 were owned by WW from new.

1934

New	Fleet No.	Re-number	Reg No.	Chassis & type	Body & type	In use	Origin	Notes
3/34	261/2/6–8	571/2/6–8	KG 3605/6/10–2	AEC Regal I	Weymann B32F	3/34 – 12/52	New	22
4/34	263–5	573–5	KG 3607–9	AEC Regal I	Weymann B32F	4/34 – 12/52	New	22
5/34	87–95		KG 3622–30	Leyland Lion LT5a	Brush B32F	5/34 – 11/50	New	23
5/34	96–104		KG 3613–21	Leyland Lion LT5a	English Electric B32F	5/34 – 11/50	New	
8/34	257–60	587–90	KG 3601–4	AEC Regent I	Weymann L48F	8/34 – 11/50	New	24
1931	105		VO 4472	Leyland Lion LT2	? B35?	10/34 – 3/50	Thomas Bros, Llanstephan	
1931	106		TH 1467	Leyland Lion LT2	? B32	10/34 – 5/49	Thomas Bros, Llanstephan	

Notes: Where shown, fleet re-numbering occurred in 1935. 22 261-8 had the company's first oil engines. Along with 87-92, they were re-bodied to B34F by Burlingham in 1946. 574's body was destroyed by fire in 1942. Their 8.8 litre engines suffered crankshaft problems and, excessive fuel consumption. Perhaps this is why no further AEC saloons arrived until 1950. Had they been satisfactory, AECs may have been as standard with WW as with SWT. 23 89 was burned out, 6/42; 90 was hired out in 1941. 24 257-60 were of all metal construction and cost £1865 each. They were re-numbered to bring the AECs together in the 500 series, leaving the 200 series for the Leyland saloons from 1936.

1935

New	Fleet No.	Reg No.	Chassis & type	Body & type	In use	Origin	Notes
7/27	370	TX 3954	Thornycroft UB	Thornycroft B32	1/35 – 5/37	FJ John, Maesteg	
7/27	371	TX 3306	Thornycroft UB	Vickers B32	1/35 – 11/38	FJ John, Maesteg	
7/28	372	TX 5837	Thornycroft UB	Thornycroft B32	1/35 – 6/38	FJ John, Maesteg	
6/29	373	TX 7602	Thornycroft UB	Thornycroft B32	1/35 – 11/38	FJ John, Maesteg	
3/35	107/8	KG 5601/2	Leyland Cub KP3	Park Royal B20F	3/35 – 11/50	New	25
4/35	109–12/20/2/3	KG 5603–6/14/6/7	Leyland Tiger TS7	B32F – see notes	4/35 – 1950-3	New	26
5/35	113–9/21/4–9/34/5	KG 5607–13/5/8–23/28/9	Leyland Tiger TS7	B32F – see notes	5/35 – 1951-7	New	26
5/35	149–52	KG 5643–6	Leyland Tiger TS7	Weymann C21F	5/35 – 1952-7	New	27
6/35	133/6/7/40–2/4/6/8	KG 5627/30/1/4–6/8/40/2	Leyland Tiger TS8	B32F – see notes	6/35 – 1952-7	New	26
7/35	130–2/38/9/43/5/7	KG 5624–6/32/3/7/9/41	Leyland Tiger TS8	B32F – see notes	7/35 – 1951-3	New	26
1928	451	TE 2861	Tilling Stevens B39	Massey 32	6/35 – 9/37	WT Jones, Bryncethin	
1928	452	KO 7648	Tilling Stevens B39	WWOC 32	6/35 – 9/37	WT Jones, Bryncethin	
8/30	453	TX 9270	Tilling Stevens B10A	W Lewis B32	6/35 – 9/38	WT Jones, Bryncethin	
4/31	454	TG 1309	Tilling Stevens B39	W Lewis B3	6/35 – 1/46	WT Jones, Bryncethin	
7/31	455	TG 1986	Tilling Stevens B39	Barnaby B32	6/35 – 1/46	WT Jones, Bryncethin	
3/32	447	TG 2990	AJS Pilot	Willowbrook 24	6/35 – 9/37	WT Jones, Bryncethin	
3/32	448	TG 3014	AJS Pilot	W Lewis B20	6/35 – 9/37	WT Jones, Bryncethin	
4/33	456	TG 5007	Tilling Stevens B39	Beadle C30	6/35 – 1/46	WT Jones, Bryncethin	
3/35	457	KG 5745	Tilling Stevens D6LA7	Beadle C32R	6/35 – 11/50	WT Jones, Bryncethin	28
4/27	—	TX 2853	ADC 416? 32		—	WT Jones, Bryncethin	12
4/28	—	TX 5044	Thornycroft UB	Hall Lewis B30D	—	WT Jones, Bryncethin	12
3/29	—	TX 6804	ADV 426? 32		—	WT Jones, Bryncethin	12
8/34	358	DW 8891	Dennis Lancet	Park Royal B32D	7/35 – 5/49	Danygraig, Risca	29

New	Fleet No.	Reg No.	Chassis & type	Body & type	In use	Origin	Notes
6/27	—	WO 402	Thornycroft A1	Hall Lewis B20F	—	Danygraig, Risca	29
1925	On hire	BO 9805	AEC Renown	United B30R	7/35 – 12/36	White's	30
1926	On hire	TX 1173	Thornycroft A1	Hall Lewis B20D	7/35 – 12/36	White's	30
1926	On hire	TX 1808	Thornycroft A1	Hall Lewis B14D	7/35 – 12/36	White's	30
1926	On hire	TX 1863	Thornycroft A1	Hall Lewis B20D	7/35 – 12/36	White's	30
1926	On hire	UH 1165/6	AEC Renown	United B30D	7/35 – 12/36	White's	30
1926	On hire	UH 1218	AEC Renown	United B30?	7/35 – 12/36	White's	30
1927	On hire	TX 2284	Thornycroft A1	Hall Lewis B20D	7/35 – 12/36	White's	30
1927	On hire	UH 2242	AEC Renown	United B30D	7/35 – 12/36	White's	30
1927	On hire	UH 2678	ADC 416	United B34D	7/35 – 12/36	White's	30
1927	On hire	YT 6056	Gilford LL166	? B26D	7/35 – 12/36	White's	30

Notes: 25 108 was requisitioned by the War Department, 7/40 – 7/43. 26 109-148 were fitted with a variety of 32-seat bodies. From new, 109-118 had Leyland bodies, 119-123 had Short Brothers bodies, and 124-148 were by Brush. 109 was re-bodied to B35F by Brush in 1936, then was requisitioned by the WD, 7/40 – 7/47; 137 was re-bodied to B34F by Weymann in 1937 and 110/21/6/41/3/4 followed in 1938 but didn't have their seating increased. Also re-bodied in 1938 but by Eastern Coachworks to B35F, were 120/4. 119/27/8/37/42/52 were re-bodied to B34F by Burlingham in 1946, except 128 which was kept at 32 seats. 111-8/22/3/5/9-36/9/40/5-51 retained their original 32 seat bodies. 116 was converted to a service vehicle in 1951. 109 was re-numbered by WD 7/40 - 7/47. 27 149-152 were 21-seat coaches and featured roof mounted luggage containers accessible via a folded steel ladder at the rear. The low seating capacity was due to the size of their luxury seats. 149 went to the WD, 7/40, and didn't return. 150 was also requisitioned from 7/40 and converted for gas burning in 1942 28 457 was requisitioned by the WD, 7/40 – 1/46. 29 358 was laid up during the war, but re-used in 1946; WO 402 was not operated. WW kept the Danygraig company going and transferred vehicles there until WW2. 30 A total of 67 White's vehicles were hired from 7/35 pending takeover of that company in 12/36.

1936

New	Fleet No.	Reg No.	Chassis & type	Body & type	In use	Origin	Notes
7/25	500–2	BO 9791/806/71	AEC Renown	United B30R	7/35 – 9/37	White's	30
11/25	504/5	UH 386/334	AEC Renown	United B30	7/35 – 9/37	White's	30, 31
3/26	374	TX 578	Thornycroft A1	Hall Lewis B20D	7/35 – 5/37	White's (since 1929)	30
3/26	503	UH 608	AEC Renown	United B30	7/35 – 9/37	White's	30, 31
3/26	507/8	UH 694/5	AEC Renown	United B30	7/35 – 9/37	White's	30, 31
5/26	506	UH 1078	AEC Renown	United B30	7/35 – 9/37	White's	30, 31
7/26	375	TX 1496	Thornycroft A1	Hall Lewis B20D	7/35 – 5/37	White's (since 1929)	30
8/26	510	UH 1395	AEC Ramilles	United B34R	7/35 – 9/37	White's	30, 31
10/26	376	TX 1810	Thornycroft A1	Hall Lewis B14D	7/35 – 9/38	White's	30
11/26	377	TX 1862	Thornycroft A1	Hall Lewis B17D	7/35 – 10/37	White's	30
3/27	378	TX 2628	Thornycroft A1	Hall Lewis B20D	7/35 – 10/37	White's	30
3/27	509	UH 2273	AEC Renown	United B30D	7/35 – 9/37	White's	30
5/27	511–3	UH 2913/813/29	ADC 416	United B34D	7/35 – 9/37	White's	30, 32
5/27	523	UH 2677	ADC 416	United B34	7/35 – 10/38	White's/Vincent	30, 32
6/27	514	UH 3045	ADC 416	United B34D	7/35 – 9/37	White's	30, 32
6/27	521	UH 3046	ADC 417	McPherson C26	7/35 – 10/38	White's	30, 32
8/27	515/6	UH 3437/339	ADC 416	United B32R	7/35 – 1937	White's	30, 32
12/27	379/8/1	UH 3844/5/67	Thornycroft A2L	Hall Lewis B20D	7/35 – 10/37	White's	30
5/28	517	UH 4730	ADC 416	United B32	7/35 – 10/38	White's	30, 32
5/28	520	UH 4732	ADC 416	United B32	7/35 – 10/38	White's	30, 32
5/28	522	DY 5014	ADC 417	Hall Lewis C28	7/35 – 11/36	White's (since 1934)	30, 32
5/28	525/6	UH 4799/31	ADC 416	United B31D	7/35 – 10/38	White's	30, 32
7/28	518/9	UH 5042/62	ADC 416	United B32	7/35 – 1936/8	White's	30, 32
1929	6	DY 5635	Leyland Titan TD1	Leyland L51R OS	7/35 – 1938	White's	30, 33
5/29	540/1	UH 6352/3	AEC Reliance	United B32D	7/35 – 11/38	White's	30, 34
7/29	542	UH 6694	AEC Reliance	United B32D	7/35 – 9/38	White's	30
7/29	382/3	UH 6719/20	Thornycroft A2L	Hall Lewis B20D	7/35 – 11/38	White's	30
8/29	524	UH 6671	ADC 426	Metcalf B30	7/35 – 10/38	White's	30, 35
6/30	441	UH 8004	Albion PMB28	Strachan B30	7/35 – 11/38	White's/Vincent	30
7/30	547/8	UH 8442/50	AEC Regal	Metcalf B30D	7/35 – 2/40	White's	30
7/31	549	UH 9924	AEC Regal	Metcalf B32R	7/35 – 3/50	White's	14, 30
8/31	550	UH 9985	AEC Regal	Metcalf B32R	7/35 – 3/50	White's	14, 30
8/31	384/5	UH 9986/7	Thornycroft AV2	W J Smith B20R	7/35 – 4/40	White's	30, 36

Continued overleaf

New	Fleet No.	Reg No.	Chassis & type	Body & type	In use	Origin	Notes
1931	579	TV 4867	AEC Regent	Park Royal H56R	7/35 – 5/49	White's	30, 37
12/31	598	KG 340	AEC Renown	Short L62R	7/35 – 11/50	White's	30
6/32	597	MV 2906	AEC Renown	Weymann H65R	7/35 – 3/50	White's	30, 38
6/32	591	MV 3161	AEC Regent	Short H65R	7/35 – 5/49	White's	30, 38
9/32	592	MV 3506	AEC Regent	Short L55F	7/35 – 3/50	White's	30, 38
3/33	599	KG 2176	AEC Renown	Short L60FD	7/35 – 11/50	White's	30
6/33	600	KG 2699	AEC Renown	Short L60FD	7/35 – 3/50	White's	30
6/33	601	KG 2700	AEC Renown	Short L60R	7/35 – 3/50	White's	30
1/36	153–60/2/3/5/6/8–70	KG 7001-8/10/1/3/4/6/6-8	Leyland Tiger TS7	B35F – see notes	1/36 – 1951/2	New	39
2/36	161/4/7	KG 7009/12/5	Leyland Tiger TS7	B35F – see notes	2/36 – 1951/2	New	39
3/36	171/2/9/83	KG 7019/20/7/31	Leyland Tiger TS7	B35F – see notes	3/36 – 1952/7	New	39
3/36	209–14	KG 7057-62	Leyland Tiger TS7	Duple C31C	3/36 – 1957/8	New	40
4/36	173–8/80-2/7/9–208	KG 7021-6/8-30/5/7-56	Leyland Tiger TS7	B35F – see notes	4/36 – 1951/3/5	New	39, 41
5/36	184–6/8	KG 7032-4/6	Leyland Tiger TS7	B35F – see notes	5/36 – 1951-3/7	New	39
5/36	215–8	KG 7063-6	Leyland Cub KPZ2	Park Royal B20F	5/36 – see notes	New	42
6/31	538	TG 1821	AEC Regal	WWOC C31	7/36 – 3/50	Gough (Welsh M'ways)	
5/32	539	TG 3387	AEC Reliance	Metcalfe C30	7/36 – 10/39	Gough (WM), Mtn Ash	
8/33	458	WN 5870	Tilling Stevens B39	Beadle 26	7/36 – 10/38	Gough (WM), Mtn Ash	
7/29	—	TX 8001	AEC Reliance	? C32	—	Gough (WM), Mtn Ash	12

Notes: 31 503-8 may have been dual entrance. 504 was exhibited at the 1925 Commercial Motor Show. 510 had a wheelbase of 15ft 9½ins, 18ins longer than the single-deck Renowns which allowed for another row of seats. 32 The ADCs were fitted with AEC engines and more reliable than the usual Daimler units. 521 was displayed at the Scottish Commercial Show. 526 was fitted with a Dorman diesel engine in 1933, but was said to be noisy and difficult to start. 525 also received a diesel engine in 1933, but this time an AEC that performed well. 33 6 was the only Leyland owned by White's and in 1935 had a Gardner oil engine. 34 540 was the prototype AEC Reliance. 35 524 was known as 'The Red Herring' and may have been obtained from AEC as a former show model. 36 384 found use with Glamorgan County Council's First Aid Unit at Barry. Its tyres were painted white as a safety aid during the blackout. 37 579 was new to Nottingham Corporation and became the first AEC Regent in the Western Welsh fleet. 38 591 was petrol-engined from new and White's first highbridge vehicle. It received an AEC 8.8 litre oil engine at a cost of £471 in 1935. 598, at nearly 30ft long and on three axles, caused a stir when new to White's and was nicknamed 'The Arcade'. It had been the largest double-decker in the area until joined by 597, and cost £1,940. 597 had been used by WW to test routes intended for Cardiff's trolleybuses. All were ex-demonstrators. 39 153-72 were bodied from new by Leyland; 173-83 by Brush; 184-208 by Roe. Re-bodying was instigated by WW who judged each vehicle by its condition. 167/206 were re-bodied to B32F by Weymann in 1937, and 203/8 followed in 1938. 175/204 were re-bodied by ECW in 1937, and 182/5 followed in 1938; all retained 35 seats. 8/9/84/90/3/5, and 202/7 were re-bodied to B34F by Burlingham in 1946, with 173/7/92/7 following in 1947, although 173/7/92 remained 35 seaters. Not all rebodies were new. 153-66/8-72/4/80-3/6-9/91/4/6/8-201/5 retained their original 35-seat bodies throughout. Brush had no part in the re-bodying programme. Two eye-catching features were the crest on top of the destination box, and the white roof. The latter wasn't a wartime safety measure, but an attempt at brightening the livery. However, white was considered unpractical for vehicles operating in the mining valleys, and gave way to red. The crest was soon banished from the roof more for practical reasons than any changing trends in design. In 1951, 172 along with 116 of 1935 were converted for use by the engineering department. They were considered to be best of their bunch and overhauled, had their chassis reinforced to take tow bars, their floors strengthened, seats removed, and windows replaced by panels and small fixed windows. When a VIP in the transport world saw them fresh out of Ely Works he likened them to trans-continental sleeping coaches and wondered if they were intended for use on the Aberystwyth express service! 40 209-14 were re-bodied as saloons by Burlingham in 1946. 212 was specially repainted with the waistband finished in solid gold leaf for an exhibition at the old Greyfriars Hall, Cardiff, in 1938. 41 219-238 and 287-306 had Weymann B32F bodies from new, while 240-286 had ECW B35F bodies. 232/50/1 were re-bodied to B35F by ECW in 1937, presumably having seen little service. 235/8/40/2/63/4/80/2/ 8/90/4/5/8/301/8 were re-bodied to B34F by Burlingham in 1946. 221-3/57 were re-bodied to B35F by Burlingham in 1946, and 220/7/53/6/73/ 97/303 followed in 1947. 224-6/8-31/3/4/6/7/87/91-3/6/9/300/2/4-6 retained their original Weymann 32-seat bodies. 241/3-9/52/4/5/8-62/5-72/4-9/81/3-6 retained their ECW 35-seat bodies. 294 was delivered in reversed livery, presumably for express service work. 239 (KG 9621) was written off when quite new and the number carried by its replacement, AUH 773, when new in 4/38. 229 and 246 were requisitioned in 7/40 and didn't return. 42 215 was requisitioned 9/40, and didn't return; 217 was hired to Monmouthshire County Council 7/41 - 3/44; 218 went to the WD 7/40 - 9/43.

1937

New	Fleet No.	Reg No.	Chassis & type	Body & type	In use	Origin	Notes
10/25	392	NY 9597	Thornycroft A1	Thornycroft B20	1/37 – 9/37	Phipps, Glynneath	
4/28	368	TX 5042	Thornycroft UB	Hall Lewis B32	1/37 – 11/38	Phipps, Glynneath	
7/28	369	TX 5872	Thornycroft UB	Hall Lewis B32	1/37 – 11/38	Phipps, Glynneath	
11/28	440	TX 6346	Guy BB	Guy 30	1/37 – 11/38	Phipps, Glynneath	
5/29	393	TX 7523	Thornycroft A6	Thornycroft B24	1/37 – 5/37	Phipps, Glynneath	
10/29	439	TX 8412	Gilford 1680T	Smith 32	1/37 – 9/37	Phipps, Glynneath	
6/30	366	TX 9873	Thornycroft LC	Metcalfe B32	1/37 – 4/40	Phipps, Glynneath	
6/31	367	TG 1796	Thornycroft BC	Thornycroft B32	1/37 – 5/38	Phipps, Glynneath	
1/32	395	CG 459	Thornycroft Daring RC6	Strachan L51R	1/37 – 5/49	Phipps, Glynneath	
6/35	394	ANY 560	Thornycroft Handy	Wadham B20F	1/37 – 1/46	Phipps, Glynneath	
3/37	241–50	KG 9623-32	Leyland Tiger TS7	see notes	3/37 – 1952-4/7	New	41
3/37	401/2	KG 9640/1	Bristol JO5G	ECW B32F	3/37 – 3/54	New	

New	Fleet No.	Re-number	Reg No.	Chassis & type	Body & type	In use	Origin	Notes
?	396		EX 2844	Thornycroft A12	? C20	4/37 – 11/39	Green & White, B'gend	
3/27	435		TX 1465	Gilford Swift	? 20	4/37 – 11/38	Green & White, B'gend	
4/29	436		GU 4179	Gilford Swift	? 32	4/37 – 3/40	Green & White, B'gend	
1929	461		DE 7335	Bean W	? 20	4/37 – 8/37	Green & White, B'gend	
6/30	460		YC 9732	Commer 6TK	Hoyal C20	4/37 – 4/40	Green & White, B'gend	
7/30	437		GJ 8375	Gilford Swift	Wycombe 26	4/37 – 9/39	Green & White, B'gend	
9/30	438		WX 5360	Gilford 1680T	? 32	4/37 – 3/40	Green & White, B'gend	
3/31	450		TG 1098	Guy BB	Guy 30	4/37 – 9/37	Green & White, B'gend	
7/31	449		TG 1895	Guy BB	? 30	4/37 – 9/37	Green & White, B'gend	
12/31	464		TG 2542	Bedford WLB	? 20	4/37 – 4/40	Green & White, B'gend	
1931	463		YD 2495	Bedford WLB	Heaver 18	4/37 – 4/40	Green & White, B'gend	
8/32	462		TG 3963	Bean B	? 26	4/37 – 1/46	Green & White, B'gend	
2/35	465		TG 9427	Bedford WTL	? 24	4/37 – 1/46	Green & White, B'gend	
4/35	466		ANY 133	Bedford WTL	Phillips 20	4/37 – 1/46	Green & White, B'gend	43
8/35	459		ATX 39	Albion PH114	Phillips 20	4/37 – 1/46	Green & White, B'gend	
6/36	467		BNY 708	Bedford WTB	Duple 26	4/37 – 11/50	Green & White, B'gend	
4/37	434		CY 9092	Gilford Swift	Metcalfe B20R	4/37 – 5/37	Green & White, B'gend	
5/37	219-31/51-7		KG 9601-13/33-9	Leyland Tiger TS7	see notes	5/37 – 1952/3/4/7	New	41
6/37	232-6		KG 9614-8	Leyland Tiger TS7	see notes	6/37 – 1953/4/7	New	41
7/37	237-40		KG 9619-22	Leyland Tiger TS7	see notes	7/37 – 1953/7	New	41
3/28	472	362 7/38	TX 4978	Star Flyer	Spicer 25	7/37 – 1938	Pencoed O.Co., B'gend	
2/30	496	7 1/46	DV 4114	Leyland Lion LT1	Brush B30F	7/37 – 11/50	Pencoed O.Co., B'gend	
5/30	469		TX 9608	Bean W	? 20	7/37 – 8/37	Pencoed O.Co., B'gend	
1/31	497	9 1/46	DV 8082	Leyland Lion LT2	Park Royal B32	7/37 – 3/50	Pencoed O.Co., B'gend	
3/31	498	10 1/46	DV 8508	Leyland Lion LT2	Park Royal B32	7/37 – 3/50	Pencoed O.Co., B'gend	
1932	470	360	VJ 4256	Commer Corinthian	Smith 26	7/37 – 1939	Pencoed O.Co., B'gend	
1932	471	361	WM 2322	Star Flyer	Spicer 25	7/37 – 1939	Pencoed O.Co., B'gend	
7/32	468		TG 3789	Bedford WTB	Grose 20	7/37 – 1/46	Pencoed O.Co., B'gend	
1/34	363/4		TG 6652/1	Guy Conquest	Guy B31	7/37 – 1/46	Pencoed O.Co., B'gend	
1/35	365		TG 9289	Guy Vixen	Hiscock B26	7/37 – 1/46	Pencoed O.Co., B'gend	
9/37	264		AKG 307	Leyland Tiger TS8	see notes	9/37 – 7/54	New	41
10/37	258-63/5-76		AKG 301-6/8-19	Leyland Tiger TS8	see notes	10/37 – 1952-4/7	New	41
11/37	277-97		AKG 320-9/31-41	Leyland Tiger TS8	see notes	11/37 – 1952-4/7	New	41
12/37	298-306		AKG 342-50	Leyland Tiger TS8	see notes	12/37 – 1953/4/7	New	41
12/37	403		AKG 330	Bristol L5G	ECW B32F	12/37 – 3/54	New	41

Notes: 360-2 were re-numbered in 7/38 and 7/9/10 in 1/46 41 See explanation in 1936 notes. 43 466 was hired by the RAF, 1/42 - 1/46.

1938

New	Fleet No.	Re-number	Reg No.	Chassis & type	Body & type	In use	Origin	Notes
4/38	239		AUH 773	Leyland Tiger TS8	ECW B35F	4/38 – 12/53	New	41
7/38	307/8		AUH 634/5	Leyland Tiger TS8	ECW B35F	7/38 – 1954/7	New	44
3/26	374/5		TX 648/9	Thornycroft A1	Hall Lewis B20D	7/38 – 1938/9	AH Evans, Barry	
10/25	370		NY 9664	Thornycroft A1	Hall Lewis B19D	7/38 – 9/39	S Harfoot, Barry	45
4/27	379		UH 2697	Thornycroft A2	Hall Lewis B20D	7/38 – 1/46	S Harfoot, Barry	45
8/27	378		TX 3960	Thornycroft A2	NCME B20	7/38 – 10/38	S Harfoot, Barry	
12/27	377		WO 1002	Thornycroft A1	Hall Lewis B20D	7/38 – 1/46	S Harfoot, Barry	45
5/28	359		HD 3434	Dennis E	Brush B30F	7/38 – 1/46	S Harfoot, Barry	45
1930	495	2	DV 7424	Leyland Lion LT2	Park Royal B31F	7/38 – 5/49	S Harfoot, Barry	45
6/33	381		TG 5659	Thornycroft Ardent	Smith B20D	7/38 – 1/46	S Harfoot, Barry	
7/33	380		TG 5558	Thornycroft Ardent	Smith B20D	7/38 – 1/46	S Harfoot, Barry	45
12/34	481		NJ 4932	Bedford WLB	Duple B20F	7/38 – 1/46	FL Harfoot, Barry	
4/27	434		WM 543	Vulcan Blackpool 3XB	Vulcan B20D	7/38 – 11/38	WJ Knight, Barry	
1929	494	1	HD 3765	Leyland Lion LT1	Brush B30F	7/38 – 5/49	WJ Knight, Barry	46
7/31	461		TG 1971	Commer G2	Norman B20F	7/38 – 11/38	WJ Knight, Barry	
7/38	469-80		BBO 301-12	Bedford WTB	Duple B20F	7/38 – 11/50	New	47
9/38	13/4		BBO 315/6	Leyland Tiger TS8	Weymann B32F	9/38 – 7/54	New	44
10/38	11/2/5/25-8		BBO 313/4/7/27-30	Leyland Tiger TS8	Weymann B32F	10/38 – 1954/6/7	New	44

Continued overleaf

219

New	Fleet No.	Reg No.	Chassis & type	Body & type	In use	Origin	Notes
11/38	16–24/9/30	BBO 318–26/31/2	Leyland Tiger TS8	Weymann B32F	11/38 – 1954/6/7	New	44
11/38	326/9/30	BBO 333/6/7	Leyland Tiger TS8	Weymann B32F	11/38 – 1954/6	New	44
2/30	5	DV 4116	Leyland Lion LT1	Hall Lewis B32D	11/38 – 3/50	JH Hill, Barry	48
3/30	351/60/1	WN 2738/9/41	Dennis EV	SWT B32R	11/38 – 1/46	JH Hill, Barry	48
6/30	4/6	DV 5483/4	Leyland Lion LT2	Hall Lewis B31D	11/38 – 1950/49	JH Hill, Barry	48
2/31	3	DV 3899	Leyland Lion LT1	Weymann B35F (1934)	11/38 – 11/50	JH Hill, Barry	48
7/31	482	TG 2005	Bedford WLB	? B20F	11/38 – 11/40	JH Hill, Barry	48
3/35	483	TG 9651	Bedford WTL	Duple C26F	11/38 – 11/50	JH Hill, Barry	48
11/29	——	TX 8556	Chevrolet LQ	? B14	——	JH Hill, Barry	12
5/30	——	WN 2999	Dennis EV	SWT B32R	——	JH Hill, Barry	12
12/38	327/8/31–5	BBO 334/5/8–42	Leyland Tiger TS8	Weymann B32F	12/38 – 1954/6/7	New	44

Notes: Fleet re-numbering occurred in 1943. 12 and 41 see earlier notes. 44 307 and possibly others ran for a time in reversed livery around 1947-50 for use on private hire to cover vehicle shortage. 308 was re-bodied to B34F by Burlingham in 1946. 11-30 and 326-35 had swept-down bodywork beading. 45 359/77/9/80 were delicensed 10/38 – 3/40. 359 was new to Yorkshire Woollen District. 370 passed to Monmouthshire CC as an ambulance. 495 was new to Devon General, delicensed 7/38-1/46, re-numbered 2 on body conversion, then delicensed again from 1/49. 46 494, new to Yorkshire Woollen District, was withdrawn in 1939, re-numbered 1 in 1943 and re-instated, then delicensed from 2/47. 47 469 was hired by the RAF, 1/42-1/46; 478/9 were requisitioned, 7/40 – 10/43. 48 482 continued as stores van V15 until 6/49. 3-6 were new to Devon General. 3-5 were delicensed 11/39-1/46, re-bodied and re-instated until 1950. 6 was delicensed 11/39-1/46 and re-instated until 5/49 but not re-bodied. 483 was delicensed 11/49-2/51. 351/60/1 and WN 2999 were new to SWT; 351 was delicensed from 6/39; 360 from 11/39 and 361 from 1/39.

1939

New	Fleet No.	Reg No.	Chassis & type	Body & type	In use	Origin	Notes
8/26	369	TX 1621	Thornycroft A1	Hall Lewis B20D	1/39 – 9/39	JH Woodfield, Barry	49
2/39	312/5/6/21–4	BBO 893/6/7/902–5	Leyland Tiger TS8	Brush B32F	2/39 – 1954/6/7	New	50
4/39	314/8–20/5	BBO 895/9–901/6	Leyland Tiger TS8	Brush B32F	4/39 – 1954/6	New	50
5/39	309–11/3/7	BBO 890–2/4/8	Leyland Tiger TS8	Brush B32F	5/39 – 1954/6/7	New	50
5/39	703	BUH 53	Leyland Tiger TS8	ECW B35F	5/39 – 6/54	New	50
6/39	700–2/4/5/9/10/3/4	BUH 50–2/4/5/9/60/3/4	Leyland Tiger TS8	ECW B35F	6/39 – 1954/6/7	New	50
7/39	706–8/11/2/5–9	BUH 56–8/61/2/5–9	Leyland Tiger TS8	ECW B35F	7/39 – 1954/6/7	New	50
11/39	720/1	CBO 105/6	Leyland Tiger TS8	ECW B35F	11/39 – 1954/6	New	50
5/35	—	ANY 500	Dennis Lancet	? B32	—	D Probert ?	12
5/31	—	TG 1694	Guy OND	? 20	—	J David, Aberkenfig	12
?	—	UT 7327	Leyland Lion TS2	? 29	—	J David, Aberkenfig	12

Notes: 12 Not operated by WW. 49 369 was a driver trainer from 10/39. 50 309-25 and 700-19 and possibly 720/1 featured similar bodywork styling to 11-30 and 326-35 of 1938. At least 310 and 314 were reduced to 24 seaters, painted in reversed livery and used as coaches after the war, until the supply of new coaches was restored. 314 (at least) had an adapted version of the WW logo with 'on tour' motto instead of destination blind.

1940

New	Fleet No.	Reg No.	Chassis & type	Body & type	In use	Origin	Notes
2/40	738	CBO 517	Leyland Tiger TS8	ECW B35F	2/40 – 7/54	New	
3/40	722–37	CBO 501–16	Leyland Tiger TS8	ECW B35F	3/40 – 1954/6/7	New	51
5/40	743–53/5–72	CBO 522–32/4–51	Leyland Tiger TS8	ECW B32F	5/40 – 1954/6/7	New	
6/40	739	CBO 518	Leyland Tiger TS8	ECW B32F	6/40 – 7/54	New	
8/40	740–2	CBO 519–21	Leyland Tiger TS8	ECW DP32F	8/40 – 1954/6	New	51
10/40	602/3	CKG 124/5	AEC Regent I	ECW L31/25R	10/40 – 6/56	New	52
10/40	773–9	GCD 666–9/72/4/5	Leyland Titan TD7	Park Royal H53R	10/40 – 1956	New	53

Notes: 51 750 was re-bodied to B34F by Burlingham in 1946. 742/51/2/4/6 were requisitioned from new; all but 754 were lost, and sole survivor 754 didn't arrive until 9/49. 756/7 were requisitioned by HM Forces and not put into service until 1946. 52 602/3 were 8.8 litre Regents, part of a larger order interrupted by the war. These chassis arrived in April 1940, just as ECW's Lowestoft factory was evacuated. Supply then dried up and it was agreed that WW would store the chassis and the sets of body parts which had been made up. It was decided to complete the pair with two of the lowbridge sets of parts, and they were completed in September/October. The balance of parts held at Central Works amounted to at least 12 further bodies which, with the exception of 604 in 1942, were not finished until 1946. 53 773-9 were intended for Southdown but had suffered war damage at Park Royal and had to be rebuilt. They were part of a batch of 27, the remainder being split between Crosville and Cumberland.

1941

Note: With wartime restrictions at their height, no vehicles could be sourced for the fleet in 1941.

1942

New	Fleet No.	Reg No.	Chassis & type	Body & type	In use	Origin	Notes
2/42	604	CKG 288	AEC Regent I	ECW H31/25R	2/42 – 6/56	New	54
2/42	605/7	CKG 289/91	AEC Regent I	N. Counties L31/24R	2/42 – 3/56	New	
2/42	606	CKG 290	AEC Regent I	N. Counties H31/24R	2/42 – 6/56	New	
10/42	484–8	CKG 433–7	Bedford OWB	Duple UB30F	10/42 – 1950/2/3	New	55
11/42	489–93	CKG 438–42	Bedford OWB	Duple UB30F	11/42 – 1950/2/3	New	55

Special Notes:
It is thought that a number of double-deckers were borrowed from South Wales Transport at around this time.

Notes: 54 It is thought that 604 may have been the third vehicle which utilised the ECW parts stored at Ely since 1940. 55 The 12 Bedfords (494/5 arrived in 2/43) were unwanted but necessary as heavier vehicles simply weren't available; they were the only vehicles of an order for 40, the balance being cancelled in 3/42. The issue of the registration series CKG 443-56 could not be attributed to Western Welsh.

1943

New	Fleet No.	Reg No.	Chassis & type	Body & type	In use	Origin	Notes
2/43	494/5	CKG 459/60	Bedford OWB	Duple UB32F	2/43 – 1950/2	New	56
5/43	366/7	CKG 430/1	Guy Arab	Park Royal UH56R	5/43 – 1956	New	56
6/43	368	CKG 457	Guy Arab	Brush UL55R	6/43 – 6/56	New	56
9/43	369	CKG 458	Daimler CWG5	Brush UL55R	9/43 – 12/51	New	56

Notes: 56 The limited number of 1943 deliveries consisted of wartime utility vehicles, designed and allocated by the Ministry of Transport in conjunction with the Ministry of Supply. They were very austere looking vehicles, box-like with no rounded corners, fitted with wooden slatted seats and painted dark grey. The issue of registration CKG 432 was not attributable to Western Welsh.

1944

New	Fleet No.	Reg No.	Chassis & type	Body & type	In use	Origin	Notes
8/30	362	TG 156	Guy ONDF	Guy B20D	1/44 – 1/46	Waters, Barry	
1932	8	OD 1833	Leyland LT5	Weymann B31F	1/44 – 3/49	Waters, Barry	

1945

New	Fleet No.	Reg No.	Chassis & type	Body & type	In use	Origin	Notes
1/45	372	CKG 607	Guy Arab	Park Royal UH56R	1/45 – 3/56	New	
2/45	370/1/3–5	CKG 605/6/8–10	Guy Arab	Park Royal UH56R	2/45 – 1956	New	

Vehicles on hire:
Fifteen Leyland LT2s from Ribble Motor Services were hired from 10/45 and were taken into stock during 1946 as Nos 1001–15.

1946

New	Fleet No.	Reg No.	Chassis & type	Body & type	In use	Origin	Notes
10/30	1001–5	CK 4497/502/6/17/20	Leyland Lion LT2	Leyland B30F	10/45 – 3/50	Ribble 1140/5/9/60/3	
10/30	1006–10	CK 4523/30/3/4/7	Leyland Lion LT2	Leyland B30F	10/45 – 3/50	Ribble 1166/73/6/7/80	
10/30	1011–5	CK 4547/9/50/4/5	Leyland Lion LT2	Leyland B30F	10/45 – 3/50	Ribble 1190/2/5/7/8	
4/46	612/3	CKG 792/3	AEC Regent II	ECW L53R	4/46 – 3/59	New	57
5/46	614–7	CKG 794–7	AEC Regent II	ECW L53R	5/46 – 3/59	New	57
6/46	610/1	CKG 790/1	AEC Regent II	ECW H31/25R	6/46 – 3/59	New	57
6/46	608	CKG 788	AEC Regent II	ECW H31/25R	6/46 – 3/59	New	57
7/46	609	CKG 789	AEC Regent II	ECW H31/25R	7/46 – 3/59	New	57
8/46	618–20	CKG 798–800	AEC Regent II	ECW H31/25R	8/46 – 3/59	New	57
10/46	798/9/802/3	CUH 798/9/802/3	Leyland Tiger PS1	ECW B35R	10/46 – 1/60	New	58
11/46	800/1/4–11	CUH 800/1/4–11	Leyland Tiger PS1	ECW B35R	11/46 – 1-2/60	New	58
12/46	812–5	CUH 812–5	Leyland Tiger PS1	ECW B35R	12/46 – 1-2/60	New	58

Notes: 57 608-620 had been ordered in 1939 but their production was suspended due to the outbreak of war. Due to the shortage of skilled staff and materials, 12 complete sets of body parts were received piecemeal and stored at Ely until 1946 when the chassis became available.

Continued overleaf

They were sent to ECW where six normal-height and six lowbridge vehicles were constructed, together with one additional vehicle appended to the original order. 58 780-877 were the first complete new 'heavyweight' saloon since 1940. Progress in engine design was such that the small 7.4 litre capacity of the PS1 was more efficient than the 8.6 litre engines in the previous TS8s. 798-877 featured co-ordinated fleet and registration numbers, a first for any bus operator in Wales. Unfortunately, not only were the PS1s a long time in coming, but many, particularly those from Weymann, suffered body rot brought about by the use of unseasoned wood. There was also an issue over the Weymann's poorly-aligned windscreens, which were positioned below driver eye level. Remedial work was done by Longwell Green at Bristol. A further order was placed with Burlingham for the re-bodying of 10 saloons. Despite the introduction of matching registration and fleet numbers, the similarity between the CKG and CUH series was extremely confusing. A further order was placed with Burlingham for the re-bodying of 10 saloons.

1947

New	Fleet No.	Reg No.	Chassis & type	Body & type	In use	Origin	Notes
1/47	816-9	CUH 816-9	Leyland Tiger PS1	ECW B35R	1/47 – 1/60	New	58
2/47	820-3/8/30	CUH 820-3/8/30	Leyland Tiger PS1	ECW B35R	2/47 – 1960	New	58
3/47	824-7/9	CUH 824-7/9	Leyland Tiger PS1	ECW B35R	3/47 – 1960	New	58
4/47	831/3	CUH 831/3	Leyland Tiger PS1	ECW B35R	4/47 – 11/60	New	58
5/47	832/4-9	CUH 832/4-9	Leyland Tiger PS1	ECW B35R	5/47 – 1960	New	58
5/47	780-92	CKG 830-42	Leyland Tiger PS1	Weymann B32F	5/47 – 1959/60	New	58
6/47	793	CKG 843	Leyland Tiger PS1	Weymann B32F	6/47 – 1/60	New	58
6/47	840-3	CUH 840-3	Leyland Tiger PS1	ECW B35R	6/47 – 1960	New	58
7/47	844/5/8	CUH 844/5/8	Leyland Tiger PS1	ECW B35R	7/47 – 11/60	New	58
8/47	846/7/9-54/6	CUH 846/7/9-54/6	Leyland Tiger PS1	ECW B35R	8/47 – 11/60	New	58
9/47	855/7/8/67	CUH 855/7/8/67	Leyland Tiger PS1	ECW B35R	9/47 – 11/60	New	58
10/47	859-66/9/71	CUH 859-66/9/71	Leyland Tiger PS1	ECW B35R	10/47 – 11/60	New	58
11/47	868/70/2/3	CUH 868/70/2/3	Leyland Tiger PS1	ECW B35R	11/47 – 11/60	New	58
11/47	794-7	CKG 844-7	Leyland Tiger PS1	Weymann B32F	11/47 – 1959/60	New	58
12/47	874-7	CUH 874-7	Leyland Tiger PS1	ECW B35R	12/47 – 11/60	New	58

Notes: 58 Refer to notes for 1946.

1948

New	Fleet No.	Reg No.	Chassis & type	Body & type	In use	Origin	Notes
9/48	622	DKG 622	AEC Regent III	Brush H56R	9/48 – 1/61	New	59
10/48	621/3-32	DKG 621/3-32	AEC Regent III	Brush H56R	10/48 – 1960/1	New	59

Notes: Nine Leyland TS7s from Yorkshire Woollen District were hired from 4/48 and were taken into stock during 1/49 as Nos 1328-36. Refer to 1949 for full details. 59 The Regents were the start of a large order by Western Welsh standards, the use of double-deckers being seen to be a quicker solution to addressing the wartime capacity shortages. However, most were of necessity to be of lowbridge layout and therefore not the easiest vehicles for conductors to work. 626 was converted to a tree-lopper upon withdrawal from regular service in 11/60.

1949

New	Fleet No.	Reg No.	Chassis & type	Body & type	In use	Origin	Notes
1935	1328-36	HD 5608-16	Leyland Tiger TS7	Roe B32F	4/48 – 12/51	Yorkshire Woollen 328-36	
1/49	878-83	DKG 878-83	Leyland Tiger PS1	Willowbrook B32F	1/49 – 1961/2	New	
2/49	884-6/8/9/92	DKG 884-6/8/9/92	Leyland Tiger PS1	Willowbrook B32F	2/49 – 11/62	New	
5/49	890/9	DKG 890/9	Leyland Tiger PS1	Willowbrook B32F	5/49 – 11/62	New	
6/49	887/91/3-8/900/1	DKG 887/91/3-8/900/1	Leyland Tiger PS1	Willowbrook B32F	6/49 – 1961/2	New	
7/49	940/1	DKG 940/1	Leyland Titan PD2/1	Leyland L27/26R	7/49 – 1963	New	
8/49	942-9	DKG 942-9	Leyland Titan PD2/1	Leyland L27/26R	8/49 – 1963	New	
9/49	754	CBO 533	Leyland Tiger TS8	ECW B32F	9/49 – 1/57	New	51
11/49	902-13/6/21/4/5/9/32	DKG 902-13/6/21/4/5/9/32	Crossley SD42/7	Willowbrook B32F	11/49 – 1960-2	New	60
12/49	914/5/7-20/2/3/6-8/30/1/3-9	DKG 914/5/7-20/2/3/6-8/30/1/3-9	Crossley SD42/7	Willowbrook B32F	12/49 – 1960-62	New	60

Notes: 51 See 1940 notes. 60 Crossleys 902-39 were bought due to Leyland delays. They were troublesome and saw little use, most were delicensed for long periods from 1956 after concerns about their handling. 904/9/19/31 were allocated to Ely Works during 1960/61, the only time Ely had a licensed allocation of vehicles other than coaches. They were sent around depots replacing vehicles going through works. All had gone by 1962.

1950

New	Fleet No.	Reg No.	Chassis & type	Body & type	In use	Origin	Notes
3/50	500	EUH 500	AEC Regal III	Windover C28F	3/50 – 8/63	New	61
3/50	508–11	EUH 508–11	AEC Regal III	Windover C30F	3/50 – 7/63	New	61
4/50	501/2/4	EUH 501/2/4	AEC Regal III	Windover C28F	4/50 – 8/63	New	61
5/50	503/6	EUH 503/6	AEC Regal III	Windover C30F	5/50 – 8/63	New	61
5/50	505/7	EUH 505/7	AEC Regal III	Windover C28F	5/50 – 8/63	New	61
8/50	950–62/5	EUH 950–62/5	Leyland Titan PD2/3	Leyland L27/26R	8/50 – 1963/69	New	62
9/50	963/4/6–73	EUH 963/4/6–73	Leyland Titan PD2/3	Leyland L27/26R	9/50 – 1962–4/69	New	62
9/50	637/8	EUH 637/8	AEC Regent III	Weymann L27/26R	9/50 – 1963	New	63
10/50	633/4/9/40/2/3	EUH 633/4/9/40/2/3	AEC Regent III	Weymann L27/26R	10/50 – 1962/3	New	63
10/50	645–51/3–6	EUH 645–51/3–6	AEC Regent III	Weymann L27/26R	10/50 – 1962/3	New	63
11/50	635/6/41/4/52	EUH 635/6/41/4/52	AEC Regent III	Weymann L27/26R	11/50 – 1962/3	New	63

Notes: 61 500-11 were the first full-fronted coaches operated by the company, with seats for the driver and courier fitted either side of the engine cowling in the front compartment. They were later converted to DP33F. 62 950-73 were the first bus bodies to the newly approved 8ft width. They were used, although not exclusively, on the Cardiff to Neath limited-stop service, where they received a great deal of favourable comment from passengers and staff. 960/8/71 were retro-fitted with rear platform doors as back up for 974-9, which followed in 1951, and enjoyed an extended life, lasting until 1969. 63 637-52, along with 950-73, were surely the classic double-deckers of all time. Dual sourcing of vehicles was rare for WW who, unlike the Welsh municipal operators, weren't obliged to buy local produce or be impartial in their accountability to ratepayers. But it occurred here in 1950, then again in 1953 with the heavyweight underfloor saloon order being split between AEC and Leyland. Even then the company stuck rigidly to its beloved Weymann bodywork for both types. Finally in 1963, the order for highbridge double-deckers was split once again between AEC and Leyland.

1951

New	Fleet No.	Reg No.	Chassis & type	Body & type	In use	Origin	Notes
5/51	404–8	FUH 404–8	Leyland Olympic HR44	Weymann B44F	5/51 – 1963	New	64
5/51	415/17	FUH 415/17	Leyland Royal Tiger PSU1/13	Weymann B44F	5/51 – 1964	New	65
6/51	409–10	FUH 409–10	Leyland Olympic HR44	Weymann B44F	6/51 – 1963	New	64
6/51	418	FUH 418	Leyland Royal Tiger PSU1/13	Weymann B44F	6/51 – 1964	New	65
7/51	411–3	FUH 411–3	Leyland Olympic HR44	Weymann B44F	7/51 – 1963	New	64
7/51	414/6/9/20/3/4/7/30/4	FUH 414/6/9/20/3/4/7/30/4	Leyland Royal Tiger PSU1/13	Weymann B44F	7/51 – 1964	New	65
8/51	425/8/9/31–3/5/6	FUH 425/8/9/31–3/5/6	Leyland Royal Tiger PSU1/13	Weymann B44F	8/51 – 1964	New	65
8/51	974–9	FKG 974–9	Leyland Titan PD2/1	Leyland L27/26RD	8/51 – 1963/8/9	New	66
9/51	421/2/6/37/8	FUH 421/2/6/37/8	Leyland Royal Tiger PSU1/13	Weymann B44F	9/51 – 1964	New	65

Notes: 64 404-13 were of integral design, the bodies had an underframe to which the engine, axles and other units were attached. They were fitted with the Leyland 0.600 engine modified for horizontal operation. 65 414-438 were Royal Tigers which had a conventional chassis on which a separate body was mounted. They were also fitted with the same modified engine. 66 974-9 were delivered with semi-coach type seats and enclosed platforms for use on the Cardiff to Carmarthen route. By the mid-1960s they were relegated to lighter duties in West Wales.

1952

New	Fleet No.	Reg No.	Chassis & type	Body & type	In use	Origin	Notes
8/48	524–7	JOD 611–4	AEC Regal 9621A	Duple C32F	11/52 – 1959	Devon General	67
3/49	528–35	JOD 615–22	AEC Regal 9621A	Duple C32F	11/52 – 1959/61	Devon General	67
11/52	540/5/53	GUH 540/5/53	AEC Regal IV 9822S	Weymann B44F	11/52 – 1965	New	68
12/52	551/5/6	GUH 551/5/6	AEC Regal IV 9822S	Weymann B44F	12/52 – 1965	New	68

Notes: In January only 23 petrol-engined vehicles were left in a fleet comprised of 40 per cent saloons and 80 per cent double deckers of post-war construction. The fleet total in August 1952 stood at 610. 67 524-35 were ex-Devon General and acquired for private hire work. 531-5 were repainted in red and ivory dual purpose livery 9/59-1/60 and retained until 1961. 68 The chassis or chassis-less debate of 1951 appeared to settle towards the traditional, but now the supplier came under scrutiny. Leyland's Royal Tiger had won round one, but of the 50 saloons on order for 1952/3, 20 were to be on AEC Regal Mk IV chassis (540-559). It was a fruitless exercise as, by the end of 1953, the lighter Tiger Cubs began arriving.

1953

New	Fleet No.	Reg No.	Chassis & type	Body & type	In use	Origin	Notes
1/53	541–4/6–50/2/4//7/8	GUH 541–4/6–50/2/4/7/8	AEC Regal IV 9822S	Weymann B44F	1/53 – 1965	New	
2/53	439–44/7	GUH 439–44/7	Leyland Royal Tiger PSU1/13	Weymann B44F	2/53 – 1965	New	
2/53	559	GUH 559	AEC Regal IV 9822S	Weymann B44F	2/53 – 1965	New	
3/53	445/6/8–56	GUH 445/6/8–56	Leyland Royal Tiger PSU1/13	Weymann B44F	3/53 – 1964/5	New	69

Continued overleaf

New	Fleet No.	Reg No.	Chassis & type	Body & type	In use	Origin	Notes
3/53	512-7	GUH 512-7	AEC Regal IV 9822S	Willowbrook C39C	3/53 – 1964/5	New	70
4/53	457–61	GUH 457–61	Leyland Royal Tiger PSU1/13	Weymann B44F	4/53 – 1965	New	69
5/53	462-4	GUH 462-4	Leyland Royal Tiger PSU1/13	Weymann B44F	5/53 – 1965	New	
6/53	465-8	GUH 465-8	Leyland Royal Tiger PSU1/13	Weymann B44F	6/53 – 1965	New	
6/53	519-21/3	GUH 519-21/3	Leyland Royal Tiger PSU1/16	Willowbrook C39C	6/53 – 1964/5	New	70
7/53	518/22	GUH 518/22	Leyland Royal Tiger PSU1/16	Willowbrook C39C	7/53 – 1965/7	New	70
10/53	1001-3/5-7/21/3/4	HUH 1-3/5-7/21/3/4	Leyland Tiger Cub PSUC1/1	Weymann B44F	10/53 – 1965-7	New	71
11/53	1030	HUH 30	Leyland Tiger Cub PSUC1/1	Weymann B44F	11/53 – 1967	New	71
12/53	1004/14/6/25/34/9	HUH 4/14/6/25/34/9	Leyland Tiger Cub PSUC1/1	Weymann B44F	12/53 – 1965-7	New	71
12/53	1040/3/8/50	HUH 40/3/8/50	Leyland Tiger Cub PSUC1/1	Weymann B44F	12/53 – 1965-7	New	71

Notes: 69 439-42/6/58 were later equipped for one-man operation. 70 512-23 were the first coaches with underfloor engines and were built to the newly-permitted dimensions of 30ft long by 8ft wide. 518/9 were reseated to 32 in 3/55 to augment 500-2/4/5/7/39 on extended tour work. They reverted to 39 seat in 10/57 in anticipation of delivery of 101-6, but 518/9 were further reseated to 34 in 3/58 before finally reverting to 39 seats in 12/59. 522 was something of a celebrity, being reseated to 25 in 9/64 for disabled party hire, then increased to 27 seats in 3/65 for football team hire, before reverting to 39 seats in 10/65 prior to sale. It was the only vehicle of its type repainted in the blue and ivory dual purpose livery, in 9/64. 71 1001-1050 were the first of the company's legendary fleet of Tiger Cubs. They were fitted with the economical 0.350 engine and had 44-seat all metal bodies. They were also the last Western Welsh vehicles to feature interior finish in BET blue. These buses marked the start of the replacement of the veteran Leyland TS7 and TS8 models, of which more than 300 had been placed in service in 1935-9. 1001-1130 & 469 were delivered with full-height cab doors, but were soon replaced by short doors. 1030/40/2/6/50-3/5/6/60/3-6/8-73/6-83/7-8/101/2/4/7/9/10/3/9/20/4/5/7/9/30 were equipped for one-man operation progressively from 10/58. 1093 and 1114 were early casualties following accidents in 1964.

1954

New	Fleet No.	Reg No.	Chassis & type	Body & type	In use	Origin	Notes
1/54	1008/11/5/20/6/8	HUH 8/11/5/20/6/8	Leyland Tiger Cub PSUC1/1	Weymann B44F	1/54 – 1966/7	New	70
1/54	1031/3/6/8/41/2/5-7	HUH 31/3/6/8/41/2/5-7	Leyland Tiger Cub PSUC1/1	Weymann B44F	1/54 – 1965-7	New	70
2/54	1009/10/2/3/7-9/22	HUH 9/10/2/3/7-9/22	Leyland Tiger Cub PSUC1/1	Weymann B44F	2/54 – 1965-7	New	71
2/54	1027/9/32/5/7/44/9	HUH 27/9/32/5/7/44/9	Leyland Tiger Cub PSUC1/1	Weymann B44F	2/54 – 1965-7	New	71
4/54	1055/74	JBO 55/74	Leyland Tiger Cub PSUC1/1	Weymann B44F	4/54 – 1966/7	New	71, 73
5/54	1051–3/6/63/73/88/9	JBO 51–3/6/63/73/88/9	Leyland Tiger Cub PSUC1/1	Weymann B44F	5/54 – 1965	New	71, 73
6/54	1054/7–62/4/8/71/2	JBO 54/7–62/4/8/71/2	Leyland Tiger Cub PSUC1/1	Weymann B44F	5/54 – 1965-8	New	71, 73
6/54	1075/7/92/3/5	JBO 75/7/92/3/5	Leyland Tiger Cub PSUC1/1	Weymann B44F	6/54 – 1964/6/7	New	71, 73
1949	536	JDF 87	AEC Regal III 9621E	Plaxton C33F	6/54 – 1958	Streamways, Penarth	
4/50	538	JTX 384	Commer Avenger I	Plaxton C33F	6/54 – 1956	Streamways, Penarth	
7/52	537	LTX 413	AEC Regal III	Plaxton FC37F	6/54 – 1961	Streamways, Penarth	72
7/54	1065-7/9/70/6/8-80	JBO 65-7/9/70/6/8-80	Leyland Tiger Cub PSUC1/1	Weymann B44F	7/54 – 1965-7/9	New	71, 73
7/54	1084-7/91/114	JBO 84-7/91/114	Leyland Tiger Cub PSUC1/1	Weymann B44F	7/54 – 1964	New	71, 73
11/47	562	HAD 477	Leyland Tiger PS1/1	Plaxton C33F	7/54 – 1958	Cridlands, Cardiff	74
1/49	568	EBO 431	Bedford OB	Duple C29F	7/54 – 1956	Cridlands, Cardiff	74
1/49	564/5	EBO 800/1	Maudslay Marathon 3	Duple FC33F	7/54 – 1959	Cridlands, Cardiff	74
4/49	566	EKG 259	Maudslay Marathon 2	Plaxton FC33F	7/54 – 1956	Cridlands, Cardiff	74
3/50	560	EUH 862	AEC Regal III 9621E	Duple C33F	7/54 – 1961	Cridlands, Cardiff	74
3/51	567	FKG 725	Maudslay Marathon 3	Plaxton C37F	7/54 – 1961	Cridlands, Cardiff	74
5/51	563	FUH 240	Leyland Tiger PS1/1	Strachans FC33F	7/54 – 1961	Cridlands, Cardiff	74
1/52	561	GBO 750	AEC Regal IV 9821E	Strachans C39C	7/54 – 1962	Cridlands, Cardiff	74
5/52	569	GKG 600	Bedford SB	Duple C33F	7/54 – 1956	Cridlands, Cardiff	74
8/54	1094/7/101/3/8	JBO 94/7/101/3/8	Leyland Tiger Cub PSUC1/1	Weymann B44F	8/54 – 1965-8	New	71, 73
8/54	1112/5/29	JBO 112/5/29	Leyland Tiger Cub PSUC1/1	Weymann B44F	9/54 – 1967	New	71, 73
9/54	1081/2/90/9	JBO 81/2/90/9	Leyland Tiger Cub PSUC1/1	Weymann B44F	9/54 – 1967	New	71, 73
9/54	1100/2/9–11/9/20/5	JBO 100/2/9–11/9/20/5	Leyland Tiger Cub PSUC1/1	Weymann B44F	9/54 – 1966-8/71	New	71, 73
10/54	469	JUH 469	Leyland Olympian LW1	Weymann B44F	10/54 – 1971	New	73
10/54	1083/96/8	JBO 83/96/8	Leyland Tiger Cub PSUC1/1	Weymann B44F	10/54 – 1965/6	New	71, 73
10/54	1104-7/13/6-8/21-4/6/7	JBO 104-7/13/6-8/21-4/6/7	Leyland Tiger Cub PSUC1/1	Weymann B44F	10/54 – 1965-9	New	71, 73
11/54	1128	JBO 128	Leyland Tiger Cub PSUC1/1	Weymann B44F	11/54 – 1965	New	71, 73
10/46	570	JHA 261	Leyland Tiger PS1/1	Harrington C33F	11/54 – 1958	Ebsworth, Laugharne	
1/47	980	CTH 828	Leyland Titan PD1	Leyland L27/26R	11/54 – 1959	Ebsworth, Laugharne	
4/49	573	ETH 785	Crossley SD42/7	Davies C33F	11/54 – 1958	Ebsworth, Laugharne	
6/49	983	FBX 35	Dennis Lance 108 K3	Davies H30/26R	11/54 – 1958	Ebsworth, Laugharne	
9/49	571	FBX 491	Leyland Tiger PS1	Davies C33F	11/54 – 1958	Ebsworth, Laugharne	

New	Fleet No.	Reg No.	Chassis & type	Body & type	In use	Origin	Notes
1/50	572	FBX 754	Leyland Tiger PS1	Davies DP35F	11/54 – 1958	Ebsworth, Laugharne	
6/50	981	FTH 445	Leyland Titan D2/1	Leyland L27/26R	11/54 – 1959	Ebsworth, Laugharne	
5/51	982	GBX 808	Leyland Titan PD2/1	Leyland L27/26R	11/54 – 1963	Ebsworth, Laugharne	
5/52	470	GTH 956	Leyland Royal Tiger PSU1/13	Leyland B44F	11/54 – 1965	Ebsworth, Laugharne	
9/53	471	JBX 220	Leyland Royal Tiger PSU1/13	Leyland B44F	11/54 – 1965	Ebsworth, Laugharne	
7/37	984	TH 9010	Leyland Titan TD5	Leyland L27/26R	—	Ebsworth, Laugharne	12
12/54	1130	JBO 130	Leyland Tiger Cub PSUC1/1	Weymann B44F	12/54 – 1967	New	71, 73
1954	On hire	168 DMU	AEC Monocoach	Willowbrook B45F	10/54 only	Demonstrator	75

Notes: 71 See notes for 53 72 537 was repainted into dual purpose livery in 11/59. 73 469 was exhibited at the 1954 Commercial Motor Show and together with 1051-1130 was equipped with two-speed rear axles in 1954/5, when they were reclassified LW1T (469), and PSUC1/1T (1051-1130). 469 was renumbered 1469 in 1964 and went on to lead a remarkably long life for a prototype, withdrawal not occurring until 1971. 74 With the exception of 561, these ex-Cridlands vehicles continued to run in 1954 in their original livery, 561 was painted red and ivory in 1954, 567 in dual-purpose style in 1955, the remainder except 568 were painted in ivory and red in 1955, as was 561 in 4/57. 568 was not painted in Western Welsh livery and was not used after 1954. 560/7 and possibly 563 were repainted in dual-purpose livery late 1959 or early 1960. 75 168 DMU was exhibited in shell form at the 1954 Commercial Motor Show, and after completion it was demonstrated to Western Welsh. The Monocoach was basically a chassis-less Reliance, being AEC's attempt at reducing weight and thus improving fuel consumption. Leyland's offering was, of course, the Olympian which would enter service in reasonable numbers with the company.

1955

New	Fleet No.	Reg No.	Chassis & type	Body & type	In use	Origin	Notes
1952	539	KUH 539	AEC Regal IV	Willowbrook C34C	5/55 – 1965	Cridlands	76

Notes: 76 1955 was a lean year for new vehicles. The only factor to account for this is that up to and including 1954, the post-war intake had at last made up for the unavailability of new vehicles during the 1940s, and there was now a short hiatus before the post-war re-bodied TS7s and TS8s needed replacing. Nevertheless, in February, 112 saloons and 23 double-deckers were classified as life-expired and authorised for scrapping over the following two years while orders were placed for £505,000 worth of vehicles in 1956. Meanwhile, 539's unbodied chassis, acquired in 7/54 with Cridlands, was sent to Willowbrook and received a body identical to Western Welsh. Its capacity was increased to 39 in 1960.

1956

New	Fleet No.	Reg No.	Chassis & type	Body & type	In use	Origin	Notes
3/56	1202/4/7/9	LKG 202/4/7/9	Leyland Olympian LW	Weymann B44F	3/56 – 1967/70/1	New	77
3/56	1210/3/5/6/20/1	LKG 210/3/5/6/20/1	Leyland Olympian LW	Weymann B44F	3/56 – 1971	New	77
3/56	657–64	LKG 657–64	AEC Regent V D3RV	Park Royal L31/28RD	3/56 – 1970-2	New	78
10/46	576	DBO 133	AEC Regal I	Harrington C33F	4/56 – 1958	E R Forse, Cardiff	79
6/48	577	FJW 328	AEC Regal III	Plaxton C33F	4/56 – 1958	E R Forse, Cardiff	79
7/48	589	AGL 70	Dennis Lancet J3	Jeffreys C33F	4/56 – 1958	E R Forse, Cardiff	79
2/49	584	EBO 600	Daimler CVD6SD	Plaxton C32F	4/56 – 1958	E R Forse, Cardiff	79
3/49	578	EKG 250	AEC Regal III 9621A	Harrington C33F	4/56 – 1961	E R Forse, Cardiff	79
5/49	579	EKG 650	AEC Regal III 9621E	Harrington C33F	4/56 – 1961	E R Forse, Cardiff	79
5/49	594	JNY 654	Foden PVSC6	Burlingham FC33F	4/56 – 1958	E R Forse, Cardiff	79
1/50	582	JRW 837	AEC Regal III 9621A	Plaxton C33F	4/56 – 1961	E R Forse, Cardiff	79
4/50	590	FBO 350	Dennis Lancet J3	Davies C33F	4/56 – 1958	E R Forse, Cardiff	79
4/50	580	FBO 360	AEC Regal III 9621A	Harrington C33F	4/56 – 1961	E R Forse, Cardiff	79
6/50	581	FBO 690	AEC Regal III 9621A	Harrington C33F	4/56 – 1961	E R Forse, Cardiff	79
6/50	585	FBO 750	Daimler CVD6SD	Harrington C33F	4/56 – 1958	E R Forse, Cardiff	79
6/50	591	FBO 850	Dennis Lancet J3	Davies C33F	4/56 – 1958	E R Forse, Cardiff	79
7/50	586	FBO 900	Daimler CVD6SD	Harrington C33F	4/56 – 1958	E R Forse, Cardiff	79
7/50	592	FBO 975	Dennis Lancet J3	Davies C33F	4/56 – 1958	E R Forse, Cardiff	79
2/51	574	FUH 50	Crossley SD42/7	Duple C33F	4/56 – 1958	E R Forse, Cardiff	79
3/51	575	FUH 123	Crossley SD42/9A	Burlingham FC37F	4/56 – 1961	E R Forse, Cardiff	79
4/51	593	FUH 375	Dennis Lancet J3	Davies FC37F	4/56 – 1958	E R Forse, Cardiff	79
2/52	583	LTG 533	AEC Regal IV 9821E	Burlingham C39C	4/56 – 1962	E R Forse, Cardiff	79
3/53	587/8	HBO 699/700	Daimler Freeline D650HS	Plaxton C39C	4/56 – 1962	E R Forse, Cardiff	79
2/43	376	FDE 496	Guy Arab I 6LW	Brush L28/27R	4/56 – 1958	Green's, H'west	80
3/43	377	FDE 569	Guy Arab I 6LW	Brush L28/27R	4/56 – 1957	Green's, H'west	80
11/43	378	FDE 737	Guy Arab II 6LW	Brush L27/28R	4/56 – 1958	Green's, H'west	80
2/44	379	FDE 828	Guy Arab II 6LW	Strachans L27/28R	4/56 – 1958	Green's, H'west	80
6/44	392/3	FDE 960/1	Bedford OWB	Duple B32F	4/56 – 1958	Green's, H'west	80
7/46	987	GDE 834	Leyland Titan PD1A	Burlingham L27/28R	4/56 – 1959	Green's, H'west	80

Continued overleaf

New	Fleet No.	Re-number	Reg No.	Chassis & type	Body & type	In use	Origin	Notes
2/47	337		HDE 414	Leyland Tiger PS1	Strachans B35F	4/56 – 9/59	Green's, H'west	80
4/47	338		HDE 544	Leyland Tiger PS1	Strachans B35F	4/56 – 1959	Green's, H'west	80
9/47	988/9		JDE 7/8	Leyland Titan D1	Leyland L27/26R	4/56 – 1960	Green's, H'west	80
6/49	681		LDE 500	AEC Regent III 9621A	Bruce L27/26R	4/56 – 1962	Green's, H'west	80
7/49	682		LDE 501	AEC Regent III 9621A	Bruce L27/26R	4/56 – 1962	Green's, H'west	80
8/49	990		LDE 602	Leyland Titan PD2/1	Leyland L27/26R	4/56 – 1962	Green's, H'west	80
9/49	382/3		LDE 600/1	Guy Arab III 6DC	Barnard L27/26R	4/56 – 1960/58	Green's, H'west	80
9/49	991		LDE 603	Leyland Titan PD2/1	Leyland L27/26R	4/56 – 1962	Green's, H'west	80
9/49	384		MDE 300	Guy Arab III 6DC	Strachans L27/28R	4/56 – 1961	Green's, H'west	80
3/50	595/6		MDE 301/2	AEC Regal III 9621A	Strachans B35F	4/56 – 1961	Green's, H'west	80
10/51	992		NDE 800	Leyland PD2/12	Leyland L27/28R	4/56 – 1963	Green's, H'west	80
1/53	484		PDE 390	Leyland Royal Tiger PSU1/9	East Lancs B44F	4/56 – 1964	Green's, H'west	80
4/54	397/8		RDE 996/7	Bedford SBO	Duple C36F	4/56 – 1959	Green's, H'west	80
6/54	993		RDE 998	Leyland PD2/12	Leyland L28/27R	4/56 – 1969	Green's, H'west	80
5/55	597/8	267/8	UDE 97/8	AEC Reliance MU3RV	Park Royal DP43F	4/56 – 1968/9	Green's, H'west	80
5/55	599/600	269/70	UDE 99/100	AEC Reliance MU3RV	Park Royal B44F	4/56 – 1969/8	Green's, H'west	80
5/36	985		WN 9475	Leyland Titan TD4	Leyland H30/26R	—	Green's, H'west	80, 12
11/37	986		CDE 782	Leyland Titan TD5	Burlingham L26/26R	—	Green's, H'west	80, 12
3/39	336		CWN 346	Leyland TS8	Duple C32F	—	Green's, H'west	80, 12
9/42	385		FDE 440	Bedford OWB	Duple B30F	—	Green's, H'west	80, 12
9/42	386		FDE 441	Bedford OWB	Duple B28F	—	Green's, H'west	80, 12
2/43	387		FDE 550	Bedford OWB	Duple B32F	—	Green's, H'west	80, 12
2/43	388		FDE 551	Bedford OWB	Duple B30F	—	Green's, H'west	80, 12
7/43	389		FDE 679	Bedford OWB	Duple B32F	—	Green's, H'west	80, 12
7/43	390		FDE 680	Bedford OWB	Duple B30F	—	Green's, H'west	80, 12
8/43	391		FDE 692	Bedford OWB	Duple B30F	—	Green's, H'west	80, 12
6/44	394		FDE 962	Bedford OWB	Duple B30F	—	Green's, H'west	80, 12
7/44	380		FDE 829	Guy Arab II 6LW	Strachans L27/28R	—	Green's, H'west	80, 12
9/44	381		GDE 33	Guy Arab II 6LW	Roe L27/28R	—	Green's, H'west	80, 12
4/48	395		JDE 889	Bedford OB	Duple B30F	—	Green's, H'west	80, 12
6/49	396		LDE 400	Bedford OB	Duple B30F	—	Green's, H'west	80,12
5/56	1201/3/5/6/8		LKG 201/3/5/6/8	Leyland Olympian LW	Weymann B44F	5/56 – 1969-71	New	77
5/56	1211/7-9/22-4/6		LKG 211/7-9/22-4/6	Leyland Olympian LW	Weymann B44F	5/56 – 1969/71	New	77
6/56	665-79		LKG 665-79	AEC Regent V MD3RV	Park Royal H33/28RD	6/56 – 1969-72	New	78
7/56	1200/35-8		LKG 200/35-8	Leyland Olympian LW	Weymann B44F	7/56 – 1967/9-71	New	77
8/56	472-82	1472-82	MKG 472-82	Leyland Tiger Cub PSUC1/2	Willowbrook DP41F	8/56 – 1968-71	New	81
8/56	1133		MUH 133	Leyland Tiger Cub PSUC1/1	Weymann B44F	8/56 – 1971	New	82
8/56	1227/9/30/3/4/9		LKG 227/9/30/3/4/9	Leyland Olympian LW	Weymann B44F	8/56 – 1969/71	New	77
9/56	1212/4/25/8/31/2		LKG 212/4/25/8/31/2	Leyland Olympian LW	Weymann B44F	9/56 – 1969/71	New	77
9/56	483	1483 5/64	MKG 483	Leyland Tiger Cub PSUC1/2	Willowbrook DP41F	9/56 – 1970	New	81
9/56	1131/2/4-40		MUH 131/2/4-40	Leyland Tiger Cub PSUC1/1	Weymann B44F	9/56 – 1966/9-71	New	82
11/56	1141-50		MUH 141-50	Leyland Tiger Cub PSUC1/1	Weymann B44F	11/56 – 1969-72	New	82
11/56	1152-4/6/8-62		MUH 152-4/6/8-62	Leyland Tiger Cub PSUC1/1	Weymann B44F	11/56 – 1967/70-2	New	82
12/56	1151/5/7/63-70/2-4		MUH 151/5/7/63-70/2-4	Leyland Tiger Cub PSUC1/1	Weymann B44F	12/56 – 1971/2	New	82

Notes: Re-numbering, where shown was in 1963/4. All 1956 saloons came with full height cab doors which were replaced by short ones. 12 see 1929. 77 1200-39 were outwardly identical to the 1131-80 series of Tiger Cubs. When new, 1200-5/7-22/32-4/8 were fitted with Leyland 0.350 engines, while the remainder had 0.375 engines. 1200-3/5/7/8/12/6/23/37/9 were fitted for one-man operation after 10/58. 1237 was cannibalised in 1967 following an accident. 1213 was loaned to Rhondda in 1969. 78 657-64, WW's first Regent Mk Vs had powerful 9.6 litre AV590 engines and were fitted with Park Royal, 59-seat lowbridge bodies. These were followed by 665-79, highbridge 61-seaters, but despite the extra weight were fitted with the smaller AV470 engines. All had platform doors, a feature included on all WW double-deckers after this date. 657/8/64/8/72/8 were withdrawn in 1971, but re-instated for use as driver trainers and retained PSV licences for occasional service. 658 received Rhondda fleet names in 1971. 677 was the first of its type to be withdrawn in 1969 following an accident. 79 574-94 initially retained Forse livery. Most received WW coach livery. 578-82 were relegated to dual-purpose and repainted wine red and ivory in late 1959 or early 1960. 578-81 had their Harrington dorsal fins removed, possibly at the same time. 585 was fitted with an AEC 7.7 litre oil engine in 1956/7. 80 Green's vehicles featured a green light, fitted at public request, to identify the company's buses. Many delicensed Green's vehicles never carried WW fleet numbers and were not even moved from Haverfordwest. Of the Bedfords and Guys, only 382/3/97/8 received fleet livery. 484 was later fitted for one-man operation. 597-600 were the first AEC Reliances with WW, 597/8 being the first semi-coaches with high-back seats. In 1957 the latter became the first to carry wine red and ivory DP livery. As 267/8, they were downgraded for bus work by 3/66, and painted all over red. They must have made an impression, as from 1958 this type became the mainstay of the coach fleet for the following decade. 81 472-83 were ordered for the Cardiff to Aberystwyth express service and had rear luggage lockers. Delivered in bus livery, repainted wine red and ivory from early 1957. All converted to one-man work after 10/58. As 1472-83 they were repainted in bus livery by 12/65. 82 1131/3/5-7/40-3/6-9/51/3-5/7/63-7/70/2/5/6/9/80 were fitted for one-man operation after 10/58. 1137/9/46/52/3/6/64/5/8/71 were fitted with towing hitches between 1969 and 1972. 1136 was an early casualty in 1966.

1957

New	Fleet No.	Reg No.	Chassis & type	Body & type	In use	Origin	Notes
1/57	1175/9	MUH 175/9	Leyland Tiger Cub PSUC1/1	Weymann B44F	1/57 – 1969/71	New	82
2/57	1171/6-8/80	MUH 171/6-8/80	Leyland Tiger Cub PSUC1/1	Weymann B44F	2/57 – 1970/1	New	82
3/57	680	MUH 680	AEC Regent V LD2RA	Park Royal H41/32RD	3/57 – 1971	New	83

Notes: 82 see notes for 1956. 83 680 was one of the first 30ft long Regents built and the first with fully automatic gearbox. It was shown at the 1956 Commercial Motor Show. The upper deck was mainly fibreglass and built for easy removal, possibly the first vehicle so equipped, but there is no record of it being used as an open-topper and the roof was later fixed permanently. The automatic gearbox was not a success and the vehicle was converted to semi-automatic. Until arrival of the Atlanteans in 1960, 680 was the longest double-decker in the fleet and for many years was confined to the Cardiff to Porthcawl route.

1958

New	Fleet No.	Re-number	Reg No.	Chassis & type	Body & type	In use	Origin	Notes
1/58	101		OUH 101	AEC Reliance MU3RV	Harrington C34F	1/58 – 1966	New	84
2/58	102-4		OUH 102-4	AEC Reliance MU3RV	Harrington C34F	2/58 – 1966/8	New	84
2/58	106		OUH 106	AEC Reliance MU3RV	Harrington C36F	2/58 – 1966	New	84
3/58	105		OUH 105	AEC Reliance MU3RV	Harrington C34F	3/58 – 1966	New	84
3/58	107-12		OUH 107-12	AEC Reliance MU3RV	Harrington C39F	3/58 – 1967/8	New	84
4/58	113-8		OUH 113-8	AEC Reliance MU3RV	Harrington C39F	4/58 – 1967/8	New	84
5/58	485-9	1485-9	OUH 485-9	Leyland Olympian	Weymann DP41F	5/58 – 1971/2	New	85
11/58	490	1490	OUH 490	Leyland Olympian	Weymann DP41F	11/58 – 1971	New	85
1956	683		PBO 683	AEC Bridgemaster B3RA	Park Royal H41/27RD	11/58 – 1971	New	86

Notes: 84 101-18 were the first AEC Reliances new to WW. Compared to earlier Regals and Royal Tigers their light weight allowed for a smaller, easier to handle and cheaper to run engine, and paved the way for successive coach deliveries until the late 1960s. They received Harrington Wayfarer IV bodies; 101-6 were known as the Ambassador Class and 107-18 the Capital Class until 1963. 106 won second prize in Class D at the 1958 British Coach Rally at Brighton, the first time WW had entered. Only one mark separated the coach from the winner, from SWT. 101/2/4-6 were re-seated to 38, and 103 to 41, in early 1964. 101/2/4-6 were relegated to dual-purpose work from 5/66, 107/9/12 from 5/67, 103/10/3/4 from 10/67, and 108 from 11/67, although no structural or livery changes took place, the change from red to blue coaching colours had taken place by then. 111/5-8 were never downgraded. 85 485-90 were the second and final batch of Olympians built for WW and finished as semi-coaches in the new wine red and ivory livery. They were the first WW vehicles to feature three-track route number blinds with yellow numerals. Surprisingly, in view of 490 being exhibited at the 1958 Commercial Motor Show, 485-90 were the last of the type to be built. As 1485-90, they were relegated to bus duties in 4/67, and gained bus livery. 86 683, the first of 20 allocated to WW, was to the shorter overall length of 27ft 8ins and shown at the 1958 Commercial Motor Show. The others, 684-702, were 28ft and followed in 1959. All had platform doors and three-track route indicators.

1959

New	Fleet No.	Re-number	Reg No.	Chassis & type	Body & type	In use	Origin	Notes
1/59	684-91/3/5		PBO 684-91/3/5	AEC Bridgemaster B3RA	Park Royal H41/27RD	1/59 – 171	New	86
2/59	692/4/6-8		PBO 692/4/6-8	AEC Bridgemaster B3RA	Park Royal H41/27RD	2/59 – 1971	New	86
3/59	699-702		PBO 699-702	AEC Bridgemaster B3RA	Park Royal H41/27RD	3/59 – 1971	New	86
8/59	1240-5		SBO 240-5	Leyland Tiger Cub PSUC1/1T	Park Royal B43F	8/59 – 1970/2/NBC	New	87
9/59	1246-51		SBO 246-51	Leyland Tiger Cub PSUC1/1T	Park Royal B43F	9/59 – 1972/NBC	New	87
10/59	1252-62		SBO 252-62	Leyland Tiger Cub PSUC1/1T	Park Royal B43F	10/59 – 1972/NBC	New	87
11/59	1263		SBO 263	Leyland Tiger Cub PSUC1/1T	Park Royal B43F	11/59 – NBC	New	87
11/59	491-5	1491-5	SBO 491-5	Leyland Tiger Cub PSUC1/2T	Park Royal DP41F	11/59 – 1972/NBC	New	88

Notes: Pleased with the 1958 intake of AEC Reliances, a further order was placed, this time with Weymann coach bodies. These were to be of a design unique to WW, and delivered over the following two years. 86 see notes for 1958. 87 1240-63 were fitted with Eaton two-speed rear axles, and the first new WW buses with pay-as-you-enter equipment including drop-down signs and flashing indicators. Another first was compressed air-operated doors. 1240/4/9/58 had been fitted with towing hooks by 4/71, 1249 was taken into engineering department stock in 11/72. 1259 was repainted in 9/72 in BET red livery but received NBC style fleet names. 88 491-5 also featured Eaton two-speed rear axles. As 1491-5, they were downgraded for bus work in 5/67, gaining bus livery between 9/67 and 12/68. 496 completed the batch in 1/60 and carried many experimental features.

1960

New	Fleet No.	Re-number	Reg No.	Chassis & type	Body & type	In use	Origin	Notes
1/60	301-4/6-12		TUH 301-4/6-12	Leyland Atlantean PDR1/1	Weymann L36/34F	1/60 – 1972	New	89
2/60	305		TUH 305	Leyland Atlantean PDR1/1	Weymann L36/34F	2/60 – 1972	New	89
1948	1554/6/7/9-62/4-6		JUO 554/6/7/9-62/4-6	AEC Regent III	Weymann H30/26R	1960	Devon General	90

Continued overleaf

New	Fleet No.	Re-number	Reg No.	Chassis & type	Body & type	In use	Origin	Notes
12/47	2901/22/43/54, 3015		EWN 344/6/8/9/54	AEC Regent II	Weymann L27/26R	1960	SWT	91
2/49	6116/6617		FCY 342/7	AEC Regal III	Willowbrook B34F	1960	SWT	91
1949	2108, 3109/10		FWN 802–4	AEC Regal III	Willowbrook B34F	1960	SWT	91
4/60	2		TUH 2	Albion Nimbus NS3N	Harrington DP30F	4/60 – 1970	New	92
5/60	119–24		TUH 119–24	AEC Reliance 2MU3RA	Weymann C36F	5/60 – 1968/9	New	93
6/60	1,3–5		TUH 1,3–5	Albion Nimbus NS3N	Harrington DP30F	6/60 – 1966	New	92
7/60	6–15		TUH 6–15	Albion Nimbus NS3N	Harrington DP30F	7/60 – 1966	New	92
7/60	496	1496	SBO 496	Leyland Tiger Cub PSUC1/1T	Park Royal DP41F	7/60 – 1973	New	94
8/60	16–23		TUH 16–23	Albion Nimbus NS3N	Harrington DP30F	9/60 – 1966/7	New	92
10/60	24		TUH 24	Albion Nimbus NS3N	Harrington DP30F	10/60 – 1967	New	92
11/60	1265/9–71		UKG 265/9–71	Leyland Tiger Cub PSUC1/12	MCW DP41F	11/60 – 1972/3/NBC	New	95
11/60	313/6/9		VKG 313/6/9	Leyland Atlantean PDR1/1	Weymann L37/33F	11/60 – NBC	New	96
12/60	314/5/7/8/20–2		VKG 314/5/7/8/20–2	Leyland Atlantean PDR1/1	Weymann L37/33F	12/60 – 1974/NBC	New	96
12/60	1264/6–8		UKG 264/6–8	Leyland Tiger Cub PSUC1/12	MCW DP41F	12/60 – 1972/3	New	95

Notes: 89 301-12 were WW's first Atlanteans and also the last double deckers to feature two cream bands in their livery. The entire batch was sold to China Motor Bus of Hong Kong in 1972 and had extra upper-deck radiators fitted to assist cooling. 301, which became CMB's PDR1, was fitted with an exhaust brake by WW at CMB's request. 90 1554/6/7/9-62/4-6 were bought from Devon General to release WW lowbridge double deckers for the Milford oil terminal contract. They operated from Cardiff, Barry and Bridgend in their original livery but with WW fleet names and numbers. They cost the company £175 each. 91 2901/22/43/54, 3015, 6116/617, 2108, 3109/10 were purchased from SWT in 5/60 also for Milford. All except one operated in original livery, but with WW fleet names and numbers which incorporated the SWT numbers, but with additional figures. 92 Although structurally identical with 30 semi-coach type seats, Nimbuses 1 and 3-23 were classed as buses and delivered in bus livery with crests in place of fleet names, while 2 and 24 were classed as dual-purpose until 11/65 and delivered in wine red and ivory. 24 was exhibited at the 1960 Commercial Motor Show. No 2 appeared at the Brighton Coach Rally and was repainted in blue and ivory by 4/67, then standard bus livery in mid-1969. Later, 2 and 10 had their curved windscreens replaced by flat ones. 93 119-24, together with 125-30 of 1961, were known as the Cambrian Class until 1963. It was originally intended that 119-24 would feature the coat-of-arms of each of the six Welsh counties. However, permission from all the councils was not forthcoming and so the idea was dropped. The body design of these vehicles together with 131-9 of 1961 was unique to WW, being designed jointly by Weymann and WW's own engineering department under chief engineer FA Mason. The number of side pillars was reduced for improved vision, and ventilation was provided by the latest hopper-type ventilators inspired by the Midland Red motorway coaches. 124 was sent to the Brighton Coach Rally in April, fully spruced up with white-walled tyres, but failed to gain an award. Some thought the concave windscreens ungainly, and the rear windows hideous, especially when compared to the Harrington Cavalier. 125-139 had improved rear styling when new a year later. 122 became dual purpose from 10/67, and the rest followed in 10/68, but there were no structural changes. 94 496 was far from the standard Park Royal-bodied Tiger Cub. It had several experimental features: leaf-air suspension, Dunlop disc brakes, an air-operated windscreen wiper, and an experimental Clayton/BET underfloor heating and ventilation system, the eventual success of which led to incorporation of a modified system in the 1965/6 Tiger Cubs 1361-74. The wiper was also a success and became a standard fitment on all WW vehicles. The disc brakes also proved successful but due to the reluctance of manufacturers to fit such brakes, 1496 (as renumbered in 2/63) remained the only vehicle to be so fitted. The only disappointment came with the air suspension, which caused the vehicle to be out of service for long periods and eventually to return to standard leaf springing. 95 1264-75 were demoted to bus duties in 5/67 and had bus livery between 9/67 and 1/68. 1264/5/70/1/4/5 were later equipped for one-man operation. 96 313-31 were fitted with offside illuminated advertisement panels.

1961

New	Fleet No.	Re-number	Reg No.	Chassis & type	Body & type	In use	Origin	Notes
1/61	323–31		VKG 323–31	Leyland Atlantean PDR1/1	Weymann L37/33F	1/61 – NBC	New	96
1/61	1272–5		UKG 272–5	Leyland Tiger Cub PSUC1/12	MCW DP41F	1/61 – 1972/3	New	95
5/61	25–48		WKG 25–48	Albion Nimbus NS3AN	Weymann DP30F	5/61 – 1967–71	New	97
5/61	125–30		WKG 125–30	AEC Reliance 2MU3RA	Weymann C36F	5/61 – 1969/70	New	98
5/61	131–9		WKG 131–9	AEC Reliance 2MU3RA	Weymann C39F	5/61 – 1970	New	98
7/61	1276–9	276–9	WKG 276–9	AEC Reliance 2MU3RA	Willowbrook DP41F	7/61 – 1972	New	99
8/61	1280–87	280–7	WKG 280–7	AEC Reliance 2MU3RA	Willowbrook DP41F	8/61 – 1972	New	99
8/61	300		YBO 300	Ford 402E	Ford B10	8/61 – 1965	New	100
12/61	336/9		XUH 336/9	Leyland Atlantean PDR1/1	Weymann L37/33F	12/61 – NBC	New	101

Notes: 95 and 96 Refer to notes for 1960. 97 25-48 were delivered fitted for one-man operation and, like 1-24 of 1960, had bus livery with crests in place of fleet names on their sides. They were bodied by Weymann to Harrington design, virtually identical to their cousins. They differed from the original batch by having a six-speed gearbox, improved interior lighting and door control. The sixth gear was an overdrive for use on long flat stretches of road and was probably never engaged on the roads for which the vehicles were intended. All were classed as buses from new. Delivery of these brought a total of 48 such vehicles to WW, the largest number for any operator. Regrettably they were to prove unreliable, and withdrawals began as early at 1966. 98 125-30, along with 119-24 of 1960, were known as the Cambrian Class until 1963, while 131-9 were known as the Celtic Class and unlike the earlier batch didn't have individual reading lights. 125-139 had modified seats and improved body styling and together with 119-124 made a total of 21 coaches with bodies unique to WW. This concluded the naming of new coaches and the idea wasn't perpetuated after 1961. 125-9 were considered to be dual-purpose vehicles from 10/69, but without any structural changes; 130 had already gone. 99 1276-87 were delivered in the dual-purpose wine red and ivory livery for express service, but to augment the summer coach fleet, were repainted in ivory with red lining between 12/62 and 4/63, and re-numbered 276-87 at or around that time. 276/7/80/4/6 reverted to their original livery between 8/64 and 10/64, while the remainder were painted in the new blue and ivory livery between 10/64 and 6/65. All except 280 were downgraded and painted in bus livery between 9/69 and 6/71; 280 received blue and ivory livery in 10/69 then bus livery in 7/71. 100 300 was used for staff transport at Ely Works, although licensed as a PSV. 101 332-66 were fitted with offside illuminated advertisement panels. The Atlantean had become a favourite with road staff but the bane of the maintenance staff. They had their share of teething problems, but these were overcome through collaboration with the manufacturers and WW's engineering staff. By 1966 reliability compared well with other vehicles.

1962

New	Fleet No.	Reg No.	Chassis & type	Body & type	In use	Origin	Notes
1/62	332/4/7/8/40/4	XUH 332/4/7/8/40/4	Leyland Atlantean PDR1/1	Weymann L37/33F	1/62 – NBC	New	101
2/62	333/5/41-3/5-7	XUH 333/5/41-3/5-7	Leyland Atlantean PDR1/1	Weymann L37/33F	2/62 – NBC	New	101
10/62	349/50/2/6/7	349/50/2/6/7 ABO	Leyland Atlantean PDR1/1MkII	Weymann L37/33F	10/62 – NBC	New	101
10/62	360/2-5	360/2-5 ABO	Leyland Atlantean PDR1/1MkII	Weymann L37/33F	10/62 – NBC	New	101
10/62	601-18	601-18 BBO	Leyland Leopard PSU3/2R	Willowbrook B54F	10/62 – NBC	New	102
11/62	348/51/3-5/8/9	348/51/3-5/8/9 ABO	Leyland Atlantean PDR1/1MkII	Weymann L37/33F	11/62 – NBC	New	101
11/62	361/6	361/6 ABO	Leyland Atlantean PDR1/1MkII	Weymann L37/33F	11/62 – NBC	New	101

Notes: 101 refer to notes for 1961. 102 601-18 were the first 36ft long, 8ft 2½in wide vehicles new to Western Welsh and delivered in all-over red bus livery. They were fitted with double-width doors and powered by a horizontal 0.600 engine with a four-speed semi-automatic gearbox. All were later equipped for one-man operation. 602 was exhibited at the 1962 Commercial Motor Show. 612 went to SWT in 1972.

1963

New	Fleet No.	Reg No.	Chassis & type	Body & type	In use	Origin	Notes
3/63	705/7/9-11	705/7/9-11 CUH	AEC Regent V 2MD3RA	N.Counties H37/28F	3/63 – NBC	New	103
4/63	703/4/6/8/12	703/4/6/8/12 CUH	AEC Regent V 2MD3RA	N.Counties H37/28F	4/63 – NBC	New	103
4/63	140/1	140/1 DBO	Leyland Leopard PSU3/3RT	Duple Northern C49F	4/63 – 1971	New	104
5/63	142/3	142/3 DBO	Leyland Leopard PSU3/3RT	Duple Northern C49F	4/63 – 1971	New	104
6/63	1300/2/4	300/2/4 CUH	Leyland Tiger Cub PSUC1/11	Marshall B45F	6/63 – 1972	New	105
6/63	918/9	918/9 DBO	Leyland PD2A/27	Weymann H37/28F	6/63 – NBC	New	106
7/63	1303/5-8	303/5-8 CUH	Leyland Tiger Cub PSUC1/11	Marshall B45F	6/63 – NBC	New	105
7/63	902/8	902/8 DBO	Leyland PD2A/27	Weymann H37/28F	7/63 – NBC	New	106
7/63	911/3-5/7/20	911/3-5/7/20 DBO	Leyland PD2A/27	Weymann H37/28F	7/63 – NBC	New	106
8/63	1301	301 CUH	Leyland Tiger Cub PSUC1/11	Marshall B45F	8/63 – NBC	New	105
11/63	900/1/3-7/9	900/1/3/7-9 DBO	Leyland PD2A/27	Weymann H37/28F	11/63 – NBC	New	106
11/63	910/2/6	910/2/6 DBO	Leyland PD2A/27	Weymann H37/28F	11/63 – NBC	New	106
1962	On hire	4559 VC	Daimler Fleetline	Northern Counties	4/63	Demonstrator	

Notes: Re-numbering occurred in 1963, to place all the AEC saloons and dual-purpose vehicles in a 2XX series, and all the Leyland saloons and dual-purpose vehicles except 601-18 in a 1XXX series. Although organised in January, vehicles received new numbers as detailed: February: 487/93/6 to 1487/93/6; 597 to 267; 1280 to 280 March: 472/94 to 1472/94; 1279/81/2 to 279/81/2 April: 491 to 1491; 1278/83-7 to 278/83-7 May: 489/95 to 1489/95; 1276/7 to 276/7 June: 477/85 to 1477/85 July: 473/4/90 to 1473/4/90 August: 492 to 1492 September: 598/9 to 268/9; 478/81 to 1478/81. 103 703-12 were the first to feature a two-tier destination which became standard on all new buses. 712 was equipped for one-man operation in 9/70 but not approved for use. The Regents were seen as a return to proven technology after the persisting teething troubles of the Atlanteans. 104 140-3 were 'Alpine Continental' bodies to the newly permitted dimensions of 36ft long by 8ft 2½ins wide. They were delivered in ivory with only a hint of wine red around the windows, this being described as maroon by WW. They had two-speed rear axles. Ventilation was by blowers controlled by the passenger. In addition to the roof vents, a louvre-blind sunlight was fitted at the front dome. This was the one and only time WW specified it. Also unique to WW was the one-piece front windscreen. These vehicles were never intended for extended tours, but were based from new at Cardiff, Crosskeys and Neath for use on day and half-day tours and excursions. They were repainted in the blue and ivory dual-purpose livery in 1965. Later they saw use on the former N&C service. 105 1300-8 saw the Tiger Cub now powered by Leyland's 0.400 engine and introduced Marshall bodies to WW. They were fitted for one-man operation from new. 1300/1/7 had towing hitches by 1972. 106 900-20 were the last traditional Leyland double-deckers for WW, bringing the total of PD2s operated to 67. They were allocated to Cardiff, Barry and Bridgend.

1964

New	Fleet No.	Reg No.	Chassis & type	Body & type	In use	Origin	Notes
2/64	144-6	ABO 144-6B	AEC Reliance 2MU3RA	Harrington Grenadier C36F	2/64 – 1971	New	107
3/64	147-9	ABO 147-9B	AEC Reliance 2MU3RA	Harrington Grenadier C36F	2/64 – 1971	New	107
5/64	1328-33	ABO 328-33B	Leyland Tiger Cub PSUC1/11	Willowbrook B45F	5/64 – NBC	New	108
6/64	1309-16/8-21	ABO 309-16/8-21B	Leyland Tiger Cub PSUC1/11	Willowbrook B43F	6/64 – NBC	New	108
7/64	1317/22/3	ABO 317/22/3B	Leyland Tiger Cub PSUC1/11	Willowbrook B43F	7/64 – NBC	New	108
7/64	1324-7	ABO 324-7B	Leyland Tiger Cub PSUC1/11	Willowbrook B45F	7/64 – NBC	New	108
10/64	713	BKG 713B	AEC Renown 3B3RA	Northern Counties H38/29F	10/64 – NBC	New	109

Notes: Vehicles re-numbered in 1964: January 480/8 to 1480/8 May: 479/82/3/6 to 1479/82/3/6 June: 600 to 270 July: 469 to 1469 November: 475 to 1475. There was no 1484 as 484 (PDE 390) was withdrawn after an accident. 107 144-9 had Grenadier bodies and were the last coaches delivered in ivory and red. Like future deliveries until 1968, they were 32ft long and ideal for negotiating rural roads featured on tours and excursions. Their bodywork had panoramic windows and Cirrus leather cloth moquette seats. Light luggage could be stored on stainless steel, nylon meshed racks. They were reseated, first to 38 in the winter of 1965/6, then to 40 a year later except for 148, which lasted as a 38-seater until 1/69. They received the new ivory and blue livery as early as 1965/6. 148 had an experimental foot-controlled exhaust brake in 1965. 108 1309-33 had Leyland 0400 engines, 5-speed gearboxes and 30ft 6 inch long bodies to the modern BET standard by Willowbrook and continued links with that builder. 1309-23 were fitted for one-

Continued overleaf

man operation from new and featured pram/luggage pens. 1324-33 had boots instead of on-board pens, and were the last vehicles delivered to WW without one-man operation equipment. 1328-33 were delivered in all over ivory with red window surrounds to augment the private hire fleet although they only had bus seats. They received standard bus livery in 1965. 1315/6/8 were fitted with towing hitches in 1971/2. 1312 was scrapped in 1971 and didn't survive to be transferred to NBC. 109 713 was exhibited at the 1964 Commercial Motor Show. It was the first Renown to be bodied by Northern Counties, which was owned for many years by the Welsh-based Lewis family. The new Renown replaced the Bridgemaster but retained its general layout. The main difference was the adoption of a separate chassis frame and suspension system. It was, however short-lived as by late 1965 AEC had announced that production was to cease once existing orders had been completed.

1965

New	Fleet No.	Reg No.	Chassis & type	Body & type	In use	Origin	Notes
2/65	153	DBO 153C	AEC Reliance 2MU4RA	Plaxton Panorama C36F	2/65 – NBC	New	110
2/65	714/6-8/20/2/4/7	BKG 714/6-8/20/2/4/7C	AEC Renown 3B3RA	Northern Counties H38/29F	2/65 – 1972/NBC	New	109
3/65	715/9/21/3/5/6	BKG 715/9/21/3/5/6C	AEC Renown 3B3RA	Northern Counties H38/29F	3/65 – NBC	New	109
3/65	150-2/4	DBO 150-2/4C	AEC Reliance 2MU4RA	Plaxton Panorama C36F	3/65 – NBC	New	110
4/65	155	DBO 155C	AEC Reliance 2MU4RA	Plaxton Panorama C36F	4/65 – NBC	New	110
5/65	1334-48	DBO 334-48C	Leyland PSUC1/11	Park Royal DP41F	5/65 – 1972/NBC	New	111
8/65	1349-55	DBO 349-55C	Leyland PSUC1/11	Park Royal B43F	8/65 – 1972/NBC	New	112
9/65	728-30	DBO 728-30C	AEC Renown 3B3RA	Northern Counties H38/29F	9/65 – 1972/NBC	New	109
9/65	1356-60	DBO 356-60C	Leyland PSUC1/11	Park Royal B43F	9/65 – 1972/NBC	New	
11/65	1361/3/5/7	FUH 361/3/5/7C	Leyland PSUC1/11	Park Royal B43F	11/65 – 1972/NBC	New	113
1965	On hire	KTD 551C	Leyland Atlantean PDR1/2	Park Royal H41/33F	5/65	Demonstrator	

Notes: The fleet total was 639 in December. At 281 the Tiger Cub tally was Britain's biggest. Vehicle 476 became 1476 in February 1965. 109 see notes for 1964. 110 150-5 had AH470 engines, six-speed gearboxes and were fitted with 31ft 10 inch long Panorama bodies featuring the largest windows of any coach at the time. Seating was increased to 38 in the winter of 1965/66, and 40 a year later. 111 1334-48 were the first Tiger Cubs delivered in the new blue and ivory livery and had chrome bumpers and rear luggage lockers. They became familiar on express and limited stop services proving popular with drivers and passengers. 1339/40/2/8 were repainted into red and ivory, 6/71-7/71; 1334/7/43/6 received bus livery, 4/72-5/72. 112 1349-55 had a luggage compartment behind the cab and aluminium mouldings on front and rear skirts, giving the appearance of bumpers. 113 1361-74 were fitted from new with Clayton/BET heating and ventilation trialled on 1496. Delivery was completed in Jan 1966. 1360/2 were fitted with towing hooks in 1971/2.

1966

New	Fleet No.	Reg No.	Chassis & type	Body & type	In use	Origin	Notes
1/66	1362/4/6/8-74	FUH 362/4/6/8-74D	Leyland PSUC1/11	Park Royal B43F	1/66 – NBC	New	113
2/66	158	GKG 158D	AEC Reliance 2MU4RA	Plaxton Panorama C38F	2/66 – NBC	New	114
3/66	160	GKG 160D	AEC Reliance 2MU4RA	Plaxton Panorama C38F	3/66 – NBC	New	114
4/66	156/7/9	GKG 156/7/9D	AEC Reliance 2MU4RA	Plaxton Panorama C38F	4/66 – NBC	New	114
5/66	161	GKG 161D	AEC Reliance 2MU4RA	Plaxton Panorama C38F	5/66 – NBC	New	114
7/66	1376-80	HBO 376-80D	Leyland PSUC1/12	Marshall DP41F	7/66 – 1972/NBC	New	115
8/66	1375/81-4	HBO 375/81-4D	Leyland PSUC1/12	Marshall DP41F	8/66 – NBC	New	115
9/66	1385-9/91/2	HBO 385-9/91/2D	Leyland PSUC1/12	Marshall B43F	9/66 – 1972/NBC	New	
10/66	1390/3/4	HBO 390/3/4D	Leyland PSUC1/12	Marshall B43F	10/66 – 1972/NBC	New	
10/66	731-6/8-40	HKG 731-6/8-40D	AEC Renown 3B3RA	N.Counties LH38/29F	10/66 – 1973/NBC	New	
11/66	737	HKG 737D	AEC Renown 3B3RA	N.Counties LH38/29F	11/66 –NBC	New	
1963	On hire	824 SHW	Bristol FLF	ECW LH70F	3/66	Bristol O.Co.	116

Notes: 113 See notes for 1965. 114 156-61 had AH470 engines, six-speed gearboxes and 31ft 10 inch Panorama bodies. They were all reseated to 40 by 1/69. 115 1375-84 were based on the design of the previous year's semi-coaches and delivered in blue and ivory. Although bodied by Marshall, they differed only in having Clayton/BET heating and ventilation and being fitted for one-man operation. 1375/9 received red and ivory livery during 10/71-11/71. 1380 was fitted with a four-speed Leyland synchromesh gearbox from new, but later received a standard five-speed Albion unit. It was the first Western Welsh dual-purpose vehicle to receive NBC poppy red and white livery in 10/72. 116 A Leyland-engined Lodekka from Bristol Omnibus (Bristol No. C7131) was hired in March and employed on service 302 between Cardiff and Porthcawl for eight days. The main purpose was to compare its fuel consumption figures and performance with those of the Atlantean. The Lodekka had previously been an untried possibility and largely restricted to THC companies. It had a reputation for reliability but was never a driver's favourite. The trial was unsuccessful and no orders resulted.

1967

New	Fleet No.	Reg No.	Chassis & type	Body & type	In use	Origin	Notes
2/67	162-4	JBO 162-4E	AEC Reliance 6MU4R	Plaxton Panorama C38F	2/67 – NBC	New	117
3/67	165/6	JBO 165/6E	AEC Reliance 6MU4R	Plaxton Panorama C38F	3/67 – NBC	New	117
7/67	201-8	KKG 201-5E/206-8F	AEC Reliance 6MU3R	Marshall DP41F	7/67 – 1972	New	118
8/67	209-13	KKG 209-13F	AEC Reliance 6MU3R	Marshall DP41F	8/67 – 1972	New	118

New	Fleet No.	Reg No.	Chassis & type	Body & type	In use	Origin	Notes
9/67	214/5	KKG 214/5F	AEC Reliance 6MU3R	Marshall DP41F	9/67 – 1972	New	118
10/67	1395–7	LUH 395–7F	Leyland PSUC1/12	Marshall B43F	10/67 – NBC	New	
11/67	1398–1408	LUH 398–408F	Leyland PSUC1/12	Marshall B43F	11/67 – NBC	New	119
12/67	1409–14	LUH 409–14F	Leyland PSUC1/12	Marshall B43F	12/67 – NBC	New	119
1966	On hire	LYY 827D	AEC Swift	Marshall	6/67	Demonstrator	

Notes: 117 162-6 were Panorama 1s with AH505 engines, six-speed gearboxes and exhaust brakes. They were reseated to 40 in the winter of 1970/1. 118 201-15 had AH505 engines and five-speed gearboxes and were delivered in blue and ivory dual-purpose livery. They were the last AECs WW bought new. The split between E and F suffixes came as a result of the change of month to August. This time a more even split occurred than with saloons 1361-74 in 1965/66. 203/6/7/15 were repainted red and ivory between 7/71-9/71. 213 was the first in NBC poppy red and white dual-purpose livery in 11/71. 119 1399 was fitted with a Voith automatic gearbox and hydraulic retarder in 9/68, which was a UK first demonstrated at the 1968 Commercial Motor Show. In 4/71 it received a standard manual gearbox from the dismantled 1312. 1414 was the 349th and final Tiger Cub delivered to the company.

1968

New	Fleet No.	Reg No.	Chassis & type	Body & type	In use	Origin	Notes
2/68	167–71	LUH 167–71F	Leyland Leopard PSU3/3RT	Plaxton Panorama C49F	2/68 – NBC	New	120
4/68	1	MBO 1F	Bristol LHS6L	Weymann DP30F	4/68 – NBC	New	121
5/68	172	LUH 172F	Leyland Leopard PSU3/3RT	Plaxton Panorama C49F	5/68 – NBC	New	120
1967	On hire	LAE 770E	Bristol RELL6G	ECW B40D	3/68	Demonstrator	122

Notes: 120 167-72 marked a return to Leyland chassis for coaching requirements. They had 0.600 engines, four-speed synchromesh gearboxes, two-speed rear axles, and 36ft long Panorama 1 bodies. 121 Due to unreliability of the 1960/1 Albion Nimbuses, a Bristol LHS chassis was bought for evaluation in 12/67 and fitted with the reconditioned body of WKG 27. A Leyland 0.400 engine was fitted which developed 125bhp at 2,400 rpm, the same rating as those of Tiger Cubs, so the LHS wasn't short of power. The conventional handbrake was replaced by a spring parking brake, a feature gaining popularity on goods chassis but previously unknown on a Bristol. The Weymann body required little alteration other than the moving back of the rear wheel arch. Interior improvements included fluorescent lights and air-operated door. The work was done at Ely and extensive trials undertaken with a view to a follow-up order to replace remaining Nimbuses. In blue and ivory, it was the first WW vehicle to receive reflective number plates. The livery changed to red and ivory in 1/72. Despite extensive publicity and interest shown, no further LHS chassis were ordered and it remained unique. 122 Another Bristol entered service early in the year – RELL6G demonstrator LAE770E. This was fitted with an ECW bus body in brown and cream livery and was loaned for evaluation. Based at Crosskeys and Cwmbran depots, this vehicle, with its Gardner engine and the dual-door body layout, was unfamiliar to WW eyes, but was well received by road staff and passengers alike.

1969

New	Fleet No.	Reg No.	Chassis & type	Body & type	In use	Origin	Notes
4/69	173–8	OUH 173–8G	Leyland Leopard PSU3A/4RT	Plaxton Pan. Elite C49F	4/69 – NBC	New	123
5/69	619–21/3/5–8	PKG 619–21/3/5–8G	Leyland Leopard PSU3A/4R	Marshall B51F	5/69 – NBC	New	124
6/69	622/4/9–38	PKG 622/4/9–38G	Leyland Leopard PSU3A/4R	Marshall B51F	6/69 – NBC	New	124
8/69	367–76	PKG 367–76H	Leyland Atlantean PDR1/3	N. Counties H42/31F	8/69 – NBC	New	125

Notes: 123 173-8 had Panorama Elite bodies and were fitted with 0.600 engines, five-speed semi-automatic gearboxes, and two-speed rear axles. Exhaust brakes, previously fitted to AEC Reliances, were now a first for Leyland. WW fitted 176-8 with experimental Webasto oil heaters, which gave a quicker warm-up without running the engine. The result was a batch of front line 70 mph coaches capable of climbing the steepest hills. 124 619-38 had 0.600 engines and four-speed semi-automatic gearboxes. Electrically heated windscreens replaced the usual demister, a first for WW. They carried their fleet names on the forward cantrail panels. Another new idea was the addition of side body mouldings to carry slide-in advertisements below the windows. During 1970, 635 featured decorative aluminium mouldings, as a trial for the body styling of 1501-10 which followed in 1971. 125 367-76 were the first WW Atlanteans fitted with drop-centre rear axles. This was a major improvement over earlier Atlanteans for as well as simplifying driveline arrangement, a lower floor level was achieved, permitting conventional highbridge seating within a body built to lowbridge dimensions. Special dispensation regarding the minimum height for the government's newly-introduced bus grant was obtained from the Ministry of Transport. The original height qualification had been set at 13ft 8 ins, which would have precluded the purchase of these vehicles but this was revised to 13ft 5ins, allowing them to be purchased for universal operation under the bus grant scheme. All 10 were fitted with periscopes in the cabs, and Northern Counties increased the luggage space by dispensing with the unpopular longitudinal seats in the lower saloon. 367/74-6 were equipped for one-man operation in 9/70.

1970

New	Fleet No.	Reg No.	Chassis & type	Body & type	In use	Origin	Notes
5/70	179–84	SKG 179–84H	Leyland Leopard PSU3A/4RT	Plaxton Elite C49F	5/70 – NBC	New	126

Notes: All new and repainted vehicles now carried Rhondda-style fleet numbers. The fleet total recorded in December, prior to the Rhondda and N&C transfers, was 527. 126 179-84 were an even greater advancement on the previous year's Panorama Elite coaches. They featured five-speed gearboxes, two-speed rear axles, power-assisted steering, exhaust brakes, power door and Webasto heaters.

1971

New	Fleet No.	Re-number	Reg No.	Chassis & type	Body & type	In use	Origin	Notes
11/56	422–4		UNY 5–7	AEC Regent V MD3RV	Weymann H33/28R	1/71 – 1971/2	Rhondda Transport	
1/59	2363–77		XTG 363–77	Leyland Tiger Cub PSUC1/1	Weymann B44F	1/71 – 1972/3/nbc	Rhondda Transport	
1/61	2378–80		378–80 GNY	Leyland Tiger Cub PSUC1/2T	MCW DP41F	1/71 – 1973/nbc	Rhondda Transport	127
1/61	445–53		445–53 GTX	AEC Regent V 2D3RA	MCW H39/31F	1/71 – 1972	Rhondda Transport	
6/61	2381–5		381–5 KTG	Leyland Tiger Cub PSUC1/1T	Park Royal B45F	1/71 – NBC	Rhondda Transport	
6/61	454–64		454–64 KTG	AEC Regent V 2D3RA	MCW H39/31F	1/71 – 1972	Rhondda Transport	
5/62	465/8		465/8 MTX	AEC Regent V MD3RV	MCW H37/28F	1/71 – 1972	Rhondda Transport	
7/62	466/7		466/7 MTX	AEC Regent V MD3RV	MCW H37/28F	1/71 – 1972	Rhondda Transport	
12/63	469/73/7/8		469/73/7/8 UNY	AEC Regent V 2MD3RA	N.Counties H37/28F	1/71 – NBC	Rhondda Transport	
1/64	470–2/4–6		470–2/4–6 UNY	AEC Regent V 2MD3RA	N.Counties H37/28F	1/71 – NBC	Rhondda Transport	
5/64	2386–91		386–91 WTG	Leyland Tiger Cub PSUC1/11T	Willowbrook B45F	1/71 – NBC	Rhondda Transport	128
5/64	2392–4		392–4 WTG	Leyland Tiger Cub PSUC1/11T	Willowbrook DP41F	1/71 – NBC	Rhondda Transport	129
8/65	479–90		ETX 479–90C	AEC Regent V 2MD3RA	N.Counties H37/28F	1/71 – NBC	Rhondda Transport	
3/66	2300–3		HTG 300–3D	Leyland Tiger Cub PSUC1/12T	Marshall B45F	1/71 – NBC	Rhondda Transport	
10/66	492/3		KNY 492/3D	AEC Regent V 2MD3RA	N.Counties H37/28F	1/71 – NBC	Rhondda Transport	
11/66	491/4/5		KNY 491/4/5D	AEC Regent V 2MD3RA	N.Counties H37/28F	1/71 – NBC	Rhondda Transport	
4/68	2319		RTG 319F	Leyland Leopard PSU3/2R	Willowbrook DP49F	1/71 – NBC	Rhondda Transport	
6/68	2304–15		RTG 304–15F	Leyland Tiger Cub PSUC1/12T	Marshall B45F	1/71 – NBC	Rhondda Transport	
6/68	2316–8		RTG 316–8F	Leyland Tiger Cub PSUC1/12T	Marshall DP41F	1/71 – NBC	Rhondda Transport	129
5/68	2320/1		RTG 320/1F	Leyland Leopard PSU3/2R	Willowbrook DP49F	1/71 – NBC	Rhondda Transport	
9/68	496–501		RTX 496–501F	Leyland Atlantean PDR1A/1	N.Counties H42/31F	1/71 – NBC	Rhondda Transport	
7/69	502–11		VTG 502–11G	Leyland Atlantean PDR1A/1	N.Counties H42/31F	1/71 – NBC	Rhondda Transport	
7/70	2322/3	107/8	YTX 322/3H	Leyland Leopard PSU3A/4RT	Plaxton Pan. Elite C49F	1/71 – NBC	Rhondda Transport	130
8/70	2324	109	YTX 324H	Leyland Leopard PSU3A/4RT	Plaxton Pan. Elite C49F	1/71 – NBC	Rhondda Transport	130
10/54	2334		PNY 371	Leyland Tiger Cub PSUC1/1T	Weymann B44F	—	Rhondda Transport	12
11/54	2340/3/9		PNY 377/80/6	Leyland Tiger Cub PSUC1/1T	Weymann B44F	—	Rhondda Transport	12
12/54	2350–2		PNY 387–9	Leyland Tiger Cub PSUC1/1T	Weymann B44F	—	Rhondda Transport	12
12/55	2353–6		SNY 231–4	Leyland Tiger Cub PSUC1/1T	Weymann B44F	—	Rhondda Transport	12
1/58	425–44		VTX 425–44	AEC Regent V	Weymann H37/33F	—	Rhondda Transport	12
4/65	103/4		CTX 985/6C	AEC Reliance 4MU3RA	Duple Commander C51F	1/71 – 1972/3	Neath & Cardiff	131
2/68	105		PTX 830F	AEC Reliance 6MU4R	Plaxton Panorama C41F	1/71 – NBC	Neath & Cardiff	131
3/69	106		UNY 831G	AEC Reliance 6MU4R	Plaxton Pan. Elite C51F	1/71 – NBC	Neath & Cardiff	131
7/60	101/2		WWN 190/1	AEC Reliance 2MU3RV	Harrington Cavalier C41F	—	Neath & Cardiff	131, 12
1/71	512–20		BTG 512–20J	Leyland Atlantean PDR1A/1	Alexander H42/31F	1/71 – NBC	New	132
1/71	1512/4		TKG 512/4J	Leyland Leopard PSU4A/2R	Willowbrook B45F	1/71 – NBC	New	133
2/71	1513/6		TKG 513/6J	Leyland Leopard PSU4A/2R	Willowbrook B45F	2/71 – NBC	New	133, 134
3/71	1501		TKG 501J	Leyland Leopard PSU4A/2R	Willowbrook DP41F	3/71 – NBC	New	133, 134
3/71	1511/5/7–20		TKG 511/5/7–20J	Leyland Leopard PSU4A/2R	Willowbrook B45F	3/71 – NBC	New	133
4/71	1502–10		TKG 502–10J	Leyland Leopard PSU4A/2R	Willowbrook DP41F	4/71 – NBC	New	133, 134
4/71	2325–34		BTX 325–34J	Leyland Leopard PSU4A/2RT	Willowbrook B45F	4/71 – NBC	New	134
5/71	801–20		UKG 801–20J	Bristol RELL6L	Marshall B51F	5/71 – 1971/2	New	135
6/71	377–85		VUH 377–85J	Leyland Atlantean PDR1/3	Alexander H41/31F	6/71 – 1971/2	New	136
8/71	185/6		VUH 185/6K	Leyland Leopard PSU3B/4RT	Plaxton Pan. Elite C49F	8/71 – NBC	New	137
9/71	190		VUH 190K	Leyland Leopard PSU3B/4RT	Plaxton Pan. Elite C49F	9/71 – NBC	New	137, 138

Notes: 12 see notes for 1929. 127 2378-80 were downgraded to buses in 6/71 without structural change and painted in bus livery between 6/71 and 12/71. 128 2388's body dated from 5/70, its original was destroyed in a runaway accident at Penrhys. 129 2316 was the only Rhondda vehicle repainted in blue and ivory dual-purpose livery, in 5/71; 2317/8/94 received red and ivory livery in 6/71-7/71. 130 2323/4 were repainted in ivory and blue coach livery in 10/71, but 2322 retained ivory and green Rhondda coach livery until sold to Western National, 1/72. They were re-numbered 107-9 in 11/71, but 107 was a paper exercise only. 131 101-6 were the WW share of N&C, control of which passed to SWT in 4/69 but not absorbed until 1/71. They were given fleet numbers 112/3, 158/9, 129 and 172 respectively by SWT. 101/2 had Cavalier bodies and not used by WW. 103/4 had Commander bodies and were repainted into ivory and blue in 11/70, in anticipation of the transfer. 105 had Panorama 1 bodywork and received WW coach livery in 3/71; it was downgraded to dual-purpose livery in 3/71. 106 was a Panorama Elite which gained coach livery in 3/71. 132 512-20 were ordered by Rhondda and delivered in their livery with their fleet numbers. 520 was the first WW double decker painted in NBC livery, in 9/72. 133 1501-20 were to have been numbered 501-20, but the numbers were used by Rhondda vehicles. They were shorter than the average Leopard. 1512/4/6 carried their intended numbers for a brief period. 1501-10 were the last dual-purpose vehicles delivered in blue and ivory. 134 2325-34 were ordered by Rhondda, delivered in their livery and were to have been numbered 325-34 in their fleet. 135 With the exception of special-build 1 (MBO1F) of 1967, 801-20 were the first Bristols to enter service with WW since 1937 . All 20 were delivered to Ely, but 806-20 were immediately transferred to SWT, whose order for AEC Swifts had been diverted to London Country. It is believed that a further order for 10 RELL6Ls was cancelled. 136 377-85 were the first Alexander bodies ordered by WW, but only 377-81 were operated. 382 was licensed but along with 383-5 stored at Ely, then transferred to East Yorkshire Motor Services, Hull, in 8/71. A tenth vehicle, to have been 386 (VUH 386K) was delivered direct to East Yorkshire and all five were re-registered AAT 395-9K. Even those that did enter service had a short life with WW, 377-81 being transferred to Western National in 4/72. 137 185-90 featured larger Leyland 0.680 engines and were the first with the new block capital fleet name from new.

1972

New	Fleet No.	Reg No.	Chassis & type	Body & type	In use	Origin	Notes
2/72	187	VUH 187K	Leyland Leopard PSU3B/4RT	Plaxton Pan. Elite C49F	2/72 – NBC	New	137
3/72	188/9	VUH 188/9K	Leyland Leopard PSU3B/4RT	Plaxton Pan. Elite C49F	3/72 – NBC	New	137/8
3/72	1521/2	XBO 521/2K	Leyland Leopard PSU3B/4R	Marshall DP47F	3/72 – NBC	New	138
3/72	1537/9/42–4/6–51/3	XBO 537/9/42–4/6–51/3K	Leyland Leopard PSU3B/4R	Marshall B51F	3/72 – NBC	New	138
4/72	1523–5/7–9	XBO 523–5/7–9K	Leyland Leopard PSU3B/4R	Marshall DP47F	4/72 – NBC	New	138
4/72	1533–5/8/40/52/4	XBO 533–5/8/40/52/4	Leyland Leopard PSU3B/4R	Marshall B51F	4/72 – NBC	New	138
5/72	1526/30	XBO 526/30K	Leyland Leopard PSU3B/4R	Marshall DP47F	5/72 – NBC	New	138
6/72	1532/6	XBO 532/6K	Leyland Leopard PSU3B/4R	Marshall B51F	6/72 – NBC	New	138
7/72	1531/41/5	XBO 531/41/5K	Leyland Leopard PSU3B/4R	Marshall B51F	7/72 – NBC	New	138
1963	107/8	TCK 720/4	Leyland Leopard PSU3/3RT	Harrington Cavalier C49F	2/72 – 1973/4	Ribble	139

Notes: 137 see notes for 1971. 138 1521-30 were delivered in red and ivory but had blue upholstery and rear luggage lockers. 1531-54 had pram pens. Marshalls also fitted improved Clayton heating systems and heated windscreens. A feature of these, along with 185-90, was the raised driving compartment, which at six inches higher than previous deliveries, gave improved forward vision. Leyland had used Atlantean steering and braking components on their PSU3B chassis. 139 107/8 were ex-Ribble Motor Services, Preston, in 12/72. They featured Cavalier style bodywork, the first and only such vehicles operated by Western Welsh. 107 entered service in 3/73 and spent most of its time with the company on hire to Red & White Services. 108 entered service in 4/73. Both were practically life-expired and despite attention at Ely would be hard pressed to reach 40mph!

1973

Notes: No new vehicles entered the fleet in 1973. The fleet total in December 1973 had reduced further to 468.

1974

New	Fleet No.	Reg No.	Chassis & type	Body & type	In use	Origin	Notes
2/74	UC1/274	RBO 191/2M	Leyland Leopard PSU3B/4RT	Duple Dominant C49F	2/74 – NBC	New	140
2/74	UC474	RBO 194M	Leyland Leopard PSU4B/4RT	Duple Dominant C41F	2/74 – NBC	New	140
3/74	UC374	RBO 193M	Leyland Leopard PSU3B/4RT	Duple Dominant C49F	3/74 – NBC	New	140
3/74	UC574	RBO 195M	Leyland Leopard PSU4B/4RT	Duple Dominant C41F	3/74 – NBC	New	140

Notes: 140 UC1-574 were fitted with Duple Dominant Express bodies and were the first vehicles to be delivered in NBC National white coach livery. They were originally to have been numbered 191-5 but carried UC1-574 from new, although the new numbering scheme was not implemented until August. They were fitted with bus-type folding doors thus qualifying for the Bus Grant available at that time. These coaches marked the last of the true Western Welsh vehicle orders, but were hardly to the standard of previous years' deliveries. As 1974 drew to a close the first batch of Leyland Nationals was delivered.

Unique in the fact that it was the only Western Welsh PSV to carry a fleet number, but never a fare paying passenger, this Ford Thames 402E 10-seat minibus was bought new in August 1961. It was used to carry staff between offices and depots in the Cardiff area.
AB Cross

Operators absorbed by Western Welsh

From its earliest days, Western Welsh set its sights on the removal of competition, not only from its stage carriage routes, but from its rivals in the tours and private hire business. The resulting list of small — and not so small — operators that were absorbed is lengthy for an operator of the company's size, but not unreasonable in terms of the territory covered. There was a long period of consolidation after the war, but when confidence in the future was regained in 1953, the businesses acquired were far more significant. As far as can be ascertained, the list that follows is complete, although not all the finer details are known. In many cases, moves towards takeover began many years before completion.

Date	Company/trading name	Base	Principal route	Cost	Vehicles acq'd/used		Note
11/29	Tresillian Motors	Penarth	Cardiff – Pontypridd	£6,500	10	7	
11/29	HJ Cridland t/a Cridlands	C'diff & P Talbot	C'diff–P'pridd; PT-G'corrwg	£33,000	21	21	
1/30	G Paskin	Brecon	Brecon – Trecastle	?	?	0	
5/30	Edwards Bros	Carmarthen	Carmarthen – Narberth	£700	1	1	
7/30	A Bowen t/a All Blue Express	Carmarthen	Carmarthen – Llandeilo	£650	1	1	
10/31	Griffiths & Davies Ltd	Newbridge	Local stage service	?	4	2	
2/33	J R Adams	New Quay	Local stage service	?	0	0	
7/33	Fred Jones	Erwood	Brecon – Llandrindod Wells	?	1	0	
8/33	Morgan Weeks	Porthcawl	Local stage service	?	0	0	
10/33	Francis Motors	Porthcawl	Porthcawl – Pontypridd	£2,550	?	?	A
11/33	Lewis & James Ltd t/a Western Valleys	Newbridge	Newport – Ebbw Vale	—	40	40	B
11/33	EVMS (Barretts) Ltd t/a Eastern Valleys	Pontnewynydd	Newport – Pontypool	—	37	37	B
4/34	William Petter	Carmarthen	Carmarthen – Llandeilo	?	0	0	C
10/34	Thomas Bros	Llanstephan	Carmarthen – Llanstephan	£1,850	2	2	
1/35	FJ John	Nantyfyllon	Local stage service	£11,500	11	4	
6/35	WT Jones t/a Express Motors	Bryncethin	Local stage services	£15,000	12	9	
7/35	J Jones & Co t/a Pontyberem M S	Pontyberem	Llanelly – Carmarthen	?	?	?	
7/35	Beavis t/a Danygraig O S Ltd	Risca	Newport – Machen	£6,000	2	1	D
2/36	Bert Langley	Abersychan	Local stage service	£1,500	0	0	
7/36	Jabez Gough t/a Welsh Motorways	Mountain Ash	Cardiff – Aberystwyth	£7,000	4	3	E
12/36	Thos White t/a White's; CJ Vincent	Cardiff & Barry	Barry – Cardiff – Pontypridd	£85,000	67	56	F
1/37	Phipps Motors Ltd	Glynneath	Neath – Aberdare – Merthyr	£15,000	10	10	G
4/37	Green & White Services Ltd	Bridgend	Local stage services	£13,025	17	17	
7/37	Pencoed Motor Co Ltd	Bridgend	Local stage services	£10,000	11	11	H
11/37	Osborne Services	Neath	Neath – Banwen	£11,000	0	0	I
7/38	FL Harfoot (Mrs)	Barry	Local stage service	£1,950	1	1	
7/38	S Harfoot & Sons	Barry	Stage, excursions & tours	£8,900	8	8	
7/38	J Isaac	Barry	Local stage service	£1,900	0	0	
7/38	A H Evans	Barry	Local stage service	£3,250	2	2	
7/38	W J Knight	Barry	Stage, excursions & tours	£4,100	3	3	
10/38	JH Hill & Sons	Barry	Stage, excursions & tours	£9,000	11	9	
1/39	JH Woodfield	Barry	Local stage service	£2,000	1	1	J
4/39	J David & Son	Aberkenfig	Local stage service	£1,250	2	0	
1/44	RJ Guppy	Barry	Local stage service	£2,834	0	0	
1/44	A Morgan	Barry	Local stage service	£2,834	0	0	
1/44	A Waters	Barry	Local stage service	£2,834	2	2	
1/44	A Williams	Barry	Local stage service	£2,834	0	0	
1/44	J Williams	Barry	Local stage service	£2,834	0	0	
4/53	AH Jones t/a Greenline	Kenfig Hill	Kenfig Hill – Porthcawl	£2,000	0	0	
4/54	Streamways Ltd	Penarth	Excursions & tours	£20,000	4	3	K
6/54	Cridlands Ltd	Cardiff	Excursions & tours	£15,000	10	10	L
12/54	Ebsworth Bros Ltd	Laugharne	Carmarthen – Tenby	£27,500	11	10	
4/56	ER Forse t/a Forse's	Cardiff	Excursions & tours	£75,000	21	21	
12/56	Green's Motors Ltd	Haverfordwest	H'west – Milford Haven	£55,000	44	29	
8/59	{Prendergast Motors {T J Harries & Sons	Haverfordwest} Milford Haven}	Local stage services	£2,000	0	0	M
8/63	Mid Wales Motorways	Newtown	Newtown – Cardiff	£2,000	0	0	N
12/70	Rhondda Transport Co Ltd	Porth	Local stage services	£457,174	160	128	
1/71	Neath & Cardiff L C Ltd (N&C Express)	Cardiff	Cardiff – Swansea	£16,177	6	4	O

Notes: LC Luxury Coaches. MS Motor Services. OS Omnibus Services. A Rhondda Transport paid £400 of the cost. B Both the Lewis & James and Barrett company names survived until 1933. C WW took over the goodwill via Daniel Jones who shared the route, Petter being in liquidation. D Continued as a separate company until 1941. E Gough's Welsh Motorways was part of the Red & White Group whose Aberystwyth express service was acquired by agreement, along with three of Gough's vehicles. F There had been a hiring agreement since 7/35; the name continued until 1938. G Continued under the Phipps name until 1938. H Continued as a separate company with hired vehicles until 9/41. I WW took over the goodwill of the Osborne company, purchased through SWT. J Operated as a driver trainer until 1940. K One vehicle did not materialise; WW management were later censured for allowing Streamways to default on trading debts including failure to supply this vehicle, at a cost of £3,000. L This was the Cridlands coaching arm which remained from the 1929 takeover, and assets included a new chassis which WW sent for bodying in 1955. M Prendergast and Harries were in common ownership. N The goodwill of the Mid Wales company's express service to Cardiff was purchased jointly with Crosville. O The Neath & Cardiff company was split between SWT and WW, and the number of vehicles absorbed by WW was proportionate to the Cardiff end of its operations.

Vehicles transferred to South Wales Transport

The depots at Neath and Haverfordwest together with the local services that operated from them were transferred to the NBC's South Wales Transport subsidiary in 1/72 and 3/72 respectively.

WW Fleet No.	Reg No.	SWT Fleet No.	Transferred	Withdrawn	Notes
1139	MUH 139	301	3/72	1974	
1166/71	MUH 166/71	327/32	7/71	1972	i
1200/17/9/21/33	LKG 200/17/9/31/33	328/9/33/30/1	7/71	1972	i
1242/8/57/8/62/4/5/75	SBO 242/8/57/8/62	302–5/41	3/72	1972–4	
1264/5/75	UKG 264/5/75	342–4	3/72	1973	
1244	SBO 244	334	1/72	1973	ii
276/7/82/3	WKG 276/7/82/3	256–9	1/72	1972–7	
612	612 BBO	507	3/72	1977	
1300	300 CUH	345	3/72	1974	iii
103	CTX 985C	158	3/72	1976	
718/20	BKG 718/20C	877/8	1/72	1977	
1335/40/52/5/60	DBO 335/40/52/5/60C	346–50	3/72	1976/7	
1348	DBO 348C	335	1/72	1977	
728/9	DBO 728/9C	879/80	1/72	1977	
1377/8/84/91/4	HBO 377/8/84/91/4D	336–40	1/72	1976–9	
201–15	KKG 201–5E/206–15F	201–15	1/72	1977–9	
367/74–6	PKG 367/74–6H	901–4	3/72	1982	
629	PKG 629G	508	3/72	1981	iv
801–5	UKG 801–5J	643–7	1/72	1982–4	
806–20	UKG 806–20J	625–639	5/71	1982–4	i

Notes: i 1166/71, 1200/17/9/21/33 and 806-820 were separate transfers and not part of the exchange of West Wales operations ii Transferred as a towing vehicle iii To towing vehicle upon withdrawal iv Further used as trainer until 1984.

Vehicles transferred to Crosville

The depots at Newcastle Emlyn and New Quay, together with the Lampeter outstation and associated services, passed to NBC's Crosville subsidiary in 4/72.

WW Fleet No.	Reg No.	Crosville Fleet No.	Transferred	Withdrawn	Notes
1146	MUH 146	STL930	4/72	1974	
1247/56	SBO 247/56	STL931/2	4/72	1975/6	
1274	UKG 274	STL933	4/72	1976	
282/3	WKG 282/3	SAA983/4	4/72	1974	i
1344/51/3/4/9/63	DBO 344/51/3/4/9/63C	STL934–9	4/72	1976/7	
1376	HBO 376D	STL940	4/72	1976	

Notes: i 282/3 came via South Wales Transport.

Vehicles transferred to Jones Aberbeeg

WW Fleet No.	Reg No.	Jones Fleet No.	Transferred	Withdrawn	Notes
179	SKG 179H	Retained 179	4/74	1983	i
109	YTX 324H	Retained 109	3/73	1983	i

Notes: i Then transferred to National Welsh, 1/81.

Vehicles transferred to NBC (Western Welsh/National Welsh)

These vehicles operated in the Western Welsh/National Welsh NBC fleet from 8/74 and were initially given the fleet numbers shown. Many of the vehicles listed were subsequently renumbered. This list includes the vehicles absorbed from the Rhondda and Neath & Cardiff fleets.

WW Fleet No.	Reg No.	NBC Fleet No.	Withdrawn
1240/3/5/6/50–3/9–61/3	SBO 240/3/5/6/50–3/9–61/3	U33–4459	1975/6
1495	SBO 495	U4559	1975
1270	UKG 270	U160	1975
313–20/2	VKG 313–20/2	LR1–8/1060	1975/6
323–31	VKG 323–31	LR1–961	1976/7
332–66	XV 332–47, 348–66 ABO	LR1–3562	1975–8
601–11/3–8	601–11/3–8 BBO	U13–2962	1977–9
1301–8	301–8 CUH	U16–2363	1975–8
703–12	703–12 CUH	H1–1063	1975–8
900–20	900–20 DBO	H11–3163	1975–80
1309–11/3–33	ABO 309–11/3–33B	U4–2764	1975–9
713	BKG 713B	L164	1980
714–7/9/21–7/30	BKG 714–27C, DBO 730C	L1–1365	1976–80
150/1/4	DBO 150/1/4C	UD1–365	1977
152/3/5	DBO 152/3/5C	UC1/2/465	1977
1334/6–9/41–3/5–7/9/50/6–8	DBO 334/6–9/41–3/5–7/9/50/6–8C	U28–4365	1977–80
1361/5/7	FUH 361/5/7C	U18/21/366	1979/80
1362/4/6/8–74	FUH 362/4/6/8–74D	U19/20/2/4–3066	1979/80
156–61	GKG 156–61D	UC1–666	1977
1375/9–83	HBO 375/9–83D	UD1–666	1976/81
1385–90/2/3	HBO 385–90/2/3D	U31–866	1978–80
731–8/40	HKG 731–8/40D	L1–966	1978/9
162–6	JBO 162–6E	UC1–567	1977–9
1395–1414	LUH 395–414F	U1–2067	1979/80
167–72	LUH 167–72F	UC1–668	1979/80
1	MBO 1F	U168	1975
173–8	OUH 173–8G	UC1–669	1980–3
619–28/30–8	PKG 619–28/30–8G	U1–1969	1980/1
368–73	PKG 368–73H	LR1–669	1980–4
180–4	SKG 180–4H	UC3–770	1982–4
185/6/90	VUH 185/6/90K	UC1–371	1983/4
187–9	VUH 187–9K	UC1–372	1983/4
1501–10	TKG 501–10J	UD1–1071	1980–4
1511–20	TKG 511–20J	U1–1071	1980–4
2325–34	BTX 325–34J	U11–2071	1980–4
1521–30	XBO 521–30K	UD1–1072	1983/4
1531–54	XBO 531–54K	U1–2472	1981–3
(191–5)	RBO 191–5M	UC1–574	1981
469–78	469–78 UNY	H1–1064	1975–8
479–90	ETX 479–90C	H1–1265	1977/9
491–5	KNY 491–5D	H1–566	1978/9
496–501	RTX 496–501G	HR1–668	1980–2
502–11	VTG 502–11G	HR1–1069	1980–3
512–20	BTG 512–20J	HR1–971	1981–4
2300–3	HTG 300–3D	U39–4266	1980/1
2304–15	RTG 304–15F	U2–1368	1980
2316–21	RTG 316–21F	UD1–668	1980
2364/5/7/70–2/4–7	XTG 364/5/7/70–2/4–7	U46–5559	1975/6
2380–5	380 GNY, 381–5 KTG	U9–1461	1976
2386–91	386–91 WTG	U28–3364	1976–7
2392–4	392–4 WTG	UD1–364	1975/7
105	PTX 830F	UD768	1978
106	UNY 831G	UC769	1978

The Parcels fleet

While much has been reported about the company's fleet of buses and coaches, it wasn't always realised that there was another fleet — the parcel vans — and although its size was in no way comparable with the main PSV fleet, it too was of high quality and boasted the latest and best vehicles.

From 1920 until 1925 South Wales Commercial Motors carried parcels on their buses, and a system of agents along the routes saw to their collection and delivery. Then in 1925 two Trojan 10 cwt vans were purchased and the first direct deliveries commenced from consignor to consignee. One van was based at Penarth Road, while the other operated from Bridgend depot for collection in that area. A year later, two Model T Fords were added to the fleet, and as a consequence, the areas and districts served were also increased. By the end of 1927 another two Fords had arrived and the parcel department's operational area extended from the Eastern and Western Valleys of Monmouthshire, Newport, Cardiff, Penarth, Barry and Bridgend, to the Bridgend Valleys.

In the slump year of 1928, the service was almost entirely withdrawn with only one van being retained at Cardiff. The surplus staff transferred to the traffic side, where most were to remain. The year 1930 brought about a resumption of the service on a limited scale when two Morris 25 cwt vans were acquired. Four years later, two Bedford 30 cwt and one Austin five cwt vans entered service. The latter was popularly known as The Bug, and these three vehicles remained in service throughout the war years, when they were used to carry stage props between service camps for the Entertainments National

Paint shop apprentices P Jones and F Caple, with van No. 23 (LBO 304F), a Commer KC painted in the peacock blue and royal ivory coach colours. This was significant as Commer was the vehicle manufacturer linked closely to the start of SWCM operations. *Viv Corbin*

Service Association (ENSA). These survived until 1950, when they were replaced by two 25 cwt Austins and a 10 cwt Morris Commercial, which joined a Bedford K new in 1949. By 1950 the compact parcel fleet consisted entirely of post-war vehicles, each of ultra-smart appearance in the company's colours and fully sign-written. The fleet was once again replaced in the late 1950s, when three Fordson 30 cwt vans, and a smaller Ford 400E were purchased. In turn, these were replaced by the final generation of Western Welsh parcels vehicles, in the form of two Ford Thames Traders in the mid-1960s, together with the final van for the company, a 1967 Commer KC which appeared in the coach fleet colours of blue and ivory.

New	In	No.	Reg No.	Chassis	Body	Out	Notes
12/29	new	V9	UH 7206	Morris	Parcel van	7/35	
6/28	1930	V2	YW 5364	Morris Z2	Parcel van	by 7/33	Ex – GWR bus 1100
6/28	1930	V3	YW 5367	Morris Z2	Parcel van	by 1935	i
12/34	new	V10	KG 5100	Austin 7hp	5cwt Parcel van	8/50	
6/35	new	V11	KG 6334	Bedford WS	30cwt Parcel van	8/50	
6/35	new	V12/3	KG 6335/6	Bedford WS	30cwt Parcel van	8/50	
9/49	new	V15	EUH 430	Bedford K	30cwt Parcel van	7/58	
6/50	new	V16	FBO 924	Austin K8	25cwt Parcel van	5/58	
7/50	new	V18	FBO 925	Austin K8	25cwt Parcel van	12/56	Written off
7/50	new	V17	FBO 998	Morris Commercial J	10cwt Parcel van	1/59	
11/56	new	V14	NBO 331	Ford Thames V8	30cwt Parcel van	4/64	
5/58	new	V18	PBO 845	Ford 4D	30cwt Parcel van	2/66	
6/58	new	V19	PBO 846	Ford 4D	30cwt Parcel van	10/67	
2/59	new	V20	RUH 296	Ford 400E	12cwt Parcel van	10/67	
4/64	new	V21	AKG 921B	Ford Trader	30cwt Parcel van	1969	
2/66	new	V22	FUH 837D	Ford Trader	30cwt Parcel van	1969	
2/60	10/67	V17	UKG 189	Ford Thames 400D	Parcel van	1969	ii
10/67	new	V23	LBO 304F	Commer KC	Parcel van	6/76	iii

Notes: i 3 was ex-GWR bus 1103 but came via Western National. ii UKG 189 was converted from stores van 10. iii 23 was the final parcels van and replaced No. 19. It was smartly painted in the coach colours of peacock blue and royal ivory, and featured sign-written advertisements for the company's tours on its roof as well as the side panels. It was a poignant reminder that the first service van was also a Commer, SWCM being area distributors for this manufacturer.

Service vehicles

New	In	No.	Reg No.	Chassis	Body	Out	Notes
1929	new	V8	UH 7140	Morris	Van	by 7/35	
1929	1930	V4	WO 2342	Morris	Service van	by 9/39	ii
6/25	1933	V5	YK 3832	Thornycroft A1	Lorry	by 5/36	Ex – GWR bus 938
2/29	6/33	V6	UL 4053	Thornycroft A1	Lorry	2/50	Ex – GWR bus 1478
5/25	1933	V7	XY 5374	Thornycroft A1	Lorry	7/35	Ex – GWR bus 913
1924	3/34	V1	BO 8263	Dennis	4 ton lorry	8/35	iii
7/35	new	V13	KG 6336	Bedford WS	Luton van	8/50	
1925	8/35	V1	071 BO*	Leyland SG11	Recovery vehicle	4/50	Ex – bus 5, see note iv
1931	12/36	V2	UH 9894	Morris	1 ton stores lorry	2/50	Ex – White's
8/27	10/38	378	TX 3960	Thornycroft A1	Booking office	3/40	Ex – bus 378
8/26	9/39	369	TX 1621	Thornycroft A1	Training vehicle	3/40	Ex – bus 369
9/39	new	V14	CBO 327	Bedford	12 cwt stores van	12/52	
7/31	11/40	V15	TG 2005	Bedford WLB	Lorry	6/49	Ex – bus 482
1943	9/46	V3	DBO 684*	Fordson F605	Recovery vehicle	1969	Ex – Army, see note v
5/36	3/48	V216	KG 7064	Leyland Cub	Engineers van	2/52	Ex – bus 216
1943	7/48	V4	*	Fordson F60S	Recovery vehicle	1/60	Ex – WD
5/36	8/48	V218	KG 7066	Leyland Cub	Engineers van	2/52	Ex – bus 218
?	4/51	V5	065 BO*	Leyland Retriever	3 ton canvas top	1/60	Ex – WD, see note vi
5/35	12/51	V10	KG 5610	Leyland TS7	Engineers van	2/58	Ex – bus 116
4/36	2/52	V11	KG 7020	Leyland TS7	Engineers van	3/58	Ex – bus 172
3/52	new	V12	GKG 332	Commer	8 cwt Stores van	1/60	
3/37	3/54	V9	KG 9632	Leyland TS7	Engineering van	8/61	Ex – bus 250
2/57	new	V7	NUH 767	Fordson Thames 4D	30 cwt Stores truck	2/69	
2/57	new	V8	NUH 768	Fordson Thames 4D	30 cwt Stores truck	3/70	
4/58	new	999	(LKG 694)	—	Mobile enquiry caravan		1969, see note vii
1944	2/59	V1	134 BO*	AEC Matador	4x4 Recovery vehicle	1990	Ex – RAF, see note viii
4/44	2/59	V2	358 BO*	AEC Matador	4x4 Recovery vehicle	1981	Ex – Army, see note viii
2/60	new	V10	UKG 189	Ford Thames 400D	12 cwt stores van	1969	ix
10/48	by 3/61	626	DKG 626*	AEC Regent III	Tree lopper	by 3/68	Ex – bus 626
9/61	new	300	YBO 300	Ford 400E	10 seat crew bus	2/65	licensed PSV
10/67	new	V11	LBO 926F	Land Rover LWB	Sheet-sided stores van	by 7/79	
2/69	new	V9	OUH 159G	BMC 700FG	Dropside with tail lift	by 10/79	
3/70	new	V10	SBO 911G	BMC 700FG	Dropside with tail lift	by 10/79	
4/66	1/71	V12	JTX 228D	Land Rover LWB	Stores van	3/77	Ex – Rhondda
?	1/71	V3	459 L*	AEC Matador	4x4 Recovery vehicle	1985	Ex – Army, see note x
9/59	11/72	V4	395 BO*	Leyland PSUC1/1T	Recovery tender	4/78	Ex – bus 1249, see note xi

Notes: * Vehicle ran on trade plates. Known trade plates used pre-war: 026 BO, 065 BO, 071 BO, 243 BO. i 1 was an ex-demonstrator and returned 7/21, re-registered BO 3470, as bus 40. ii V4 was of unknown origin and converted to a lorry 3/36. iii BO 8263 was Cridlands double-decker 78. iv Originally registered BT 8424, the body was the lower saloon of bus 351 (BO 7833), a Dennis taken over from Tresillian Motors, the remainder of which was scrapped in 5/34. This vehicle saw out its days in use as an engine testing facility from 1934. v Former army gun tractor; ran on trade plates from around 1950. vi Previously registered FTX 752. vii Built in Ely, this trailer was used during construction of the central bus station, Cardiff, and during the rebuilding of Bridgend bus station. It was usually towed to its place of work by Austin A40 Countryman LKG 694. viii 1 and 2 were ex-government vehicles acquired via dealers and converted at Ely Works in 1959. They were allocated to Ely and Neath respectively. They were rebuilt in 1970 after which they were kept at Bridgend (V1, using 358 BO) and Cwmbran (V2, using 355 BO). ix UKG 189 was converted to a parcels van, 10/67 and re-numbered V17. x V3 was rebuilt and fitted with an Ergomatic cab at Ely. It was based at Porth and later used 395 BO. xi Based at Bridgend and carried its original identity SBO 249.

Bibliography

Modern Transport Magazine, August 27, 1938, 'Mr A Gray' • The Omnibus Magazine Vol.34 No.179, '1963 Presidential Weekend'. • British Bus Fleets: South Wales, 1st edition 1963; 2nd edition 1966 - Ian Allan • Buses Illustrated/Buses Magazine, Fleet News 1965-1974, G W Watts - Ian Allan • Railway Motor Buses and Bus Services in the British Isles 1902-1933,- Vol 2, John Cummings - Oxford Publishing, 1980. • Western Welsh Omnibus Company Limited/National Welsh Omnibus Services Limited, Fleet History PG7 (Part 2: 1951-1981) - PSV Circle and the Omnibus Society, 1981 • History of British Bus Fleets – South Wales, David Holding and Tony Moyes - Ian Allan, 1986 • British Bus, Tram & Trolleybus Systems No 11: South Wales Transport – Alan Townsin & Chris Taylor, Transport Publishing Company 1989 • Classic Bus: 'Whatever Happened to the Western Welsh', John Dunabin, April/May 1994 • AEC Society Gazette, 'Western Welsh AECs', Gerald Truran, Issue 57, July 1999 • Classis Bus, 'Only a Western Song', Roger Davies, June/July 2004 • The Rise and Fall of National Welsh, Viv Corbin 2004/2009 • Hello... Coastal,: The story of Victoria Coach Station, Richard Paramor - Venture Publications, 2007 • Glory Days – Western Welsh, Roger Davies, Chris Taylor and Viv Corbin - Ian Allan, 2007 • The Motor Bus Operators of Barry Before 1945, Viv Corbin and Chris Taylor, 2010.

Farewell to a legend

At its zenith in the mid-1950s, Western Welsh was the largest bus operator based in Wales. Even in 1972, and despite the National Bus Company reorganisations, it remained a highly respected company that still boasted over 500 buses and enjoyed major employer status.

It is therefore all the more difficult to accept that by the end of 1974, Western Welsh had largely been consigned to history. By this date all the company's vehicle orders had been completed, and the many changes to staff and directors had engineered the demise of the old company. The assets of the Red & White NBC subsidiary were transferred to Western Welsh on January 1, 1978, all road service licences becoming registered to Western Welsh. The vehicles, however, retained R&W licences and carried 'on hire' notices in the windows. This situation remained until the amalgamated company was renamed National Welsh Omnibus Services Limited on April 27. The name owed its origin to the winning entry in a public competition. However, it was perhaps an obvious one. This new name, in keeping with the times, was applied to vehicles bilingually. Inevitably the Western Welsh and Red & White names disappeared after this.

It could never have been predicted that this new name would remain in existence for only a fraction of the time of its predecessor. By 1987 National Welsh had become the 31st company to be sold by NBC and the champagne corks popped at head office. This was no longer at Ely, but at an insignificant building at Cardiff's West Canal Wharf. However, within five years, the management buy-out team had called in the receivers and despite a few initial hopes, there was to be no reprieve for the company. By 1992 the new, as well as the old, had been consigned to history.

The Red & White name returned to buses in the Gwent/Dean area in 1984, then made a widespread return as Western Travel's trading name from 1991, and from 1993 as part of the Stagecoach Group. The Rhondda name returned in 1992, and from 1997 that too continued as part of the Stagecoach group's empire. More recently, however, the Rhondda identity was lost under the Stagecoach in Wales branding.

Sadly, apart from an attempted, short lived, resurrection by a small operator in 2000, the once proud Western Welsh name has never returned to grace the roads of south and west Wales.

Guide to behaviour in omnibuses

'Do not get into a snug corner yourself and then open the windows to admit a north-wester in the neck of your neighbour. Do not spit upon the straw. You are not in a hog-sty, but in an omnibus, travelling in a country which boasts of its refinement. Remember you are riding a distance for sixpence which if made in a hackney coach would cost you as many shillings; and that should your price elevate you above plebeian accommodations, your purse should enable you to command aristocratic indulgencies'

The Times, 1836

A big thank you!

This may be the end of the journey, the last page in the book, but it is also the most important too. It is where I am finally able to express my sincere appreciation to all those, without whose help, this book would not have been possible.

I am particularly grateful for the information contained in the Western Welsh Staff Bulletins, which its long-serving editor, Stewart Williams, gave me his blessing to draw upon, before his untimely death in 2011.

The detailed vehicle history contained in the PSV Circle/Omnibus Society's PG7 booklet was invaluable, as was Viv Corbin's excellent 2004 publication which provided details of company minutes and accounts. Viv also allowed me access to more than 200 Staff Bulletins, supplied details of the White's company, and even had records of every staff car from SWCM to National Welsh! Transport historian Chris Taylor provided much assistance towards the end, allowing me to tie up loose ends and collate a definitive fleet history.

Christine Davies deserves special thanks for her enthusiasm, hospitality and loan of memorabilia as does George Wedlake, for his unstinting encouragement, advice and insistence that his unique collection of photographs be put at my disposal; to Tony Jenkins for the loan of more bulletins, paperwork and photographs; and to the late Gerald Truran, whose family allowed me to become beneficiary of fleet and allocation lists.

Sincere thanks must go to the photographers and custodians of all things Western Welsh who had the foresight to record or preserve it all. Alan Cross, John Heighway, Malcolm Jones, Peter Keating, Andrew Mann, Gerald Mead, Paul Redmond, Mike Street, Ken Swallow, and Tony Warrener were all there at the right time and, more importantly, recorded what they saw. It is a privilege to share the results of their sterling efforts.

Thanks also to Mike Morant for making the previously unpublished material of his late brother Geoff available; to Graham Bravey, John Evans, Tony Jenkins, John Jones, Andrew Porter, Howard Roberts, Peter Smith, Gail Sydenham and Ray Thomas who threw open the pages of their many albums; to Alan Oxley at The Omnibus Society, and to the Online Transport Archive for allowing use of the wonderful images of the late Reg Wilson. All these fine people not only wanted to help, but insisted they did. This spurred me into action on several occasions and helped bring the book closer to fruition.

There are others: Byron Westlake, for his assistance with technical details; Mark Lemon, whose modelling expertise has enabled all my favourite buses to be on display in my cabinet and Jeff Phillips for trips to rallies in PTX 830F, his preserved N&C coach which, he is forced to admit, had tentative connections with Western Welsh!

In the selection of photographs, I have diligently sought permission for their use and acknowledged the various sources accordingly. Hopefully anyone ommitted on this count will draw solace from knowing their efforts will provide much pleasure for subsequent generations.

During preparation of this book, Roger Davies was gathering material for his Glory Days book on Western Welsh. From the outset we both knew the result would be something special, something that only real enthusiasm and esteem for Western Welsh could create. We have liaised throughout and hopefully have avoided too much duplication, while agreeing that where Western Welsh is concerned, you can't have too much of a good thing!

Publisher David Roberts and his dedicated team at Bryngold Books deserve a salute for the sympathetic and enthusiastic way in which they handled the editing, design and production of the book from start to finish.

Finally, I am indebted to Roy Noble for supplying such complimentary words in his wonderful foreword without hesitation after only the briefest of meetings at the atmospheric Barry Depot.

I hope this book has treated you all to an enjoyable trip back down memory lane and that it will carry the proud story of Western Welsh long into the future.

Colin Scott,
Neath, June 2012